This collection of William Empson's essays on Elizabethan and Jacobean drama is the second volume of his writings on Renaissance literature. Edited with an introduction by the leading Empson scholar John Haffenden, the contents range from famous essays on *The Spanish Tragedy, Volpone, The Alchemist* and *The Duchess of Malfi* to a sprightly piece on Elizabethan spirits. In addition, there are previously unpublished essays which revisit critical controversies, and a magnificent, provocative study of *A Midsummer Night's Dream* which ventures a major new reading of the play. 'I am attracted by the notion of a hearty indifference to one's own and other people's feelings, when a fragment of the truth is in question', Empson stated. The incomparable Empson here fights his own critical corner with unequalled zest, intelligence, and insight.

ESSAYS ON RENAISSANCE LITERATURE

VOLUME TWO

1906-

WILLIAM EMPSON
ESSAYS ON RENAISSANCE LITERATURE

EDITED BY
JOHN HAFFENDEN
University of Sheffield

Volume two

The drama

CAMBRIDGE
UNIVERSITY PRESS

Published by the Press Syndicate of the University of Cambridge
The Pitt Building, Trumpington Street, Cambridge CB2 IRP
40 West 20th Street, New York, NY 10011–4211, USA
10 Stamford Road, Oakleigh, Melbourne 3166, Australia

First published 1994

Printed in Great Britain at the University Press, Cambridge

A catalogue record for this book is available from the British Library

Library of Congress cataloguing in publication data

Empson, William, 1906–1984
William Empson: essays on Renaissance literature / edited
by John Haffenden
Includes bibliographical references and indexes.
Contents: v. II The drama.
1. English literature – Early modern, 1500–1700 – History and criticism.
2. Renaissance – England.
1. Haffenden, John. II. Title.
PR423.E56 1993   820.9′003   92–20647

ISBN 0 521 44044 0 hardback

CE

Contents

Sources and acknowledgements

The Spanish Tragedy (I) was first published in *Nimbus*, 3, Summer 1956. *Volpone* first appeared in *Hudson Review*, 21, Winter 1968–9, and *The Alchemist* in *Hudson Review*, 22, Winter 1969–70; both essays are reprinted with permission. 'Mine Eyes Dazzle' (a review of *Webster: The Duchess of Malfi*, by Clifford Leech) was first published in *Essays in Criticism*, 14:1, January 1964, and is reprinted with permission. 'Elizabethan Spirits' (a review of *The Occult Philosophy in the Elizabethan Age*, by Frances Yates) was first published in *The London Review of Books*, 2:7, 17 April 1980, and is reprinted with permission.

The remaining pieces – '*The Spanish Tragedy*: a letter' (1958), *The Spanish Tragedy* (II) (*c.* 1976), '*Volpone* Again' (*c.* 1975), *The Duchess of Malfi* (*c.* 1956–60), and 'The Spirits of the *Dream*' (*c.* 1976–84) – are published here for the first time; all are taken from Empson's typescript drafts. The nature of these essays, and the circumstances of their writing, are described in the Introduction. The title '*Volpone* Again' is Empson's; the other titles are editorial.

Editorial principles are outlined in the section on 'Sources and acknowledgements' in Volume One: *Donne and the new philosophy*. As in the first volume, and for reasons which are likewise explained therein, I have chosen to provide rather a full apparatus of notes; the occasional note by Empson himself is followed by the initials 'WE' in parentheses.

Introduction

'The plan of one Shakespeare book and then one Jonson etc. book seems to be an admirable one, settling a whole area', William Empson wrote to Cambridge University Press on 5 November 1981. 'But of course I must arrange them as real books ... '[1] He had been proposing to compile various collections of his essays since as early as 1958; but in the event, after publishing *Milton's God* (1961), he went on to compose an extraordinary number of further essays in several major areas – specifically those that have now been gathered in *Using Biography* (which he had just finished at the time of his death in April 1984), *Essays on Shakespeare*, edited by David B. Pirie (Cambridge University Press, 1987), and a heartening essay entitled *Faustus and the Censor: The English Faust-book and Marlowe's 'Doctor Faustus'*, edited by John Henry Jones (Oxford: Basil Blackwell, 1987). Furthermore, the grand assemblage of items in *Argufying: Essays on Literature and Culture* (London: Chatto and Windus, 1987) shows that Empson remained tirelessly productive in the later years: his habits of work and his output were as continuous as they were wide-ranging.

The present collection of essays on Elizabethan and Jacobean drama is the second part of a two-volume edition of Empson's work on Renaissance literature; this twofold package is designed to complement the canonical volume *Essays on Shakespeare*. In letters to friends, Empson announced this volume – which he called by the working title *Some Elizabethan Plays and their Stage* (he never quite mastered the knack of devising snappy titles) – well over a decade ago. 'The next one is about other Elizabethan playwrights', he told Christopher Ricks in November 1981; and then, in September 1982, 'The book on Shakespeare and one on other Elizabethan playwrights are to be done by CUP.'[2] Earlier still, he wrote to Ian Parsons in 1975: 'I have been delayed by various things but am

1

going on quite well now, and if I keep it up will finish "Elizabethan Plays" within a year at least. One keeps finding soft bits that need more information to carry the needed weight, but most of it is just re-writing now.'[3] The only problem, as he had notified Parsons as early as 1958, was that 'I have always worked slowly and would still do so if I didn't have to mess about being a Professor, but I hope you don't regard me as already dead.' His extended apologia – which stands as fair warning to any literary critic, whether hack or professor – figures in a letter from the following year:

literary criticism ... has become a much more powerful and interesting tool since about 1900, and many of the able literary young want to go in for it. They can I think certainly do it quite as well while employed as dons, though they must be warned against insisting they must be Professors, a capacity in which they are liable to get heavy extra chores. Bonamy Dobrée warned me like that when I was looking for a job after leaving Communist China ... I do not regret the way it fell. But at least a literary critic can become a university lecturer without feeling that he is wasting his talent, and indeed is likely to improve it that way ... I do not know how a literary critic could be in such close contact with the existing audience reaction anywhere else; he certainly won't do it by writing journalism in obedience to the hunch of an editor ... You must remember that, if a young critic makes the great renunciation, saying 'It is beneath me to read all these horrid essays', the next thing he will have to do is turn out a lot of shockingly coarse hackwork, which really is beneath him and will remain permanently in print to shame his later years. A university job does at least mean that you are free to print in a decently considered manner ...[4]

The contents of this volume range from the first item on *The Spanish Tragedy*, first published in 1956, through the bracing pieces on *Volpone* and *The Alchemist* dating from the late 1960s, to an essay on the subject of 'Elizabethan Spirits' incited by the work of Dame Frances Yates (1980). In happy addition, there are a number of previously unpublished pieces that Empson was working on during his later years, including critical analyses of works by Kyd, Jonson, and Webster (which eagerly revisit early controversies), and a capacious, imaginative study of *A Midsummer Night's Dream* which – though it survives only in ramifying and unfinished form – ventures a major new thesis on the play and its context. In fact, over half of this volume consists of essays that are published here for the first time.

Empson remarked in 1981, apparently to his own surprise: 'While in employment, I raised hares, usually reported in magazine articles, and left them to be worked out during my retirement. But I now find that a lot of unprinted and incomplete material has piled up.'[5] The material had piled up in part because he could never rest content with his own essays, but even more so because he knew that no essay could ever say the last word: every text and topic, every issue, had to be reviewed and reinvigorated. 'Besides, I am always finding mistakes in my old articles while having to read some book again for a lecture', he readily allowed;[6] likewise in the opening remarks to his Clark Lectures, delivered at Trinity College, Cambridge, in 1974: 'I am usually saying things that other people disagree with, and I need to present a much stronger case in print than I do in a lecture.'[7] Not just leftovers, but a cogent combination of argued and reargued essays: such is the sum total of Empson's long-considered, long-awaited 'Jonson etc.' volume. (In his negotiations with Cambridge University Press, Empson was always insistent that the collected editions of his essays should be so much more than 'all old-hat' pieces reprinted out of periodicals.)

As a rationalist, Empson is keen to prove the supremacy of meaning over mystery; sense and story stand head and shoulders above symbol. Thus it is not surprising to find that a fair part of his criticism is taken up with what we nowadays term the 'hidden agenda', the subtext – along with the genuine likelihood, in the context of Renaissance theatrical production, of religious or political censorship. With regard to *The Spanish Tragedy*, for instance, Empson believed that the modern reader is quite entitled to feel wary of a play-text which is framed by the story of a revenger, Andrea, who lacks a demonstrable, let alone any satisfactory, motive for revenge – since he was killed in a formal battle with the enemy. Arthur Freeman, in *Thomas Kyd: Facts and Problems* (1967), rightly insists too: 'we may assume that if Kyd knew what he was doing, the death of Castile finally is not, as some have suggested, either an accident or a gross dramatic error in the interest of pure sensationalism'.[8] Yet many critics of Kyd do seem to be complacent about these problems. A recent editor of the play has written, for example: 'Such criticism is misguided because Kyd's interest lies in the consequences, proportionate or not, of human enmity. When the play concludes in the satisfaction of Andrea and Revenge, we may feel that morally there is a good deal to deplore ... But we feel equally the bitter consistency of motive and action that has led to this point.

Kyd has dramatised, through the revenge idiom, that is to say, a rigorously coherent and emotionally convincing set of human circumstances that in the last analysis are tragic, not moralistic, in character.'[9] From Empson's point of view, such rhetoric has to be seen as a fudging, for it is the very lack of 'consistency of motive', of dramatic point, that is so vexatious, so suspicious. Empson put forward his own considered solution to this inconsistency or riddle (or this hush-up, as he preferred to think it) in a letter which appears to date from the 1970s:

> I had been trying to make sense of *The Spanish Tragedy* and *Dr Faustus*, two foundation masterpieces which are shockingly silly in the mere story, a thing only hidden from Teacher (though not from a plain-minded pupil) because of the monstrous Aestheticism which has become an Eng. Lit. Trades Union regulation. I agree now that this is impossible from the surviving texts [although he did try to argue so in his initial essay on *The Spanish Tragedy* below]; both plays ran into a lot of trouble with the censorship, and were considerably mangled, as well as being continually altered because they were in great demand. In both cases the audience *knew* that the point of the story had been cut out; this made them all the more gleeful at having the essentials of it acted; though of course other persons in the audience felt that this version had been purged. The presumption that everybody in the audience must have been stupid (or must have been a pure aesthete, at least) has blocked all grasp of the dramatic situation.[10]

The crux that has been cut out of the plot, Empson argues, is that 'Andrea has suffered the fate of Uriah; the father and brother of Bel-imperia, that is, the Duke of Castile and Lorenzo, had arranged to have him killed in battle so that they could marry her to Balthazar the Prince of Portugal.' Of course it might be held against Empson that he is vainly postulating a suppression of significance, whereas the received text, albeit corrupt and irregular in parts, betrays no positive sign of such a silencing. (He even goes so far as to make up a brief bit of dialogue for a 'lost' closet scene, in order to rediscover the clandestine original 'message' that he alone posits; and this kind of intervention, this creative interpolation, may strike many readers as an utterly illegitimate critical trick. Yet, as Empson would say, 'The reconstruction only gives enough words for a production making the plot intelligible.')[11] Empson's answer was that such a gaping absence in the play, such a telling want of dramatic point in the part of the plot that should bother Andrea the Ghost, only goes to show how successfully the censor did his job. Hence, according to Empson, the true covert story of *The Spanish*

Tragedy entered a political critique of dynastic marriages. Queen Elizabeth I, following her announcement in 1581 that she was minded to marry the Duc d'Alençon, 'was eager to prevent discussion of her private affairs, and the censor would be afraid to pass anything about murders committed to help forward royal marriages'. Empson goes on, astutely here: 'I think he cut a whole scene after III. xi, which had been followed by the now missing act-break; like the other act-breaks, it gave a reaction from the ghost, who learns here what he was sent back from Hades to learn.'[12]

Most modern critics of the play agree with Philip Edwards' argument that the copy for the first extant edition of the play, published for Edward White in 1592, contains material of two distinct kinds; and that the latter section of the play at least, following Act III, scene xiv, manifests certain elements of revision and abridgement.[13] Two further factors need to be re-emphasised by way of prefacing any estimate of the true nature of the play, and any sustainable interpretation of it: not only was White's edition a piracy of a (now lost) *editio princeps* owned by one Abel Jeffes, but it also carries the exceptionally anomalous announcement 'Newly corrected and amended of such gross faults as passed in the first impression' (as does Jeffes' edition of 1594). John Henry Jones argues: 'The "gross faults" may have been matter for ecclesiastical censorship, which would explain Whitgift's involvement, and the announcements of amendment would then have become mandatory inscriptions.'[14] Given such a persuasive crucial suggestion, maybe it is really not so outlandish after all for Empson to have tried to recover, by way of his admittedly unorthodox device of creative reconstitution, a pristine plot behind the signally corrupt text that has come down to us: to do anything less is to bow to the conditions of Elizabethan dramatic censorship. (In any case, even recent scholars who have specifically enquired into the occasions of Renaissance censorship seem to draw divergent conclusions.)[15]

Empson stated it as 'a general truth about the pleasant and economical habit of reprinting old articles that the author had better say each time how far his opinion had changed now'.[16] Moreover, the critics of the critic should always be answered, as a point of honour: 'In the learned world, a man loses his standing if he refuses to answer a plain refutation ... '[17] He himself was stubborn in his opinions and pugnacious in answering back; he loved a public tumble with his rival critics, and scorned 'literary prattle' and jargon. In truth, he could be downright rude to both friend and foe – for reasons set out at the beginning of his career, in a piece written at the same time as *Seven Types of Ambiguity*:

if you attack a view in any detail that proves you to have some sympathy with it; there is already a conflict in you which mirrors the conflict in which you take part; that is why you understand it sufficiently to take part in it. Only because you can foresee and enter into the opposing arguments can you answer them; only because it is interesting to you do you engage in argument about it.

For personally I am attracted by the notion of a hearty indifference to one's own and other people's feelings, when a fragment of the truth is in question . . .[18]

For that reason he chose, quite often, to adopt an adversarial stance in his criticism: it helped him to have a prick to kick against. However, it needs to be said that very little of Empson's argumentation is *ad hominem*, even when he is attacking a fellow critic for being crazy or 'neo-Christian' (or both): invariably, in Empson's habits of critical address, the person is turned into a peg, the proper name into a notion. Furthermore, there is frequently a helping of exuberance to leaven his critical enmities – and even his odd errors and misrepresentations.

His essays on Jonson exhibit that tendency. John Creaser, in '*Volpone*: The Mortifying of The Fox' (1975), for example, adjudged that Empson's first article on *Volpone* ventured 'an extraordinarily uneven argument';[19] Martin Butler rebukes the same piece as 'provocative and untrustworthy', and likewise rates Empson for being 'characteristically provoking' on the subject of *The Alchemist*.[20] Exactly what irks the experts may be seen in an Empson letter of about 1973 to a (not unfriendly) critic that is itself a counterblast against virtually all the other critics, the mass of misreaders.

This misreading is always of a pietistic character, but otherwise just whatever will serve. Take *Volpone* and *The Alchemist*; you say that I am obviously wrong because I do no close reading. In reprinting I had better add some detailed evidence that Ben Jonson was not a Puritan, but hated them for trying to interfere with his pleasures; I need not add any 'analysis', to show that he habitually writes in a sardonic manner, hinting that what the character on the stage admires and praises does not really deserve such praise. This work has been thoroughly done already; the question is how to interpret his intention. The story that he despised bodily pleasure, and despised all his characters for wanting to enjoy it, whereas they ought to be yearning to be pure in Heaven like Ben Jonson, strikes me as such gross farcical hypocrisy that it does not need verbal disproof. What proves my case, I think, is that the plays are so very much better when this dirty nonsense is wiped or scraped away.[21]

Accordingly, in the essay I have entitled '*Volpone* again', John Creaser is pressed into service as Empson's whipping-boy – not necessarily because he is the worst offender, but because Empson has just happened upon his article in *Essays in Criticism* and so fixes upon it for exemplary correction. In defending what he calls Jonson's jovial indulgence of 'rogue-sentiment' in the plays, Empson's seriously sustained general principle is that a good morality should celebrate pleasure sooner than lay down laws of censure. To say the least, in the face of critics who rebuke Empson for seeking (or seeming) to pull the carpet from under Jonson's supposed moral rigour, one might well prefer the opinion of Samuel Schoenbaum (Distinguished Professor of Renaissance Literature and Director, Centre for Renaissance and Baroque Studies, University of Maryland) that Empson's 'vigorously argued essays, while protesting against "the pietistic strain in Eng. Lit.", give Jonson his due as a comic dramatist'.[22]

If Empson occasionally erred on the side of burlesquing the opinions of his critical opponents, he had no need at all to fashion men of straw when he came to *The Duchess of Malfi*. There is a long tradition of critics who find fault with the Duchess merely for marrying a second husband (perhaps in order to gratify her carnal desire), or else for electing to get married in hugger-mugger manner – and against the express wishes of her jealously aristocratic brothers – to her major-domo, who is no better than a household servant: a decent, weak chap or low-born opportunist, depending on how you take him. The Duchess commits a wanton error, the argument runs, and maybe deserves her tragic fate. ('Neo-Christians' have a 'craving to scold and befoul', as Empson bemoaned.) Denigrators of the Duchess include Clifford Leech – whose monograph on the play (*Webster: 'The Duchess of Malfi'*, 1963) Empson waylays in 'Mine Eyes Dazzle' – James L. Calderwood, and Joyce E. Peterson. Empson's review of Leech, his initial outcry in defence of the Duchess, is a brief piece, and as such has received little scholarly-critical notice – perhaps because it offers righteous protestation rather more than sustained evidence or full proof. The scholar Lee Bliss remarked in a note, a decade ago, 'William Empson's bluff approach wittily dismisses detractors of the Duchess'[23] – which

seems to leave the reader to guess whether he is praising or patronising. Yet Frank Whigham, in a long and warmly argued recent
article ('Sexual and Social Mobility in *The Duchess of Malfi*', *PMLA*,
March 1985), insists upon the force of Empson's position:

> Despite documentary arguments against widows remarrying and for the
> obligations of state service, it seems unlikely that the audience is supposed
> to find the duchess's action antisocial, hubristic, and licentious, as a certain
> sector of well-known criticism claims ... Certainly the duchess's plight is
> pathetic in personal terms, but I object to seeing her as deservedly
> punished (nonetheless, as it were), chiefly because the ideology that
> grounds such a judgment – Ferdinand's ideology – is the very ideology the
> play puts most deeply in question ... Empson's irascible retort to Leech is
> essential reading on this point.[24]

It is thus a pleasure to find among Empson's papers a longer
composition on the subject of *The Duchess of Malfi*, albeit unfinished,
which is printed here for the first time. Empson seems to have begun
drafting this larger essay within a short while of the review that takes
its title from the most famous line in the play, 'Mine eyes dazzle';
and it may therefore reflect Empson's own judgment that he really
did need to present a fuller case for the defence. However, he also
evidently sat down to it for a little at a time, over a period of four
years or so, since here and there it is a touch circular and reiterative.
It is probably best to see it as being comprised of draft sections,
written in spurts, towards a substantial essay which the author never
found the time to shape into a final form. But it is possible that some
of these sections are the original mass from which he mined his initial
review of Leech. Despite its unpolished state, this further essay on
The Duchess of Malfi considerably extends Empson's work on the play
in terms both of sprightly analysis and of his engagement with the
errant modern scholars he felt compelled to chastise. As always with
Empson's criticism, the incidental insights are so marvellous that it is
virtually out of the question for an editor to cut or dovetail his
sentences, even though this piece had not yet attained a shape that
he himself found satisfactory.

   In the essays on Jonson and Webster, as in all of his criticism,
Empson resolves to locate in literature the best of all possible
feelings. Refusing to kowtow to what he once called the 'unpleasing
personal habits' of the Christian God, he labours to bring forth a
humane large-mindedness and, still better, world-mindedness.
Dogma he finds disgusting. As he held, 'It strikes me that modern

critics, whether as a result of the neo-Christian movement or not, have become oddly resistant to admitting that there is more than one code of morals in the world, whereas the central purpose of reading imaginative literature is to accustom yourself to this basic fact.'

Accordingly, Empson tends to see the Renaissance theatre as a locus of dissent, as a forum for undercutting the official line, political or religious, if not for outright subversion. Art is at odds with orthodoxy. It is small wonder then that he worked so often to explain covert literary meanings (including double-plots in drama). The final essays in this volume flow from his absorption in the weird and wonderful drama of the philosophical writings that the European Renaissance termed 'occult' – including the lore concerning the marginal place and purposes of 'daemons' (neither angels nor devils), which Empson liked to call the 'Middle Spirits'. Inspired in part by Frances Yates' *Giordano Bruno and the Hermetic Tradition* (1964), Empson steeped himself in the dissertations of Renaissance Hermetism, beginning with the seminal *Hermetica* (reputedly written by the so-called Hermes Trismegistus) and continuing into the lucubrations of Cornelius Agrippa (notably *De Occulta Philosophia*), and Paracelsus (*De Nymphis*). Modern works that helped to excite, or rather irritate, his interest include studies such as *The Invisible World* (1939), by Robert Hunter West, and *The Occult Sciences in the Renaissance* (1972), by Wayne Shumaker.

The fullest achievement of Empson's inquiry into the state of the art of English Renaissance magic is the work now published as *Faustus and the Censor: The English Faust-book and Marlowe's 'Doctor Faustus'* (1987), which was originally planned as an appendix to a projected edition of *The German and English Faust-books: Parallel Texts*, translated and edited by John Henry Jones – a project that is published, albeit in a sadly less ambitious form, as *The English Faust Book* (Cambridge University Press, 1994). Sickened by the muddle of the surviving texts of *Dr Faustus* – especially the 'harmful' status of the B-text – as well as by the sanctimoniousness of some of the play's critics, Empson attempted to reconstruct the 'original' text against the background of its known sources, the hermetic tradition, Marlowe's likeliest intentions and contemporary theatrical expectations. The result in *Faustus and the Censor* is a detailed and vigorous new reading. Faustus must no longer be seen as an overreaching dope who deserves eternal punishment: he is reinstated as a true

Renaissance hero, a resourceful and roguish magician who 'lives next door to Punch' and makes a business deal with the 'freelance' Mephistophiles. The 'mystery' of 'Meph', it transpires, is that he derives neither from Heaven nor Hell, but is a Middle Spirit, a spirit of nature; and to understand the play at all, Empson argues, you must appreciate its 'secret plan'. Empson aims to put the cat among the pietists, and the evidence from his researches and close criticism goes far to expand the possible meaning of the play. He concedes that 'most of this essay consists in scouting round for evidence, and thinking up supporting detail in plot or production'; but, even when he seems to be quite contrary, he is never less than enlivening.

The last two essays in the present collection are exciting collateral pieces, expatiating upon Empson's conviction that the Hermetic and magical lore – inherited from the ancients, mediated by sixteenth-century publications – was a vibrant source of inspiration to English dramatists of about 1590. (There is a further unpublished essay – on *The Jew of Malta* – which also relates to this elaborating interest; but unfortunately it is very obviously first-draft work, rudimentary and unrefined, and not fit for publication.) Frank Kermode, in his New Arden edition of *The Tempest* (1954), noted what he called 'a degree of interchangeability in the expressions "spirit" and "fairy"', and outlined in an appendix the elements of the spirit-world that Shakespeare must have taken from the systematic exposition of the 'dæmonic' hierarchy set out by the white magician Agrippa.[25] Empson, for his part, came to believe he had found in *A Midsummer Night's Dream* evidence to suggest that Shakespeare comprehended heterodox theories both about intermediate spirits and about the Copernican revolution even as much as twenty years earlier, in 1590. Moreover, he was convinced that his exposition of these elements would rout the pervasive, pernicious influence of the brutalising argument of Jan Kott's chapter called 'Titania and the Ass's Head' (*Shakespeare Our Contemporary*, London: Methuen, 1964). Empson wrote in a draft passage of this exhilarating long essay – which I have given the title 'The spirits of the *Dream*' –

As I understand, there is a rather shadowy body of theory for producers, encouraging them to be original by saying that a play has an under-text, a secret intention of the author which ought to be followed rather than the literal words. This has some truth and should anyhow be encouraged, because it is much better than what the producers actually do. They use the old plays as a quarry to supply a modern entertainment; very much as a statue worshipped with awe, danger and edification by a remote tribe may be mass-produced as a toy for children. This is what Kott is up to, while imagining that he is plunging to the heart of reality.

Jan Kott's effort to promote a dark, terrible, orgiastic view of the play is known to have been part of the inspiration behind Peter Brook's famously carnivalesque Royal Shakespeare production of 1970, which was in fact a sexy circus – a piece of chic, diverting virtuosity – that with benefit of hindsight we may see as a product of the all-licensing 1960s. (Nevertheless, it is odd that Kott's insistence on a grotesque sexuality in the play should have been transmuted by Brook into a nimble, inventive, but perhaps fundamentally sub-stanceless, variety-performance.)

Empson deplored the Kott and Brook perversions of the play, and in a letter to Cambridge University Press spoke of his own interpre-tation as getting at the authentic historical moment – and the genuine challenge – of Shakespeare's prescient unconventionality:

I have a long article about the *Midsummer N. D.*, offering a way out from the Peter Brook outrage upon it; the spirits of nature need to be recognised as powers, and the decisive way to do it is to make Puck fly. To do this was one of the first technical triumphs of the Globe, which has an enlarged area for crane machinery on top ... Also Puck tells us with hair-raising exacti-tude the time needed for Major Gagarin to make the first circuit of the earth in space. This cannot be a coincidence, especially as the slight error in it corresponds to the Elizabethan error in the size of the earth. [Thomas] Harriot must have arrived at this answer and been refused publication by the censor; it is agreed that he fell into some such trouble, soon after 1590, and reacted with such a tremendous sulk that he refused ever to publish again. His supporters had a slogan, and it somehow got brief mention in Shakespeare's play; but why? ...[26]

It is now widely believed, as by the editors of the latest Revels Plays edition of *Doctor Faustus* – that Marlowe must have been acquainted with the opinions on Copernicus of advanced thinkers such as Thomas Harriot, Giordano Bruno, and Thomas Digges, and exploited in his play the radically sceptical implications of the brave new astronomy (see also volume 1, *Donne and the New Philosophy*, for Empson's extensive writings on these progressive philosophers). David Bevington and Eric Rasmussen also assent to the likelihood that Marlowe penned his play at the early date of *c.* 1588–9, especially in view of the recent demand for plays about magicians and their tricks.[27] Back in the 1970s, Empson drew like conclusions about *A Midsummer Night's Dream*: in view of the nexus of interest in occult hermetism and revolutionary astronomy, magic, and Middle Spirits, he felt convinced that Shakespeare had written the earliest version of his play *not* between 1594 and 1596 (the parameters that historical critics debate to death) but by 1590.[28]

The validity of Empson's claims remains to be weighed by the learned, but I believe there can be no doubt that his passionate, wide-branching exploration of the play and its putative intellectual context, which makes the arcane freshly accessible, is a real treat. It is notable, too, that in the years since Empson's death a number of critics and literary historians have felt eager to follow the trail blazed by Frances Yates in *The Occult Philosophy in Renaissance England* (1979). To cite one recent example: John S. Mebane in *Renaissance Magic and the Return of the Golden Age* (1989) seeks to demonstrate that Marlowe, Jonson, and Shakespeare were each 'thoroughly familiar with the philosophical, social, and political implications of Hermetic/Cabalist magic, as well as with the claims of particular occult philosophers ... '[29] Perhaps Empson's most controversial contribution to the debate is his argument that Shakespeare had tumbled to the implications of philosophical occultism, and of the new astronomy, at the beginning of his career (and not only by the time of *The Tempest*, as most critics will allow); but it would surely be foolhardy for anyone to allege that Empson was out on a limb of his own invention.

David B. Pirie, when editing *Essays on Shakespeare*, took the prudent course of including in that volume only the briefer version entitled 'Fairy flight in *A Midsummer Night's Dream*' (a review of *A Midsummer Night's Dream*, ed. for the Arden Shakespeare by Harold Brooks), first published in the *London Review of Books* in October 1979. The full text survives in numerous alternative versions; and, as David Pirie pointed out, one has to 'conclude that Empson had not produced in any of these drafts a complete text he judged ready for publication'.[30] Thus, in salvaging a version of the fuller essay for publication in this volume, my principal concern has been to work towards the most advanced state of the text; but the reader must appreciate that this exercise in recovery still falls short of a state that would have satisfied Empson. I have been encouraged to print this draft essay by a letter that Empson wrote to Cambridge University Press in August 1981 in which he specifically – and excitedly – refers to 'a long essay about the *Midsummer ND* which I think much the best thing I have written about him [Shakespeare]; and so does Karl Miller, in whose magazine a summary of it appears'.[31]

Empson told Cambridge University Press in August 1981, 'my two elder brothers were no use after the age of eighty, but at that rate I may still hope for time to finish off the loose ends, as I am just reaching 75.'[32] Sadly, he lived only to the age of 77, and so was unable to complete his work to his own satisfaction. As in editing other posthumous volumes of Empson's writings, I am grateful to Hetta Empson for entrusting me with the task, and for her tremendous hospitality. I am also obliged to John Henry Jones for his supportive friendship; and to Rodney G. Dennis (former Curator of Manuscripts) and Elizabeth A. Falsey (who has undertaken the awesome task of cataloguing the Empson Papers and is therefore both my mainstay and a fast friend), at the Houghton Library, Harvard University. For their help in various capacities I am greatly indebted to Anne McDermid, Gillian Maude, Barbara Ozieblo, Christopher Ricks, Russ Sharrock, and Frank Whigham. At Cambridge University Press, Kevin Taylor has calmly steered the volumes to the line on time, in time.

I would like to express my gratitude again to the British Academy for the award of a Research Readership which enabled me to make happy progress both with this volume and with a biography of Empson; and to the Research Fund of the University of Sheffield for financial assistance.

John Haffenden

PART I:

Kyd, Jonson, Webster

CHAPTER I

'The Spanish Tragedy' (I)

It seems to me that *The Spanish Tragedy* of Kyd has been underrated through misunderstanding, as I shall try to show in this article. The question may seem remote, but the play is commonly regarded as the surviving analogue to the Ur-*Hamlet* of Kyd, so has a considerable bearing on Shakespeare's *Hamlet*; or at least on what the first audience thought Shakespeare was doing when he rewrote the old favourite, a thing which they had laughed at even before they decided it was out of date.

So far as I have seen, critics always take for granted that the ghost of Andrea has no point; Kyd was crude, and anyhow he was copying Seneca. I think the point was obvious at the time, so obvious that it did not get stated in the text. Andrea has suffered the fate of Uriah; the father and brother of Bel-imperia, that is, the duke of Castile and Lorenzo, had arranged to have him killed in battle so that they could marry her to Balthazar the prince of Portugal. Presumably they informed the enemy prince, who killed him in the battle, where he was going to be sent and how he could be recognised. There is a reason for not mentioning this (though I agree that one would expect the ghost to say it at the end) because the ghost is part of the audience, and it has been arranged by the queen of Hades that he must discover what happened to him, without being told. The culprits themselves, of course, have no occasion to mention it. If this is assumed, the audience has the interest of keeping half an eye on the ghost, to see whether he has guessed the point yet, while the ghost watches the actors and the actors watch the play-within-the-play. I do not think this bold conception has been given its due.[1]

The ghost opens the play by entering with Revenge, and makes clear at once that he knows of no reason for revenging himself. His coolness all round, indeed, compared to Hamlet's father for example, is very refreshing. (However, we cannot suppose that the

Ur-father-Hamlet was cool, since the only thing we hear about him is that he was pale and cried revenge miserably like an oyster-wife; this would at least prevent the two plays from being absurdly similar.) When alive he was at the Spanish court, he says, and was accepted as a lover by a lady above his social position, not that his position was bad; then he happened to get killed in a war with Portugal. The puzzle began when he got to the classical Hades; the officials there couldn't decide whether he was a lover or a soldier, so he was referred up in the administrative machine to the king and queen. Proserpine smiled, and asked Pluto to let her settle it; then she whispered in the ear of Revenge, and the two have arrived back on earth. Revenge says Andrea will see his Bel-imperia kill the man who killed himself (Andrea): 'here sit we down to see the mystery' (I. i. 90).[2] But on the face of it there is no mystery, and no reason why the administration of Hades should be disturbed, let alone why Proserpine should grin and whisper. The ghost also sees something else, which he is not told beforehand; Bel-imperia chooses another lover, Horatio, and Horatio is killed by her brother Lorenzo, so that there will again be no obstacle to her marrying the prince of Portugal. Surely all this has only one possible point; Andrea is to guess that her family had previously arranged, in the same way, to kill himself.

We may pause at 'Here sit we down' to ask where they sit. The text as we have it seems planned for a full Elizabethan stage, and it looks as if the play-within-the-play was done on the inner stage, with the courtly audience on the balcony, rather absurdly pretending that the spectacle was in front of them. In any case, human listeners appear 'above' at II. ii, the imprisoned Bel-imperia appears 'at a window' in III. ix, and before the play-within-the-play Hieronymo asks the duke to throw him down the key after the audience has gone up (this gives him a bit of time to harangue them before they 'break down the doors'). Thus Ghost and Revenge can't be 'above'; I take it they sit right out in front, each of them leaning against one of the pillars which held up the Heavens. This puts them on a rather homely footing, and makes clear that they are part of the audience, except that most of the time Revenge is asleep.

At I. iv, Bel-imperia hears about Andrea's death from Horatio, who captured Balthazar just after he had killed Andrea. Andrea, he says, had fought long with Balthazar, but then fate took a hand and 'brought in a fresh supply of halberdiers, Which paunch'd his horse and ding'd him to the ground'; then Balthazar 'finished' him, 'taking advantage of his foe's distress'. Bel-imperia, after Horatio has gone, finds this sufficient reason to want revenge on Balthazar, and to make Horatio her lover for the purpose:

> But how can love find harbour in my breast,
> Till I revenge the death of my beloved?
> Yes, second love shall further my revenge.
> I'll love Horatio, my Andrea's friend,
> The more to spite the prince that wrought his end.
> And where Don Balthazar, that slew my love,
> Himself now pleads for favour at my hands,
> He shall in rigour of my just disdain
> Reap long repentance for his murd'rous deed:
> For what was 't else but murd'rous cowardice,
> So many to oppress one valiant knight,
> Without respect of honour in the fight?   (I. iv. 64–75)

However, she clearly doesn't mean to kill him for his unsporting behaviour – she assumes he will have 'long repentance'; nor would the audience think it an adequate reason for the ghost to be sent back by Proserpine. The audience can, however, notice that the halberdiers arrived very opportunely; maybe they weren't sent only by fate. By the way, on the stage Bel-imperia has not yet met Balthazar; it is assumed that for dynastic reasons he is already her suitor, not that he fell in love with her on meeting her after his capture. At II. i. 45, when Lorenzo is extracting the secret of Bel-imperia's love for Horatio from her servant Pedringano, we learn that her father was angry at her love for Andrea, and that the watchful Lorenzo then saved Pedringano from being punished as a go-between, apparently to use him later; it all helps to make the fate of Andrea look suspicious. The nearest we get to an admission of the murder is in the evasive language which Lorenzo uses to Bel-imperia when he is explaining why he locked her up (III. x). He says it is essential for her honour that he should protect her from herself, so when he happened to find her with Horatio –

> Why then, remembering that old disgrace
> Which you for Don Andrea had endur'd,
> And now were likely longer to sustain,
> By being found so meanly accompanied,
> Thought rather, for I knew no readier mean,
> To thrust Horatio forth my father's way.   (III. x. 54–9)

We learn nothing about how she interprets this; she is behaving with fierce dignity, especially because of the presence of Balthazar. We do not see her again for some time, apart from two riddling answers in public, till IV. i, where she upbraids Hieronymo for not having done his revenge, threatens to do it herself, and promises to help him (prefiguring Lady Macbeth and the Queen of *Hamlet* Q1). One might think that her brother's remark had some geographical meaning, that Horatio was banished from the town by a private gate; but she would know this to be a lie; she saw the murder, said so at the time, and told about it in her letter afterwards. Thus there seems no meaning for 'To thrust him forth my father's way' except 'I killed him, as my father did Andrea'. It is meant, of course, to be the more thrilling because obscure.[3]

The idea that the duke [of Castile] is guilty appears again prominently at the end, though he has always kept up an innocent appearance. The last act of Hieronymo before he kills himself is to kill the duke; this might be merely a sign of madness, or might give him a complete revenge against the son, but I do not think the audience would find that satisfying. In any case, the ghost of Andrea is then allowed by Revenge to arrange punishments for the villains; he starts the list cheerfully with the duke, and it is clear that Revenge thinks this proper. The reason must be (though poor Hieronymo may not have been told by Bel-imperia, and the audience only know it from the phrase 'my father's way') that the duke had arranged the death of Andrea.[4]

The reason why we have this duke in the cast, brother to a childless king, is I take it simply to avoid revenge against a king, which would be too wicked on the separate ground of divine right; the king has then to be childless to make the proposed marriage of Bel-imperia dynastic. We gather from III. xiv that Lorenzo has hidden his murder of Horatio from the duke, which seems unnecessary as he must know the duke would approve; but it adds to the mystery to make the duke a complete hypocrite, and no doubt Lorenzo himself is merely keeping to his principles:

> no man knows it was my reaching fatch.
> 'Tis hard to trust unto a multitude,
> Or anyone, in mine opinion,
> When men themselves their secrets will reveal.

The effect of the speech (III. iv. 46–9) is a challenge to the audience to discover further secrets.

Going back to the scene of Lorenzo with his sister, the actors need to make clear that he is trying to break her spirit. Soon after the riddle about 'my father's way', which she ought to receive as a horrible flash of light, she asks with her usual firm dignity whether her father has not inquired for her while Lorenzo kept her imprisoned, and he breaks the formality of their dialogue (Balthazar being present) by saying he must whisper in her ear. We heard about this before she entered; Balthazar remarked that she had better be released soon because her father was asking for her, and Lorenzo said jauntily:

> Why, and my lord, I hope you heard me say
> Sufficient reason why she kept away:
> But that's all one. My lord, you love her?
> BAL.:   Ay.
> LOR.: Then in your love beware, deal cunningly   (III. x. 15–18)

and so forth; 'Jest with her gently', which in view of the other jokes in the play may be expected to mean something appalling. He might simply have told her father that she was prostrated by the murder of her lover, but why need such a story be whispered to her? I take it the audience presumed him to whisper, perhaps falsely, that he had told her father she was procuring an abortion. She could make this clear by a flash of horror and disgust, though she must recover at once her contemptuous grandeur towards both of them:

> Too politic for me, past all compare,
> Since last I saw you; but content yourself,
> The prince is meditating higher things.   (III. x. 85–7)

(i.e. 'Balthazar is too holy to have overheard you'). The play should be rather like an opera, with the end-stopped lines pronounced next door to song, so this break is a strong dramatic effect; what had to be whispered, presumably, was what could not be said in the high language of the honour of Spain. She ends the scene with a riddle about fear in Latin, and no doubt this would easily suggest Seneca and a determination to revenge.

I think, then, that the play could be produced so as to make pretty clear to the audience that Andrea had been murdered for love, but I admit that it is peculiar for the text never to say it. A mystery is dramatic, but you expect to have an answer at the end of the play, and the ghost could give it in one line. Perhaps he did, and it got dropped from the printed text. But there were several editions, the first probably earlier than the first dated one of 1594, and you might argue that even the Elizabethans would want to restore such an important omission. However, though the answer would need to be made clear to the first audiences (if only by the production), the first readers would know it already, not buy the quarto to find it. In any case, the ghost at the end could not say much about himself, because the audience has rather lost interest in his story compared to what they have seen; he settles down contentedly to the administrative work of giving the villains suitable torments in his classical Hades. He is an unusual type of ghost, and one may imagine that from the first he didn't bother to draw the moral about himself; thus perhaps recovering some of the mystery which he had otherwise so frankly thrown away.

Another peculiar thing about him is that he is entirely unjealous; to watch Bel-imperia giving herself to Horatio excites no complaint. He does indeed complain at the end of Act I that he is only shown 'league, and love, and banqueting' (I. v. 4) instead of revenge as expected (Revenge gives him a brief appalling reassurance), but presumably he would mention the infidelity of Bel-imperia if he felt it as such; and at the end of Act II he combines their names without the smallest resentment:

> Brought'st thou me hither to increase my pain?
> I look'd that Balthazar should have been slain:
> But 'tis my friend Horatio that is slain,
> And they abuse fair Bel-imperia,
> On whom I doted more than all the world,
> Because she lov'd me more than all the world.   (II. vi. 1–6)

(Revenge gives him a further reassurance.) For that matter, Bel-imperia while imprisoned (III. ix. 9–11) herself appeals to the ghost of Andrea, taking for granted that he would not mind her change to Horatio:

> Andrea, O Andrea, that thou sawest
> Me for thy friend Horatio handled thus,
> And him for me thus causeless murdered.

By the way, this almost necessitates some reaction from the ghost, so he may be presumed to have reacted elsewhere; I think Revenge ought to have to hush him, both here and at the words 'my father's way'. The appeal seems to get him worked up, though in a stupid manner, because after Act III (there are only four acts) he needs a longer interlude. He is distressed at finding all quarrels apparently quieted, and Bel-imperia agreeing to marry the prince of Portugal. The audience are to think the poor creature rather dull, because the agreement of Hieronymo is patently false, and we only hear from Bel-imperia three-and-a-half lines of harsh double-talk. Revenge, while trying to reassure him, uses an exact echo of the riddling talk of Hieronymo in III. xiii, and prepares us for more of it in IV. i:

> Nor dies Revenge although he sleep awhile,
> For in unquiet, quietness is feign'd,
> And slumb'ring is a common worldly wile.   (III. xv. 23–5)

This proves to the audience that Hieronymo is a correct revenger; and indeed a revenger always wants to be somehow Revenge in person. It is inadequate to calm the ghost, who is only made to shut up ('argue not') by being given a separate dumb show with an explanation of it. He then says

> Sufficeth me, thy meaning's understood,
> And thanks to thee and those infernal powers
> That will not tolerate a lover's woe.   (III. xv. 36–8)

Now the combination of this grand phrase with his complete friendship to Horatio cuts out all but one interpretation; the lover's woe has to be the arranged marriage. I understand that this custom was almost universal, at least in the sense that the families were expected to come to an agreement about the money affairs of a young couple; but the theatre was always in favour of the lovers as against the arranged marriage, and no doubt it was echoing a state of sentiment which often avoided harshness in borderline cases. Now, if you wanted to have a play against the arranged marriage, the royal marriages of Spain and Portugal gave the most impressive example you could find. It is clear that dynastic importance attaches to the marriage of Bel-imperia and Balthazar; as early as II. iii. 18, as a way of settling the war, the king says to the Portuguese ambassador (after referring to the dowry from the lady's father),

> ... in case this match go forward,
> The tribute which you pay shall be releas'd,
> And if by Balthazar she have a son,
> He shall enjoy the kingdom after us.

One might assume that this meant giving Spain itself to the royal family of Portugal, but he never speaks of excluding his nephew Lorenzo, and Portugal is only ruled by a viceroy, whose failure to pay tribute has caused the war. He means that Portugal would be allowed to recover its independent sovereignty in favour of a son of this marriage. The only problem is that, if Lorenzo is the heir to both Spain and Portugal, he can hardly want to commit all these murders merely in order to make his sister produce an independent heir to Portugal. He might conceivably argue, in a statesmanlike manner, that Portugal is getting too hard to hold under the present system. Presumably the audience wouldn't bother much; they would only feel sure that the marriage somehow mattered a great deal.

The question, of course, was a major one of current politics. Spain and Portugal had acquired the first maritime empires, and the pope had divided America between them. For England, the great enemy was Spain, and Spain when the play was new had recently acquired by inheritance the whole empire of Portugal. That is, Philip II took it in 1580 and made a reasonable hereditary claim; he had to send an army to Lisbon, and I gather had other grounds such as that the Portuguese had been trying to take Morocco, but the hereditary claim was an essential part. One could hardly say that he got Portugal by marriage; he got it because the more direct male heirs of that house had become too holy to produce children; but he got it by an earlier royal marriage, and that is the kind of thing the play envisages. Emanuel the Fortunate, I learn from the encyclopaedia, in whose reign the Portuguese Empire was founded, 'had pursued the traditional policy of intermarriage with the royal families of Castile and Aragon, hoping to weld together the Spanish and Portuguese dominions' [*Encyclopædia Britannica*, 14th edn., p. 279]; as indeed he did, though sexually the wrong way round for his purpose. (The arrangement, with Portugal technically independent but happening to have as its king the king of Spain, lasted till 1640.) One might think the first audiences would be in favour of Belimperia for liking brave native lovers and refusing to unite Spain with Portugal, but politically they would have to be in favour of this marriage, because it might separate Spain from Portugal. Presumably they would also be rather shocked by her because it is made so clear that she goes to bed with her lovers (among the first words of the play are 'In secret I possess'd a worthy dame'). One would assume that all the characters were a bit wicked, but the main sentiment would be against these oppressively important royal marriages (which the queen of England had been quite right to refuse);

one would take for granted that any amount of murder would be done before such a thing was arranged.

A slight suggestion that all these characters are wicked no doubt helps to bring in the idea of fate, which gets rather unusual treatment. Some critics have called the ghost a clumsy and undramatic device because, not only pointless, he has no effect on the action. In any case, it is dramatic to be able to glance at the ghost in the audience, as you might at one of your friends, and wonder whether he has got on to the point yet. But I also think it is symbolically good as expressing a moral truth. Swinburne wrote about the *Hamlet* of Shakespeare that the characters 'veer sideways to their doom';[5] this is true in general about the Elizabethan revenge play, rather than making as he supposed a contrast between the first and second quarto. May I express here my impatience with 'Fate'; it seems both logical nonsense and harmful in its historical effects. But in the story before us we can give the word a reasonable interpretation; if this family keeps on killing the daughter's suitors, one after another, to make a grand marriage, then it does seem likely to run into trouble some time. Proserpine might intelligibly smile when she told Andrea to go and see what happened next. Revengers indeed are usually presented as acting in a roundabout manner, chiefly perhaps because they dislike what they are trying to approach; and the catastrophe is usually arranged to come as much from the nature of the villains as from the loony though fascinating calculations of the revenger. In this play, for example, Lorenzo is only discovered because he is so vainly ingenious about getting his tools to kill each other off. However, though this gives us a tolerable meaning of Fate, I must admit it is not one that a revenger while in mental turmoil would accept. He wants to take part in fate; he wants to show that he is acting *as* or *like* fate, which itself evidently works in a roundabout way. Such is the doom of Old Hieronymo, but the ghost is spared it; he sits among the audience listening with some impatience while the revenger babbles about how clever and useful it is for him to be mad. I have come to think that this early play gave a more profound treatment of revenge than the later ones.

It can be presumed, I think, that the Ur-*Hamlet*, with its handfuls of speeches and the ghost crying miserably like an oyster-wife, had been written before *The Spanish Tragedy*. The French of Belleforest was an easily accessible source for *Hamlet*, and likely to be combed for material – it was a big collection of moral tales; whereas for *The*

Spanish Tragedy no source has ever been found. None could be, if it was simply an attempt to apply the technique and atmosphere of the Ur-*Hamlet* to the highly topical theme of the royal marriages of Spain. The basic idea would be 'Take a woman who revolted against one of these shocking royal marriages, and you would get a similar case of madness and revenge.' Like so many previous critics, I am putting a lot of weight on the Ur-*Hamlet* for conjectural arguments, but to do that one need not assume it was very good (indeed, it seems plausible as well as comforting to suppose that no very good Elizabethan play failed to hit print). It was a decisively important foundation, or piece of basic engineering, for the Elizabethan drama, because it showed them how to express something they wanted to (if you like, how to adapt their Seneca to the Christian conscience and the Renaissance code of honour); but Kyd would have learned a bit by experience, the year after his initial success, when he entirely transposed his material into *The Spanish Tragedy*. This would be a good reason why only the second play got printed, though no doubt there were accidental causes as well.

I am assuming that the audiences of the first period of Elizabethan drama thought revenge wicked, and that a dramatist trying to present a revenger had to reckon with the weight of that feeling. This is handled by the structure of the play, before it advances on the serious case of Hieronymo; such is the only purpose of the rather absurd sub-plot, about events at the court of Portugal. The first time human characters speak of revenge is when the Viceroy is brooding over the fate of his son if captured in the battle; a courtier suggests that the Spaniards would not make 'a breach to common law of arms', but he answers, in the first of the grand echoing lines of which the play is so full,

> They reck no laws that meditate revenge.   (I. iii. 48)

A courtier in reply calls revenge 'foul'. We then see the captured son insisting with high rhetoric (II. i. 111–33) that revenge is essential to his nature if the woman refuses the marriage which his plans demand;

> Yet I must take revenge or die myself,

he says, if she has another lover. The dramatic irony is heightened if we already suspect that he had been tipped off to kill her previous lover in the battle. In any case, he is presented early as the admittedly wicked type of man who takes revenge for granted, therefore as very unlike the final revenger Hieronymo.

Some critics have said that in a crude play like *The Spanish Tragedy* the revenger is simply mad, whereas the whole subtlety and profundity of Shakespeare consisted in introducing doubt as to whether the hero was mad or not. This sounds likely, but I believe it is now generally admitted to be wrong. It underrates the general moral background of the audience, apart from their native wits; and the questions which were being discussed in the theatre, in a theatrical manner as one might expect, had a good deal of practical importance. I want now to advance on a rather lengthy attempt to prove that Hieronymo is just like Hamlet in being both mad and not mad, both wise and not wise, and so forth.

The last action of Hieronymo, before the trick by which he secures a knife to kill the duke and himself, is to bite out his tongue lest tortures force him to confess his secret. Many critics have complained at the 'sensationalism' of this, particularly as he seems to have no secret to tell.[6] I think they would have discovered the point if they had allowed themselves to speak with less restraint; the incident is wildly absurd, as it was meant to be, because Hieronymo has just told the bereaved fathers everything he possibly could.

> And to this end the bashaw I became
> That might revenge me on Lorenzo's life,
> Who therefore was appointed to the part
> And was to represent the knight of Rhodes,
> That I might kill him more conveniently.
> So, Viceroy, was this Balthazar, thy son,
> That Soliman which Bel-imperia
> In person of Perseda murdered:
> Solely appointed to that tragic part,
> That she might slay him that offended her.
> Poor Bel-imperia miss'd her part in this,
> For though the story saith she should have died,
> Yet I of kindness, and of care to her,
> Did otherwise determine of her end:
> But love of him whom they did hate too much
> Did urge her resolution to be such. (IV. iv. 130–45)

Nothing could seem madder than this professorial tone, patiently explaining at length what is already obvious, with a pedantic satisfaction in making clear where there were little errors of detail. But at last, when he has finished telling everything, a great wave of revulsion comes over him; there is something he must never tell, at all costs; so he bites out his tongue. This is very imaginative, I think, and the whole point of it is that he is now completely mad. The reason why critics have not found this obvious, I suspect, is that they were ready to assume the old play would commit any absurdity, just to have some more blood splashing about, and also ready to let the development of the character be obscured by Jonson's additions. Jonson removed the incident of biting out the tongue and put in some poetical mad talk instead; no doubt it had come to seem too absurd altogether, *too* un-life-like, by 1600. But really his additions, as a whole, made the old play much *more* un-life-like, because he was going all out to satisfy 'the modern convention' of the revenge play. He makes Hieronymo raging mad as soon as he finds his son dead, and from then on another splendid bout of madness is inserted at each convenient point; then each time we return to the old text and find him sane enough to carry on his plot. But in the crude old play he is only gradually pushed into madness, just as he is only gradually pushed into revenge; he disapproves of both, but cannot keep them from him; a long period of grizzling over his wrong and puzzling over his duty has to be gone through, and all this time he is getting madder. Just before he gets to the deed of blood his wife kills herself because he hasn't yet done it; this ought to be enough to show that he is assumed to feel powerful resistances against it. And after he at last has done it, instead of being 'pleased and eased' as he boasts, he is for the first time completely off his rocker. Presumably the audience knew that a man would be unable to bite out his tongue unless in a highly abnormal condition. All this makes a much more human and sensible picture of revenge and its madness than you get from the play with Jonson's additions, though I confess that the old version would be very hard to put over on a modern audience, as no doubt Jonson felt about his own audience. The theatre of Kyd was presumably very formalised both in acting style and in the way the audience was meant to interpret; they were to feel that biting out the tongue symbolised something true, rather than that this individual had already convinced them he had a character likely to do it.

The contrast between the periods looks rather more definite if one considers Jonson himself. We know from Henslowe's accounts that he was twice paid to write additions to Hieronymo, in 1601 and 1602, and it seems clear that this marks an attempt by the Admiral's Company to offer an adequate counter to Shakespeare's *Hamlet* (incidentally I think Shakespeare was also offering further 'additions' in the second year). Some critics carry their reverence for style so far that even with the accounts in front of them they refuse to believe Jonson wrote the existing additions, because they aren't 'in Jonson's style'; so Henslowe must have paid somebody else for better additions than Jonson's, and these are what got printed. From what we know of Henslowe it is extremely unlikely that he tossed money about in this manner, and I don't think it at all unlikely that Jonson could write in a different style if he was challenged and paid to. He was then 29, rather struggling for his position, and a very clever man. It does him great credit that he could write so wonderfully in the high Elizabethan romantic manner:

> Confusion, mischief, torment, death and hell,
> Drop all your stings at once in my cold bosom,
> That now is stiff with horror: kill me quickly:
> Be gracious to me, thou infective night,
> And drop this deed of murder down on me:
> Gird in my waste of grief with thy large darkness,
> And let me not survive to see the light
> May put me in the mind I had a son.   (First addition, 45–52)

(this is Hieronymo when he has just discovered the corpse); but one can understand that he did not want to print it in his collected edition. No doubt he didn't himself know quite how far his tongue was in his cheek; but in any case he was trying to satisfy a demand, he was writing to a very clear-cut 'convention'. Whereas, when Kyd wrote the old version, the convention had not yet been established; he needed to make his basic development of character much more reasonable and in accordance with serious moral opinion, even though the incidents he used would be less realistic. This view, I submit, gives a consistent explanation of the difficulties of the texts.[7]

I must admit that Hieronymo speaks of revenge soon after he has discovered the body. He has twenty lines of lament before his wife enters, then:

> ISABELLA. What world of grief – My son Horatio!
>   O where's the author of this endless woe?
> HIER.   To know the author were some ease of grief,
>   For in revenge my heart would find relief.
>
>   (II. v. 38–41)

He tells her that he will keep the bloody handkerchief till he takes revenge, and tells her to dissemble her sorrow for the present: 'so

shall we sooner find the practice out'. It seems to be the lament of
the mother which puts this practical idea into his head. Even so,
they both appear to be thinking in terms of law; as when Isabella
says 'The heavens are just, murder cannot be hid.' It is only when
the heir to the throne is found to be implicated that normal justice is
assumed to be impossible. The discovery of the body is at the end of
Act II; in III. i, we are taken away to see the viceroy of Portugal
doing injustice because of the false witness of a villain, and the
victim says

> Nor discontents it me to leave the world,
> With whom there nothing can prevail but wrong. (III. i. 33–4)

Then scene ii begins with the famous soliloquy of Hieronymo
denouncing all the world, as

> Confus'd and fill'd with murder and misdeeds.   (4)

The whole scene is darkening. He feels he is being dragged into
revenge; both night and day, he says, are driving him to seek the
murderer, and

> The ugly fiends do sally forth of hell,
> And frame my steps to unfrequented paths,
> And fear my heart with fierce inflamed thoughts.   (16–18)

These lines can only mean that he partly suspects the whole process
of revenge to be a bad one. Next the letter falls, written by the
imprisoned Bel-imperia in her blood to accuse her brother. Hieronymo like Hamlet is suspicious of this first evidence, and warns
himself that it may only be intended to prevent his revenge by
inducing him to make a false accusation against Lorenzo, which
would endanger his life. In spite of this caution to himself, he
immediately does excite the suspicion of Lorenzo, who enters at
once, and Lorenzo therefore sets to work to cover his tracks by
killing both his accomplices. This is done by getting one of them,
Pedringano, to kill the other, and then having him hanged for it;
Pedringano believes till the last moment that Lorenzo will get him
off. We next see Hieronymo in scene vi, acting in his function as
judge; he begins by bemoaning that 'neither gods nor men be just to
me' (10). The refusal of Pedringano to pray before he is hanged
(actually because he can see the boy holding the box which he
believes to contain his pardon) draws from Hieronymo his most
splendid sentence against the revengeful mind.

I have not seen a wretch so impudent!
O monstrous times, where murder's set so light,
And where the soul, that should be shrin'd in heaven,
Solely delights in interdicted things,
Still wand'ring in the thorny passages
That intercepts itself of happiness.
Murder, O bloody monster – God forbid
A fault so foul should scape unpunished.
Despatch, and see this execution done:
This makes me to remember thee, my son.   (III. vi. 89–98)

In a way it is dramatic irony against Hieronymo, who fails to apply this reflection to himself. But it is not heavily against him; he is speaking as a judge, and we are not meant to think him wrong for wanting justice to be done. By the way, there is evidence here that our text at any rate leaves out stage directions, because no use is made of the boy standing by with the box. When Pedringano demands life 'by my pardon from the king', and the hangman replies (104)

> Stand you on that? then you shall off with this
> *He turns him off.*

It is clear that Pedringano must point at the boy with the box, who opens it with hearty laughter showing it to be empty, before the hangman dare proceed. A critic may reasonably impute other omitted 'business' elsewhere, such as might clear up the mystery about Andrea.

In scene vii, Hieronymo in soliloquy is a noticeable degree crazier; he has

> Made mountains marsh with spring-tides of my tears,
> And broken through the brazen gates of hell.
> Yet still tormented is my tortur'd soul.   (8–10)

Then the hangman brings a letter written by Pedringano in prison, begging Lorenzo to hurry up, and pleading for himself 'I holp to murder Don Horatio, too' (39). Hieronymo is now convinced that the letter written in blood was true; and by the way he hasn't learned it by any of the subtlety he proposed – the prison letter is merely handed on to him as the officiating judge. For that matter, Hamlet's pretence of madness in Saxo does not let him find out who the murderer is (a thing universally known), and even in Shakespeare it at most only makes the king act suspiciously – what convinces Hamlet is the play-within-the-play. Hamlet in Saxo has superfine senses (like the fairy-story princess who was black and blue from the pea under the nineteen mattresses), and Belleforest makes this 'rational' by explaining he was a magician. Shakespeare may have been drawing on this tradition for the piercing and testing quality of the mad talk of his Hamlet, but I don't suppose it was much use to the Hamlet of Kyd. The main thrill about his talk was that he could tell the truth without being believed.

Hieronymo deduces from this accident that Heaven is arranging to punish the murderer by letting out the truth (lines 48 and 56). He is still thinking as a judge, and can say as such that 'naught but blood will satisfy my woes' (68); indeed, not only does he still hope to get this blood lawfully, but he noticeably refuses to threaten that he will otherwise get it unlawfully.

> I will go plain me to my lord the king,
> And cry aloud for justice through the court,
> Wearing the flints with these my wither'd feet,
> And either purchase justice by entreats
> Or tire them all with my revenging threats.   (69–73)

There should I suppose be a dramatic pause after 'Or'. We next see him, after three more scenes, on his way to the court for this procedure; and he is now, perhaps from reflecting on the difficulty of it, at a stage where passers-by call him mad. He goes out and comes back (a mark of folly on the stage used by Hamlet in talking both to Ophelia and to the queen). The passers-by ask him the way to Lorenzo's house, and he describes it as going to hell; this appears simply to denounce Lorenzo, but also means that his own going there puts him on the path of wickedness.

> A darksome place and dangerous to pass:
> There shall you meet with melancholy thoughts,
> Whose baleful humours if you but uphold,
> It will conduct you to despair and death.   (iii. xi. 16–19)

He begins the next scene by rejecting two methods of suicide as an unreliable source of revenge – this is not as stagey as it may appear, because many suicides actually are done to punish other people (institutionally among the Japanese); and it was a necessary partial justification of the revenger that he should be willing to die. In his appearance before the king (this is scene xii) he is too easily shuffled aside by Lorenzo; one would think the letter of Pedringano need only be shown. It would be fussy to deny that Kyd is unskilful at this crucial point of the play, unless our text has been curtailed. But the story is not absurd; Hieronymo's nervous condition might well prevent him from making his accusation except in so violent a form as to sound mad, and the first audiences might recognise more easily than we do that he had a practical danger – if he produced at once his evidence against the heir to the throne, it could simply be taken from him and destroyed. He does win the sympathy of the king, who proposes to look into his case later (line 100). As the chief object of Hieronymo is to speak to the king away from the brother and nephew, this means that his choice of mad behaviour nearly succeeded. (Of course, in one way he can't help being peculiar, but in another way he is trying to make use of it.) But the king only says this after he has gone, and then refers the matter to the duke, who has Lorenzo at the interview; so that Hieronymo again feels that his case is hopeless.

He next comes in (scene xiii) 'with a book in his hand' like Hamlet, because he is grappling with the theory of revenge. I want to maintain that his arguments were meant to seem mad to the audience, or at least tragically deluded; such is the point of development he ought to have reached, and he is at least very confused about the well-known difficulties of his topic. But you may say that the audience was confused too, and I confess that there is at least one point in the play where we are inclined to think both author and audience very simple. It is at the end of Act I; to establish the position of Hieronymo as court playwright, we have him showing a masque to the king and the Portuguese ambassador, consisting of three English knights who capture two Portuguese kings and one Spanish king. Both dignitaries accept this with high chivalry, saying that, as even little England can win, one ought to accept calmly the fortunes of war. This seems childlike unreality, but I suppose any members of the audience who thought so would be content to take it as charming; in any case, it comes early, before the play is too serious for it. I do not think we need impute the same careless effrontery to the discussion of Hieronymo about revenge. He begins with the Scripture text 'Vindicta mihi' (I will repay, saith the Lord), which meant that men must not do this work of God, and contrives to twist it into meaning only that a revenger ought to delay until God gives him a good opportunity. Having used Latin for this Bible text, he can move smoothly over to Seneca as if the two had equal moral

authority; but his next bit of Latin has to be twisted equally
violently before it will suit his purpose. The line became a stock one
for the Elizabethan drama, either in quotation or in echo, but I
doubt whether it was ever again so starkly misused.

> *Per scelus semper tutum est sceleribus iter*;
> Strike, and strike home, when wrong is offered thee.   (6–7)

Clytemnestra says this when nerving herself to kill Agamemnon, and
has just remarked that her chance of taking 'the better way' has
already gone; she has already behaved so badly that her only chance
of safety lies in further crime. Nobody but Hieronymo ever took it to
mean that a good man, when a crime is done against him, ought to
commit an immediate crime in reply. Even so, his interpretation
contradicts the one he has just made from the Bible text; he deduces
now that he ought to revenge at once, instead of waiting till God
gives him a good opportunity. He encourages this view by a baffling
argument that the duty of 'patience', which of course was prominent
in medieval thought, was really a recommendation to suicide. This
is supported by a third Latin quotation, about fate; this time from
the *Troades*, when poor little Astyanax is hidden in a tomb and told
that, even if the Greeks catch him there, he has at least got his tomb
handy. Hieronymo manages to deduce:

> . . . let this thy comfort be,
> Heaven covereth him that hath no burial.
> And to conclude, I will revenge his death!
> But how? not as the vulgar wits of men,
> With open, but inevitable ills,
> As by a secret, yet a certain mean,
> Which under kindship will be cloaked best.   (III. xiii. 18–24)

'Not with open injuries, as men do, but with inevitable ones, as Fate
does' – such has to be the grammar, and the effect is that he proposes
to become Fate in person, so he must act by roundabout and
unexpected methods, as one must agree that Fate appears to do. The
lines go straight on to a solution of the problem whether to delay,
and here I think the audience *must* have been meant to realise that
he is talking nonsense, even if they were meant to be rather stunned
by the bits of Latin.[8]

> Wise men will take their opportunity,
> Closely and safely fitting things to time:
> But in extremes advantage hath no time,

And therefore all times fit not for revenge.
Thus therefore will I rest me in unrest,
Dissembling quiet in unquietness,
Not seeming that I know their villainies,
That my simplicity may make them think
That ignorantly I will let all slip:
For ignorance, I wot, and well they know,
Remedium malorum iners est   (25–35)

In extremes advantage hath no time can only mean, I submit, 'in such a
hard case as mine waiting is useless, because there will never be a
safe opportunity'; and indeed all cases suited to revenge plays are
'extreme' like this, because the revenger is so desperate that he is
ready to die as soon as he has succeeded – this is necessary, to make
the audience respect him however much they think him wrong. But
this created a difficulty for the other requirement of the theatre, that
he is needed to argue and delay; and here the knot is cut (by a
complete contradiction in the next line) with a bold absurdity
intended to make the audience realise that he is mad. Now that he
has settled his problem the poetry sounds very contented; he enjoys
thinking how subtle he will be, and manages to extract a kind of cosy
gloating out of a third tag from Seneca, which is again off the point.
Oedipus was saying, with courageous public spirit, that the reason
for the plague must necessarily be found, whatever its
unpleasantness to himself; this is very remote from the idea of hiding
by flattery an intention of private revenge. After thus consistently
showing the informed spectator that he is hopelessly confused, he
ends the speech with the one argument that the audience would
respect; that he cannot work in any other way, because if he showed
any 'menace' to his enemies they would 'bear me down with their
nobility' (38).

Some petitioners now enter to see the judge, and for the first time
he is violently crazy, as the speech has prepared us to find him; he
rips up their expensive documents, and then patters away saying
'catch me' (Shakespeare copied this twice, separating the two
elements of the madness of the revenger; we get the grim humour of
the pretence in Hamlet – 'Hide fox, and all after' – and the pathos of
its reality in Lear, waving his boots in his hands.) It is in the next
scene that we see Hieronymo fail in his last chance of getting public
justice, the interview with the duke of Castile (the audience thinks
he is right in suspecting the duke to be a hypocrite, but also that a

saner man would have made some attempt); then we advance on the final act, where he agrees on revenge with Bel-imperia and has only to plan the method with a lunatic and presumably unnecessary cunning.

I hope this is enough to show that the old play gives a graduated advance towards madness and revenge, taking for granted that only great and prolonged forces would have driven such a character into such a crime. It might not seem to need much proof, but a rival theory has been growing up, of a kind which I call 'neo-Christian', that the Elizabethans considered their theology to be in favour of revenge, and that we would too if we weren't rotted with 'humanitarianism'. I find something rather alarming in this fashion for savagery among dons. Actually, I take it, the clergy regularly said that revenge was very wicked, but the soldiers tended to say that a man's honour might require it; an audience would not have only one opinion, but would broadly agree on feeling that, while revenge was nearly always very wicked, a point might come where it was almost inevitable. Indeed, so far as we still find the plays good, we do so because they reflect this breadth of feeling. As for Hieronymo, who has worried about it as much as he ought to have done, the pretence of a classical next world might leave room for doubt, but still he is definitely not damned at the end of the play by the supernatural characters who distribute punishments in Hades; indeed the Ghost calls him 'good Hieronymo' (IV. v. 11).

It could be said, however, that the second crop of Elizabethan revenge plays, around 1600, was itself a rather similar fashion; Marston makes a pet of a hero in a monstrous fit of sulks [*Antonio's Revenge*], in some way that Kyd does not.[9] Shakespeare in rewriting *Hamlet* seems to have been following a trend, and, though he certainly didn't abandon himself to it, I rather suspect he cut out the 'moral' of the old play, in the course of bringing it up to date. This obvious moral, from the surviving plot, is that Hamlet ought not to have spared Claudius at prayer, at least for the reason he gave; being the rightful king, it was his duty to kill a criminal usurper, but even a king had no right to try to send a man to hell (as by refusing absolution before he was executed). Hamlet went too far about revenge, and this was fatal to him. He is already an alarmingly tricky character in the sources, and Kyd needed to invent some crisis which would turn his story into a tragedy. If you admit that *The Spanish Tragedy* is not pointless, this moral for *Hamlet* seems one which Kyd might well have invented. Shakespeare of course would assume it to be well known, so that the chief effect of not mentioning it in his version was to raise a further mystery about the real motives of the character. Many critics of the last century, including Bernard Shaw, thought that Shakespeare couldn't say plainly what he thought about revenge because he was morally so much in advance of his coarse audience; and I should fancy they were right, except that he was about ten years behind it.

CHAPTER 2

'The Spanish Tragedy': a letter

Derek Roper, a colleague in the Department of English Literature at Sheffield University, took issue with a number of points in the preceding essay on The Spanish Tragedy. *Empson responded with the following letter, which ends by adumbrating the theory of censorship expounded in the next piece.*

13th October 1958

Dear Roper,

I have been mulling over the play and your comments on my theory. None of your objections seem to me decisive except one, a rather important one. You are probably right in thinking

> To thrust Horatio forth my father's way.   (III. x. 59)

means 'out of his way'; it is FORTH B. 2. in the *OED*, from out of, e.g. 'He went forth his desk.' Lorenzo has just been telling Bel-imperia that the king and their father were coming privately to consult with Hieronymo, and that he had come first to arrange the meeting; so it is just his style of pride to say 'I murdered Horatio to remove a disgusting object from my father's path' – except that now he doesn't even literally admit the murder of Horatio. There is now no approach to admitting the murder of Andrea, and we need not even be sure that the ghost of Andrea guesses it before the end. I still think this must be the point of the presence of the ghost, even granting that he and Revenge are only a 'frame'; but the point just gets taken for granted.

You feel this is absurd, and it does seem very odd; but the whole suggestion of the 'atmosphere' is that the court of Spain is poisoned with criminal secrets, though it always behaves with such formal grandeur that they as it were couldn't be mentioned. The style of course is frightfully stiff, and we tend to assume that this is just early Elizabethan drama, but it was also very well fitted for describing what they thought about the court of Spain. Secrets keep being hinted at; I notice now that Lorenzo, when saying he guesses Hieronymo knows who murdered his son, adds:

A guilty conscience, urged with the thought
Of former evils, easily cannot err. (III. iv. 14–15)

Surely we are expected to be curious about his former evils.

You wrote that Proserpine in the production 'suggests that the Ghost might enjoy seeing Balthazar himself killed', as he [Balthazar] had killed him in battle. No, she doesn't, she grins and whispers; then Revenge cheers up Andrea by saying that at least he will see Balthazar killed, and also find out what 'the mystery' was – that is, surely, why the underworld have been puzzled how to classify him. Certainly the ghost sticks to the idea that he wants at least to see Balthazar killed, but he makes clear that he finds the whole procedure pretty baffling. It is no use your saying that ghosts were conventionally blood-thirsty, because the question is whether this early ghost was a conventional one. Certainly he ends, in his rather fatuous way, by saying he is pleased about the whole sequence of deaths, listing them in order; but this is merely because the whole affair is cleared up and he is permitted to reward the good ones, whom he loves. By the way, it isn't quite such nonsense as you thought to have him send Bel-imperia

... to those joys
That vestal virgins and fair queens possess (IV. V. 21–2)

Presumably she counts as an honorary queen rather than an honorary virgin; she was princely minded to select her two lovers rather than submit to the wicked royal marriage. I don't say that this is very good, but it would prevent the audience from thinking the line farcical.

You were saying that surely Bel-imperia would tell what she knew when released, and could not be told more secrets than she knew already (the murder of Andrea as well as of Horatio). She says her brother is

Too politic for me, past all compare; (III. x. 85)

and when he ends the scene by saying

Nay, and you argue things so cunningly,
We'll go continue this discourse at court (III. x. 104–5)

he means to imply feelingly 'you wouldn't dare'. He says at the beginning of the scene that he can safely release her now that the nine-day's wonder of the murder is overblown (xi), which seems absurd as the king hasn't even heard of it (III. xii. 61–2), but we presume they are accustomed to hushing such things up. I take it the main idea is that she can't expose him, both because she has no evidence but her own assertion and because she would be exposing her love-affair by making it. Anyhow, she knows that the court is determined to ignore what she says and force her into the royal marriage. You were saying that the play ignores this aspect; well, her father begins II. iii by saying he will force her into the marriage, and the king then says the heir of it will be the king of Portugal. The audience needed no more; Balthazar himself of course firmly ignores it and claims to be pathetically in love with her, even while he is murdering her lover, because that is the grand manner of his Iberian honour. The one moment when she 'comes to life', by the way, is where she tries to save Horatio from being murdered by crying

> I lov'd Horatio but he lov'd not me   (II. iv. 58)

– a sacrifice of her pride, which is normally the chief motive of a Spanish character.

I was interested to see, going over the play again, that the sub-plot accuses Alexandro of murdering Balthazar in the battle. This gives a point to the tiresomely lengthy sub-plot, which I had thought was merely wanted to show how wicked revenge is and how usual in the Iberian peninsula; no, it brings in the idea of killing a man on your own side under cover of a battle, and this makes it easier to guess that this was what happened to Andrea. You say that the general's first account of the battle in I. ii doesn't mention that Balthazar had a troop of halberdiers up his sleeve to finish off Andrea; therefore, you feel, it can't be important when the eye-witness Horatio describes them in I. iv. But this is just what is suspicious; the Spanish general was not in the plot, but Castile and Lorenzo had tipped off Balthazar how to be ready to kill his rival in the battle. Surely this is a consistent development.

I agree that one can't say what motives Hieronymo has for killing Castile at the end, because he is at last definitely mad; my point is that this early audience would be surely moralistic, and wouldn't want to have Castile killed, let alone have Revenge approve of the killing and a punishment arranged in Hades, unless he had been shown to deserve it. I still think that, and still think the peculiar situation of the ghost must have been meant to have its obvious explanation in view. But I must say I am shaken by your explanation of 'my father's way'; it looks as if the explanation of the mystery never comes to the surface at all though it is planned for all along. One might I suppose fall back on the irritating theory that our text is cut; or your theory that Kyd left ideas lying about which he didn't use in his final version. I might enquire whether anything has come to light about the history of the text; there was a quarrel about the property in it, as I remember.

Thanks for your notes.

W. Empson

CHAPTER 3

'The Spanish Tragedy' (II)

The story of the Ghost, as we have it in our surviving text, seems very incomplete and confused, and would be actively pernicious if taken as moral advice, when the play was new. Fredson Bowers said he was meant as a moral warning *against* revenge, but he is close to the other revenger, Old Hieronymo, who is deliberately put into a test-case situation where almost anyone would consider revenge a duty.[1] Also an expectation is aroused but never gratified. The play opens with the ghost explaining himself to the audience, so far as he can; he has been sent back to earth from the classical underworld because the officials there could not decide whether he died as a lover or a soldier; if as a lover, he can go to the Elysian fields and be with Bel-imperia. His case was moved up and up in the legal hierarchy till it reached Pluto, whose wife grinned and whispered in his ear, and on her advice this ghost has been sent back to learn the answer. He is led by Revenge in person, who says: 'Here sit we down to see the mystery' (i. i. 90).[2] But the mystery is never solved, and we do not even hear whether the ghost is adjudged to have died as a lover. It is hard to see how Proserpine would arrange that, however willing she is, as he has told us that he was killed in a battle against the Portuguese. At the start, he is entirely cool, with no idea that he deserves a revenge; he is not quite a Bernard Shaw character, because he is impressed at the torments suffered by the wicked in this underworld, but he is not himself in any danger of them. His mind is undarkened. But as the play goes on he acquires a craving to be revenged (he can only watch, not take part, and he is evidently accustomed to action); till at the end, when practically all the characters are killed, he is especially delighted with 'good Hieronymo' for killing (when mad) the duke of Castile, against whom we have heard nothing except that he disapproved of his daughter's love-affair. The ghost does also want to be revenged on the man who killed him in battle, but that is not specially important to him; and indeed, if the rules were to be changed, so that death in battle created a duty of revenge for the survivors, about half the male population would be wandering about, seeking hopelessly for the enemy soldier who killed uncle.[3] I would readily agree that the habit of brooding over one's wrongs is a grave mental disease, eminently deserving satire; but if the play is meant to provide this it is very badly planned. So far from that, I think there is an obvious solution to the 'mystery' – Andrea was betrayed by his own side in the battle, so as to clear the way for a diplomatic marriage between Bel-imperia and the prince of Portugal. If only this point is made clear, the whole elaborate structure of the play becomes straight-forward.

I said this in an article about twenty years ago [see above], but the thesis was rightly considered incredible, because I had no idea how the answer could have got dropped from the play. I said it was so obvious that it did not need saying; or at least it could be said very shortly, and perhaps one line had got dropped out. But of course this is not how the theatre works; one might as well say that the murders at the end were so obvious that they might just as well be left out. I never did think of censorship as the obvious solution here; it was at last forced into my mind as the only way to explain the much more radical and baffling case of *Dr Faustus*, and then I could hardly help applying it also to the *Tragedy*. It is unfortunate that the two great foundation works of the Elizabethan theatre both happened to get mangled in this way, encouraging the later plays to become more boiling and irrational than they need have been – after being hacked about, both of these plays became exasperating to reason, and only to be justified as explosions of passion. However, the *Tragedy* is easier to put right, and the reason for making the cut will more readily be accepted; debate about *Dr Faustus* will certainly continue, but I may hope I am clearing the *Tragedy* up.[4]

In 1581, Elizabeth made a public announcement that she would marry the Duc d'Alençon, her 'frog', who was considered peculiarly unsuitable, besides being a Roman Catholic; and there was much public alarm.[5] But it could not be publicly discussed, not even by parliament.[6] Unlike the censorship of books, that of plays was directly under the control of the queen [through the Master of the Revels]; she had made her own appointment (Edmund Tilney) in 1579, before there was much stir in the public theatres. We may be sure she gave him a standing order, when the question came up, that no criticism of royal marriages must appear in plays.[7] The duke died of typhoid in 1584, and the *Tragedy* is agreed to be later, but not very much. Kyd might well think that the crisis was over, and anyway that his story was entirely unlike the affairs of the queen; and Tilney would probably answer that he was letting him get away with a dangerous amount, cutting only the passage that couldn't possibly be allowed, and would be considered a belated attack on the earl of Leicester. Probably neither of them would reflect that the moral effect of the whole play was being altered very queerly; and, indeed, the company would make sure that this official cut was widely known, so that the first audiences would be sufficiently abreast of the plot before the play began. It is a very likely thing to have happened, as I ought to have seen long ago.

Another bit of history is needed to show why the play was really topical, as apart from why the censor thought it was topical; and that had better be put here, before starting on the text.[8] The take-over of Portugal by Spain in 1580 looked a deadly blow against England; the pope had divided the new worlds between Spain and Portugal, and now Philip had combined them. He too thought it a serious step, as in the same year he 'claimed the right to exclude foreigners from Asia and Africa' as well as America. Elizabeth knighted Drake in harbour that year for sailing round the world and returning with Spanish loot, and next year (1581; of course she had to reach agreement with the sultan) established the Levant Company, with trading depots in Aleppo, Damascus, and Alexandria. That is how the *Tiger* came to be sailing to Aleppo in *Macbeth*. She also raised the fine for not going to church on Sunday from 1/- a week to £20 a month. From then on it is a straight run to the sailing of the Armada, with two major conspiracies defeated and the execution of the Queen of Scots; also the killing of William the Silent. And all this heightening of the scene was merely because Philip II had *inherited* the result of a long previous royal marriage. (There was some token fighting, as in the play, but it was hard to raise much enthusiasm against an admitted legal claim.) In the same way, the admitted right of Spain to devastate the Low Countries, the modern Holland and Belgium, depended solely upon a previous royal marriage; and England might have got into the same position if Queen Mary had succeeded in breeding by Philip II. There was really a great deal to be said against these royal marriages, and a plucky girl like Bel-imperia who stood out against them deserved strong support, as indeed did Elizabeth if she would stick to it. As she had become 50 in 1583, the danger from a child by a Catholic marriage was probably over; but still, if you were looking round for a case where revenge might genuinely appear as a duty, the murky background of these royal marriages might well appear the first place to look. One other bit of history seems needed here; during this time of the build-up to the Armada, there was an attempt at killing the queen, and her leading officials signed a document, which was firmly publicised [the Bond of Association, 1584], saying that if the pope or the king of Spain killed Elizabeth, they in their turn would see to it that the pope, or the king of Spain, was killed. There were no later well-attested attempts on her life; and a reader of the play needs to know about this success. Many students, both in England and America, take for granted that revenge cannot really occur among Christians, being totally discredited; and so they think that a revenge play must be a merely arty thing, a 'convention' which imitates the literature of the pagans. All the time the newspapers they read deafen them with incessant threatening tom-toms; probably this century has seen more monstrous revenges, and a greater proportion of minds tormented by the belief that they have been wronged, than ever before. But also, we have become accustomed to being protected by police; the idea that Elizabeth's officials may have done right to express an intention to commit revenge, all together, is one that the student does not want to envisage. But the whole point of this play, as originally conceived, is to be a discussion drama. I do not say that Kyd was a clever man, as Marlowe was, but he is miles more intelligent than his modern students have been laboriously trained to suppose.[9]

I am next to look at the textual evidence. *The Spanish Tragedy* is supposed to have four acts, very curiously planned as to length; omitting the additions, they number about 570, 360, 1250, and 530 lines. The third is more than twice as long as any of the others, so it is inherently likely that another act-division was once there. It becomes practical certainty when one realises that there is no Elizabethan four-act play. I learn this from the sheer book on the subject by W. T. Jewkes (*Act Division in Elizabethan and Jacobean Plays 1583–1616*, 1958), who points out that the university wits, young graduates who began to write for the theatres during the 1580s, attached importance to the five-act structure of late classical

Roman comedy, but the acting companies did not;[10] so that some of the texts give only confused reminders of it, and some give no indications of it at all. There are two other plays which appear to have four acts: Lodge's *Wounds of Civil War* prints 'Actus Quartus. Scena Prima' after line 1308, and again 'Actus Quartus' after line 1936, and Peele's *Jack Strawe*, which has only 930 lines, puts only 'THE KING'S PARDON' before its final act (pp. 216, 230). One can readily believe that a great deal of cutting was needed to put a decent face on this part of the story. There are also irregular act-divisions in *The Three Ladies of London* (only Acts I and II marked), *Battle of Alcazar*, and *David and Bethsabe* (pp. 110, 127–8). But such cases give no reason to suppose that the author, if he intended acts at all, intended any other number than five. Indeed, the Renaissance was happy to revere both classical authority and number-magic, so that all kinds of reasons for having five acts were invented and admired, but no one considered whether a particular story might be better treated in four.

I need next to offer a reason for thinking that the cut was made by the official Tilney, not by a whimsical producer. In this play the act-structure has peculiar importance, because the ghost speaks at the end of each act, and never elsewhere. He does not know the secret at the beginning of our third act, where he is merely rather more fractious than before, but he does at the end of it, because he says to Revenge: 'thanks to thee and those infernal powers/ That will not tolerate a lover's woe' (III. xv. 37–8). The whole question, when the play began, was whether he should be classed as a soldier or a lover; now it is decided, and of course the lover's woe is the arranged marriage. Thus the missing interlude has to be the one where he learns the mystery; and surely no producer would want to cut out that alone. He might consider the whole structure of inter-ludes by the ghost too stiff, and sweep them away; but he would not sweep away the only interesting one. On the other hand, this would be the natural place for the ghost to make some general remarks against the customs of the royal marriage. And on the other hand, one might expect the royal censor to forbid the whole play; but we happen to know how Tilney proceeded, by his note written on the disputed text of *Sir Thomas More* [c. 1592–3]. This is a bit of good luck, because no government publishes evidence about its censor-ship procedures (so I cannot be blamed for not producing it). He is discussing references in the play to an insurrection of London apprentices, and is not at all inclined to suppress the whole thing; one feels he wouldn't mind writing the new bits himself. He must have been rather too lenient, because he let through several things in his time which caused great trouble; but no doubt Elizabeth was sensible in wanting a man who would act as a real go-between. He says, in the brief moment when we hear him:

> Leave out the insurrection wholly and the cause thereof, and begin with Sir Thomas More at the Mayor's sessions, with a report afterwards of his good service done, being Shrieve of London, upon a mutiny against the Lombards, only by a short report and not otherwise, at your perils.

He had also made some changes in the text on his own account. He seems just the sort of man who might have demanded this cut, and spared the rest of the play.[11]

I want now to glance through the play, showing how much better it is if you are allowed to know the plot. Some critics have felt that the scenes at the court of Portugal are irrelevant padding, though of course consonant with the general tone of gloom. However, a villain reports falsely that the prince of Portugal has been killed in the battle by a leading Portuguese who wants the throne for himself; he shot Balthazar while pretending to shoot the enemy general over his shoulder. It should be recalled that battles often give an opportunity for private murders, usually among compatriots. Before this scene and after it we have two eye-witness accounts of the death of Andrea, one by the Spanish general to his king, the other by Horatio to Bel-imperia. The general says the battle had remained in doubt till 'Don Andrea, with his brave lanciers' broke the Portuguese line and caused a retreat, but then Prince Balthazar 'brought rescue', so there was heavy fighting,

> And in that conflict was Andrea slain.   (I. ii. 71)

The prince, 'insulting over him,/ Breath'd out proud vaunts' (73–4), and this made Horatio challenge him to single combat; he beat the prince from his horse, thus capturing him. Horatio's account is chiefly meant as comfort to the mistress of Andrea; he says Andrea and Balthazar had a long equal combat (whereas the general thought Balthazar was stronger); but then 'Nemesis, that wicked power' became envious of Andrea, so she

> Brought in a fresh supply of halberdiers,
> Which paunch'd his horse and ding'd him to the ground.

Then young Don Balthazar with ruthless rage,
Taking advantage of his foe's distress,
Did finish what his halberdiers begun ...   (I. iv. 21–5)

So Horatio had to recover the body, and he captured Balthazar. Only the general mentions the triumphant insults of Balthazar, 'sounding to our reproach' (I. ii. 74) – he thinks of them as nationalist sentiment, whereas they are more likely if Balthazar has destroyed an obstacle to his dynastic marriage. To say that it was 'Fate' – remarkably bad luck – might excite suspicion even nowadays, and Elizabethans were more ready than we are to recognise that fate was a pagan conception, ill-fitted to the providence of God. However, these are very slight grounds for suspicion; the main fact is that we have been told the story twice (three times, counting the false one), so that we expect it to deserve attention. Bel-imperia says that it was 'murd'rous cowardice ... Without respect of honour' (I. iv. 73–5) for so many men to attack Andrea, and the general says that Horatio did challenge Balthazar to single combat (I. ii. 76–7), so it was current practice among these people, but nobody says that Andrea had done it. None of the men encourage Bel-imperia in her idea that the death was unsporting (apart from the one line 'Taking advantage of his foe's distress'), and even she has no idea of killing Balthazar in revenge for it – she will make him 'Reap long repentance for his murd'rous deed' (I. iv. 72). Unless the ghost overhears evidence for a real plot against him, therefore, he has no grounds to claim revenge at all.

It may be supposed that more indications of treachery had been introduced at this early stage, which the censor had cut; but he would see no need to. After all, Horatio in the second act undoubtedly is killed to remove an obstacle from the marriage of Bel-imperia, and this was not too shocking; the trouble with the ghost had been that, in the first shock of discovery, he had talked about royal marriages in general, thus coming under the ban. I think indeed that the scarf of Bel-imperia, which Andrea was wearing round his arm (I. iv. 42), was mentioned in the final discovery; it was used to alert the Portuguese, an identification. But this was to give the feeling 'It all fits in' rather than 'I ought to have guessed'. We should remember, the administrators in Hades themselves could not be sure whether Andrea died as a lover or as a soldier, and they must have a good deal of experience. We gather that information was sent to the Portuguese commander, who passed it on to Balthazar; but Andrea went to the heart of the battle himself, not waiting to be sent there like Uriah, and the general might well have decided that reinforcements needed sending, at the crisis, even without this murky note from the enemy royals. Discovering the plot makes the ghost very angry, as an act of dishonour in the family he owes allegiance to, but it is greatly to his advantage; we find at the end that he is going to the Elysian fields with Bel-imperia, which was what he was sent back on earth to secure. There is no need to suppose a power of prophecy in the Queen of Heaven; when she grinned and whispered in her husband's ear, she said: 'This family is sure to go on murdering the daughter's lovers, and if Andrea is sent back to watch he will see the next one killed. They cannot go on like this without running into trouble some time.' Here indeed we have the sense in which everyone believes in fate. The advantage of having the ghost in the play, though he is unable to have any effect on the human story, is that he represents the other main strand of opinion. So far from being an artificial literary convention, the duty of revenge was a built-in conflict for the society of the time. Military officers would tell you that you ought to defend your honour, even if you were sent to hell for it; whereas the clergy and the lawyers would say that you ought to accept the amount of revenge doled out to you by the king's law. Such was their interpretation of 'Vengeance is mine, saith the Lord'; it broke down in cases of royal crime, which were therefore of special interest to the theatre. The conflict had long been present but was heightened by the Renaissance code of honour. Hieronymo is a judge, accustomed only to approve revenge by process of law, and to find he has a duty of extra-legal revenge against the heir to the throne is so horrible to him that it sends him slowly mad; but all the time the previous victim is quite at home with the idea of revenge, and much irritated by his delay. The connexion in the plot, the fact that the same criminal design is upsetting both of them, is surely essential if the ghost is not to appear merely otiose; and his presence is wanted to express the other side of the debate.

Though the air is so thick with wrongs, the author does not regard any character as simply a villain, being interested in how they would justify themselves. The most contemptible is the prince, especially when he appeals for sympathy as a forlorn lover, soon after murdering the second of his rivals; but even here he is merely playing his cards carefully, as his father would wish him to do – relations with ladies are governed by rules, which one must learn. Even his crimes are committed with the same complacency. The author for his engineering of human sentiments in the audience needed to make Balthazar sufficiently disagreeable, so that we respect Bel-imperia for rejecting him with violence and desperation, and yet he must not stand out; it is done very adroitly. Pedringano is of course a minor character, but his motives for choosing villainy are treated with the same coolness. He is a family servant, with no special duty to Bel-imperia, but he tries to be loyal to her when her brother questions him (II. i). However, when threatened with death, and as he owes a duty to the family, and owes Lorenzo gratitude for extra pay, he decides it is allowable, as well as being somehow fun, or sporting, to work for Lorenzo, and he is still deluding himself into thinking so up to the moment when Lorenzo has him hanged (III. vi). Marlowe became a master of this grim pathos or harsh sympathy, but Kyd had done it first. His other merits have been well recognised, but his style has tended to obscure his firm sense of character. And the author who treated the characters so cannot have thought the final judgments of the ghost at all sensible. He condemns Pedringano to boiling Acheron and endless flames, but even the Spirit of Revenge does not literally say that he will make Pluto do all that, while not denying that there is a penalty, when he ends the play with:

> I'll there begin their endless tragedy.

Bel-imperia, after hearing Horatio's report of the death of Andrea, appoints Horatio her next lover, and tells the audience when he has gone that this will 'further' her revenge upon Balthazar (I. iv. 66). One might suppose that the incident typed her as a wicked foreign aristocrat, eating up one man after another, in the minds of the first audiences. Among the first words of the play we heard 'In secret I possess'd a worthy dame' (I. i. 10), and this was intended to make the audience feel sure that she went to bed with her lovers; because in any other sense of that important word Bel-imperia possessed Andrea. But she does not eat them. If she had chosen a third lover, after Horatio had been murdered in her presence, then she would have been challenging a fool to risk death. That is why she accepts her doom of a royal marriage, at which both must die before consummation. When she accepts Horatio she has no idea that her first lover has just been murdered *because* she had accepted him, and the audience have not yet been told. They regard her as a brave girl resisting an arranged marriage. Very likely it is a slight cover-up in saying 'further my revenge', when his eloquence and noble sentiments and evident devotion to Andrea have made him particularly attractive to her; all we can say is that the ghost recognises the affair without any resistance, only assuming at the end that Horatio will not come to the Elysian fields with himself and Bel-imperia. It never occurs to this pasteboard figure, one can hear a Leavisite critic grumble, that she is only attractive to men because of her social position, though it only offers them death. But this does occur to Bel-imperia; she cries out while her lover is being murdered:

> O save his life and let me die for him!
> O save him brother, save him Balthazar:
> I lov'd Horatio but he lov'd not me.   (ii. iv. 56–8)

The play was rather like an opera, or at least it made its points by single ringing lines at big moments; I suppose the critics have ignored this moment because it seems emptily theatrical, or even perfunctory, but a sacrifice of her dignity would mean a great deal to her. The murderers ignore it because it is useless; but it proves that she understands the situation. Maybe the young men accept her advances only because they are afraid of being called cowards if they don't; so, after this disaster, she will not choose a third one. (She knows there was trouble from her father about the first lover, though she is not sure he was killed on purpose.) The line was put in to clear this point, and allow the audience to admire her without reservation for fighting a dragon.[12]

I am maintaining that Kyd is a more intelligent author than readers usually think, judging from the formality of his style; so I need to explain away the final scene of the first act. To establish Hieronymo as a man accustomed to devise court entertainments (prepared for the final scene of all), we have him showing a masque to the king and the Portuguese ambassador, consisting of three English knights who are said to have defeated two Portuguese kings and one Spanish king. The King of Spain accepts this with high chivalry, saying that, as even little England can win, one should remain calm under the fortunes of war. The ambassador merely uses the third case to back his own side, but the king assures Hieronymo that his device has pleased both of them. All the comments are propaganda for England, but the ambassador's, coming third and last, are the strongest:

> This is an argument for our viceroy,
> That Spain may not insult for her success,
> Since English warriors likewise conquer'd Spain,
> And made them bow their knees to Albion.   (I. iv. 168–71)

This seems childlike unreality, or else a coarse attempt to win the mob. One must realise that it was written for an audience expecting the Armada, half expecting conquest and conversion with rack and fire. There is no need to work up hatred against Spaniards; that is already in good supply; rather, one should keep in mind their virtues. Monstrously cruel and pig-headed, of course, but they have their code of honour; you want to get on the high-minded side of them. (Incidentally, that is why they are so prone to revenge.) One of the gong-like single lines in the first act establishes this major theme:

> Yet shalt thou know that Spain is honourable.   (I. ii. 137)

All the same, no Spaniard except the holy and almost imbecile king (who does not know till the end even that Horatio is dead) utters such unpatriotic or philosophical sentiments, and Hieronymo designed the masque only to please him. The ghost, a plain military officer, is irritated by it to the point of uttering his first grumble (I.v). A modern producer may reasonably choose to cut this brief scene, but there is no need to; it does not matter at this stage if the audience laugh; probably some people did in the first audiences.

I have not yet considered where the ghost and Revenge sit. As they are very much part of the audience, it is tempting to make them lean against the two pillars in front, quite at home. But then the ghost is too prominent; he cannot seem indifferent to the performance, and yet must not distract attention from it; besides, a ghost must not lose his mystique, even if he is an engagingly unpretentious one. They should be together in one of the bay windows at the two sides of the upper stage (the other is used for the imprisoned Bel-imperia to drop her letter from), and the ghost should seldom demand attention. I would not rule that he may react only when he has words to say, but his noises should be brief and immediately intelligible; our only serious interest in him is to learn whether he has guessed the answer yet. He opened the play with an address from the balcony, and was led by Revenge up to this window: 'Here sit we down to see the mystery' (I. i. 90). We hear nothing from him till the end of the first act, and then find him much crosser than he was at the start. Fredson Bowers might say that he is already corrupted by the craving for revenge. Probably he disliked the masque, and anyhow he has been accustomed to activity; it is tiresome to sit and watch, and the scene is not what he was told to expect. A serious dislike for Balthazar he does express, but we need not suppose that is new; he would have heard Balthazar exult over him before killing him, as his horse was first crippled by the halberdiers. He does not demand revenge, but Revenge gives him a brief appalling reassurance. It would be as well to have some brief piece of military music, a trumpet voluntary for instance, after the Induction and repeated after each of the act-breaks, to insist on the formality of the design.[13]

The second act is the shortest, with no scene in Portugal; it is concerned with the murder of Horatio and the despair of his father. The second murder has no puzzle about it; the purpose is admittedly to secure a royal marriage, and Lorenzo (Bel-imperia's brother, nephew of the king) plots it frankly with Balthazar. The king is in favour of the marriage, and makes a large offer to promote it; he says to the ambassador:

> in case the match go forward,
> The tribute which you pay shall be releas'd,
> And if by Balthazar she have a son,
> He shall enjoy the kingdom after us.   (II. iii. 18–21)

I have known experts on the play who stuck to it that this means the kingdom of Spain, or rather totally refused to let the politics be real. Of course the king could not give away Spain to the issue of a foreign prince, while actually in the presence of his brother who was the heir. But Balthazar and his son would be legitimate kings of Portugal, apart from the superior claim (by primogeniture) of the Spanish royal line. Balthazar will still have to describe himself as viceroy, though freed from the humiliating demand of tribute; but his son, when he inherits, will be absolute king of Portugal. This is plain enough, but you may well ask whether it is sensible; would the next heirs, brother Castile and nephew Lorenzo, be at all keen to renounce such a large part of their inheritance? So keen that they would commit murder for it? Castile perhaps, but hardly Lorenzo. One might argue that the English were deluded by their own propaganda here. In their dismay, they called the swallowing up of Portugal very unnatural, sure not to last; not remembering that a similar fate for Scotland was already looming up. On this view, nothing but expense and disorder could ever follow from direct Spanish rule over Portugal, but to have grateful cousins in power there should provide a bulwark. The view of Philip II was not so statesmanlike, and the Spanish control of Portugal lasted only for sixty years; but maybe that was only because of a weakness in Spain which he could not have expected. I only claim that the political theory taken for granted by Kyd, so far from being fatuous, is more serious or large-minded than any that one can find in the later and more 'life-like' Elizabethan plays. We may deduce that Lorenzo is not being fatuous when he seduces Balthazar into helping him with the murder of Horatio, though he could not need such help and boasts of never sharing a secret with anyone; what we see is the future king of Spain making a committed accomplice of the future ruler of Portugal.

Some remarks about the staging may be fitted in here. Act I scene ii, or the first scene after the ghost on the balcony, needs the throne, so the back curtain is opened, but it is closed while the king is doing private justice after line 60 – he and the group concerned wander forward, and the others withdraw. The curtain reopens on the same throne but with different blazonry for the court of Portugal. All seems clear till Act II scene ii, when the lovers meet in the open, outside the curtain, and the villains listen on the balcony. Thus scene iii can open on the court of Spain. But scene iv is the bower, with a pergola strong enough for Horatio to be strung up on it and then stabbed (or if a dummy only, then the more need to conceal it); shrubs in tubs are also required, if the words praising the bower are not to sound nonsense. Here we seem to have two inner scenes with elaborate settings jammed together; but there are two ways to solve it, and probably both were used. The king at the end of his council-meeting speaks privately to his brother, for ten lines, and the curtain would close on the throne; then they go out on one side, and the lovers enter on the other side, merely on their way to the bower – for ten lines, till Pedringano is told to 'watch without the gate' (II. iv. 10). Then the curtain opens, and they are within the bower without more ado. It remains in sight till the end of the act, when the interlude with the ghost gives time for reopening on the court of Portugal. After that we are on the apron stage, needing no curtain.

Before the bower disappears (to have it carried out by stage hands, after those pathetic speeches, really would involve a risk of giggles), Hieronymo speaks 14 lines in Latin (II. v. 67–80), which have probably entailed rejection of the play by many an otherwise willing producer. They were very likely cut from the original public performances.[14] The last three of them contain the dramatic point – Hieronymo decides not to kill himself just yet, standing beside the corpse of his son, because he has a duty of revenge – and there are enough well-known Latin words, suiting the business with the sword, to make the intention quite plain. He describes it as saying a 'dirge', and we may presume that he is not actually puzzling whether to stab himself; after all, he has just told his wife to help him carry the body home; but then he pauses, feeling the need for some act of dedication. (To argue that they carry the body home because the company hadn't a curtain seems to me beneath reply.) However, this cut version is not as weighty as Kyd intended, and there is a very good bit in the first addition, twenty lines before, not at all unlike Kyd, which might sensibly be called in. (The rest of this first addition is extremely phoney madness, unlike Hieronymo at any time, and incredible at his first moment of shock; it urgently needs keeping out, and I would not recommend using any of the later additions.) The addition then follows these lines of Kyd:

> Come Isabel, now let us take him up,
> And bear him in from out this cursed place.   (II. v. 64–5)

But then he drops the legs, leaving her holding the arms and head. He turns to face the emptiness.

> Be gracious to me, thou infective night,
> And drop this deed of murder down on me:
> Gird in my waste of grief with thy large darkness,
> And let me not survive to see the light
> May put me in the mind I had a son.
> (He half turns back)
> I'll say his dirge, singing fits not this case.
> (He sets his sword unto his breast)
> *Emoriar tecum, sic, sic juvat ire sub umbras.*
> (He holds his sword erect before him)
> *At tamen absistam properato cedere letho,*
> *Ne mortem vindicata tuam tum nulla sequatur*
> (here he throws it from him and bears the body away.)

I think that would be accepted; the English is big enough to carry the Latin. He is himself rather small, and the wife helps with the body.

What seems almost impossible to present to a modern audience is that Hieronymo, in thus dedicating the remainder of his life to revenge, is thinking merely of a legal process; that he can only get it by murder, because the law will not work against royalty, comes as a great shock to the old judge; he only gradually finds out, and it has not yet entered his mind at all. My students at Sheffield very often assumed that everybody knows revenge is wicked, so anybody who wants it must be a bad man; the extent to which they were surrounded by legal revengers, let alone the monstrous self-righteousness of the illegal ones a bit further away, had been successfully hidden from them. Nor is it easy to make clear that the ghost, though seriously annoyed by this time, still makes no claim that anything deserving revenge had been done against himself. His words follow directly upon the departure of the parents:

> Brought'st thou me hither to increase my pain?
> I look'd that Balthazar should have been slain:
> But 'tis my friend Horatio that is slain,
> And they abuse fair Bel-imperia,
> On whom I doted more than all the world,
> Because she lov'd me more than all the world.   (II. vi. 1–6)

(He is entirely without jealousy.) Revenge gives him a brief appalling reassurance.

In the third act, as Lorenzo is making fatal efforts to avoid discovery, there is a certain amount of grim military fun; and it is important to realise that Kyd is capable of making jokes on purpose. The basic joke is that Lorenzo destroys himself by his plots to make himself safe, and would probably have been safe if he stayed quiet; there is also incidental humour in the results, such as the plucky but deluded trust of Pedringano in his master. That this is a joke gets patiently explained to the audience by the 'boy with the box' who stands beside the gallows (Pedringano imagines it to hold his reprieve, but the boy knows it is empty):

Will 't not be an odd jest, for me to stand and grace every jest he makes, pointing my finger at this box, as who would say, 'Mock on, here's thy warrant.' Is't not a scurvy jest, that a man should jest himself to death? Alas, poor Pedringano, I am in a sort sorry for thee, but if I should be hanged with thee, I cannot weep. (III. v. 13–19)

I am not sure why, but the flatness of it has a kind of beauty, perhaps from being so unforced. In any case, the Machiavellian behaviour of Lorenzo has been absurd from the start, and we need not blame the author for the weakness of his plot. Lorenzo imprisons his sister immediately after the murder, knowing he cannot do it for long (even his father is not in his confidence), but hoping that she will cool down after a few days of reflection. This of course prevents her from cooling down, and she pushes out through a crack in her window a letter written in her blood and addressed to Hieronymo which accuses her brother. It is very doubtful whether she would have betrayed her brother to a plebeian father if she were still being treated as one of the family; though probably she had already decided, if forced to marry the prince, to kill both him and herself. After this decision, all the plans made by the various men are inherently fatuous; but Lorenzo's plans get him killed.

The joking of Pedringano with the hangman works up to a shocking climax; he asks him to ask all the spectators to pray for him, and this the hangman says he will gladly do, but Pedringano says he has remembered now that he has no great need at this time. Hieronymo interrupts the hanging (at which he is present as the judge who passed the sentence) to make a speech that seems to mean more than he intends:

> I have not seen a wretch so impudent!
> O monstrous times, where murder's set so light,
> And where the soul, that should be shrin'd in heaven,
> Solely delights in interdicted things,
> Still wand'ring in the thorny passages
> That intercepts itself of happiness.   (III. vi. 89–94)

It never occurs to him that this applies to his own struggle to achieve extra-legal revenge, because he regards that merely as a painful duty; but it seems wilful to deny that it occurred to the author, and that the producer should try to make it observable for the audience. However, the author of course didn't mean to deny that Hieronymo really had a duty of revenge.

The gallows of course must be on the inner stage, though most of the actors in the scene would be on the main stage, so that the curtain may close upon this gadget; then we have Hieronymo alone on the main stage. He is deeply frustrated and noticeably madder; he now believes that all grass has stopped growing because of his woes, or says he does (III. vii. 7) – he was not talking like that before.

Then the hangman brings him some papers found among the effects
of Pedringano, including a letter sent to his patron begging for the
reprieve to come in time, and the whole matter is now clear to
Hieronymo. He cannot suppose the letter a plot against him, as he
did the letter from Bel-imperia. (And, if you say the plot is absurd,
because Lorenzo would have arranged to remove the man's final
writings, the answer is that Machiavellians are regularly found
absurd, because their schemes are too hard to complete.) But he is
still not willing to admit the possibility of extra-legal revenge.

> But wherefore waste I mine unfruitful words,
> When naught but blood will satisfy my woes?
> I will go plain me to my lord the king,
> And cry aloud for justice through the court,
> Wearing the flints with these my wither'd feet,
> And either purchase justice by entreats
> Or tire them all with my revenging threats.   (III. vii. 67–73)

The actor of course should pause after 'Or' before the character
signs off with this shocking anti-climax. The ghost groans, tormented by his weakness. At once we see the wife of Hieronymo –
'She runs lunatic' – bitterly ashamed of her husband for not finding
the murderer (she and her maid had better be on the inner stage),
and then Bel-imperia, equally indignant, appears at the upper
window on the left, upbraiding Hieronymo for being 'so slack in thy
revenge'. She once knew a real man:

> Andrea, O Andrea, that thou sawest
> Me for thy friend Horatio handled thus,
> And him for me thus causeless murdered.   (III. ix. 9–11)

She ends with:

> ... force perforce, I must constrain myself
> To patience, and apply me to the time,
> When heaven, as I have hop'd, shall set me free.   (12–14)

It is a threat of suicide if the marriage is forced upon her. The ghost
is at the upper window on the right, and it is impossible not to expect
him to react to this cry. At this point he begins to shake the stands of
his bow-window, like a gorilla shaking the bars of its cage.

The next scene, releasing the lady, is perhaps the best written in
the play and would be even more exasperating to him. Lorenzo tells
the suitor to 'deal cunningly':

And if she hap to stand on terms with us,
As for her sweetheart, and concealment so,
Jest with her gently: under feigned jest
Are things conceal'd that else would breed unrest. (III. x. 20–3)

And at once she comes, denouncing them for their ill-treatment of her, but never mentioning the lover she was found with. Lorenzo says that locking her up was a kindness, because her father is exasperated with her; she has seen no sign of it, she says (indeed, we never hear him admit to knowing about her second affair), and has he not asked for her? Her brother says he will whisper in her ear how he explained her absence; presumably his story was that she had been getting an abortion. Her answer has a fine flash of contempt: 'content yourself, / The prince is meditating higher things' (86–7). The prince does cut a sordid picture in this scene, perhaps most at the end, where he moans with gentle elegance like a figure of pastoral. But the effect is sinister; we are left with the impression that they can force the marriage upon her somehow, or rather leave her with no resort but death. The ghost is growling a good deal.

The back curtain closes (the scene was an elegant room in the duke's house), and Hieronymo potters onto the open stage, shiftlessly – he told us in III. ii. 50 that he will in future 'hearken near the Duke of Castile's house', that is, haunt the gate to learn what he can. Two Portuguese, walking on from the other side, ask the way to this house (no doubt they want to pay their respects to the returning ambassador), and Hieronymo is now mad enough to tell these strangers that the house is in hell. They laugh, and he laughs, at his description, and they go on, still looking for the house. He goes out by the other door, more purposefully now, as his speech has made him think of something to do. Plainly, I submit, this is where the missing scene was placed; it has been well prepared for. The back curtain opens, showing the same elegant room in the duke's house, and hell it really is. I have to invent the words.[15]

It has a tapestry on the back wall, a small table, a few elegant chairs, a locked cupboard. The ambassador is just sitting down at the table, and the duke is fetching a decanter and two glasses out of the cupboard. (This is to emphasise that he has sent the servants away, but also he is unusually unbuttoned in manner).

DUKE.　All is in train, my dear Ambassador. (*drinks*)
　　　　Thank heaven that my message to you was enough.
　　　　(*Whimsically*) I was glad to learn that Bel-imperia's scarf

Had proved sufficient to pick out Andrea.
(*Gulps and rises, slowly.*)
So now my headstrong daughter will obey.
AMB.   (*Also rising*) By sure my master will show gratitude.
DUKE.   (*Sharply – maybe the man is an ass*)
My brother must not hear a word of this.
(*Ambassador nods knowingly but seems crushed.*)
The curtain closes.

There is a great roar from the ghost, who has listened at first with
disgust and surprise but then with keen satisfaction. He had thought
that these people were villains but too hard to catch; now he has
caught them (a revenger always feels he is somehow Revenge in
person). And, as regards his own affairs, it is now certain that he
died as a lover, not as a soldier, and can go with Bel-imperia to the
Elysian fields: it is no occasion to be cross. He receives the congratu-
lations of Revenge complacently. But he did in the original text
make a speech denouncing the arranged royal marriage as an
institution, while protesting total loyalty to the queen. He would
come onto the central balcony for all this, and return to his window,
bowing to the audience, with his usual trumpet fanfare. I cannot
invent his speech, and what is more I don't think the modern
audience wants to hear it. The Ghost need only make a great roar,
expressing both indignation and delight. But perhaps it would be as
well, not to confuse anyone in the audience, to have an Elizabethan
lord chamberlain walk onto the balcony and announce that what
the Ghost said at this point has been cut by direct order from Her
Highness. I don't think this would feel a false note; in its way, the
moment is rather a jolly one.

However, the audience must not go out and have drinks here; two
intervals can be allowed, after the second act and the fourth, but not
here, after the third, because the other revenger is also just reaching
his crisis. As soon as the trumpet fanfare is over, Hieronymo comes
pattering back onto the open stage, carrying two means of killing
himself, but these are toys which no longer interest him. He had
been thinking of taking his appeal to the King of the Afterlife, and
for this of course he must be dead; but now he realises he had better
appeal to the king of Spain first. (He is now talking to an invisible
friend, called 'sir', which is generally considered strong evidence of
madness.) Then as he expected he sees the king coming to the duke's
house, but he becomes frightened, and runs to the side of the stage,

peeping out. These antics prevent the audience from feeling too much lack of realism in what happens. The back curtain opens again, discovering the duke and the ambassador, who are still waiting for him; and the king, with a few grandees, including Lorenzo, enters the room. He sits down and asks the ambassador at once for the reply of the king of Portugal (described of course as 'our viceroy' [III. xii. 25]). But Hieronymo shouts out his interruption at once, demanding justice. How does Hieronymo get there, except with the staging I have described? Lorenzo easily shuffles him aside as a lunatic, though he shouts out again after the major affairs have been handled; and then it turns out that the king has never even heard that Horatio is dead. He is entirely charitable to the madman, and says he will look into the case further before stopping his salary (III. xii. 100–1); but Hieronymo has already left the room in despair, judging it impossible to break through the fence surrounding the mind of this king. We may feel he has spoiled his chances by going mad, but he clearly cannot do it in his present mental state. What is so remarkable and lifelike about Kyd's treatment is that he allows the apparent madman to be completely sensible underneath. Getting into the presence of the king, and finding himself treated as a lunatic there, is naturally a severe shock; it makes him reconsider his whole position; he decides he will have to *use* his madness, he will have to pretend friendship with his victims and take advantage of their uneasy concessions to his folly (III. xiii. 20–44). The ghost, of course, does not understand this at all, and assumes that the tiresome zany has ratted; hence the explosion of the ghost at the end of the fourth act, which has to be hushed by a rather elaborate procedure from Revenge. If you understand Hieronymo, you understand that the interview with the king is what has settled him upon his implacable path.

This will sound rather high-flown, and I am afraid the dramatic effect really is rather hard to get across to an audience, so I am glad I can offer a more actor-like reflection. A madman on the stage must at least offer surprise (whereas really, as a rule, they are dreadfully fixed); Shakespeare learned a lot from Kyd, and Hamlet never once appears without causing surprise. The addition of the Painter scene intrudes here, and it is so good that the original surprise has been obscured. The next thing, after the madman has been driven out with jeers from the courtly meeting (and the courtly meeting, after its agreed conclusion, has been hidden by the back curtain), is:

Enter Hieronymo with a book in his hand.   (III. xiii)

This carries a ring for the modern reader because it was parodied by Shakespeare's Hamlet, to excellent effect, but it had been much more straightforward when Old Hieronymo did it first. (He is carrying his own notebook, with selected quotations in it.) At first Hieronymo seems entirely sane; he is behaving like a professor, an academic lawyer, considering the historical precedents about revenge. But then, if you know about his Latin quotations, you realise that he is getting it all completely wrong. At the third level, however, this discovery is outfaced; though his mind is so jumbled, the conclusion it arrives at is very defensible, and he holds it with entire firmness until he dies. I do not see how a modern audience can be helped over this obstacle; but still, if his speech with a book is allowed to come immediately after he has failed with the king, it makes the point that he has changed his policy, and will now try for a secret and in ordinary terms treacherous revenge.

Then we have another bout of his madness, tearing the leases of the petitioners, and it should be clear that his behaviour is now merely a release for his feelings, since he has become resolved, whereas before it expressed a painful conflict. I wish I could say that the words make it clear enough. The last twenty lines or so of the Painter scene [Fourth Addition] ought to be used because they are so central and basic for Elizabethan drama; they only need moving forward a short distance. But it would be absurd to give any further rulings to a modern producer; Hieronymo's madness was considered great fun, and the crucial point of change in his character was already ignored when Jonson wrote his additions around 1601.[16] The modern producer will need cuts anyhow. What I hope he will convey is the strength of mind, the range of understanding, of the original conception. These final bits of raving had better be ended with the end of the Painter scene (after a sufficient lead-in, but it needs cutting), because there you get a rational comment on the process of running mad, and it helps to show that his mind is now made up. The Painter is told to paint him when mad, after other instructions, and asks whether this is the end.

O no, there is no end: the end is death and madness. As I am never better than when I am mad, then methinks I am a brave fellow, then I do wonders: but reason abuseth me, and there's the torment, there's the hell. At the last, sir, bring me to one of the murderers: were he as strong as Hector, thus would I tear and drag him up and down. (Fourth Addition, 163–9)

He goes out beating the Painter, and the back curtain opens on another committee arranging the royal marriage (our III. xiv). The statement does not consider why the procedure is helpful (Jonson had not an analytic mind), but it feels like a summing-up. Shakespeare read more into it, and used it in *King Lear*:

> the worst is not
> So long as we can say 'This is the worst'.   (IV. i. 27–8)

The Portuguese emissaries have already agreed to the proposal from Spain, so the meeting is short, but it gives them an occasion for the viceroy to renounce his throne in favour of his son, thus giving Bel-imperia the title of queen as soon as she is married. Don Pedro the brother of the viceroy is introduced merely to add grandeur to the ceremonial (probably he did more in an earlier version, and anyway in the original First Part). But this is only a brief glimpse of the world of grandeur, and then the back curtain closes on the throne, leaving the duke and his son on an empty stage. He scolds his son for unkindness to Hieronymo, and says that if the old man chose to denounce him to the king it would cause a scandal. The duke at least knows that Horatio has been murdered, but appears to know nothing more (53–72). This scene is much more telling if we have already seen him admit to the betrayal of Andrea; we are to regard him as an impenetrable hypocrite, and yet his warning must be taken to show that Andrea lost heart too easily. Bel-imperia comes in, grimly telling lies to her princely lover, and presumably intending to kill herself; we do not know that she had had any contact with Hieronymo since she pushed the letter out of the window. Hieronymo comes in, and tries to follow his new policy of becoming accepted as a friend of the family, but this at once runs into an obstacle. The duke having the Spanish grandeur talks extremely slowly, but the revenger is all on wires:

CAST   Hieronymo, the reason that I sent
       To speak with you, is this.
HIER.   What, so short?
       Then I'll be gone, I thank you for't.
CAST   Nay, stay, Hieronymo! Go call him, son.   (III. xiv. 124–7)

This is not too stiff; indeed, the stiffness which the theme requires is being mocked, and Hieronymo continues to do it, deceiving both father and son (one might complain) too easily. However, they are

so sure he is mad that they cannot suspect he is plotting. Kyd is
establishing the formula for Hamlet and suchlike; the revenger
cannot help acting queerly, but he uses it to carry through his plans.

However, the ghost cannot be expected to understand this; during
Act IV, he could make no sense of Hieronymo's lecture, thought his
indulgence in madness merely tiresome, and took his sane behaviour
for a sell-out, so he now touches his greatest depth of despair.
Revenge gives him a dumb-show, presumably on the balcony, to
relieve his feelings, and this rather surprisingly restores his confidence:

> Sufficeth me, thy meaning's understood,
> And thanks to thee and those infernal powers
> That will not tolerate a lover's woe.   (III. xv. 36–8)

(If there is something that deserves punishment about his woe as a
lover, surely his death in battle must have been rigged, to secure the
royal marriage.) The fourth act is short, but this does not feel bad if
it marks a decisive change of policy in Hieronymo (indeed, one
might suspect the mad scenes of padding); on my count, the five acts
go 570, 360, 750, 500, 530. The second contains the murder of
Horatio and the lament of his father, and probably no spectator has
felt it inadequate. The long Act III runs easily (with jokes and plots)
till it begins its calculated blows for the ghost, and then makes no
real division before the fourth, but rather a double crisis. We enter
the fifth act feeling sure that the end has been decided.

The unexpected, however, can still occur. The first scene is the
long-delayed meeting between Hieronymo and Bel-imperia, and it
turns out that she has decided to kill the murderers of Horatio
whether his father does or not. This is bound to reduce the dignity of
the revenger, and it already seemed obvious that Hieronymo could
kill his enemies with much less fuss, if prepared to die soon after. He
apologises to her, and only asks to be allowed to do it in proper form.
She agrees to help him, and almost at once Lorenzo comes and asks
him to arrange private theatricals for the wedding festivities. He
seems to have been expecting it, as his plan is ready at once; Lorenzo
wants to keep him in good humour, on the duke's instructions, and
this appears to be the only advantage that his madness has brought.
It seems to have become a rule for later stage revengers that their
madness and artfulness were not as useful as they comforted themselves by supposing; they 'veer[ed] sideways to their doom'.[17]

However, what they really needed was a smart flashy revenge, one that would make talk; a type of which the theatrical revenge, actually done while acting a part, was the supreme exemplar. The case for private revenge only arose when the public revenge supplied by the law failed to work, and there a good man always wanted to appeal to public opinion; everyone must know why he had done murder, and the only way to make them talk was to do it in an interesting way. It was necessary to kill himself as soon as his revenge had succeeded: in the theatre, the audience would not otherwise accept him as a worthy man: and in real life it would often be the only way he could avoid a slow death by torture. The breakdown of law was most often caused by the bold actions of royalty, and *The Spanish Tragedy* is rather keen to insist that the Iberian royalties were particularly ready with torture in such cases. If you are killing yourself in order to tell people something, you naturally want to make sure they will pay attention after you are gone. The modern distaste for 'theatrical' behaviour is dubious anyhow, but in this type of case it is patently unfair.

Deeper and more tormenting defences of revenge have been offered by our modern theologians, as when Professor Helen Gardner writes in 'Milton's "Satan" and the Theme of Damnation in Elizabethan Drama':

We accept the justice by which the tragic hero is destroyed. Indeed if it were not for the justice we should have no pity for him. The acceptance of the justice makes possible the pity, and the pity calls for the justice without which it would turn to loathing. But the cause must be secret in tragedy ... what is hateful in the tragic world is that Eternal Justice should argue.[18]

Perhaps this is not one of the tragedies she had in view, but it was the father of many of them; and she appears to speak of 'the tragic hero' in general. Hieronymo would not thank her for this degree of charity; he considers that he has brought himself after long struggle to carry out a painful duty, and two supernatural characters praise him for it at the end. But the idea that a tyrant might be in the wrong simply cannot occur to such critics. C. S. Lewis went the whole way, in the chapter 'Hell' of his *Problem of Pain*. In an earlier chapter, he is saying, he has maintained:

that all punishment became unjust if the ideas of ill-desert and retribution were removed from it; and a core of righteousness was discovered within the vindictive passion itself, in the demand that the evil man must not be left perfectly satisfied with his own evil, that it must be made to appear to him what it rightly appears to others – evil. (*The Problem of Pain*, London: The Centenary Press, 1940, p. 108)

[*Partitudo interrupta: Empson's draft essay breaks off at this point.*]

CHAPTER 4

'Volpone'

A good deal of standardisation of opinion and critical method became necessary when Eng. Lit. became a large profession, and I think the results are often mistaken; but it is naturally hard to make my colleagues agree with any such judgment. The best opportunity is where the credibility gap appears at an unexpected place – where the university teachers or examiners feel slightly appalled at the apparently orthodox opinions which the children (whose school-teachers usually retain more hold upon their loyalty and affection than any later teacher) write sturdily down. When I first met Professor L. C. Knights, which was fairly recently at Gambier, Ohio, there was some mention of the yearly examinations, and he said, 'The very saddest time of all.' I said, 'You mean you find the students haven't followed what you told them?' 'Well, of course, there is that too', he said, 'but sometimes, you know, they have'. This delicacy of feeling proved at once that he was not a Leavisite in any harmful way. Thinking it over, I doubt whether he had literally said these things which he did not like to read in an answer; they would be deductions from his position, or parodies of it, which he had not foreseen the need for a warning against. I fancy that the salutary shock which he adumbrated here arises more frequently about Ben Jonson than about any other standard author. The argument has a more direct impact upon an English than an American professional, because in England a large proportion of the students who are being prepared to read Eng. Lit. at university have to pass examinations in either *Volpone* or *The Alchemist* (to which the same troubles apply in a rather different way); but many of my American colleagues would feel the same shock if faced with the same documents.

What the children write down is a good deal hotter and cruder than most of the stuff in the textbooks, but it is the same grand muddle which appeared so novel and charming about half a century ago. They write: 'Volpone is a miser. The play does nothing but denounce misers, and he is the worst one, because he worships his gold. All the characters are loathsome except the young couple, and they are subnormal because they talk in a conventional poetic style; but Volpone is the most loathsome, as he blasphemes. Jonson had a theory about plays, that they ought to make you sick of being wicked, and the reason why his plays are so good is that they make you sick. They are written in poetry which is meant to excite contempt and nausea, and that is why it is such good poetry. Good people enjoy these plays very much, though they are in pain all the time, aching for the tortures to begin.' It is extraordinary to me that a man can 'mark' a large number of these answers straight on end and still believe what they say.

At first I thought I knew an immediate reply: that Volpone cannot be a miser, because he offers to lavish upon Celia his whole fortune – he is a 'dashing' lover, which was an equally familiar type, and a quite different one. But my opponents had been properly indoctrinated, and would readily answer that this minor error in characterisation, necessary for the plot, was not risked till the 'type' of Volpone had been established firmly. I made a point of asking whether the students who wrote and argued like this had ever seen a performance of 'Punch and Judy', at the seaside perhaps, and they all said they had, though of course only long, long before. So it is not true that there had been any 'failure of tradition', only that a false tradition, like a cuckoo's egg, had been imposed.

Jonson himself was prone to instruct his audiences, knowing that he had often been misunderstood, and *Volpone* as he planned it begins with a prologue telling the audience to laugh. Laughing is good for them, he says, and he is not attacking any individual sinners at the moment:

> All gall and copperas from his ink he draineth,
>   Only a little salt remaineth,
> Wherewith he'll rub your cheeks till, red with laughter,
>   They shall look fresh a week after.   (33–6)

Physiological reactions vary with period and fashion a great deal more than we easily realise, and maybe some cheeks actually did go on looking red for several days after the explosions of laughter caused by seeing the famous farce. But, even granting that what the author announces is incredible, a man who chose to start off like this could not have intended what the modern students describe – a play of almost unbearable horror, regularly screwing itself up to points which are still more nearly unbearable. It seems plain to me that the pietistic strain in Eng. Lit., as it has developed during the last forty years or so, regularly produces crippled or perverted moral judgments, wholly out of contact with the basic tone of feeling of the older works which they purport to interpret; and I have to say this in a general or pompous way, because I find that when I make jokes intended to say it lightly they are regarded as merely in bad taste.

It was quite frequent on the sands, as I remember, for one of the kids to bellow because 'Punch' was too hard to take, and this unfortunate would be carried away by its nurse; but the elder children, when I was one, proud that they could take it, would laugh on till the final hanging of Punch as their Victorian parents had done at the same age. I have been secretly afraid of the theatre ever since, but I feel I know what it is about. However, the harshness is not invariable; 'rogue sentiment' does not have to be offset by this primitive bitter flavour. The first audiences of *The Winter's Tale* (and they were Jonson's public too) enjoyed seeing Autolycus pick pockets, and readily agreed that he was at bottom a good man, who would help the lovers and thus forward the plot; though in real life they would have got him hanged if they had caught him. You may decide that rogue sentiment is a rather silly self-indulgence, but that is no reason for blinding yourself to its frequent occurrence in plays.

After the Prologue, the curtain opens on Volpone worshipping his gold, a handsome piece of rhetoric, intended of course to establish the main theme powerfully at once. I agree that the references, though classical rather than Christian, are meant to imply that worshipping gold is a bad thing; and at first the audience necessarily supposes that Volpone is being satirised, since he is the only character yet in view. But an actor, however much he has been lectured by symbolist critics, feels bound to treat the soliloquy as satire intended by the character. The mind of Volpone needs to be presented as powerful and rather sinister; to make him an earnest gold-worshipper would reduce him to a quirky eccentric. Mosca then starts flattering Volpone, and the audience must assume, while rapidly picking up the social situation, that what he says is what Volpone likes to be told – it gives a slightly unusual, therefore less boring, kind of dramatic exposition. They hear at once that Volpone is morally much better than the other rich men in Venice, never hurting the poor at all, and is positively the opposite of a miser because his occupation and his delight is to cheat misers as they deserve. No wonder we found him mocking them to himself – Jonson expects the audience to reinterpret the 'imagery' when it appreciates the 'character'. The presumption of our modern literary critics that no audience could jump this little fence amounts to presuming that all audiences are subhuman.

I do not mean to deny that the lead-in of the play is consistent with its whole plot and setting; indeed, the setting made the plot seem almost credible. London was jealous of Venice, as an aggressive leader of international maritime trade, because London wanted to do that on a bigger scale. 'Terrible pigs, that tyrannous Council of Ten; they never think of anything but money' – Jonson could rely upon getting this reaction even from businessmen in his audience, while most of the audience were enjoying the play as a satire upon businessmen. Naturally, Volpone is tainted by the society which has produced him, and seems unable to imagine any directly good way of life – cheating the cheats is about all he can rise to. As the play develops, this comes to seem pathetic; but one cannot feel sure that the effect is intended, because the frame of mind of Jonson is so close to that of his hero. The story goes that he conceived this play (as a triumphant popular farce) and the *Masque of Blackness* (as delightful for the court) together in a debtors' prison, and felt confident that they would set him up, as they did. So far as he identifies himself with Volpone it is because of the enthusiasm of his own break-through into fortune, which he need not be supposed to regard morosely.

We next meet the three unappetising deviants, dwarf, eunuch, and hermaphrodite, whom Volpone keeps for his amusement or pleasure, and I can't deny that he seems here particularly short of ideas for gracious living. But as Velasquez was just then painting the similar figures who satisfied the court of Spain it would be hard to argue that Jonson was malignantly making his satire worse than the reality. We are hampered in reading, here and later (e.g. the rhymes here about the previous incarnations of the hermaphrodite, and later the prose speech of Volpone as mountebank), by a fault which is regularly corrected in production; Jonson used to add words for the printer whenever he felt touchily proud of an effect which had failed on the stage, and these bits need taking out again. The audience would accept three hours from Shakespeare but only two and a half from Jonson, and he was in an uneasy relation, resentful though admiring, to his older and more experienced rival. Now, Shakespeare had been winning all hearts by the breadth of poetry of his clowns, and Jonson had never quite accepted them – nor would we, if we had to meet them. It is cheerful to imagine the immense decisiveness with which the present Elizabeth would silence her royal clown, if forced to have one. Still, the formula of Erasmus was well within the powers of sympathy of Jonson, and the final lyric of the scene here ('Fools, they are the only nation' [1.ii.66ff]) comes off very well. Nowadays many critics assume that the first audiences would regard the scene as an attack on the top-class habit of keeping a resident clown, and this, I do submit, is quite unhistorical. So far from that, the mountainous scholar would be simpering as he held the pose in his spangled tights; he would expect to be as much loved for it as Feste or Touchstone. How cross he would be if he heard our modern experts praise the scene because it excites so much disgust. We should maybe praise Jonson for bringing a bit of reality into the theme of the pet lunatic, but we cannot say that he meant it to stand out as satire; after all, no Elizabethan playwright except Shakespeare was good at writing the mad talk which they felt to be somehow needed.

The Broken Compass (1958) by E. B. Partridge is a book always on the university shelves which firmly encourages the delusions of the students. It is impossible to realise, I think, that his remarks about the 'imagery' take for granted that you accept passively the words on the page, and never imagine yourself producing the play, telling the actors what to do:

Mosca ... answers Corvino's question about Volpone's children by saying that the dwarf, the fool, and the eunuch are only a few of Volpone's many bastards [1.v.47]. Of course, Mosca may be talking loosely ... So far as the imagery is concerned, whether or not he is telling the truth does not matter, because the connection between Volpone and his 'family' is made in the listener's mind.[1]

This presumes that the listener is imbecile, so much broken-down by the loathsome theory of Imagism that he is unable to recognise even a farcically plain human situation. What you see on the stage, when Mosca tells this lie to Corvino, is Volpone wrestling not to betray his trick by exploding with laughter; Mosca has told it merely in order to tease him. At least, there is no other effective way to act the thing, but I recognise that a decisive moral judgment has to be made before the producer accepts the obvious here. A pietistic reader immediately gulps down the bit of scandal (though not because of 'imagery' – that is only an excuse; *what* image?). But the type of spectator Jonson relied upon getting was eager for the horrible old miser to be deceived, and regarded his pious affectation of shock on hearing the scandal as further gross hypocrisy. This spectator was not tempted to believe the scandal, because for him it was not even part of the 'atmosphere'. Mallarmé and Verlaine, it seems fair to remember, did not employ their treasured symbolism to insinuate scandal, as at a cats' tea-party; this bold application of the method was invented by our own pious Establishment critics. But maybe the great anti-intellectual movement did rather deserve to be misused.

Volpone is an extremist or desperate character, I do not deny; that is why he is equipped to show us the commercial hell of Venice; but he is on our side against it, as the earlier literary guides through hell had always been. We are expected to feel a basic sympathy for him, as for Punch; and this is the chief source of the poetry of the play. Simple-minded readers, and I too, expect poetry to have a certain warmth and expansiveness, even a feeling of generosity, though this may perhaps be given merely by a process of generalisation, a sudden insight into life as a whole. The modern refusal to recognise this in Jonson is unfair to him. Towards the end of the first act, when the second horrible old miser totters away after being cheated, Volpone bounds from his sickbed and generalises about them:

> So many cares, so many maladies,
> So many fears attending on old age,
> Yea, death so often called on ...   (i. iv. 144–6)[2]

and yet they are still so eager to cheat for money that they have become absurdly easy to cheat. Volpone here is remarkably unlike what the students say; he is brooding like an archangel over the self-torturing folly of mankind. Mosca is evidently accustomed to sentiments like this, though he feels more at home when encouraging the sense of triumph:

> VOL. Dispatch, dispatch – I long to have possession
> Of my new present.
> MOS.   That, and thousands more,
> I hope to see you lord of.
> VOL.   Thanks, kind Mosca.
> MOS. And that, when I am lost in blended dust,

And hundred such as I am, in succession –
VOL.   Nay, that were too much, Mosca.
MOS.   You shall live,
       Still to delude these harpies.
VOL.   Loving Mosca!
       'Tis well. My pillow now, and let him enter.   (I. ii. 117–24)

The golden glow of this poetry is rare in Jonson's plays, and depends
here upon a moral sympathy, even if a mixed and fleeting one, from
the audience to the comic hero. Mosca and Volpone are right, as
well as clever and brave, to cheat the grandees of Venice. To
become morally independent of one's formative society in this way is
the grandest theme of all literature, because it is the only means of
moral progress, the establishment of some higher ethical concept.
Our modern neo-Christian critics seem to imply that what Jesus
Christ did, let alone Robin Hood and Huckleberry Finn, is particularly contemptible to them; they assume that any established
orthodoxy must be supported. I suppose this movement was prophe-
sied by Wyndham Lewis in *The Art of Being Ruled* (1926), which
recommended for us (whatever he meant by it) a total subservience,
ready to lick the boots of any policeman in power. No one would
deny that to set oneself up as morally independent carries great
dangers, even in minor cases, and a play on the topic needs to
present them firmly. None the less, the very basis of the operation of
Volpone is the familiar sentiment about the highwayman or the
bootlegger, which though it feels obvious to the whole audience is
rather complex. Surely it is peculiar that these scholarly critics, who
claim to be recovering for us the grand old tradition which we have
lost, have less understanding of it than the first man they might ask
in the street, and talk as if they were androids from Andromeda.

   Going back to the incident of the hero in triumph, just quoted: the
audience was sure to laugh because he is shown loving his male
flatterer, who must give him a kiss before the words ''Tis well'.
Volpone indeed hungers for the love of Mosca whenever he is
triumphant, though he is also ready to enjoy the ladies, and lets drop
in Act V that Mosca is no use for sodomy. Italians were assumed to
be highly sophisticated in such matters, but the main story here did
not seem foreign at all. The life of a successful criminal is miserable
unless there is someone he can boast to while he drinks, telling his
secrets, and he is bound to love this person because his social
isolation does not allow him any other intimacy; and yet this person,

by the mere logic of having excluded the rule of law, is committed to betraying him. I never feel sure about the logic of this, and wicked gentry often dodged it, but it was accepted as common experience. Consider the Jew of Malta, who after losing his daughter buys a Turkish slave. He at once wins the heart of this earnest affectionate man by boasting of his crimes, and the slave betrays him merely because he cannot bear not to boast of his good luck in getting such a wonderfully wicked master. The betrayals of Volpone by Mosca, and of Mosca by Volpone, are I think somehow richer and deeper, but even so Jonson would regard them as interesting examples of this well-known and accepted moral.

The English visitors need not have much interpretation piled onto them; their chief effect, being ridiculous in a relaxed and fairly homely manner, is to lighten a play which would otherwise be too tense for a comedy. They do show the importance of Venice in the minds of Londoners; Sir Politic imagines himself to be a spy, and it is assumed that this is a recognised line of endeavour. Also, to a slight extent, the contact of these everyday figures with the fantastic Volpone, who is almost too much an antique Roman even to be a Venetian, helps to make him a contact-man for the audience too. This is not done by making him friends with Lady Would-be, but by making him laugh at her from the same side as the audience. Always a man of restless and powerful intelligence, he is I think the first character in English literature who is bored by a literary critic. (Hamlet had already been shown as bored, but as a literary critic he is himself fairly boring.) When Lady Would-be threatens to cheer the sick-bed of Volpone by a survey of the Italian poets, he is almost driven to betray his secret by leaping up and escaping, or so he tells Mosca afterwards to express the violence of his boredom. Mr Partridge has a splendidly absurd sequence here, which I hope I may be allowed to follow, though it makes a slight digression. As Volpone is expecting to enjoy Celia soon after his chat with Mosca, another danger from the visit of Lady Would-be occurs to him:

> I fear
> A second hell too, that my loathing this
> Will quite expel my appetite to the other.   (III. iii. 27–9)

Mr Partridge finds here a striking piece of symbolism (p. 91): 'Hell, to this animal, means a loss of appetite; heaven, a gratifying of it.' A more refined type of man, I readily agree with my brother critic, would have found his heaven in hearing from Lady Would-be such a lecture as we both give. But shortly afterwards Mr Partridge has an opposite complaint against Volpone, who remarks to Mosca, in a moment of triumph after cheating an old miser, that 'the pleasure of all womankind's not like it' (v. ii. 11):

Here is the perfect perversion of the sexual instinct ... [G]reed and vanity and a debased intelligence have so far deranged his normal instincts that the joy of life comes not from giving joy to others but from giving pain.[3]

At least, then, the animal is no longer blamed for being sunk in his instincts, and incapable of the pleasures of the human mind. But also, Volpone intends a hyperbole; he thinks well of the pleasure to be gained from womankind, and used this to say that the moral pleasure to be gained from penalising a corrupt grandee is especially great. Compassionate Mr Partridge himself, and moral Ben Jonson too, and the whole audience so far as they can be won over, are all committed to this same line of interest, even if it is true that they had better have stayed in bed with their wives. The denunciation is thus particularly absurd here, but also it distracts attention from the main point, that Volpone is designed to work as a contact man, sufficiently at home with the London audience to show them Venice.

Naturally, for this purpose he must also be at home in Venice, and there need to be moments when he behaves with a convincing amount of native wickedness. To make him absurd is then the only way to save his popularity, and this is unflinchingly done. The main case is the attempted rape of Celia; traditionally he has been found absurd enough there not to revolt a predominantly male audience, though I have never found it possible to alter the mind of a female student who already considered him a monster. Rape is even more unpopular in the theatre than elsewhere, and the incident is a direct cause of the downfall of Volpone; delicate handling is required. Volpone first loves Celia on hearsay only; her beauty is reported by Mosca, in a handsome speech – he must have been told to scout round; it is part of the vanity of Volpone to enjoy the greatest beauties. But also to win their hearts; it does not occur to him that she might *want* to refuse him – to that extent, the attempted rape is merely a technical one. To find the rich old husband willing to sell her, instead of having to be cheated, was a great extra pleasure for Volpone; it showed he deserved to be cheated even more than

Volpone had supposed. The lady herself, he still assumed, he could woo with his real charms, chief among them his poetic imagination. I am not sure what Jonson felt about this, or meant the audience to feel, but I expect he considered the behaviour of Volpone straightforward. He offers Celia classical charades in expensive fancy dress, and a modern reader is not surprised when she treats his speeches as merely gabble adding to her torment. But Jonson himself had just discovered that he could handle the court by this method, and win a comfortable life by it for a long while. I expect he could hardly imagine wooing a lady in any other way. And then again, there is a rather puzzling whole-heartedness in the lyrical effect when Volpone offers Celia

> A diamond, would have bought Lollia Paulina,
> When she came in like star-light, hid with jewels.
>
> (III. vii. 195–6)

Puzzling, I mean, if you assume that Jonson despised his characters for feeling this kind of enthusiasm. I think he felt it himself very readily. The phrase here is easily turned into contempt, because only a very ugly woman could need to be totally hidden behind her jewellery; but the poet writes with the genuine bated breath of the crowd standing outside to watch the great ladies make their entries. Lollia achieved mention for her splendour during the days of Augustus; and Jonson, it seems to me, like a number of earlier Renaissance scholars, admired Imperial Rome in a way which we now find remote. He thought that modern science was just beginning to get us back to that paradise, that magnificent technology which had somehow got lost in the Dark Ages; he is helping to recover our birthright when he imagines unheard-of luxuries. (The assumption that he too was complaining against science for being irreligious is therefore peculiarly absurd.) Indeed, the whole story of Volpone is in a way a complement to seventeenth-century Venice, because it was recognisably borrowed from Imperial Rome.

Whether attractive or not, the wooing fails because of the simple piety of the girl, who had already accepted misery when her father sold her to a rich cripple. With needling pathos, Celia makes any offer she can think of to Volpone if only he will spare her virtue, and of course she will then also 'report him virtuous'. This has an electric effect, because, as the audience is expected to realise, he has been operating all along from a peculiar code of honour:

VOL.   Think me cold,
       Frozen, and impotent, and so report me?   (III. vii. 260–1)

Such is the threat which forces him to lay hands upon her, and the
virtuous young man at once bounds out of hiding to interrupt him.
Since this young man has also learned a more important secret, that
Volpone is not dying and only pretends it to win legacies, Volpone is
next found bemoaning to Mosca the prospect of 'beggary and
infamy'. But surely it was not a reputation for sexual potency which
he has been building up for the last three years by pretending to be
at death's door? The audience liked hearing about absurd points of
honour, and here they are given a specially absurd one; then
Volpone and Mosca go into a childish huddle for comfort, confessing
and making excuses to one another. It amounts to a fairly elaborate
protection for Volpone, to prevent the audience from swinging
against him.

     Mosca seems an undeveloped character, but this is not a fault of
the author, nor yet an illustration of a profound theory that all
characters ought to be undeveloped. One might indeed complain
that one or two of Mosca's comments are too magnificent to belong
to him:

> Bountiful bones! What horrid strange offence
> Did he commit 'gainst nature in his youth,
> Worthy this age?   (IV. vi. 89–91)

(that is, making him deserve to become this horrible old man); but
such rhetoric can be viewed as simply imitated from his master, for
whose feelings he has a real sympathy; also, it helps to keep up a
uniformity of tone. Apart from that, the plot requires Mosca to be a
conventional-minded parasite, actually trying to be a 'typical' one,
because this is what causes his downfall. At the start of Act III, the
correct point for the 'crisis' of the design, he tells us what a clever
parasite he is, and we find at once that he has overplayed his hand.
He planted the good young man as a witness to something else, but
events move too fast, and now the witness knows that Volpone is not
dying. Disaster is only averted by the splendid impudence of Mosca
at the trial, aided by the contemptible behaviour of the misers; but
the nerve of Volpone is shaken by having to appear in court, and
this causes his fatal error, which begins Act V. After being carried
home, he looks round for a yet more reckless action, to recover his
nerve:

'Fore God, my left leg 'gan to have the cramp,
And I apprehended, straight, some power had struck me
With a dead palsy. Well, I must be merry   (v. i. 5–7)

– or fear will give him a disease; so he drinks, and as usual on the
stage the effect is immediate:

'Tis almost gone, already – I shall conquer.
Any device, now, of rare, ingenious knavery,
That would possess me with a violent laughter,
Would make me up again!   (v. i. 13–16)

That is, not only his chief pleasure, but his basic confidence, his
assurance that his view of the scene around him is correct, comes
from being able to fool in a spectacular manner these great world
bankers, so as to prove that he completely understands their folly. It
is plain here that Jonson was not still operating on the crude theory
about 'humours' which he had used earlier while struggling and
frustrated. Unless you accept Volpone as an unusual character,
almost as complicated as those of Shakespeare which the same
audience enjoyed, the story is merely incredible. Be this as it may,
after Volpone and Mosca have boasted together a little, tenderly,
though Mosca rallies him a bit to calm his fears, he signs a will
leaving Mosca his entire fortune and tells Mosca to announce that
he is dead. It is done with no expectation of further gain, merely to
torment the expectant misers and induce them to act still more
absurdly. Mosca comes to feel uneasy about this, after dismissing
three misers with insults one after another, while he works away at
his accounts and Volpone (like the author as usual) peers
delightedly from the wings; Mosca suspects that they may feel too
insulted to continue the arrangement after the truth becomes
known; but Volpone feels certain that they will swallow any insult to
get his fortune.

As it happens, then, what destroys Volpone is a superstitious fear,
while on trial in court, that he has been genuinely made a cripple by
'some power' [v. i. 6], the guardian angel of the state of Venice
perhaps. This would recall to early audiences the corresponding
movement in the mind of Macbeth, whose throat had become so dry
while murdering Duncan that he found he could not say 'Amen'
when the guard said 'God bless us'. But why couldn't he? he asks his
wife with his unnerving self-pity, while it is obvious that he was
lucky to be unable to betray his presence. I think that Jonson copied

this detail from Shakespeare's play, which had only just been brought out, merely because he considered it true to life – another bit of evidence that *Macbeth* was written before *King Lear*. But the dating does not affect the present argument; I only say that, as the mind of Volpone was so close to the mind of Macbeth, at a crucial point which would be recognised by the Globe audiences, they cannot have regarded him simply as a humour.

After the third miser has been sent away with a flea in his ear, Volpone bounds out of hiding and takes the final step which ensures disaster:

> VOL. Bid him eat lettuce well. My witty mischief,
> Let me embrace thee. O, that I could now
> Transform thee to a Venus – Mosca, go,
> Straight, take my habit of *clarissimo*,
> And walk the streets; be seen, torment 'em more;
> We must pursue, as well as plot. Who would
> Have lost this feast?   (v. iii. 102–8)

The difficult rhythm of the last sentence, addressed directly to the audience, is best treated as a vast sigh of content.

> VOL. I could now but think on some disguise
> To meet 'em in, and ask 'em questions.
> How I would vex 'em still, at every turn!
> MOS. Sir, I can fit you.
> VOL.   Canst thou?
> MOS.   Yes, I know
> One o' the *commandadori*, sir, so like you;
> Him will I straight make drunk, and bring you his habit.
> (v. iii. 110–15)

Thus Volpone will be outside, disguised as a humble policeman, with his servants assured that he is dead and taking orders from his accredited heir. He might induce them to recognise him, but this would be at the cost of admitting that he was not at the point of death, which would lose him the three legacies. He is handing Mosca the ideal situation to betray him (exposing a servant to temptation, as my mother used to say). Indeed, Mosca might claim later to have only protected Volpone's interests by refusing to recognise him. But Mosca seems to look at him as a chess-player might do at an opponent who is sacrificing his queen: 'Did you really mean to do that? Well, I must take the obvious advantage, whatever you have in mind'; so he captures the queen. At first he only demands half, but when Volpone rejects this with indignation he becomes absorbed in the fun of trickery and conflict – he has no idea that he is breaking Volpone's heart, or at least exasperating the pride which in a Venetian grandee is even more dangerous. In the final trial, he orders Volpone the supposed policeman to be whipped for insolence to himself, now in Volpone's place; perhaps he feels that the extravagance of the presumption makes him safe, because no one could suspect he is doing it. Jonson is careful not to let the farce become weepy at the climax, and Volpone merely asks the audience to agree with him that 'if I confess, / It cannot be much more' [v. xii. 82–3]; but it is, and the real reason why he chooses to confess is that he has nothing left to live for, and would prefer to be wronged under his own high name. As he abandons his disguise Mosca gives a last whimpering cry of 'Why, patron!'; he had not believed that anything could make the father-figure turn against him. The court of Venice is shown as grossly venal, and naturally outraged by flippancy about wills; it orders Volpone to be crippled by irons till he is as decrepit as he has pretended to be. He is led out with the grim stoical last line, faintly reminiscent of Iago, 'This is called mortifying of a fox' (125). It sounds as if some practical operation was called that, but I do not know what.

It has been argued that the play is the tragedy of Volpone, and this question largely turns on whether you decide that Mosca has broken his heart. A lady student pointed out to me that Mosca, when Volpone tells him to invent an excuse for not showing his supposed corpse, answers stoutly: 'I'll say it stunk, sir' [v. ii. 78]. Considering what the pretence has been, this is the correct excuse, and Mosca evidently enjoys his work on the whole; but an actor could fairly present him as getting tired of being hugged and kissed all the time. Jonson himself might tell the actor to do it, since his feelings on the subject were mixed. As one often finds with manly men, who need pleasure with coarse vigorous women (and resent the pretentions of ladies), he was very susceptible to elegant courageous lads, and inclined to denounce sodomy in other people so as to cover this up. But the English audience expected sodomy in raffish Italians, and Jonson does not treat the matter as at all crucial. Another conviction of the first audience would be more decisive for the motivation: that the rulers of Venice are immensely proud aristocrats, though of course all 'in trade'. Jonson was no good at presenting aristocratic dignity, any more than romantic love, and preferred to take the mickey out of them, but he could rely on his audience to presume that Volpone, though a rebel, kept his class pride; and as this supplies his motive a modern producer should put it back. Telling the audience that Mosca is no use for pleasure ('O, that I could ... ' [v. iii. 103]) cannot be intended to forestall scandal because it is delayed till the last Act – it comes just before their feelings for one another become decisive. I think its function is to make clear that this love is of a comparatively dignified kind, the love of a criminal for his accomplice to whom he boasts, nobly undemanding in any other way; but it is still doomed, especially in a man with a code of pride.

You may have noticed that my last paragraph set out to shoo away the feeling of tragedy but ended by yielding to it. I have next to recall the real end of the play. Some of my readers can perhaps remember (long, long ago) seeing *Peter Pan*, in which Tinker Bell, though dying of poison, will recover if the audience believe in fairies – 'clap if you do'. Tired of sitting still, the children save the life of Tinker Bell every time. This device had presumably been learned from the end of the *Beggar's Opera*, which also allows the audience to give a reprieve. In *Peter Pan* they are only asked to confess a habit of day-dreaming, I think; but in the *Beggar's Opera* the first audiences were asked to confess that they were half on the side of the rebels, they half agreed that they ought to overthrow the government of Walpole. It was a display of careless ease, but the call for applause was bound to have a certain fighting political point. This in turn had been taken from *Volpone*, one of the few Jacobean plays still revived; and there, I think, in its rough prejudiced way, the device amounted to a vote for English law against Continental law. The English had long been proud that their legal procedure did not admit torture (Shakespeare uses the belief, with the vagueness that was needed, at 2 *Henry VI*, III. i. 120); and indeed Volpone could hardly even be detained under English law, except for masquerading as a policeman. You are not asked to believe that Volpone is a good character, but that the wicked laws of Venice inherently produce characters like him – and like Shylock, for that matter. No English audience would want to cripple Volpone, as the Venetian bench did, for making Venice ridiculous; they can be trusted to let him off, thus dispelling the clouds of tragedy which have gathered over the last act, from the intensity of the reactions of these odd characters. Jonson invented the device, likely enough, just to preserve decorum; to make the farce end like a farce though it had become so gripping. All the same, the pardon of Volpone is given the dignity of political language, and some other members of the first audience would be likely to take it seriously. Our moralising school, on the other hand, cannot face the actual end of the play; such critics hardly ever admit its existence:

> ... though the Fox be punished by the laws,
> He yet doth hope there is no suffering due
> For any fact which he hath done 'gainst you.
> If there be, censure him – here he doubtful stands.
> If not, fare jovially, and clap your hands. (v. xii. 153-7)

Better results really might be expected, morally as well as aesthetically, if they would fare more jovially.

CHAPTER 5

'Volpone' again

An article by Mr John Creaser ('*Volpone*: The Mortifying of The Fox', *Essays in Criticism*, July 1975) allows priority on some points to an earlier article by me, but disagrees with me on others.[1] The agreements have not done him much good, as he murders the play all the same. I need to plead for its life more effectively than I have done so far.

We agree that the first incident, of Volpone worshipping his gold, 'cannot be taken at face value', and Mr Creaser decides that it is 'a knowing act of self-adoration' (pp. 333–4); having thus pin-pointed the flaw in the hero, he scolds him for it till the final scene. But the start of a play has its own requirements, called the Exposition. The audience have come expecting satire, and at first they are bound to think that Volpone is being presented as the 'type' of Avarice; but when he turns and speaks to his servant he confidently blames other people for avarice, so he is the satirist here. In real life it would be odd to tell Mosca what he already knows, a mark of vanity perhaps, but here everybody wants Volpone to define his activity, and give what defence of it he has; even the schoolboy, though severe by tradition upon show-offs, would not blame him for it here. During the last act, I don't deny, we may reflect that there has always been something unstable about Volpone, but to have made this mistake at the start is no help in understanding him. Many readers do fail to realise that he is not worshipping but satirising, whereas an actor of the part, knowing it as a whole, feels that he cannot help treating the first words as satirical.

Critics have often said that the speech is blasphemous, and that this made the audience hate Volpone at once; in the same way, Mr Creaser remarks that the Golden Age was 'a then living myth' (p. 334), so that only a bad man could joke about it. But you could not be burnt alive for a joke about the Golden Age, or the sun-god

82

either; the learned fun of Volpone is about pagan beliefs, which were
a legitimate field for play. (How extraordinarily misleading the
conventions of Eng. Lit. Crit. are, in how many ways!) However, he
does use some Christian terms at the end of the speech, when he is
turning towards Mosca and preparing to be indignant about his
rivals:

> Riches, the dumb god ...
> ... even hell, with thee to boot,
> Is made worth heaven! Thou are virtue, fame,
> Honour, and all things else! ...   (I. i. 22, 24–6)

This is plainly satire, and he goes on to tell Mosca that he will not
take part in the activities usual for a rich man of Venice:

> I ... have no mills for iron,
> Oil, corn, or men, to grind 'em into powder ...
> I turn no moneys in the public bank;
> Nor usure private ...   (I. i. 35–6, 39–40)

Mosca interrupts to say that he avoids more obviously brutal
oppression as well, so could make his point more strongly:

> MOS. You loathe, the widow's or the orphan's tears
>   Should wash your pavements, or their piteous cries
>   Ring in your roofs, and beat the air for vengeance –
> VOL. Right, Mosca, I do loathe it.
> MOS.   And, besides, sir ...   (I. i. 49–52)

In itself, the flattery of Mosca proves nothing, but the interruption
by Volpone, eagerly agreeing that he hates the tyranny of big
money, is a device for convincing the audience that his revulsion is
active and real. Nothing happens afterwards to cast doubt on this
exposition – quite the contrary; and it is normally expected to give
basic information. I do not know what reason Mr Creaser could
provide for cold-shouldering the moral sentiments of the hero; he
seems merely to feel that his dignity requires him to despise Volpone,
especially for his lack of moral sentiments; because an establishment
critic regards any character who revolts against tyranny as a
show-off, addicted to 'self-adoration'. The morality of Jonson was
not as sordid as all that.

In accordance with this programme, he next denounces Volpone
for cowardice; but here he is too absurd.[2] Most of us do not realise
till the end of the play what a great risk Volpone is running, but we

already hear him expect branding and disfigurement in Act III; and he does all this, not out of need for the money, but as a 'demonstration', or for fun, or because Venice exasperates him. The result is death by torture. What would the hero Creaser, in his own life, find brave enough to be acceptable? The case is so bad, I think, that the palliation ought to be admitted at once. A reader should always estimate the intention of a writer, and the theory forbidding him to do it has done great harm; but there are special difficulties when an author is writing pastiche. Mr Creaser had a good article about Marvell in *Essays in Criticism* a few years ago, without any such taint;[3] and maybe in the present case he merely set out to follow the rules of the grand Eng. Lit. manner, as one might patiently construct a sonnet. It is more likely that the disciples, as they preen and posture, actually experience the bad feelings which they have chosen to ape; but Mr Creaser may be able to carry this spiritual risk, as a heavy drinker may have a strong liver. Even so, his reader must first consider the words on the page.

Volpone does not keep up appearances before Mosca (if that is showing off) and often expresses fear to him. But (a) if a man regularly says he is afraid of doing something, and then always does it, you are mistaken to think him a coward; (b) an audience needs to be told when something reckless is being done; and (c) begging Mosca to comfort him is part of his loving play with Mosca; after the attempt at rape, it helps to keep the audience from thinking him too much of a brute. Mr Creaser thinks it cowardly of him in Act III to ask Mosca whether he had been spotted in his disguise as a mountebank, after his safe return;[4] then he blames him even more severely for becoming reckless in Act V. He has one real argument, such as would have impressed the first audiences if it were valid: that Volpone 'collapses at Bonario's intrusion' (p. 346). But Volpone on his sick-bed is unarmed, whereas Bonario has a sword, which he uses on Mosca as he goes out ('Enter Mosca, bleeding' [III. viii]). This by the way is why the line 'Forbear, foul ravisher! libidinous swine!' [III. vii. 267] is not really so feeble as many critics tell us; they think of the poetry as always being intoned or crooned, whereas these phrases are adequate if muttered between clenched teeth as Bonario first breaks the clinch and then hunts Volpone round the nooks of the Elizabethan stage. Seeing Volpone dodge a sword would not make him contemptible to an audience acquainted with swords, though it might help, again, to make him seem less of a brute.

Mr Creaser's craving to patronise Volpone gets a good start as soon as the exposition is over, when some comic rhymes composed by Mosca in favour of being a fool are recited by Volpone's fool, dwarf, and hermaphrodite (I. ii). These, the critic explains, are merely 'praise of the cleverness of the whole coterie' (p. 341), therefore flattering to Volpone also. How about those paintings by Velasquez of the imbecile dwarfs kept at the court of Spain, brooding in an eerie silence; were they the 'coterie' of the king of Spain? And what about all the lords in Shakespeare who accept this fashion of keeping fools; are they equally contemptible? I agree that Jonson is clumsy about it, but I expect he was behaving just like Mr Creaser here, struggling to follow a bad fashion that does not suit his talent. To suppose that Johnson was rebuking King James for keeping a clown would surely be a long way outside Mr Creaser's intention. All the same, I grant that the bleak contempt of Volpone for his fools is one of his few disagreeable traits. He manages not to laugh when Mosca tells a dupe that they are all his bastards, but if Lady Would-be had called them his coterie he would have exploded.

Mr Creaser of course prepares these earlier details for his interpretation of the end of the play. In the scene before the last, Volpone recognises he is in a jam, and curses himself for his folly:

> To make a snare for mine own neck! . . .
> Out of mere wantonness! O, the dull devil
> Was in this brain of mine when I devised it,
> And Mosca gave it second; he must now
> Help to sear up this vein, or we bleed dead.   (v. xi. 1, 4–7)

It is Voltore who has made trouble, when jeered at for not being Volpone's heir; and Volpone (pretending to be dead) knows he is now in a dangerous position; all depends upon Mosca remaining loyal. Perhaps he will fail to be loyal, because he is silly, but if he fails both of them will die. Mr Creaser's comment on these lines, couched in the hideous jargon of his tribe is: 'significantly he also senses that he had lost self-control' (p. 350). But it is impossible to think of words in which Volpone could express the idea attributed to him. Immense control of his body is always at his command when he is acting, and when he thinks of a line of action he feels inspired. Usually he is glad after being inspired, but this time the spirit was a dull devil; obviously that was not his fault, and anyway he is only considering the future. There is no repentance about it at all.

It is important for Mr Creaser to deny this. What Volpone had was a 'coterie', he is forced to assume, because there never was anybody in all history except high-minded lower-middle-class persons, worrying about their consciences, living in suburbs; and as to lords, of course there never were any lords, you stick to the words on the page. His remarks are almost like what George IV would say if he had been transported to the court of the Emperor of China. However, there is always a surprise in another man's reading, and I was shaken for a moment when Mr Creaser quoted the final line of this very dramatic penultimate scene:[5]

> When I provoked him, then I lost myself.   (v. xi. 22)

Volpone foresees his fall, and the reason for it is something to do with Mosca. Mr Creaser assumes that Volpone has long been subordinate to his house-mate, always clearing a plan beforehand with Mosca, but just for once he has acted on his own, naturally annoying Mosca, so he is afraid. This cannot survive a glance at the text. Volpone decides, in his lordly manner, and tells his decision to Mosca; Mosca gives a warning, as is his duty, and when overruled is at once ready in helping the plan forward; so he was not *provoked* in the sense of 'offended'. What Volpone has at last realised is that he has given Mosca a great temptation, to keep the property for himself; *provoke* here has the archaic sense 'act so as to cause temptation' (*OED*, PROVOKE 4; Shakespeare 'Beautie prouoketh theeves sooner than gold'). It was a well-known fact that one should avoid exposing servants to temptation; can it really not be known any longer? Then we have a more crucial point, very near the end, when Volpone is deciding to abandon disguise. Mr Creaser thinks that this marks an important change in his character, so that he stops being a coward.

> VOL.   ... If I confess,
>   It cannot be much more.
> 4TH AVOCATORE.   [*To Mosca*] Sir, are you married?
> VOL. They'll be allied anon; I must be resolute.
>   *He puts off his disguise*
>   The Fox shall here uncase.   (v. xii. 82–5)

Mr Creaser says (p. 351):

his sardonic gaiety here is an expression of achieved courage; his aside 'I must be resolute' (line 84) shows it still costs him an effort to concentrate his will in this way.

But plainly it means: 'I must be ready at once, before they are allied, with some decisive action' (*OED*. RESOLUTE 9). This gives him a partial excuse for a fatally wrong decision, in line with his recent craving to jeer openly at the disappointed millionaires. Why does Mr Creaser not call this a loss of self-control, as he did that? Only sixty lines before, Volpone saved himself by the sudden invention of an immensely bold trick ('see, see! He vomits crooked pins!' [v. xii. 24-5]), and the only trouble now is that Mosca has become intoxicated with triumph. Volpone is not likely to tell himself, as Mr Creaser expects him to: 'Don't go on being such a coward as you have been all through the play so far.' At this rate, any man could be proved a coward.

I have now considered most of Mr Creaser's contentions, except the first one, that Volpone suffers from self-adoration. It is rather like answering a swear-word. I agree that he is like Punch. The bouncing showmanship of Volpone makes him popular with an audience, Mr Creaser readily admits, and for that matter (he goes on) most of the successful characters of Jonson do the same.[6] The accusation dissolves; of course it had a kind of relevance, like Tolstoy saying that King Lear is frightfully embarrassing. I ought to point out a particularly absurd example. When a critic fully realises, says Mr Creaser, that Volpone

arouses reactions of some complexity, then certain fluctuations in his conduct throughout the final act – the only one which does not begin with a speech of self-praise – become easier to see and to account for. (p. 345)

Now surely the clause added between dashes, about speeches of self-praise, has no point unless Volpone makes them. Two are by Politic Would-be and one by Mosca, leaving to Volpone only the initial satire against his dupes. No act of the play begins with a speech of self-praise by Volpone. I suppose Mr Creaser just misread one of his notes, and when writing the note was reflecting that other characters suffer from self-adoration, as well as Volpone; even so, it leaves one a bit dubious about his complex reactions.

Still, I think he does understand the traditional view pretty well, and intends to destroy it. He rightly quotes the poet Swinburne (p. 346):

I admire as a master-stroke of character the haughty audacity of caprice which produces or evolves his ruin out of his own hardihood and insolence of exulting and daring enjoyment. (*A Study of Ben Jonson*, London: Chatto and Windus, 1889, p. 42)

Swinburne of course admired an aristocrat, especially when he acted in defiance of the other aristocrats, taking the side of the people; and there is good reason to admire Volpone on both counts. It would not occur to Swinburne to ask what actual help such a man brought to the people, or whether he had made sensible plans; the mere display of his sentiments, the work of propaganda, might be the best he could do. One cannot, I agree, go all the way with his enthusiasm. Still, this view of the play is what a number of his critics have felt to raise the farcical deceptions into a larger air, and make Volpone an inherently interesting character; I do not think there is any literary reason why we must be told this is a misreading, and my opponents dare not put forward the political one, that such a hero would be a bad influence on the kids. I may be told that it is absurdly unhistorical to read Jonson as if he had read Marx. I find I have handy an excellent Pelican *What is History?* (Harmondsworth, Middx., 1961) by E. H. Carr: he says (p. 133) that there was an important social revolution during the middle years of the twentieth century, 'comparable with' something very familiar:

that which, in the fifteenth and sixteenth centuries, inaugurated the rise to power of a new class based on finance and commerce, and later on industry.

Jonson considered it the duty of a writer to expose evils of that sort, and was prone to quote classical authority for it; he was probably rather glad to have such a good example, but he knew it had to be treated gingerly so that it could not be passed off as a farce, not to annoy the king. You may say he had no business to give himself such airs, living as a parasite on the court, but he would have argued back. So far there is no problem, and the moral judgment of Mr Creaser is even more perverse than usual when he tries to make us cry over the poor old money-tyrants, spoken to so rudely by Volpone, even openly tormented;[7] the first audiences would have been waiting for that. But as to what the first audiences would think about Venice, though I am sure Mr Creaser is wrong, I have to confess I have no dossier; I will try to make or find one later, if I am spared.

Swinburne accepted Volpone as extremely aristocratic, one of a rare but famous type. Mr Creaser denies that Venetian grandees were aristocrats at all; everyone knew they were in trade, practically artisans; in fact some of them were glass-blowers (p. 334). Well, the chief pleasure of Emperor Joseph II of Austria was making toffee, and glass-blowing is a great deal more distinguished; but either is compatible with an exclusive social system. Long before Jonson wrote, Venice had established a 'Libro d'Oro', a Social Register, to leave no doubt about which families were within the charmed circle. Anyhow, the grandeur of the Venetian style of painting, and the yearly marriage of Venice to the sea, would make it absurd to pretend that they lacked dignity. One might argue that their claims were excessive, and that by Jonson's time the real 'world bankers' lived in Hamburg, but at least the theatre kept up the tradition that Venetians were grand; it is clear that the cloak which marks Volpone as a clarissimo strikes awe, and Mosca seems almost blasphemous when he puts it on. Jonson is not good at fine shades, and we generally see Volpone when he has cast his grandeur aside; but he is quite willing to snatch it up again at need, and the actor should allow him to. Indeed, if we are told which bits had struck Mr Creaser as 'self-adoration', they would probably turn out to be moments when Volpone is being particularly external, and acting up to his real position in the world. At any rate, it is the Creaser view which is the fanciful paradox, whereas the Swinburne view accepts the obvious.

There is only one problem about Volpone, where a producer needs to make a decision: why is his behaviour so different in the last act? Always a modest speaker, he says (when the act begins) that he felt frightened at the trial, and needs a good laugh now to recover his nerve; but what he does is more like a challenge, and seems to lead straight on to his final unmasking. Till Act V he is at least pretending to deceive the misers for money, but now his only admitted motive is that good laugh. A coward who acts recklessly when he gets rattled would be possible in a novel, no doubt, but he seems very inadequate for this play. Surely another explanation is in easy reach, if you are willing to attend to the guidance given at the start. He *wants* to be found out; only with part of his mind, but an increasingly demanding part. First he wants his dupes to know how much he despised them, and how much they deserved to be cheated; but that rapidly brings him back to the lawcourt, and then he wants all Venice to know how much he despises them. On both occasions the lawcourt is the chief source of these feelings; he finds its pretensions so impudent. But he is not self-righteous about it; at least, not inclined to make a positive claim for his own motives, which would be out of place. He feels that his enemies ought to be kicked out of his way. An unexpected appeal to some extraneous authority would be very much in his style.

Swinburne was especially pleased by this because he liked both the contrasting sides of it, the populist sympathies and the lordly behaviour. But he assumes it is familiar; he has no idea that he has invented an interpretation of Volpone, and indeed this is the only plausible one. It is quite compatible with disliking Volpone, and believing that this type of man has never done anything but make trouble; but it does make the character hold together.

Mr Creaser says that the final scene '*is* a triumph, even though the ending has invariably been interpreted as a humiliation' (p. 350). I was keen to know how he can make this out; after cold-shouldering the epilogue, he gets very little help from the words. They need a close look. Volpone is disguised as a kind of policeman, and Mosca wears his robe as clarissimo, but they can exchange brief remarks unheard by the lawcourt. At Mosca's entry, Volpone takes for granted they are still allies:

> VOL. Mosca, I was a'most lost; the advocate
> Had betrayed all; but now it is recovered.
> All's o' the hinge again – say I am living.
> MOS. What busy knave is this!   (v. xii. 52–5)

– and he explains that he himself is very busy about the funeral of his dear patron. Before the hubbub at this news has died again, he is saying:

> MOS. Will you gi' me half?
> VOL.   First, I'll be hanged.   (v. xii. 63)

Within four lines he has capitulated: 'Thou shalt have half.'

> MOS. Whose drunkard is this same? speak some that know him –
> I never saw his face. [*Aside to VOLPONE*] I cannot now
> Afford it you so cheap.   (v. xii. 68–70)

The replies of Volpone now begin to risk exposure for both of them, and Mosca can hardly be blamed for asking to be relieved from the impudence of this low person. He does not ask for him to be whipped; Third Advocate does that. Mosca says: 'I humbly thank your fatherhoods', and Fourth Advocate starts trying to arrange a marriage for his daughter. This is what makes Volpone say 'I must be resolute', and he 'uncases'. 'Patron!' says Mosca, and again, after

Volpone has exulted over him, 'Why, patron!' It is in part a cry for mercy, though necessarily past hope; but even more, I think, of surprise: 'I thought you loved me so much that you could never betray me.' He has been 'playing chicken', and did not expect it to go so disastrously far. The second of these cries follows an insult from Volpone that is genuinely contemptuous but not so much impressive as flip – 'my substance shall not glue you, / Nor screw you, into a family', he tells Mosca (one of the families in the Book of Gold, no doubt). It is a heart-rending cry, but one can hardly blame Volpone for being spiteful; to refuse half, and thus ruin both of them, was shockingly silly of Mosca, and yet this kind of silliness was just what he in the past had found so charming about the young man – 'Rare, Mosca! how his villainy becomes him!' he had said in Act V scene iii, as he watched Mosca at work exasperating the misers. Then he insults his three dupes, with venom but briefly, and asks for sentence. He can hardly hold the stage while the sentences drag on for thirty lines, except for a brief drip of venom when Mosca is condemned, 'I thank you for him' (v. xii. 115), followed by his own condemnation. He is 'taken from the bar' and says (125):

> This is called mortifying of a fox.

Then there are thirty lines on the punishments for the three dupes; and that, if you consider the epilogue merely an advertisement, is the end of the play.

Mr Creaser is thus committed to building up the one-line epigram, which has now to signalise an important change in Volpone's character and thus make him dominate the scene. Mortifying, he says, is a 'superbly complex pun', and he lists a number of possible meanings, such as 'making meat and game tender for the table by keeping it raw until it is "high" – although the fox is, of course, inedible' and 'disposing of property for religious, charitable or public purposes (a Scots legal term)' (p. 352). But he makes no attempt to fit them together, to find a point for the pun.[8] From what he says (p. 351) about the final Yeats and *The Revenger's Tragedy* ('We die after a nest of dukes'), a Stoical meaning should be in the list, but there is no sign of one; nor yet of the splendid phrase of Yeats: 'no tragedy is legitimate unless it leads some great character to his final joy' (*Explorations*, London: Macmillan, 1962, pp. 448–9). I am not sure what to make of this, but it is a distinct help in the present case; because Volpone is so very plainly not one of the characters in view. The audience are almost driven to laugh at him, after he has confided to them that 'if I confess, / It cannot be much more' (v. xii. 82–3), because the effects *are* much worse, and all he has gained is the ruin of the only man likely to help him. But his code of honour was what drove him into this mistake, though it would not occur to him to say so. I find this last scene so very good, so bare and so fiercely true, that any smearing of fashionable holy-thoughts over it excites nausea.

The extra meanings of *mortify*, so far as I can see, merely work as camouflage for Mr Creaser; all he wants is the standard Christian meaning of the word; so that a suddenly converted Volpone is saying: 'I welcome this slow and agonising death, because it will enable me to attain eternal bliss.' If said plainly, this would be recognised at once as grossly out of character, and therefore as false sentiment. Owing to our literary convention of evasive sanctimoniousness, which refuses to specify a religious tenet, or even a religion, I cannot be sure what is in question; but presumably if Volpone has been suddenly converted he now thinks he was wrong before. Does he now think it a good thing to have the widow's and the orphan's tears washing one's pavements? The change of opinion must have been immensely rapid; why is there no sign or mention of it?

However, I could not deny that, when Christianity is taken for granted, its terms often get used casually, and it is almost certain that Volpone wanted to sound wise when he said *mortify* here. One must realise that he is on show; he has received a terrible sentence, and his enemies will be watching to see if he can take it in the proper style. He would regard coolness, and passing the matter off with a joke, however bad, as part of his code as a grandee; though most men of any class seem to have risen to it. I hope there was a phrase *mortify a fox* meaning 'temper the steel of a sword' (*OED*, FOX 6); this would make the line quite good, though I have never come across an example. Its function hardly allows it to be very good, because it is a stopgap, before the great surprise is swung on the audience. He says: 'Many people will say this trouble will do me good; I only say, however bad it is, I won't give in to it.' One should feel that he is manly enough to deserve his rescue, which follows as soon as the court rises – he has reflected that he can take advantage of happening to be in a theatre.

Maybe Mr Creaser agrees with my estimate of the resultant

meaning, and then we only disagree about the degree of impress-
iveness which even a good actor could give to the line. There is room
for doubt, because when he is trying to recommend his view of the
'superbly complex pun' he calls it 'a characteristic exploitation of a
religious term' (p. 352). It was the communists, of course, who first
'exploited' the double meaning of this word, for developing natural
resources or robbing the people; but Mr Creaser's school, hungry for
any means of double-talk, have long taken it over. So Volpone is still
sneering at Christianity, when he reaches his apotheosis, is he? Then
why is he so much better? And for that matter, when did he ever
sneer at Christianity before? The conviction that he is a blasphemer
comes into Mr Creaser's essay several times, but it seems to depend
entirely on his identification of Christianity and the pagan myths
(both are 'religion'). I looked through the text with curiosity, and
find Volpone to be placidly orthodox, though of course willing to use
pious language to deceive bad men. It is only by refusing to admit
that Volpone could sincerely disapprove of the establishment that
Mr Creaser involves himself in inventing a Volpone who is a
nerve-racked self-accusing criminal, driving himself to keep his
conscience at bay by blasphemy. There are only a few Christian
remarks by Volpone. He tells Voltore in the third scene that he is
dying, and 'I am glad I am so near my haven' (I. iii. 30): obviously
there is no sneering about this, only acting. Lady Would-be in Act
III, scene v reduces him to telling Mosca 'For hell's sake, rid her
hence' (11), because she is so boring; this does not mean that
Volpone and Mosca are both devils, but that it is hell to have to
listen to an establishment literary critic. (By the way, it is interesting
that he accepts the social duties of his position; he feels he has to
remain polite to the foreign visitor.)

There is a more interesting case at the end of Act III, when the
rape has been stopped and several faces need putting straight;
Mosca goes off with Corbaccio and Voltore, saying:

> MOS. Patron, go in and pray for our success.
> VOL. Need makes devotion; Heaven your labour bless.
>
> (III. ix. 62–3)

Here for once an actual comment is made on religious activity, but it
implies no scepticism at all; Volpone is in trouble, and he says
'people pray when they are in trouble', so he prays. Of course
it is rather flip, but that was recognized as quite different from

blasphemy. In Act V, scene ii, gloating over their successful deception of all three dupes, Mosca remarks that each of them is so eager to believe in his own success that they resist any evidence against it – 'Like a temptation of the devil' (28) breaks in Volpone, and certainly this thought might lead him eventually to a sceptical position, but so far it merely shows him familiar with the accepted religion of his place and time. He does not admit at the end that he has done anything wrong (though of course he might speak differently to his confessor), and he would be very angry to find Mr Creaser patronising him as a converted man, wonderfully transformed by the rod of justice, on the sole evidence of a complex pun.

I agree with Mr Creaser that some kind of rehabilitation of Volpone is needed at the end, and only disagree with his belief that he can still have it after debunking the epilogue. He says (p. 353):

An actor's direct appeal for applause is a device that evokes a mood of gaiety and harmony which is out of keeping with tragedy's darker sense of waste and loss.

Yes, and that proves it is in very bad taste here, if we are to believe that Volpone will move straight on to a death very similar to a crucifixion. (All aesthetes assume that the story of a play is merely a peg to hang moral and 'poetry' on, so they refuse to enter the play and get nothing from it.) The truth is, the words have to do more than Mr Creaser allows, or they would be too outrageous; in a performance where they could not be given weight, before the king for instance, they would simply be omitted. We hear that the Globe was hung with black for tragedy; surely the audience would feel exasperated if a supposed comedy turned out to be a particularly needling tragedy? Volpone says:

> The seasoning of a play is the applause.
> Now, though the Fox be punished by the laws,
> He yet doth hope there is no suffering due
> For any fact which he hath done 'gainst you.
> If there be, censure him – here he doubtful stands.
> If not, fare jovially, and clap your hands. (v. xii. 152–7)

The words are scrupulous, I agree, in refusing to admit that this is anything but a routine bit of salesmanship. I might claim an ambiguity of syntax from the punctuation; if you stop at the third line, obeying a comma which is otherwise unnecessary and almost ungrammatical, he clearly means that he hopes to avoid suffering altogether. And he stands there *doubtful*; if he knows he is next to begin an agonising death, whether the audience clap or not, there can be no large doubt in his mind. This remarkable invention by Jonson did not go unnoticed, we may be sure, because it is used again in *The Beggar's Opera*, using much plainer language. Jonson indeed might have disclaimed invention here and claimed a high authority. The scholar Creaser remarks that Jonson seems not to have known how unorthodox his ending was, regarded as an imitation of Latin Comedy; but surely his claim to be specially moral in this play was merely another manoeuvre to outface the Puritans; and he would be well aware that a final pardon by a god was quite orthodox in Greek Tragedy. The people also are a god. Volpone when 'taken from the bar' is held by guards in large shining chains back centre, and speaks his one line about 'mortifying' (gangrene from the treatment to which he is condemned is, I agree, meant to be in view). Thirty lines later, after the ravenous speech of a lawyer clamouring for blood, the guards lead him impassively to the front of the apron stage, where he speaks the epilogue. When the audience clap, the guards unlock his chains, and he waves gayly, delighting in his freedom. All the other actors hurry away behind the back curtain, which is closing; the music strikes up, and the men dance on for a jig.

In this sketch of the closing scene I have assumed that all went well; the audience did clap, and so Volpone was freed. But why should they clap the person Mr Creaser describes, a coward and a cheat, suffering from almost insane vanity, of disgusting personal habits, who has made a sordid and offensive misuse of a high position? He might be brought out to be hissed, but that is not what the words presume. Mr Creaser, as I understand, admits that the audience liked Volpone much better than he thinks proper, and presumably that the author had intended them to; this raises an almost metaphysical question – are we to say that everyone had always been out of step except our Creaser? Even so, might we not think that so widespread a literary delusion is itself a proper object of critical inquiry? The remarks about Falstaff by Maurice Morgann in the late eighteenth century [*Essay on the Dramatick Character of Sir John Falstaff*, 1777]: that the audience take him at three levels, on the first level believing that he has been exposed as a coward, on the second that he is an artful schemer who knows how the prince can be amused, and on the third that the personal life behind his triumphs

is an unpleasant and miserable one– surely that is immensely closer
to what actually happens than any of the posturing by Mr Creaser
and his school. But it is not concerned with the politics of the case,
probably important even there, but frankly important in the case of
Volpone. Indeed this technique invented by Jonson, of breaking out
from the frame of make-believe, has I think always been used for a
political or quasi-political appeal to the audience; it could hardly be
effective with any other.

What can be the purpose of such an ending, and why did Jonson
only use it in this play? Because a sympathetic spectator, responsive
to the politics, who has not forgotten the firm statements at the start,
will be thinking: 'It's a fine jape, but they'll never let him get away
with it. Not them; not if he makes a fool of their bloody wills. They'll
torture him in the end.' If you had been feeling this, you would be
glad to clap as a firm pretence that you were setting him free. It does
not feel like wishful thinking, because it is so sardonic, and also it is
like casting your vote; but it also has the effect that you go out feeling
more cheerful. Actual capitalists, who think this line of sentiment all
wrong, need hardly be considered; they would be rather few in
number, with the sentiment of the house against them. (Of course the
play needed to be set, not in London, but in a town generally blamed
by London for avarice and usury.) Also there would be a large part
of the audience who were not committed to either side, but well
aware of Volpone's faults; they enjoy the play by indulging in
'rogue-sentiment', imagining they are on the side of the bold rebel,
but recognising it as a pretence. To them the pretence of letting him
off at the end, by their own choice, feels quite in keeping; in a way
they have abetted him, so they cannot want him tortured, or admit it
at any rate, and to end by breaking the dream (which had been
getting rather near to nightmare) gives an assurance that it is unreal.
Of course, the same spectator might be taking it both ways; the audience is not radically divided, as in Verrall's Euripides. I think this
double structure is what makes the device feel so solid here.

I ought perhaps to make a final attempt to grapple with the saying
of Yeats, recalled by Mr Creaser; 'no tragedy is legitimate unless it
leads some great character to his final joy'. I do not like it, but do not
feel it can be ignored. However, it is no trouble in this case, as it
serves to make even more clear that Volpone is not a tragic character,
and the efforts of Mr Creaser cannot make him one. This is why the
frame of the drama had to be broken to make the end satisfactory.

CHAPTER 6

'The Alchemist'

Probably it is a delusion caused by ignorance, but my impression is that, in the case of this one play, I stand alone like Abdiel against the forces of night. A number of critics have written quite sensibly about *Volpone*, but in *The Alchemist* (I suspect they feel) the crude formula becomes too hard to resist. There seems no way of jolting its adherents, making them willing to recognise the actual merits of the play. Hence it is unusual to deny that Jonson hates and despises all the characters in *The Alchemist*, either for being fools or for being knaves, because he is so moral. And yet the two plays are very alike, in their general tone as well as their electrically geared-up construction – they are the most frequently revived of Jonson's plays, and I agree that they are much the best. The producer of either play, it will be found, never tries to implement our established critical theory about it (not even making it like non-Euclidean geometry), because the audience is sure to reject that. The case is thus rather odd, and might throw some light on the presumptions of Eng. Lit. in general.[1]

The reason for the difference, I think, is that teachers feel *The Alchemist* to be hiding something worse than *Volpone*, needing more urgently to be kept from the students. The romantic appeal of *Volpone* is felt as a tender indulgence even while it is being ignored by an effort of hypocrisy, but somehow *The Alchemist* is felt to have harshly unwelcome 'values' lurking within; this makes it even more urgent for the critic to insist that Jonson has no 'values', in that he despises all the characters he describes. The term 'values', it seems as well to point out, has the serious function of helping us to recognise the variety of the world. The chief use of reading imaginative literature is to make you grasp that different people act on different ethical beliefs, whereas the chief use of critical jargon is to obscure this basic fact, making you feel at home where you are not. Jonson in this play has a splendid range of characters with wildly different values, and the effect is very funny, but if you think he despises them all you are taken aback when he begins to express his own. However, to let him be morally active does not make him a scold; indeed, *Bartholomew Fair* strikes me as rather too permissive, too like the comic Dickens – the audience is expected to love the eccentrics so much that it merely wants them to troop back onto the stage, each repeating his fixed gimmick. It is not the sterner morality but the clockwork plots of the two great farces that haul them up into the cold exhilarating air of the mountains.

Even so, one cannot get on with *The Alchemist* without accepting its moral. This might seem easy to grasp; the play sets out to dissuade its audiences from superstitious belief. But nowadays the rivetting home of the chains of superstition upon captive children is regarded as the prime duty of an educator; so naturally this activity of Jonson, though the critics are always trying to invent ways to tell us how moral he is, cannot be recognised as moral at all. 'Do you imagine he was like H. G. Wells?' I shall be asked with exasperated astonishment. Only like Wells on a few plain-man issues, I grant, because he was also prone to the seductive role of the working-class reactionary. But in this play we find him solidly and consciously backing a progressive cause; and I do not see why he should not be respected more for it than Shakespeare in *Macbeth*, lavishing his art upon an encouragement for James to torment old women. I do not, indeed, think we need be so solemn as is now usual over the repeated claims of Jonson to be an improving author. The theatre was under Puritan attack, and to provide a defence for himself and his fellows was one of the uses of his learning. He would expound the classical defence whenever convenient; it should apply, of course, to all good playwrights. Evidently he believed in it, but it would not actually deflect his mind while he was being inspired to create a farce. On the other hand, when the structure of a play required a moral, the doctrine enabled him to present one with vigour; and that is what we find going on here.

Both *Volpone* and *The Alchemist* depend for their intended effect upon rogue-sentiment, upon making the audience half-sympathise with the tricksters. I think this was helped in *Volpone* by the jealousy of London at the maritime trade of Venice, but anyway jealousy at rich businessmen would excuse quite a lot. In the more homely setting of *The Alchemist*, the audience are to feel: 'People oughtn't to be such mugs. If a man can be cheated by obvious rogues like this, he deserves it. They may be doing him a kindness by teaching him a bit more sense.' The fun was permissible as in a good cause; and this at least explains why the rogues don't have to be punished at the end.[2] The sentiment comes out strongly in the poetry at III. iii, the right place for a high boast before the fall. Doll on returning to the house says to the exultant Face:

> ... lord general, how fares our camp?
> FACE.   As, with the few, that had entrench'd themselves
> Safe, by their discipline, against a world, Doll:
> And laugh'd, within those trenches, and grew fat
> With thinking on the booties, Doll, brought in
> Daily, by their small parties.   (III. iii. 33–8)[3]

We ought to share in the sense of glory here. But the two rogues are pretty flat and straightforward; Jonson feels that Doll is too good for them, but she cannot make much difference, and the main interest has to arise from their dupes.

The play begins, like *Volpone*, with a prologue telling the audience they are supposed to laugh. As always, Jonson intends to better them, but here nobody need be offended, because nobody need admit that he is one of the people laughed at. Jonson is no longer writing about an imaginary Italy:

> Our *Scene* is *London*, 'cause we would make known,
>   No country's mirth is better than our own.
> No clime breeds better matter, for your whore,
>   Bawd, squire, impostor, many persons more,
> Whose manners, now call'd humours, feed the stage ...

The sentence goes on *And which*, so *for* has to mean 'as providing' not 'because' – it does not introduce a clause explaining why England is good for comedy. The confusing grammar perhaps helps to imply a joke, that the English are good comic material for bad reasons (as when Hamlet's madness is said not to matter in England, where all the men are as mad as he), but even so this would be a cosy bit of disguised self-praise. The audience is being put in a good humour at the start; and for that matter Jonson had just returned to the Anglican Church, so he was rather inclined to draw attention to his patriotism. He had no need to tell the major reason, known to all, why England might be expected to produce amusing eccentrics – because it was a uniquely free country (even if they had little reason

to believe so). It is thus very absurd to make this passage mean that
Jonson the Morose despised his own countrymen even more than he
did the rest of mankind.

The first two dupes presented to us, Dapper the clerk and
Drugger the shopkeeper, are silly chaps who take up little time,
though they should be acted as earnestly and patiently deluded.
Drugger needs a little magic to make his shop pay, and he is let off
lightly; Dapper has the worst time, because his object in wanting
magic to win bets is to be admired by men friends of better class. It is
a democratic or Dickensian moral; if Dapper had only wanted to
make money, Jonson would never have driven him into such fierce
shame. For the Puritans he feels real enmity; they wanted to close
the theatres and interfere with his private life, and he is trying to
make mischief, though not lying, when he presents them as inherently traitors intriguing against the king. One does not much hate
them, because they are so funny, but they are allowed no spark or
decent feeling. On the other hand Sir Epicure Mammon is
genuinely admired for being so advanced and public-spirited; he is a
patron of the new sciences, which already excited great hopes, and
such a man deserved respect not only for his generosity but for his
readiness to make a fool of himself – plainly, if he met with any
success, it could only be by luck. He enters at the start of Act II, and
Act I closes with a fanfare of glowing praise for him by Subtle, too
good as poetry to be meant as spiteful or jeering:

> He will make
> Nature asham'd of her long sleep: when art,
> Who's but a step-dame, shall do more than she,
> In her best love to mankind, ever could.
> If his dream last, he'll turn the age to gold.   (I. iv. 25–9)

Mammon himself is always generous-minded, and speaks much the
best poetry throughout the play. His most absurd scene has nothing
to do with science; it is when he proposes marriage to Doll, accepting her as an aristocrat who studies philosophy in retirement:

> DOLL. Blood we boast none, sir, a poor Baron's daughter.
> MAM.   Poor! And gat you? Profane not. Had your father
> Slept all the happy remnant of his life
> After that act, lien there but still, and panted,
> H' had done enough to make himself, his issue,
> And his posterity noble.   (IV. i. 43–8)

It is of course very absurd, but to think him contemptible for it would be mean-minded; and Jonson had no such temptation, as he considered that Doll really had got high courage and the power of command – not admiring Doll, but admiring ladies, was what he found absurd in the man's delusion, and a part of the artisan audience would agree.[4]

Mammon of course expects luxury, as well as world power, from the chemical operation; and here I meet a grave obstacle. Nowadays everybody seems to take for granted that Jonson loathed and despised luxury, and indeed only mentioned it here to express his hatred and contempt for science, which was already known to be irreligious and materialistic. The critics do not, I think, offer evidence for this interpretation, because they find it obvious from the 'whole tone' of Jonson as they read him. And they read him so, no doubt, because they are sure that all other seventeenth-century poets hated and belittled such achievements of science as had yet occurred. It is a pleasure to be able to report that all this is false, and that the small-mindedness which it imputes needs only to be sponged away. (In fact, it is rather hard to see why the poets felt that so much had already happened.) And then, if you read what Drummond of Hawthornden reports about Jonson, or Izaak Walton, for instance, it is surely hard to remain confident that he had a holy contempt for bodily pleasure; and their gossip does not seem malignant, though they probably exaggerate for fun. One should remember, too, that the Golden Age of Latin literature, the time when the authors lived whom Jonson genuinely did revere and never ceased to emulate, was notorious for its impudent luxury, which had chiefly meant a display of power; obviously, to win it back would mean a final recovery from the Dark Age. To see this play as when new, I have come to feel, one needs to unwind layer behind layer of false assumptions, rucked and rotting together about a foot deep, as Fenollosa unwound them from the Yumedono Kwannon, the most beautiful statue in the world. Of course, none of this is meant to deny that Mammon is a shockingly silly man, who ought to have been able to see through Subtle, and ought anyway to have attended to what his friend Surly told him.

Anyhow, an audience commonly feels at home with Mammon, whereas poor Kastril really does need a bit more appreciation. He has recently inherited three thousand a year from land, a great deal then, and he feels that the position brings with it obligations; he

must become terrifically sporting, an expert in the technicalities of
duelling, and any other line that may be required. The obligations
indeed have become so heavy that they might drag him loose from
the position; he at least listens without protest when Face insinuates
that he had better sell the estate and use the capital to set himself up
as a leading London trickster (III. iv). It is useless to scold Kastril as
irresponsible and sybaritic; he is hag-ridden by his imaginary duties,
accepting an early death but terrified that he may fail to die in
proper style. This is a case in which the 'values' of the modern
literary critic, for reasons which are about two centuries old and
quite creditable to him, make him blankly unable to read the text.
He has never met a young man like that; well, nor have I, or Ben
Jonson either I should fancy, because they cropped up mainly under
the Regency; but Jonson is grasping the first stage of a historical
development there.

In the play, what matters is his affection for the character; it
decides the structure. Jonson takes for granted that poor Kastril has
been badly educated – his impulses have been almost fatally mis-
directed – but that the impulses themselves are splendidly good; he
deserves, if ever man deserved, to escape from the suicide into which
he is driving himself with frank cries of pain and fear. This gives the
play its happy ending; Kastril is saved at the last moment by a quite
unexpected twist of his psychology. He finds that the middle-aged
businessman is what he really admires, so now he need not be a
gangster leader, only another businessman; he and Lovewit can play
tricks together for ever after. It is very like the deep thankfulness
with which Fielding, acting as a family lawyer, allots good luck at
the end to Tom Jones, which Tom fully deserved though he was so
very unlikely to have stumbled across it in real life. A modern
audience, I should think, would accept this if it were firmly enough
presented to them. It does not involve any intellectual sell-out to the
ethical claims of the businessmen (that is, a good production need
not). Surely the discovery of Kastril, that they are quite criminal
enough for an aristocrat to admire them, ends the play to the
satisfaction of all concerned.

A few years ago I was asked to address a large audience of young
people who were just going to take an 'A level' exam in this play,
which would partly decide whether they went to a university; and
the vocal ones were sure the play simply tells us that Kastril was a
coward. It made me realise the strength of the opposition. I suppose

they felt that a man who wants lessons in how to be a bully is necessarily a coward (and duelling can no longer be recognised as a sport). But if a man frequently tells you that he is afraid of doing something, and then invariably does it, you are mistaken to think him a coward; and if Kastril had not told the audience that he realised his plan to be next door to suicide they would only have thought him a fool. But probably the effect of the final scene, at the time, turned on a social detail now forgotten. Kastril enters dragging and beating his sister, angry because she has married Lovewit and has thus not even become a 'lady' (as by marrying a knight); Lovewit advances upon him:

> LOV. Come, will you quarrel? I will feize you, sirrah.
>   Why do you not buckle to your tools?
> KAS.   God's light!
>   This is a fine old boy, as e'er I saw.
> LOV. What, do you change your copy, now? Proceed,
>   Here stands my dove: stoop at her, if you dare.
> KAS. 'Slight, I must love him! I cannot choose, i'faith!
>   And I should be hang'd for 't. Suster, I protest,
>   I honour thee, for this match.
> LOV.   O, do you so, sir?
> KAS. Yes, and thou canst take tobacco, and drink, old boy,
>   I'll give her five hundred pounds more, to her marriage,
>   Than her own state.
> LOV.   Fill a pipe-full, Jeremy.   (v. v. 131–41)

Lessons in fencing have been the most important part of Kastril's education, and we have often seen him stumbling over the sword he wears. But a businessman, not being expected to defend his honour, did not carry a sword, any more than he carried 'tools', like an artisan. He advances upon the young gentleman unarmed, in the mere confidence that he is the new ruling class. Or perhaps that is dragging in more social significance than we need here; the bare fact of his coolness is what leaves Kastril, who has always been much impressed by these tools, morally disarmed. Also his sister has run and sheltered from him behind Lovewit, who threatens him to defend her; this is hard for him to resist. Of course you may still think Kastril a great booby, but if you act him as a coward you have to leave out nearly all the points of this concentrated little scene.

The poet Yeats has pluckily recorded, in *On The Boiler*, that he was bowled over by businessmen in very much this style (though on a different plane), as soon as he had reached enough political eminence to encounter them. 'When I was first a member of the Irish Senate', he is recalling, some of the members had been nominated, not elected:

In its early days some old banker or lawyer would dominate the House, leaning upon the back of the chair in front, always speaking with undisturbed self-possession as at some table in a board room. My imagination sets up against him some typical elected man, emotional as a youthful chimpanzee, hot and vague, always disturbed, always hating something or other.[5]

The spontaneous admiration, indeed, was what got him into very odd political company, where he never felt at home. One might say that the play is a prophecy; Kastril regularly has been bowled over by Lovewit ever since, and it has been rather a bad thing. But one need not, I think, go on to say that Jonson analysed the first stirrings of capitalism.

Another point where Kastril is like Yeats, making him very unlike the stock cowardly swashbuckler, is his desire to build up all his new acquaintance into legends, so that he feels surrounded by the kind of life he admires. This point of character is firmly established at his first appearance, as soon as he has finished mentioning his income:

> FACE.   Is your name Kastril, sir?
> KAS.   Aye, and the best o' the Kastrils, I'd be sorry else,
> By fifteen hundred, a year. Where is this Doctor?
> My mad tobacco boy, here, tells me of one,
> That can do things. Has he any skill?   (III. iv. 13–17)

We in the audience have just been hearing the modest hopes of Drugger for his shop, and feeling that they hardly deserve the help of a magician; so it comes as a shock to find him considered reckless and romantic. The note of loony aspiration or high-mindedness is habitual to Kastril, so that he does not seem feeble even when he says, childishly, 'do you think, Doctor, I e'er shall quarrel well?' (end of Act IV). He quarrels well enough in the next act – to be sure, Surly refuses to fight out of contempt, and Ananias gives unwitting help; but then Surly is tough and has a fortune at stake and is keen to expose the rogues. One cannot think Kastril merely ineffective after he has driven out Surly.

Some critics have argued from the name that the character is meant to be despised. A kestrel is a small kind of hawk, which was not trained like the large ones for aristocratic sport, and as it did damage could be regarded as vermin. The term *coistrel* for a low trouble-maker was derived from it, and no doubt *Kastril* was simply a local pronunciation. The young man is a notably unaristocratic squire, meant to be absurd; but no hawk is really contemptible. The kestrel is the windhover. Kastril knows he is not very big or strong; it is only his unquenchable desire for glory that makes him hurl himself into trouble, with his feathers all scuffed up. Ordinary men take a rather different view of him in each generation, and it chiefly turns on how much we need him to fight in our defence. Jonson had himself killed a man in a duel, and was partial to brave young cocks; he would think it very odd of us not to be glad when Kastril is saved.

Much more puzzle arises over Surly. As the name implies, he is an honest man of the sort Jonson liked; not only intelligent enough to see through the cheats, he also labours to expose them in the public interest, or at least to help his friend Mammon. The author is attacking popular superstition exactly as Surly does; but he makes Surly look a fool for it. Surly in order to overhear the cheats dresses himself as a Spanish nobleman (who knows no English), and does so well that they try to marry him to Kastril's sister – Kastril wants this, knowing that the Spaniards are far ahead of the English at the game of aristocracy. Left alone with her, he scolds her and tells her that any other man would have raped her (apparently this would secure her money, because she could only recover her reputation by marrying him):

SUR.   For y' are a handsome woman: would y' were wise, too.
        I am a gentleman, come here disguis'd,
        Only to find the knaveries of this citadel,
        And where I might have wrong'd your honour, and
           have not,
        I claim some interest in your love. You are,
        They say, a widow, rich: and I am a bachelor,
        Worth naught. Your fortunes may make me a man,
        As mine ha' preserved you a woman. Think upon it,
        And whether I have deserv'd you, or no.
PLI.   I will, sir.   (IV. vi. 7–15)

The moral atmosphere being so firmly like Dickens, one expects this good deed to be rewarded with an ample competence. But Lovewit on his return takes the lady and her fortune for himself; he then 'rallies' Surly, apparently literally for not having raped her

when he got the chance. Kastril has stumped off to search the house
for his sister, and Lovewit explains that she

> ... should ha' marry'd a Spanish Count, but he,
> When he came to 't, neglected her so grossly,
> That I, a widower, am gone through with her.
> SUR. How!   Have I lost her then?
> LOV.   Were you the Don, sir?
> Good faith, now, she does blame y' extremely, and says
> You swore, and told her, you had ta'en the pains,
> To dye your beard, and umber o'er your face,
> Borrow'd a suit, and ruff, all for her love;
> And then did nothing. What an oversight,
> And want of putting forward, sir, was this!   (v. v. 49–55)

The plot is winding up rapidly, but Surly snatches a moment to say

> Must I needs cheat myself,
> With that same foolish vice of honesty!   (v. v. 83–4)

before he goes out to search for Face, saying he will beat him if he
catches him. The reconditioned Face opens the door and bows him
out, saying

> ... in troth, they were strangers
> To me, I thought 'em honest, as myself, sir.   (v. v. 88–9)

So we are forced to join in laughing at Surly, who is not even
allowed to stick to saying he behaved like a gentleman.

C. G. Thayer (1963) is the only critic I happened to come across
who recognised this problem (most of them just assume we are
meant to despise the whole cast); he says:

> In Mammon and Surly, then, we have the willing victim and the jealous
> rival. Surly is dishonest, but is outraged that Face and Subtle should be
> dishonest too, and this feeling of outrage leads to his attempt to unmask
> them, with disastrous results for himself. This is a fairly complicated
> matter: Surly is one of those ironic commentators who would be effective if
> he were moral.[6]

A wild flight of fancy, and yet, come to think of it, there very likely
was a Victorian melodrama which plugged home this tiring plati-
tude. How totally unlike *The Alchemist* it must have been. To make
Mr Thayer's point, the other characters must have been ready to
believe Surly, so that he would have succeeded in exposing the
cheats, had they not already known him to be smirched; from

practically the first scene, we must observe the ladies as they pass him in silence labouring not to touch him with their crinolines. But nobody even hints at this idea, and no character however unsmirched could get heard against the hullabaloo of Kastril and Ananias combined (IV. vii). Also Surly cannot be trying to cheat Mammon, as a 'rival' to Subtle, because Mammon knows all about him, or at least gives us the only insinuations against him. I would even deny that Surly meets 'disastrous results'; he only escapes a marriage which would have been painful to him – the type of woman he wants would have responded to the approach he made. Admittedly, this refined thought is not insisted upon by the play, but it is less remote from the play than the refined thought of my opponent.

Mammon tells Surly, when they first appear, that he is going to make all his friends rich, and he rather spreads himself on the disagreeable things, very unsuited to poor Surly's character one would think, that Surly will never have to do again. He begins with the really splendid phrase

> You shalt no more deal with the hollow die,
> Or the frail card   (II. i. 9–10)

and seems next to envisage his pimping for rich young men. On the stage, Surly had I suppose better spit and look round defiantly; he is not going to confess to it, whatever it was. Mammon himself is fairly well off and quite respectable; his friends are assumed to be of the same class, though some of them get driven to unfortunate shifts. In fact, this is meant to be the world of *Vanity Fair*, though Jonson is no good at marking fine shades of gentility. Most of the ways of earning money which are now considered honest are not open to Surly, as they would cost him his status as a gentleman; cadging is about all he can do. He can also gamble, and may well have to 'deal with' people who cheat at it; the words do not have to mean that he is a cheat too. At what point giving manly advice to a young friend brought one within danger of the shameful word 'Pimp' was extremely moot. In short, Jonson is trying to present Surly not as a petty criminal but as a shabby gentleman, and Surly tells Dame Pliant he is a gentleman in his first words to her.

One part of this was very familiar to the Elizabethan mind. If a man is educated above his status, especially by being sent to a university, and does not afterwards get the white-collar job which he regards as his due, then he is sure to make trouble, probably as a revolting politician. For example, the doctrine is used to explain Bosola, at the start of *The Duchess of Malfi* (when I was young, it was always being said about Indians). Such a man is the malcontent, who makes the severe epigrams or wisecracks; Jaques was in part a parody of him but shows the character in the round. However, most playwrights insinuate that their malcontent isn't *really* a gentleman; to assume that the cadging life was quite normal for a gentleman down on his luck (for Rawdon Crawley before he had landed his governorship) would, I should think, make many people in the first audiences feel rather dubious, like ourselves.

We may now recognise that Dame Pliant is not necessarily an imbecile; she is merely a satire on ladies. Having been brought up to marry for wealth and status, she will accept any man who treats her with cool authority. The theatre was always against the arranged marriage (which may have made the operation of the custom less severe, though it went firmly on) and showed this by sympathy for girls in revolt; but to mock the type of girl who accepted it was very unusual. Jonson, it seems clear, had got on better at court with the men; they were impressed by his learning, his fighting sense of honour, and his conviviality, but the ladies found him coarse. The decisive comment on ladies here is entrusted to Doll Common, who expresses confidence when told to imitate a lady for the plot:

> I'll not forget my race, I warrant you.
> I'll keep my distance, laugh, and talk aloud;
> Have all the tricks of a proud scurvy lady,
> And be as rude as her woman.   (II. iv. 8–11)

The last clause may seem off the point, but Jonson and Doll assume that any professional who has learned the tricks will be better at them than an amateur.

It will now be plain what the 'values' are which establishment critics are so unwilling to recognise. Jonson is militantly anti-Puritan, but also anti-Cavalier from a working-class point of view; you might say he is just spiteful about ladies and gentlemen. I am not at home with this tone myself, and I think he is unfair to Surly; but one cannot be surprised if the Globe audiences found it a treat, and no doubt some of the people in our modern audiences like it better than dons do.

To make an audience accept a successful businessman as a good character is always hard, and no wonder Lovewit has to ingratiate himself at the end by jeering at Surly in a coarse manner. A critic however argues that Lovewit has 'taken the wrong turning and joined the fools' when he marries the fortune at the end, and that Jonson 'indicates' this by Subtle Irony. We are not even told where the irony comes. The duty of toeing the critical line is no doubt much eased by this rule that you can impute subtle irony wherever you like, but one would like to hear how it could be put across in production amid the uproar of the happy ending of the farce. In its quiet way, this is perhaps the most deadly interpretation of all.

Various critics have tried to show that Jonson had a deep understanding of the rise of capitalism in his time; and I agree at least that, after Volpone, the apotheosis of Lovewit needs a bit of comment. Jonson's own attitude to money, there is plenty of evidence to show, was the traditional one of the artist. An artist should flatter a king till he tosses him a bag of gold (for example, by telling James in a court masque that he is chaste because he does not keep mistresses); and when he has drunk up all that gold, in the course of his devoted labours, he should go back and flatter the king again. Many good artists have lived like this, and the procedure takes endurance as well as nerve; but it can't be a model for the rest of us, and is unlikely to give much insight into mass economic changes. Jonson understands his businessman well enough, and does not inflate him; but I think the major insights of the play, or bits of moral advice if you prefer, concern matters of vanity or social advantage, which readily distract the characters from their none the less oppressive duty of monetary gain. There is a wonderful lot of truth in it.

CHAPTER 7

'Mine eyes dazzle'

(CLIFFORD LEECH, *WEBSTER: THE DUCHESS OF MALFI*, 1963)

This handbook by Professor Clifford Leech on *The Duchess of Malfi* is scholarly and up-to-date, and also betrays a certain delicacy of feeling. As he is strictly bound by our ridiculous fashion, he has to argue that the author and the first audiences were jeering at the Duchess for her carnal lust, and the book gives the horrid little 'proofs' of it, but one feels that he dislikes the duty and mitigates it so far as he can.[1]

Since this view of the duchess cannot be presented on the stage, because an audience rejects it, the academic critics can give no help to the dramatic producers, so the dramatic critics, when the play is revived, usually praise the production for guying the sensationalism of the Elizabethans. There is a bit of tradition behind this idea, so that it gives a useful hint; the trouble about having learned the neo-Christian tradition, on the other hand, is that it cuts you off from any real tradition. Webster may sensibly be regarded as a precursor of Monk Lewis and Mrs Radcliffe, and what they are being 'sensational' about was the wickedness of Roman Catholic southern Europeans. Neo-Christian critics have to pretend that everybody has always been an Anglo-Catholic, so they have no idea of what the play meant to its first audiences.

We are commonly told that Webster and Tourneur, with their characters like 'coiling asps' (Mermaid edition),[2] were describing the harm often done by loss of religious faith to the Londoners around them. But an Elizabethan would say of *The White Devil* what a Victorian did of *Antony and Cleopatra*, 'How unlike the domestic life of *our* beloved Queen!' The English felt culturally and socially inferior beside Italians and Spaniards, and felt it a duty to try to catch up; but also took comfort in remembering that we were good and they were very wicked, partly because they had such a wicked religion. Webster would be astonished to have his Italians taken for Englishmen.[3] Not long ago the student drama society at Sheffield put on *The Revenger's Tragedy*, and I was reflecting how innocent the young people seemed, as they threw themselves into their parts with all the pleasure of fancy, when I realised with a jolt that this was what Tourneur would have done too. His aristocratic villains felt to him very remote, indeed I suspect they are often just unlifelike.

I realise that Belleforest [*Histoires Tragiques*, 1565] and Painter [*The Palace of Pleasure*, 1567], the French and English pedants who report the story, scold the duchess for marrying her butler (unlike the Italian source [Bandello]); Mr F. L. Lucas showed a firm grasp of tradition by remarking that this was ungentlemanly of them.[4] The theatre usually backs the young lovers against the arranged marriage, and the Globe theatre, having a mass audience, was ready to rebuke the pride of lineage of Aragon. Thus the duchess is a heroine; Painter or Clifford Leech would have been hooted in that theatre if they had voiced their sentiments about her.[5] One character in a play for the Globe, indeed, does talk about a romantic marriage as we are now told that everybody in the audience would have talked; it is Iago, and the playwright does not assume that the audience will agree with him. However, as Miss Bradbrook said long ago [*Themes and Conventions of Elizabethan Tragedy*, Cambridge, 1935], the play is also in part a discussion drama, like those of Bernard Shaw, questioning whether the duchess ought to have married the butler. I know this sounds very Philistine, after the great anti-intellectual movement, but any good theatre discusses matters of current interest. Still, a play can give the pleasure of debate without leaving any doubt which side the author is on. The moral of this play, driven home as with the sledge-hammer of Dickens I should have thought, is not that the duchess was wanton but that her brothers were sinfully proud.

My opponents argue that the duchess and her husband make a number of anticlerical or free-thinking remarks, which would turn the audience against them; and though she becomes pious just before her death, accepting her punishment, this only gives a further indication that we are meant to think of it as partly deserved. Rather an interesting bit of historical background is needed here. Aquinas lays down (*Sum. Theo.*, Q. 42. 1., Q. 45. 5., Q. 63. 2) that marriage, even the second marriage of a woman, is a sacrament, and its sufficient cause is consent 'expressed in words of the present' (that is, not a betrothal); the priest's blessing does not validate a marriage, and indeed is not given at the second marriage of a woman. However, not to solemnise a marriage is a sin. A footnote to the translation by the English Dominicans explains that Aquinas was giving the canon law of his time, but that clandestine marriages were declared invalid by the Council of Trent. This council, during the middle years of the sixteenth century [1563], tightened up a number of points of discipline by way of inaugurating the Counter-Reformation, and was of course not accepted by Protestants.[6] The events of the play had taken place before the change in the law, but probably most of the audience would be vague about these dates. When her brother tells her that her children are bastards, and she answers:

> You violate a sacrament o'th' church
> Shall make you howl in Hell for't. (IV. i. 39–40)[7]

she is in the right, considering her date; but anyhow a legal discussion is going on, and only the horribly flabby aestheticism of our present fashion would refuse to recognise it.[8] A fanatical Protestant, I suppose, would say that the new law arrogated power to priests and encouraged breach of promise in seducers, but the Church of England was rather inclined to favour it; a play which treated the question as open was not likely to frighten the licensing authority. The duchess and her husband are presented as reasonable and practical – 'Our sort of people', as Professor Leech rightly puts it (though the duchess is aristocratic in her exceptional courage), so the audience would think of them as souls naturally Protestant. All the phrases which have been found irreligious, and therefore likely to make the audience condemn the duchess and her husband (for example, the assumption that pilgrimages deserve no reverence), are simply Protestant.[9] Antonio, though a cautious speaker, also contrives a reference to one of the major disputed points of doctrine. Asked what he thinks of marriage, he says:

> I take 't, as those that deny purgatory –
> It locally contains, or heaven, or hell ... (I. i. 393–4)

This crack of course is meant to make him seem charming, as well as sturdily sensible and right-thinking; the idea that the Globe audience would expect him to be punished for his flippancy is very overstrained.

Modern critics usually call him cowardly, because he is so aware of his wife's danger, just as they call her responsible for her courage. But it was standard bourgeois opinion that a second husband should not be dashing or flashy; with a sober businesslike man, the theoretical objections would not be raised. Thus, in a way, his character is sacrificed to make the audience accept the duchess. To allow the separation when she goes to her brothers alone was fatal in the result, but Ferdinand loves her and has demanded to have Antonio kept out of his sight, so the plan is worth trying as a last chance; when it goes wrong, Antonio follows her with courage ('Very near my home' [v. iv. 51]). In the second scene of the play we are told he has won the ring at jousting, to prove that he is a gentleman in all but his origins. A play intended as a warning against marrying a social inferior would have to be constructed quite differently.

Professor Clifford Leech has an argument of his own to prove that the duchess is an irresponsible ruler; as usual, it goes bang in the opposite direction as soon as you examine the text. The duchess is so devoted to her city state that we never hear her personal name, and she marries the man who is already administering it in the way she approves. Naturally he spends rather more as her husband. Later on Delio asks him what people say; he says they think she is letting him get hold of a lot of her own money, unwillingly no doubt, but on the calculation that then he won't squeeze money from the people [III. i. 27–35]. That is, the people know that they are unusually well governed, or at least lightly taxed, and try to invent some amusingly bad reason for it, but even in doing so confess they realise that the duchess wishes them well. If she had married a grand husband, he would be pretty sure to squeeze Malfi for his private vanity or his quarrels. As the case stands, the only person who seems politically irresponsible is the professor.[10]

Modern critics often claim that the duchess admits, shortly before she dies, that she was wrong to marry Antonio, or at least the imagery there, having so much hell about it, makes her remarks amount to that. Such critics would also claim to be defending the high old moral tradition, now all but lost; whereas any ordinary citizen could tell that they are being quaintly low-minded. A number of people in the seventeenth century actually did meet death with saintly impertinence towards the tyrant who killed them, thanking him for the gift of martyrdom, which had done them all the good in the world: 'Minds innocent and quiet take That for a hermitage.' If anything could have knocked them off their perch, poor creatures, it would have been to have a modern neo-Christian come up and say how pleased he was to find them licking the boots of the tyrant at the last, as it made a very edifying picture. I can't tell you how old it makes me feel, to live on into this eerie cultural twilight.

When the duchess proposes marriage to her major-domo, we are usually told that he betrays ambition by accepting, but Clifford Leech is inclined to think that she tricked him into the fatal marriage; his lukewarm polite answer would not have bound him if she had not hidden a witness behind the curtain. So far from that, knowing that she is asking him to accept a post of danger, she hides the witness to make him free to refuse; in the presence of her maid, he might well feel that a refusal would make her lose too much face. We have already heard him tell a friend that he loves her, so we need not doubt it when we hear him hesitate because of the danger to her, not to himself. Both the lovers in this scene show delicacy of feeling, and the struggle of modern critics to display high-mindedness by finding something dirty in it strikes me as very queer.

We may now approach the famous incest problem, which arose because Freud expected audiences to be unconscious and English critics did not know what an Elizabethan audience would be conscious of. Elizabethans believed that Lucrezia Borgia went to bed with her brothers because, owing to her intense family pride, which was like that of the Pharaohs, she could find no fit mate elsewhere. The incestuous reflections of Ferdinand would thus be obvious to the first audiences, as a standard expression of the insane pride which is almost his only characteristic (at the start of the play, he forbids his courtiers to laugh unless he laughs first); no wonder he turns into a wolf in the last act, as one hoped he would. In short, the play has a popular Dickensian moral, against the wicked rich; whereas our critical attempt to recover the ethics of a nobler age has been limited to recovering subservient or boot-licking morals.[11]

You may answer that, although many spectators would feel an easy sentiment in favour of the lovers, their serious conviction would be that the duchess was wrong to marry her major-domo. Some would think so, no doubt; the idea that everyone held the same opinion at a given date, 'the opinion of the time', is disproved as soon as you open a history book and find a lot of them killing each other because they disagreed. But there was a reason why this question was especially open to doubt, so that hardly anyone could feel the whole truth lay with Painter and Belleforest. Many subtle pages in the Variorum edition of *Twelfth Night* offer meanings for *Strachey* in 'There is example for it; the lady of the Strachey married the yeoman of the wardrobe' [II. v. 38–9]; the answer is that Shakespeare had hunted for a meaningless word because the meaning which would be presumed was dangerous. The widow of the national hero Prince Hal, whether or not she actually married her gentleman of the wardrobe, in their brief and harried life together, had made him the ancestor of the entire Tudor dynasty. It would strike the groundlings as probable that the duchess too had made a momentous decision, and I think this explains what is usually called one of the mistakes of the play, the unhistorical choice of her surviving son by Antonio as the next duke of Malfi. English critics tend to regard dukedoms as ancestral, but the first husband of the duchess had merely been given the job, presumably through the influence of her brothers.[12] Now that they are both dead and discredited the normal influence of the town council may carry some weight, and Delio is speaking for them when he pronounces that this boy deserves the position. His horoscope would no doubt be right in predicting an early end, but I expect Webster thought of him as lasting long enough to establish a dynasty.

Perhaps I should try to make clear my assumptions about the audience. It was predominantly artisan, and the real Puritans would not come. Such an audience, like most of the population, would readily admire aristocratic courage and independence; but they would be especially prone to blame the family pride which destroys the lovers. Readily, again, they would side with their own Protestant government against wicked Spanish grandees; but the nagging theoretical Puritanism of our present mentors would be remote from their sympathies. They would welcome the detail about keeping down the taxes.[13]

CHAPTER 8

'The Duchess of Malfi'

Scholarly critics in our time have taken a great interest in the play, struggling to recover the exact flavour of opinion which it was intended to convey to the first audiences, and thus to pinpoint the spiritual wisdom which it is felt to contain; but when it is revived the notices commonly say: 'The production rightly treated this extremely sensational tragedy as almost a farce, because it is practically a parody of the Elizabethan drama.' There seems a failure of liaison here, but I expect the two parties mean nearly the same thing. Followers of Mr Eliot's tradition, it must be remembered, are very completely cut off from the real tradition; the unnatural is precisely what appears to them 'significant'. The unscholarly dramatic critic, on the other hand, will have a vague memory that *The Mysteries of Udolpho* was an early example of sensationalism, and here a bit of history is alive to him. Roman Catholic priests, with their insinuating whispers and their torture-chambers, were the basis of Protestant sensationalism, whereas Miss Muriel Bradbrook and Professor Clifford Leech have been carefully brought up not to know that the Reformation ever happened. When a misbeliever commits one of his usual villainies, they think: 'Oh goody; this is a holy Christian, so he must be giving us a subtle example of the highest morality.' But in their own way, of course, they are militantly historical; they think that everybody in the period reverenced Degree; so they assume that we are intended to despise the duchess for marrying her major-domo. The thoughts they impute to the author about his romantic story are glumly disgusting in a self-righteous manner; in fact, precisely those of Iago about the marriage of Desdemona against the wishes of her family. It is surely relevant to remember that, if these sober dons could talk to their Elizabethan opposite numbers, they would be assured that the theatre was notoriously immoral, and that to search for morals in it was about the most absurd thing they could do. That is, the theatre was in favour of the young couple, and against the arranged marriage; this has always been a basic source of popularity for a popular theatre. If you settle down to interpret Elizabethan plays in accordance with the rancid piety of Iago, there is no limit to the absurdity you may attain.

As a reaction to this, it is natural to regard the play as a Shavian discussion drama, on the question 'ought the duchess to marry her butler, or ought she not?' It makes a good discussion drama, until the imprisonment of the duchess in the fourth act; and that is the chief reason why the play is so much better than *The White Devil*. The end needs to be enjoyed or excused in some other way, probably a religious one, but the discussion is enlightened and down to earth, and assumes an audience which can follow it. Nor would the audience have a basic assurance, whatever the discussion, that the duchess was wrong; because she was the ruler of a city state, and there were no such people in England. The French collector Belleforest from whose moral tales the story is taken does, I understand, scold her up hill and down dale; but the English translator Painter is already non-committal before Webster uses his version to make her a martyr. If she is a queen, one could hardly forget that Elizabeth had considered herself free to marry Leicester, if she chose; and there was a more actual precedent. The widow of Henry V, a very famous memory, had married her major-domo, and his name happened to be Tudor.

Professor Clifford Leech, whose historical conscience made him insist that the play is largely opposed to the duchess, also says very finely:[1]

Webster indeed gives to his Duchess a splendour in [the fourth] act that makes us proud, makes us glory in the human nature that is ours as well as hers.

But this is the result of her purgation by despair, and he would not praise her before it happened. 'Webster shows us a woman at odds with life' (p. 77) – but he shows her as idyllically happy with her husband and children, and tells us that her people are content with her rule, till her brothers choose to murder the whole family. When she says under mental torment 'I am Duchess of Malfi still' (IV. ii. 142),[2] Leech comments: 'There is grandeur in the egoism, but its implications are essentially anarchic' (p. 77). Anarchic, when we never even hear the woman's name because she is so absorbed in her public function? It is not anarchic to say: 'I am still the rightful legal authority in this place, where I am being put to mental torment for the purpose of making me say that I was wrong, when I did something which was not wrong.' Shelley annoyed Mr T. S. Eliot somehow, and so the Anglo-Saxon literary critics all decided that resistance to tyranny was old hat; henceforth they must titter at it. Meanwhile the appalling historical events around them went on providing any amount of astoundingly heroic resistance to tyranny, but the critics had been forbidden to pay any attention. Slavishness was the only virtue they felt permitted to praise, even in a legitimate ruler; but here surely they were running madly far ahead of their brief. No audience that remembered Queen Elizabeth would consider the duchess anarchic; and Elizabeth certainly considered herself entitled to marry Leicester, if she chose. Leech goes on to say that 'with part of his mind Webster apparently considers her innocent', and he concludes that 'part of Webster's thought in this play is itself anarchic' (p. 78). It is much inferior, he thinks, to *The White Devil*, because that is nothing but thrills about sin, with all known stagey tricks piled up, whereas this one is actually tainted by intelligence and enlightenment, as a result of 'Webster's impatience with law and custom, of a recurrent longing for a "compassionate", undisciplined Nature' (p. 81). The chit who disobeyed her brothers even had the impudence to imagine while she is being murdered that she will go to heaven, whereas (the Professor takes for granted) any girl who disobeys her brothers ought to know that she will go to hell. Nature ought to be recognised as disgusting, and therefore any unnatural custom, however obviously harmful and malignant – female circumcision in East Africa, for example – ought to be praised and supported. For that matter, any criminal lunatic who is trying to introduce a still more horrible unnatural custom ought to be praised and supported. Here, the alert reader may notice, is the rather remote point where a too eager supporter of Mr T. S. Eliot might tangle with the public law. But it is an astonishingly crazy position anyhow. And a person who really did understand the medieval Christian tradition would never start making this card castle, since he would realise contentedly that the play is against family pride, and that Duke Ferdinand's family pride leads him into very unnatural behaviour. Instead of bristling suspiciously at every reference to nature, and writing 'compassionate' in inverted commas (I suppose this means that the truest kindness, as Dante remarked, was the creation of Hell), he would readily agree, like the modern reader, that the duchess has an almost overwhelming amount of natural law on her side. I say 'almost' merely from feeling my ignorance of what the duchess's brothers might have said if they had been more sensible and less wicked.

A graceful work of scholarship from California, *John Webster's Borrowing* by R. W. Dent (1960), gives us a definite picture of Webster's mode of operation.[3] I take it he hung around the theatres, collaborating at comedies for a living though he wasn't a spontaneous comedian, out of an immense reverence for tragedies and a craving to make an immortal name by producing one or two of them slowly from notebooks, as he succeeded in doing. He is much more like the Savonarola Brown of Max Beerbohm than any actual figure of the 1890s still remembered; he set out to imitate the plays he so rightly admired, or even to outgo them by distilling their essence. His borrowings are therefore of especial interest. They appear oddly restricted in Mr Dent's account; nothing from the Bible, and nothing from contemporary sermons, except that *The Gallants Burden* by Thomas Adams (1612) gave five passages to *The Duchess of Malfi* – no doubt it was calculated to have an interest for worldlings. What struck Mr Dent was that the sermons often borrowed from secular authors.[4] The most impressive single source for Webster was Sidney's *Arcadia*, but he only started using it halfway through the *Duchess*, his second tragedy. This is very hard to interpret, as the *Arcadia* was so famous and fashionable when he was young; he hardly seems a reading man at all. Poetry he seldom uses, even the poetry of the *Arcadia*;[5] he wants 'sentences', sententious epigrams, with bits of unnatural history perhaps. The printed text of *The White Devil* carries an address 'To the Reader', explaining that Webster is a scholar and therefore despises the reader; this is copied out from the second paragraph of Jonson's introduction to *Sejanus*.[6] One's heart bleeds for him; no wonder he only dared praise Shakespeare with Dekker for their 'happy and copious industry' ['To the Reader']. Mr Dent has a crotchet about Webster's imitations of Shakespeare, apparently denying all of them, but one would think he must mean something different; perhaps that they were vague memories, not transported through the notebook.[7] The madness of Cornelia (*The White Devil*, v. iv) is a cento from so many different mad characters in Shakespeare that an audience which can spot them is forced to laugh; I had assumed he heard them laugh, and that was why he didn't use the Shakespeare page of the notebook when he wrote the *Duchess*; but perhaps there was a more graceful reason, that he was writing for Shakespeare's company.[8] He shows good taste in selecting Shakespeare for his mad bits, though the need also betrays his incapacity to get under the skin of a madman. Mr Dent is also made quaintly indignant by Delio's characterisation of Bosola as a comic scholar, who has measured Julius Caesar's nose with a shoe-horn and so forth (III. iii. 41–7):

a functionless satiric intrusion, made worse by expansion and by inconsistency with the play's earlier treatment of both Delio and Bosola. (p. 24)

Well, it may be pretty coarse to laugh at scholars like Mr Dent, but he himself has given the evidence that Webster was an unscholarly type, who might be tempted to imagine them turning into Bosola. Oddly enough, the scholar Gabriel Harvey scribbled down his day-dreams of becoming a power behind the court like Bosola, and they have survived. English Tories were always saying when I was young that, if you educated an Indian at a university and then didn't find a white-collar job for him, you had created a revolutionary at your own expense. Such is the prosy but entirely realistic picture of Bosola, and his character seems consistent enough though probably copied from life.

There is no known source for Webster's murder-discovering wolf, which comes in both plays (*WD*, v. iv. 97; *DM*, IV. ii. 309–11). Presumably he heard it as a legend from a visitor whose homeland provided wolves; here again he appears unbookish, and decided in fastening on what suited him.

Knowing the source of a line often leaves its purport in doubt. Thus the duchess says to Antonio, at the end of her wooing scene:

> I would have you lead your fortune by the hand,
> Unto your marriage bed.   (I. i. 495–6)

Mr Dent suggests that this comes from Montaigne II. xvii: 'Concerning ambition ... it had beene needeful [to advance me] that fortune had come to take me by the hand.' That is, nothing would make Montagne ambitious, though he would have accepted any position in which he had found himself. 'Whether a source or not', Mr Dent goes on, 'Montaigne's idea harmonizes with Webster's emphasis on Antonio's "ambition"' (p. 192). This, you understand, has become an article of faith; every assertion by the playwright, however blatant, that Antonio was *not* ambitious has to be twisted round into an argument that he *was*, because otherwise the critic would have to recognise the romantic love-story. This example, I submit, is a valuable teaching device; once the student has realised what a gorgeously extravagant piece of nonsense it is, he will be able to recognise the ubiquitous similar bits of nonsense hidden under more workaday clothes. I do not, of course, think the parallel proves that Antonio was not ambitious; because I do not think it proves anything at all.

There is a textual point in v. iv. 68–9 which may have some bearing on this; I have long wanted to emend it, but no editor seems troubled. Antonio is dying, and says:

> In all our quests of greatness,
> Like wanton boys whose pastime is their care,
> We follow after bubbles, blown in th' air.
> Pleasure of life, what is't? only the good hours
> Of an ague; merely a preparative to rest,
> To endure vexation ...   (v. iv. 64–9)

I have quoted the first sentence for continuity and to discuss whether Antonio is ambitious, as some modern critics have absurdly claimed. I think there is no sign of it, even in this death-bed confession, where he has no cause to hide it. He is concerned to give a warning against ambition, leading up to the surprising line:

> And let my son fly the courts of princes. [*Dies.*]   (v. iv. 72)

This is much in character, because greatness was thrust upon him by the love of the duchess; we can understand that he does not want his son to be duke, though, for our part, Webster assumes we will take it as a happy ending to have the dying wish immediately disappointed. He says that *we*, meaning all mankind, tend to be foolishly ambitious, because it would be bad feeling in one's death-speech to claim any distinction; but he seems unable to imagine any greatness other than ease and play. The final metaphor, about as horrible as it could be I don't at all deny, is drawn from the calculations of the torture-chamber; if you want to hurt the man as much as possible, you have to let him heal up between bouts; and that is all that God is doing to us when our lives apparently have a pleasant interval. He may well speak with bitterness; he did not choose his worrying life, which kept him incessantly feeling pity for the wife he loved, and now he has failed to save her after all. I do not therefore attach great theological importance to his sentence, but at least we had better be allowed to have it; we need to remove the words *to rest*, which seem to have been added as a bowdlerisation; and then the line scans, if that is any evidence:

> Of an ague; merely a preparative
> To endure vexation.[9]

Professor Clifford Leech has an odd remark (p. 56) about the show of installing a pope, in the fourth act of *The White Devil*; it was put in to show 'that man, not altogether in vain, strives to bring order into his affairs'. He means, I take it, that practically everything else in the play except the holy ceremony happens all wrong, by fate; so Webster felt it needed a bit of earnestness. Surely it is very odd to assume that he would choose the pope for this random function. The *Duchess* also has a show, of disinstalling the cardinal of Aragon, as the emperor wants him to command an army (III. iii); one would think that men are planning here too. As soon as he is disinstalled he banishes his sister, so one might think that his office had restrained him before; but two pilgrims, whom we have no reason to disbelieve, blame the pope for seizing her dukedom (III. iv. 30–3). The purpose of Webster is rather hard to make out, but the only effect in both cases is to give a show of popish grandeur, and he may well have intended no more.

1ST PIL.   . . . who would have thought
So great a lady would have match'd herself
Unto so mean a person? yet the cardinal
Bears himself much too cruel . . .
2ND PIL.   . . . her brother show'd
How that the Pope, fore-hearing of her looseness,
Hath seiz'd into th' protection of the church
The dukedom, which she held as a dowager.
1ST PIL.   But by what justice?
2ND PIL.   Sure, I think by none,
Only her brother's instigation.
1ST PIL.   What was it, with such violence he took
Off from her finger?
2ND PIL.   'Twas her wedding-ring,
Which he vow'd shortly he would sacrifice
To his revenge.   (III. iv. 214–39)

It is clear at any rate that the pilgrims consider she is married.

The objection of her brothers to her marriage is based upon family pride; they remark indeed that they have 'the royal blood of Arragon and Castile' (II. v. 22–3), which must not be corrupted by a misalliance. This would be evident to the first audiences, and one might expect neo-Christian literary critics to find it evident too, because they are keen on the medieval tradition of denouncing pride; but they dare not side with the duchess against her brothers, because then they would be abetting modern enlightenment. The Globe audience was largely artisan, and its pride would readily reject the claims of aristocrats to be of superior breed. They were not in the least surprised when Ferdinand in the last act turned into a wolf, as he deserved; that was the chief thing they needed a fifth act for. Spain was still felt as the chief danger, and a great rival in America, whereas Italy was culturally overwhelming and a major commercial rival; but most of the rulers of Italy were Spaniards. The Spanish Borgias, for example, felt such a sinful amount of family pride that Lucrezia went to bed with her brothers because there was no fit mate elsewhere, just as if she had been the daughter of a Pharaoh. Practically everybody in the audience would know this story; the main points of the accepted political propaganda were as well known then as they are now.

This explains the frequent hints in *The Duchess of Malfi* that Ferdinand kills his sister out of a tormented incestuous desire. When I was young the unconsciousness was very prominent, and we wondered what mysterious source of wisdom could have inspired Webster to insert these subtle indications of a truth which must have remained invisible to his coarse listeners. The answer is that his coarse listeners, many of whom thought the author rather low, found the indications of incest-wishes in Ferdinand quite as obvious as the indications that he turned into a wolf. Both unpleasantnesses were thoroughly suitable, being punishments for excessive family pride. Modern critics refuse to accept the obvious here because they want to scold the duchess for her romantic marriage; but it seems possible to offer them a working compromise, and let them scold her for being as proud as her brothers.

The initial speech of Antonio, in the first scene of the play, praises the French court as recently brought to order by a new king, and Professor Clifford Leech argues that this is meant as a warning that the duchess' court is liable to get out of order (pp. 73–4). The scene is her court, but her wicked brothers are visiting her, and they are firmly blamed whereas she is praised. There is indeed a suggestion, or rather an assertion, that the faults of rulers do great political harm; but I do not know how any spectator could guess that the prosy speaker himself is the sycophant or dissolute and infamous person who will spread death and diseases through the whole land. We are given no reason to suppose that the duchess's marriage to Antonio did anything but good in her duchy. It used to be said that this speech was added to the play, about five years after its perform- ance, to express gratification at a sordid murder by a French king [in April 1617] which the English fancied to their advantage, but I am pleased to report that there is no need to suppose so.[10] Webster is anyhow an unlikely playwright to have known real secrets of state. The only person the newly returned Antonio happens to blame, as he talks to a friend in an alcove while viewing the reception, is Bosola, an unwilling creature of the cardinal (i. i. 22–8), and Bosola then happens to come up to Antonio and grumble to him about both the brothers (the Cardinal and Duke Ferdinand); so Antonio ends the scene by expressing a rather better opinion of Bosola (i. i. 75–82). A number of critics have said that Webster contradicts himself by making Antonio express these two different opinions of Bosola, whereas obviously what the dramatist has to plant is that the riddling personality of Bosola is going to go on deceiving Antonio for some time. This is a typically one-eyed complaint. But Antonio is meant to appear a sober sensible man, the right choice for the duchess, so even though he is deceived his opinion does not change very much; he still knows that Bosola is a malcontent, and his attitude to that well-known type is already settled. A university graduate who is not given a white-collar job must be expected to become politically disaffected, and probably criminal as well; what the Italian means by a malcontent's 'goodness' is presumably his *virtue*, his capacity, which will fester within him if unused. This practical and humane comment is very remote from the whelming and incapacitating sense of sin usually ascribed to Webster. One might think he considered Antonio too easy to deceive, but the truth seems to be that the playwright found the character too dull to be worth criticising. All the same, it has to be made clear that the duchess chose well; in the next part Antonio has won the prize at some form of knightly jousting, which is patently inserted to prove that he is a thorough old-fashioned gentleman, even though he is the major-domo of a royal establishment. This part also lets us meet Ferdinand, who though not yet mad is already insanely proud. He tells the courtiers that they must not laugh unless he laughs, 'were the subject never so witty' (I. ii. 45), and to the English ear this sounded outrageous; even Elizabeth wanted you to laugh of your own accord, however unfairly she might box your ears for laughing in the wrong place. Antonio again tells his friend Delio what wicked plotters the duchess's brothers are, and how divinely virtuous she is herself. We see the brothers seduce Bosola to spy on her, and then they both lecture her hysterically against remarriage. As soon as they have gone, she proposes marriage to Antonio, who accepts the hopeless burden with firm courage because their mutual knowledge of their love has already made refusal impossible. All modern critics invent reasons for claiming that he is 'ambitious' because he accepts her, but the scene is written with delicacy of feeling, and the truth is that he could not refuse her without brutality; or perhaps cowardice would be sufficient alternative. In any case, he is so far from satisfying ambition that he only accepts a tormenting duty and an early death. I think it notable that all modern critics have been stampeded by their distaste for the normal affections into such very bad feeling as they have towards Antonio. The whole sequence could not be more hammeringly simple if written by Dickens, and it insists that the duchess and her lover are the good characters of the play.

After she has accepted him she calls her servant from behind the arras and says:

> Be not amaz'd, this woman's of my counsel –
> I have heard lawyers say, a contract in a chamber
> *Per verba de presenti* is absolute marriage. (I. i . 477–9)

Now here I can offer a definite contribution, well known to historians but apparently never recognised by critics of the play. Throughout Europe, a mutual promise of marriage taken before witnesses was legally binding until the Council of Trent, in the middle sixteenth century; it would still have been binding in Italy when the duchess actually lived (she was killed in 1513), but the passionate denial of its legality by her brother may suggest that she lived in the time of Webster. The Council of Trent [1563], by way of stiffening Catholic morals in answer to the Puritans, laid down that a marriage to be legal required the services of a priest. The

Protestants kept for some time to the medieval system, which finally survived only in Scotland – hence the Gretna Green marriages of young couples escaping from legal control in England. Thus, at the time of the play, a difference about what counted as a legally binding marriage was one of the striking differences between Catholic and Protestant countries.[11] When Ferdinand catches his sister speaking before the mirror to her absent lover (III. ii), she repeatedly claims to be married, and he insists that she is living in sin. When he visits her prison in darkness, having vowed never to see her alive, he is more explicit:

FERD.   ... where are your cubs?
DUCH. Whom?
FERD.   Call them your children;
        For though our national law distinguish bastards
        From true legitimate issue, compassionate nature
        Makes them all equal.
DUCH.   Do you visit me for this?
        You violate a sacrament o'th' church
        Shall make you howl in Hell for't.   (IV. i. 33–9)

Miss Bradbrook said:[12]

The Duchess had not sought the sacrament of marriage in the Church, or that of baptism, but she is at present experiencing the sacrament of penance.

That she had denied her children baptism is merely a lunatic suspicion of her brother's; and many Protestants had reached the position of saying that a binding marriage, even if not performed by a priest, is inherently sacramental. I do not believe that a visit for scolding and exhortation was ever supposed to violate the sacrament of penance; why should it? Thus the witty crack of Miss Bradbrook cannot be sustained; even she, I presume, did not mean that this is what the duchess herself means. The duchess means to claim indignantly that she is fully married somehow, and she would still mean it even if minor holes can be picked in my defence of her assertion. At this point the Protestant audience would readily give her three cheers; she is on their side against the wicked new doctrine of the papists, by which the priests usurped a new occasion of bribes and thereby encouraged seducers to break their oaths. Our historical-minded critics have been telling us that the prejudices of the time would vilify the duchess and her romantic story, so that what a spontaneous reader gets from the play is a complete inversion of the intended effect. You find if you read a little history that this is all nonsense, and that the prejudices of the time had actually been mobilised in the duchess's favour.[13]

However, I must not deny that some of the audience would feel she was going alarmingly far:

> DUCH. What can the Church force more?
> ANT. That Fortune may not know an accident,
> Either of joy or sorrow, to divide
> Our fixed wishes.
> DUCH.   How can the Church bind faster?
> We now are man and wife, and 'tis the Church
> That must but echo this.   (I. i. 487–93)

Professor Clifford Leech found 'an independence of mind, a note of challenge, in the duchess's references to religion', and said that in this passage she was 'almost peremptory' (p. 75); perhaps he means that she has tricked the butler into marrying her, and now boasts to him that he can't get out of it. I must say I regret that this situation wasn't arranged for the beginning of *Joseph Andrews*, but to pretend that it has happened to Antonio is to ignore the earnest adoration of the duchess which he expresses to Delio in the second scene of the play. He is bound not to encourage her suit, all the more because he loves her back; if he did, he would be encouraging her in a fatally dangerous course of action. It is true that he cuts a poor figure, as a man in that position cannot help doing; but he has the merit of not trying to wriggle out of it, and he has the great advantage, derived from Fletcher perhaps, of being able to sound ringingly earnest in a quiet throw-away half-line:

> Were there nor heaven nor hell,
> I should be honest: I have long serv'd virtue,
> And ne'er ta'en wages of her.   (I. i. 438–40)

Towards the end of the play he again looks feeble, when he allows the duchess to go and appeal to her murderous brothers without him. But the only tender side of them is their family feeling, so they might relent to her alone but are certain only to be exasperated against her by the presence of him; and when this rational plan fails he follows her to almost certain death. The spectators cannot be expected to despise him when he searches for his wife in the darkened palace, and makes the tremendous answer after being stabbed to death: 'Very near my home' (v. iv. 51).

Well then, after reconsidering the character of Antonio, I think we can say why the duchess hid Cariola behind the arras. It is a peculiarly coarse misrepresentation of her character to say that she did it in order to force him into an unwilling marriage. She did it because he might want to refuse her, and it might become difficult for him to speak sincerely if he knew he was in the presence of a witness. Once he has accepted, she can call in the servant without more ado and explain that their pledge has been witnessed, but a refusal could have been treated as known only to themselves. I may be answered that the Elizabethan theatre did not deal in such delicacies; but I never said that it must; I am only answering a dirty story by showing that a clean one is more probable, and it does seem very much more probable if you can follow the delicacy of feeling of the two characters as expressed in the placid versification.

Modern critics as well as her brothers have also blamed the duchess for pretending to go on a pilgrimage, so as to escape from Malfi and join her brothers. Bosola has tricked her into telling him the secret of her marriage, and then he invents this plan for her, saying 'so you may depart / Your country with more honour' (III. ii. 309–10). *Your country* treats her firmly as a queen, if the English spectators felt any doubt. The servant Cariola says 'I do not like this jesting with religion, / This feigned pilgrimage', and the duchess says: 'Thou art a superstitious fool – / Prepare us instantly for our departure' (III. ii. 317–20). In the next scene Bosola betrays her affairs to her brothers, including the plan which he has himself proposed.

> CARD. Doth she make religion her riding-hood
>   To keep her from the sun and tempest?
> FERD.   That!
>   That damns her:- methinks her fault and beauty,
>   Blended together, show like leprosy,
>   The whiter, the fouler:- I make it a question
>   Whether her beggarly brats were ever christen'd. (III. iii. 60–5)

Webster is bad at lunatics but wonderfully good at hysterics. The listeners cannot feel encouraged to believe the suspicion about baptism, because the verse of Ferdinand gabbles so insanely. As to the first accusation, most of them would agree with the duchess that a pilgrimage to worship a saint was a superstitious practice deserving no reverence. In III. v. 71–81, while separating from her husband, she speaks with an earnest piety which I think can be described as very Protestant:

DUCH.   ... in the eternal church, sir,
I do hope we shall not part thus.
ANT.   O be of comfort!
Make patience a noble fortitude,
And think not how unkindly we are us'd:
Man, like to cassia, is prov'd best, being bruis'd.
DUCH.   Must I, like to a slave-born Russian,
Account it praise to suffer tyranny?
And yet, O Heaven, thy heavy band is in't.
I have seen my little boy oft scourge his top
And compar'd myself to't: nought made me e'er
Go right but heaven's scourge-stick.

This is before she has had the mental torments which Miss Brad-brook considers to purge her. The ruler of Malfi is fairly widely informed if she is proud not to be a Russian, and when she told her brother how her people mock at her in spite of their prosperity she drives the point home that she is not a tyrant. Here in her answer to her husband she drives home a contrast which modern critics seem unable to appreciate. He says, as anyone might do, that troubles do us good in the end. She says, and she might be quoting the gospels though a neo-Christian has never read those bits, that even so the man who brings the trouble had better never have been born. Very little pressing of her thought would make her blame tyrants who pervert religious endurance to bolster political slavery, and listeners would often think of this; but the main impression would be simply that she is convinced she is right and yet willing to believe that the victory of her wicked brothers will be used by God for some good purpose, for example sending herself to Heaven or making her son by Antonio, rather than her son by the previous duke, the next duke of Malfi.

Such is the way she talks just before her imprisonment, and it must be called tolerably pious, but there is a point during the testing process of her imprisonment when she begins cursing; it is after she has been shown what she believes to be the corpses of her husband and their elder son. However, she foreshadowed this at the moment of her arrest, when Bosola asks whether the two younger children, who are coming with their mother, can speak, and she says

No:
But I intend, since they were born accurs'd,
Curses shall be their first language.   (III. v. 114–16)

Bosola says 'Fie', meaning this is an impious way to talk, and also a
defiance to his employers; and indeed many listeners would have
held it against the duchess unless she had said with her last breath
that the little boy must be made to say his prayers. Her last words
are therefore not only a coarse piece of tear-jerking. She takes care
not to involve her children, but in herself she is an almost pure case
of defiance, in the sense which is probably still described as a crime
in the Navy. She defies her brothers, as well may be her duty since
she is the absolute ruler of a city state; and no doubt, with Bosola
whispering in her ear in prison, she comes to feel it may be her duty
as a prince to resist evil rather than to endure patiently. It is hard to
choose a point of entry to the sequence:

DUCH.   I am full of daggers:
         Puff: let me blow these vipers from me.
                  Enter servant.
         What are you?
SERV.   One that wishes you long life.
DUCH.   I would thou wert hang'd for the horrible curse
         Thou hast given me: I shall shortly grow one
         Of the miracles of pity:- I'll go pray: no,
         I'll go curse:-
BOS.   O fie!
DUCH.   I could curse the stars.
BOS.   O fearful!
DUCH.   And those three smiling seasons of the year
         Into a Russian winter, nay the world
         To its first chaos.
BOS.   Look you, the stars shine still:-
DUCH.   O, but you must
         Remember, my curse hath a great way to go. –
         Plagues, that make lanes through largest families,
         Consume them! –
BOS.   Fie lady!
DUCH.   Let them, like tyrants,
         Never be remember'd, but for the ill they have done;
         Let all the zealous prayers of mortified
         Churchmen forget them! –
BOS.   O, uncharitable!
DUCH.   Let heaven, a little while, cease crowning martyrs,
         To punish them!
         Go howl them this: and say I long to bleed:
         It is some mercy, when men kill with speed.   (IV. i. 90–110)

Mr Dent (p. 232) finds a parallel in Montaigne to 'the stars shine still': 'wee deeme our death to be some great matter, and which passeth not so easily, nor without a solemne consultation of the Starres ... *There is no such societie betweene heaven and us, that by our destinie the shining of the starres should be as mortall as we.*' That is, somewhere at the back of Webster's mind, he was recalling an argument against astrology, which tells us not to be conceited about our position in the universe. (Antonio on the other hand had his first son's horoscope calculated.) This is a slight comfort, certainly after so many critics have taken for granted that the play is all pompous groaning after fate. On this view, the duchess curses her own misfortunes rather than the world as a whole, and she is ready to laugh at herself a little after the serpent-like reply from Bosola; 'my curse hath a great way to go' really might be inspired by the humour of Montaigne. In between, for two lines, she did call for the destruction of all life, like King Lear (and I do not see why Mr Dent is not allowed to quote this parallel; it is stronger than most of those he gives, though less verbal); but now she collects her wandering mind and proceeds to rational curses against her brothers, telling Bosola to repeat the defiance to them, since its purpose is to make them kill her. I do not deny that she is meant to be considerably purged from this by the time that death is granted to her, but the audience would not regard this kind of despairing speech as particularly irreligious.

Later, the cardinal while advising Bosola how to discover Antonio tells him to follow Delio to mass:

> ... may be Antonio,
> Although he do account religion
> But a school-name, for fashion of the world
> May accompany him ...   (v. ii. 132–5)

The brothers use this as a standard slander against both the duchess and her husband; and I must grant that what we are to make of it is not obvious. It seems natural to regard them as a 'free-thinking' couple, since they make an 'unconventional' marriage; but does not this way of expressing it mobilise the audience against them? I think it is calculated to present them as souls naturally Protestant, people who would become Protestants if they had the opportunity; and this is eked out by an illogical effect of the theatre – as they are the sympathetic characters, among a lot of wicked Catholics, the Protestant audience tends to assume 'they are ordinary people like us'. Thus Bosola says with glee at a moment of discovery (II. iii. 65–6):

> ... this precise fellow
> Is the duchess's bawd,

and *precise* was a word that easily suggested Puritans; but Antonio
would only seem so to a Catholic, one may suppose, not to the
moderate Protestants in the audience. The duchess begins her proposal to him with:

> What do you think of marriage?
> ANT.   I tak 't, as those that deny purgatory –
> It locally contains, or heaven, or hell;
> There's no third place in't.   (I. i. 392–5)

Denying purgatory was the fundamental Protestant thing to do,
because the priests had been demanding money to let people out of
it, and this was what triggered off the Reformation; Antonio may
well sound vague, as it had not yet happened in his time. The
audience was of course very conscious of it, and would readily pick
up such hints to explain the accusations of the brothers. Ferdinand
himself at one point makes a rather free-thinking remark:

> Damn her! that body of hers,
> While that my blood ran pure in't, was more worth
> Than that which thou wouldst comfort, call'd a soul –
>
> (V. i. 121–3)

But this is just the materialism of a wicked Catholic, not the
incipient sectarianism which he smells out in the hero.

It is interesting that the Mermaid edition of Webster and Tourneur,
published with its introduction in the nineties, still feels entirely
contemporary; I expect we would not feel so about other topics.
Sepulchral groaning still goes on about Webster's cosmic despair
and his sickened loathing for mankind, and critics often imply that
he was an atheist without knowing it. Well, playwrights had to put
up with a good deal of slander, but I expect Webster would have
been indignant about this. (As to Tourneur, he strikes me as an even
more innocent man than Webster, pathetically struggling to
imagine whatever it can be that wicked people do.) Webster wrote
about Italian Roman Catholics like a loyal English Protestant, and
his audience reflected thankfully: 'Well, we aren't as bad as all that,
so maybe we won't be struck down yet-away.' They also felt a
fascinated curiosity about the wicked Italians, who were immensely

cultured, whereas the audience had a guilty consciousness of being boorish provincials; but this made it all the more of a comfort to be so much better in the eye of God. I suppose Webster might have expressed a pessimistic philosophy all the same, but I don't know why anybody should expect so, merely because he writes about bad men who get punished. Fate was not a thing an Elizabethan writer could take seriously, any more than Cupid, because it didn't fit into the Christian scheme. No doubt Webster really did believe that once you had got entangled with an Italian court you would be sure to find that repentance had come too late; and to this extent the remarks of the characters about fate are dramatically relevant; but it also made one feel pleased that one was not an Italian courtier. The duchess and her husband are not kept at such a distance, but surely we do not feel that life is no good, because everybody is like her brothers? We know that they are very peculiar, unlike most other people.

James L. Calderwood ('*The Duchess of Malfi*: styles of ceremony', *Essays in Criticism*, 12:2, April 1962, 133–47) points out a curious phrase of Ferdinand (II. v. 65–6):

> It is some sin in us, heaven doth revenge
> By her,

adding 'the sin is within him alone, and he knows it' (p. 144). That is, he feels guilty for desiring her. That may be, but he is speaking to his brother, and may well suppose that there is a doom on the House of Aragon; after all, the brother remarks later on, to explain Ferdinand's madness:

> You have heard it rumour'd for these many years,
> None of our family dies, but there is seen
> The shape of an old woman, which is given
> By tradition to us . . .   (v. ii. 90–3)

This is an extremely aristocratic distinction, and practically a doom already. I am not even sure that Ferdinand realises how close to incest his feelings are, since he can always describe them as concern for the purity of his own blood. But Bosola, who pries into means of tormenting others beside the duchess, must be supposed to know that he exasperates the duke by imputing lust to her:

> BOS.   . . . this restraint
> (Like English mastives, that grow fierce with tying)
> Makes her too passionately apprehend

Those pleasures she's kept from.
FERD.   Curse upon her!
I will no longer study in the book
Of another's heart ...   (IV. i. 12–17)

Bosola had just told him how noble and majestic she was in prison,
and perhaps his satisfaction at this had almost made him spare her.
Critics who quote this passage as evidence that she is lustful are
asking to be deluded by the villain – Bosola of course would not
want to lose his elaborately planned psychological experiment. At
the end of the scene he again eggs on the duke under pretence of
restraining him:

And go no further in your cruelty –
Send her a penitential garment to put on
Next to her delicate skin, and furnish her
With beads and prayer-books.   (IV. i. 118–20)

'Damn her! that body of hers,' begins Ferdinand; Mr Calderwood
seems clearly right to say (p. 145) that the mention of her skin made
him cruel again.

The standard edition of Webster, by Professor F. L. Lucas (1927),
dates from before the deluge of Mr Eliot's tradition, and on going
back to it while I wrote this piece I found that he says practically
everything I have to say, probably indeed I remembered it
unconsciously; but it needs saying again. He remarks that the
successive narrators of the story, Bandello, Belleforest, and Painter,
were 'a gentleman, a fool, and a knave': this was to point up a
remark just before that Belleforest, the French author who started
vilifying the duchess, was 'a pedant and a prig'.[14] Nowadays critics
assume that the judgments of a lower-middle-class pedant were the
judgments of everybody in the period, though they were not
accepted either by the working class or by the ruling class; I think it
hard on Mr Eliot that this has become his tradition. 'But it is
interesting to see how very little Webster borrows from Painter's
language, considering how freely he conveys from Montaigne and
Sidney', remarks Professor Lucas (Painter made a free translation of
Belleforest); and he finds a detail in Webster which might be taken
from Bandello, as Webster 'had enough Italian to quote Ariosto'
(p. 13). These are slight indications, but they do not force us to
believe that Webster was ignorant enough to take Painter as the
only tradition.

Professor Lucas is rather against the play, preferring *The White Devil* for being more full-blooded; the first pair of lovers are like soldiers, the second like martyrs, he says, but it does not occur to him that this makes them more religious; they are just melancholy (pp. 20–1). And indeed the critics in Mr Eliot's tradition are simply malcontents like Bosola and Iago, though (like those villains again) they are always insinuating that they hold some tremendously sophisticated and adult religious position.

Mr Frank W. Wadsworth, in the *Philological Quarterly* for October 1956,[15] tried to defend the duchess against Professor Clifford Leech, mainly by giving quotations to show that second marriages, and marriages beneath one's class, were not always considered bad. Remarriage was frequent in spite of the occasional savage attacks on it, he points out; and Webster seems to have planned to make his duchess satisfy the criteria which were held to justify it. She is not said to be lustful, as by Painter, her previous marriage appears to be some way off (the son by it is elsewhere), and her new husband is a very sober and undashing type. (This explains why Antonio is made so dull, and indeed has been accused of cowardice for his patience.) Mr Wadsworth grants 'the general applicability of the doctrine of degree' but asks 'whether it is possible that any part of Webster's audience would have been so enlightened that they would not automatically condemn the Duchess' (pp. 401–2); and he finds several moral quotations to the effect that true worth and a happy marriage may be found without social splendour. What a horrible world these critics have been living in; I had not realised that the mental disease of Eliot's 'tradition' had gripped them so tightly. Professor Clifford Leech's reply ('An Addendum on Webster's Duchess', *Philological Quarterly*, 37:2, April 1958) denied that he had meant that Webster merely blames the duchess:

If her human weakness were too strongly marked, we should have difficulty in admitting her status as a tragic figure. If she were wholly innocent, the difficulty would lie in our recognising her as 'one of us' or as one of the sick society of men that is presented in the play. (p. 253)

The marriage of the duchess beneath her rank

would be likely to make an audience feel that she was one of themselves, in concluding her affairs on a plane below the ideal. It would not, however, involve a sense of active 'guilt'. (p. 254)

But she is one of us because she is a naturally Protestant soul, and this makes her a martyr.

More gravely, he goes on to point out that it is not merely a matter of rank (pp. 254–5):

she is a sovereign with a duty to her small realm ... Nowhere does the duchess show any thought for her public duty. We see what her court is like in the first act, and it is evident that it needs attention. But the duchess has thoughts only for her brothers' enmity and for her love for Antonio. The effect of her behaviour is exhibited to us by Antonio himself in the third act:

> DEL. What say the common people?
> ...
> ANT. They do observe, I grow to infinite purchase
> The lefthand way, and all suppose the Duchess
> Would amend it, if she could: For, say they
> Great princes, though they grudge their officers
> Should have such large and unconfined means
> To get wealth under them, will not complain
> Lest thereby they should make them odious
> Unto the people – for other obligation
> Of love, or marriage, between her and me,
> They never dream of.   (III. i. 28–42)

He then says (p. 255) 'the irresponsibility of her behaviour' is brought home to us when she laughs with her husband while her brother is under her roof; but the Elizabethans always respected courage. What we are told about the people is that they think the duchess would make Antonio less rich if she could (therefore they think her attentive), but that she lets him take money from her because she fears he would otherwise take it from the people (therefore they think she shows loving care for them). In fact, of course, she has only given him what is practically his own, being hers (there is no suggestion that she has robbed the people for him, or that they think themselves robbed). Webster is perhaps rather too prone to affect the Machiavel in straightforward matters, but to twist this into an accusation against the duchess' government is comically malignant.

Keen though I am to defend the honour of the duchess against neo-Christian cynicism, I must agree that there is a technical likeness between the two ladies who give the plays their names. They are both 'complex characters', of a sort with which the audience had become familiar. Shakespeare no doubt had established the demand, but other authors found that they could satisfy it with less expense of spirit. The meaning of the title *The White Devil* is that Vittoria is an interesting moral paradox, good in one way though bad in another, and you are to be all the more thrilled when she switches round. The duchess had an interest of the same kind, though to us she seems plainly a good girl, and Vittoria a bad one. Recent critics have driven home that the duchess was bad for marrying the butler, but have not put the same effort into explaining why Vittoria was good. She is not of course guilty of murder; when we first see her with her lover, she at once tells him she has had a dream to the effect that their two spouses have both been killed, but an incident follows at once to make clear that this is not why he kills them. She is receiving her lover in her mother's house, to get away from the sordid husband, and Old Mother makes a clamorous entry saying 'Not in *my* house'; then the lover replies, in a very ducal manner, 'Why then, I'll have to kill the two spouses, if you won't connive at a little adultery':

> Be thou the cause of all ensuing harm.   (*WD*, I. ii. 296)

The audience would laugh, feeling that only an Italian lord could be so impudent; then it would settle down to feeling that nearly all the wickedness was on his side. Adultery she is guilty of; but the popular theatre was always against the arranged marriage of high life, and we gather that Vittoria's family have sold her to a weak old fool without getting a sufficient bribe, or rather enough grandeur to suit their temperaments and social claims. She is not exactly mercenary; she seems to forget to pay her brother his reward, and then resent the tone of his demands, rather than grudge it to him. Even this confusion, I think, would add a little to her essential virtue; which was just that she was immensely aristocratic. Modern critics have been so eager to find a subtly theological morality in these plays that they ignore the simple fondness of the audience for wild grandeur. Her permanent high courage is the same in her badinage as at her death; she somehow assumes that everything about her is grand. Considering how slowly Webster wrote, he may well have got his first conception of the White Devil from Shakespeare's Cleopatra; she makes a similar challenge to the skill of a boy actor. I think that scholarship has overreached itself about her last words, as she bleeds to death:

O my greatest sin lay in my blood.
Now my blood pays for't.   (*WD*, v. vi. 237–8)

We are always told that *blood* here means 'lust', to make it moral
enough for the critics; but that does not explain why her brother for
the first time expresses admiration for her and says she should breed
men. Blood-stock and breeding true and suchlike were perfectly
familiar uses for the word; the family of Vittoria had almost ceased
to be aristocratic, but she fought her way to the infamous splendour
which she considered her heredity to demand. No doubt both
meanings of *blood* are present, but the aristocratic one is what
extracts reluctant praise from Flamineo. This side of the aristocratic
tradition, which may simply be called the law-breaking side, has
long been opposed to Christian morals, and has regularly gone down
well with the working classes. Or, at any rate, it has in the theatre,
because swagger is a thing which both aristocracy and the theatre
exist to provide. *The White Devil* always seems to me a parody of
Elizabethan drama, because Webster was an earnest collector of the
gimmicks of that theatre and in his first 'serious' play empties his
whole rag-bag of gimmicks onto the stage, usually turning them into
double gimmicks to make sure; but at least we in our turn can be
sure that the point of them was meant to be something quite familiar
and theatrical. No wonder the characters die uttering warnings
against the life of courts, though they themselves have never flinched
from it; because we are meant to think: 'how very self-sacrificing to
go through all that misery, and with hell still to come, in order to
look so frightfully grand'. Ferdinand in the *Duchess* means the same
thing by blood in his last couplet:

FERD.   I do account this world but a dog-kennel:
        I will vault credit, and affect high pleasures,
        Beyond death.
BOS.   He seems to come to himself,
        Now he's so near the bottom.
FERD.   My sister! O! my sister! there's the cause on't:
        Whether we fall by ambition, blood, or lust,
        Like diamonds, we are cut with our own dust. [*Dies.*]   (v. v. 67–73)

He cannot simply mean 'lust' by *blood*, because lust comes next in the
list. By *we* he means his own family, or just himself and his twin; they
are so high-born that only their own foibles or products of decay can
affect them, like diamonds which can never meet a tool harder than
themselves. They must have been like Al Capone.

This kind of thing is sad nonsense, though likeable in a way; and the reason why the *Duchess* is an immensely better play than the *White Devil* is that it supplies the formula of moral paradox with an adequate theme. There really were two opinions in the audience about whether the duchess ought to marry the butler, and I suppose that, as in productions of Bernard Shaw when I was young, there would be two parties A and B in the audience, with first A going Tut-tut and the gratified B going Tee-hee, then the surprised A going Tee-hee and B in its turn, Tut-tut. I make no doubt that Webster like Shaw was on the enlightened side, but like Shaw he was concerned to give life to both sides of the debate. This of course is why the modern neo-Christian critic, ignoring all but the black notes on the piano, can make quotations purporting to show that he scolds the Duchess all along.

Miss Bradbrook wrote very well about the Duchess in *Themes and Conventions of Elizabethan Tragedy* (1935); in fact, this I think is the true faith from which the neo-Christians backslid, through their craving to scold and befoul; but it needs restating, because most readers nowadays assume she meant something different. In Act IV there is a strong suggestion that the duchess is in hell; it is an 'overshadowing metaphor ... of such force ... that the mind is suspended between accepting it as that or between [*sic*] taking it as something more'. Webster's attitude to the duchess 'is entirely sympathetic; but it is not simple'. The immediate source of the story, Painter, is not hostile but not approving; he shows the duchess and Antonio as 'led by their instincts', 'deploring the absence of an essential fitness which is not of the intelligence or the feelings alone, but which distinguishes the awakened self from the "natural man"' (pp. 197–8). Webster, on the other hand, simply 'utilised the conventional "case" against the Duchess as material for the tragedy' (p. 201).

However, I have to report that even Miss Bradbrook began the process of shrinking away from this manly acceptance of ambiguity into inventing petty accusations against the duchess; partly because Miss Bradbrook did not understand the theological politics of the secret marriage, partly because she accepted the debilitating theory of imagism which was already current when she wrote. Thus she finds that when Ferdinand pours out abuse upon his sister 'the sense of moral outrage behind the lines is so *strong* that it carries its own *force*[16] (typical imagist grammar) – but Webster's audience had none of this aesthetic flabbiness; what they heard, or knew that the other half of the audience had heard, was a Catholic monster denouncing a girl with a naturally Protestant soul, and all the filth he was spouting could only be blown back in his own face. In the same way, she says (p. 203) that though the assertions by the cardinal against his sister are 'unreliable', they 'only confirm the general temper of the early scenes'. I do not believe that we are meant to make subtle observations against the duchess in the early scenes, finding her a tiny bit short of what Henry James would have let pass muster; her behaviour is meant to be rippingly aristocratic all along, though I agree that her isolation, experience, and immaturity make the exact correctness of her decision (to marry Antonio) all the more shockingly pathetic. Miss Bradbrook said that to miss the contrast between her readiness to invent or recognise indecent jokes and 'Antonio's enthusiastic tribute to her continence' was 'to miss the complexity of the situation' (pp. 202–3). It seems impossible to reconcile this thoughtful remark with (for example) the readiness of Queen Elizabeth herself to recognise indecent jokes. But there really is a collapse of logic at the end of their wooing scene, because in spite of their being legally married in a Protestant sense she says that they will merely lie beside one another and discuss the enmity of her brothers as with a sword between them. This must be intended to placate some part of the audience, but I cannot understand which part. No modern critic has discussed the passage, because none of them would condescend to talk about anything real; the imagery and the atmosphere are the only meat refined enough for them to touch. Miss Bradbrook even sinks to saying that when Antonio accepts the offer of marriage from the duchess his decision 'has perhaps a mingling of ambition' (p. 201). This is very unjust; he says that he expects death if he accepts, and yet he accepts willingly, and no ambition is either excited or gratified. The duchess would not have asked him unless she had felt confident, and a refusal by the time she made the offer would have been brutal and cowardly, because he had already totally committed himself to it. On any other ground, clearly, he would have no duty to accept death just to please her.

The behaviour on both sides was heroic, and was admired as such by the audience; the theatre usually has been more on the side of the young couple than prose works of edification for private reading. A critical theory need not labour so hard to deny the obvious.

Thus we are told to blame the duchess for some trait of character which 'makes her also ready to dismiss the inevitable from her mind, and live from hand to mouth, equivocating pitifully with her brothers'.[17] Well, E. M. Forster was thought to express a high sentiment when he said 'The people I admire most behave as if they were immortal and society eternal', and so was whoever said

> Let determined things to destiny
> Hold unbewailed their way.
> [*Antony and Cleopatra*, III. vi. 84]

What would have been better than the course she follows? It would be useless to plead with the diabolical brothers, and they are likely to get themselves killed quite soon; she has several years of happiness, and they only live just long enough to murder her. I agree however that the 'combination of experience and immaturity [in the duchess] is a piteous thing'.[18]

Her approach to death is perhaps more important:

> ... nought made me ere
> Go right but Heaven's scourge stick.   (III. 5. 92–5)

This is an entirely new mood for the Duchess, and it is one which grows upon her. She never acknowledges that her brothers have the right to judge her; but she does acknowledge that she is in need of a corrected judgment. It is in this development of the Duchess that the interest of the prison scenes lie, and by this they are saved from being merely sadistic exhibitions. (Bradbrook, *Themes and Conventions of Elizabethan Tragedy*, p. 204)

To say they have no other interest is a bit much; but certainly the tragic heroine needs to prepare her soul for death if she is to be whole-heartedly admired. By the word *acknowledge* Miss Bradbrook implies that the brothers did have the right to judge her; did they have the right to kill too, I wonder? A Christian did not have to be so slavish as this amounts to; she could humble herself before God well enough without yielding to the tyrant. I can agree that the subtle corruption of Bosola makes him genuinely well fitted to be her spiritual director as she prepares for the death which he has brought upon her, but this is well calculated to set the teeth of a Protestant sharply on edge. When she expresses indifference to the means of her death, and adds 'any way, for heaven-sake,/ So I were out of your whispering' (IV. ii. 222–3), the Protestant audience thinks of priests in dealing with English captives in Spanish torture-chambers; it accepts the 'degrees of mortification' planned by Bosola as really turned by the duchess to her spiritual good, but in themselves they are a grim parody. Miss Bradbrook felt rather impatient with the stupid modern reader, who could not realise how holy the prison scenes were; it never occurred to her that there was a slight disagreement about religious matters in Webster's time.

What happened to the Duchess was as little deserved as what happened to Lear: neither of them get common justice; by the end of the play neither of them desire it. (p. 209)

A tiny bit too much pious resignation, perhaps; they still desire at the end the common justice of sparing the children's lives, and if they did not the audience would not think them even holier.

I have now to examine the contradictions and confusions which all critics have found in the play, and must first say that they were very likely to occur; Webster added a bit at a time, copying out his 'sentences' from notebooks, devoting himself to the magic of the individual phrase or at most the individual scene, therefore he was almost certain to be inconsistent. I was surprised to find that all inconsistencies vanish. But it might be added that if you write slowly you have time to tidy up.

The most famous one derives from the stage direction (IV. i):

Here is discovered, behind a traverse, the artificial figures of Antonio and his children, appearing as if they were dead.

If Webster was Shakespeare, we would simply print 'and his child'; that would be the established text, too familiar to be doubted, though there would be ample examination questions about the apparatus. I feel confident that it is only a misprint. The trouble arises because the duchess at the moment before she is strangled wants her little girl to be given cough mixture and her little boy to be made to say his prayers before they sleep. The elder boy (making three children in all) had stayed with his father, in a forlorn attempt to keep some of the family alive; to present her the 'figures' of these two absent ones as dead is in a way imaginatively credible – they are remote, as in a vision or on the telly – but to mix up with them the corpses of the two babies she had last seen only half an hour ago would be out of keeping; for one thing, these would have to be much fresher corpses. Miss Bradbrook however insists that

The conviction that all the children are dead is behind the heavy despair of 4.2; it justifies the complete hopelessness of that scene as compared to 4.1, its whole fixed and rigid grief. (p. 210)

She might well feel certain that the two babies she has still to care for are also doomed. Miss Bradbrook however is positively cross about her attention to them:

She had been in a peace 'beyond hope and beyond despair': this touch of 'humanity' is as out of place as it is offensive in itself. (p. 210)

Miss Bradbrook was pretty young when she made this crack; I doubt whether she would still carry the unnaturalness of the neo-Christian tradition to the point of actually despising the duchess for carrying out a practical duty before she is martyred. There is in any case plenty of Christian tradition to praise the duchess for it. But of course what Miss Bradbrook felt was that Webster was cheating like Dickens; in fact this one misprint was practically enough to turn her against the author altogether:

The felicitous phrase is there for its own sake; or, at most, the touching sentiment, the poignant feeling is there for *its* own sake, without any regard to the structure of the feelings as a whole. (p. 210)

I think this could reasonably be said of *The White Devil*, his first ambitious piece, into which he packed all the tricks he had learned; but it isn't true of *The Duchess*, his second and final serious effort, into which we may expect him to have distilled whatever wisdom he had. His shade is forever gibbering with fury at the printers for putting 'children' instead of *child*.

Professor Clifford Leech, following on from Miss Bradbrook, supposed that the duchess had repressed the memory of the murder of her children, so recently presented to her (p. 86). This is to his credit, but the idea strikes me as quite unpresentable in the theatre, whereas to correct the stage directions is a help for the producer – a man and boy corpse are just presentable, four corpses inevitably give a cluttered appearance. Even Webster would have known the effect would be absurd.[19]

There is also a misprint about the reference to the duke of Malfi [Alfonso Piccolomini], the Duchess's son by her first husband (III. iii); Ferdinand lets drop that he is young, as we may expect from the youth of his mother, so his mother is a kind of caretaker, ruling during his minority only. But at the end of the play we find that the duchess' elder son by Antonio has survived and will inherit the duchy. I confess I thought for years that this was a mistake by Webster, obviously not a man much acquainted with high life, who might easily forget the technicalities of inheriting a title. But in the Italy that Webster was writing about one did not merely turn to Debrett if wondering who was the next duke; we find that the sturdy noble Delio, who spoke the first words of the play and has listened patiently all along, is naturally the man who speaks up at the end and tries to make the best arrangement still possible:

> Let us make noble use
> Of this great ruin; and join all our force
> To establish this young, hopeful gentleman
> In's mother's right. These wretched eminent things
> Leave no more fame behind 'em than ...   (v. v. 110–14)

In short, nothing that the wicked brothers of the duchess planned for will survive them. We hear nothing about her son by the duke of Malfi, but we know that she was rapidly left a widow after an arranged marriage (presumably to an old monster) and then chose a good man for her second husband, whose son is likely to be a fit ruler. The worthy nobles who do not stick their necks out but see to it that a decent ruler is appointed are determined to appoint Antonio's son, and ignore the previous claimant whose wicked supporters are now all dead. The actual appointment was made by a town council vote, and not inherited by a legal document; the whole situation was a great deal more democratic than the donnish commentators like myself are even able to envisage.[20]

The delay of the brothers in their revenge, so that the duchess has three children though her secret was betrayed at the birth of the first one, has been found tiresomely incredible and is not in Painter; Webster evidently recognised that Bosola once put on the job would not be likely to miss the first childbirth, and put this right without any worry about the resulting strain on the calendar. But the wicked brothers have to struggle all the time even to keep their heads above water; it is likely enough that they simply weren't at leisure to torment their sister when they first learned her secret and exploded with indignation. A few more of the perfunctory references to their indebtedness to the Jews would be enough to fill the gap; though I agree that the flippancy of Elizabethan playwrights about time is not a thing they should be positively praised for.

I do not believe he is flippant in this way about the motives of Ferdinand for tormenting his sister, though one ought to recognise that the effect in the theatre is almost to boast that the author is flippant, when the villain is made to wonder, with an intimate moodiness, whether there is really any reason why he should be playing the part of a villain. His chief purpose at the time is to refuse to pay his tool:

> I bad thee, when I was distracted of my wits,
> Go kill my dearest friend, and thou hast done't.
> For let me but examine well the cause:
> What was the meanness of her match to me?
> Only I must confess, I had a hope,
> Had she continu'd widow, to have gain'd
> An infinite mass of treasure by her death:
> And that was the main cause ... her marriage! –
> That drew a stream of gall, quite through my heart.
>
> (IV. ii. 279–87)

It was Shakespeare, of course, who had discovered that you could make the puppets tell the audience that they don't understand their own motives, as in the electrifying cases of Hamlet and Iago, and Webster follows the technique like a disciple; one could not be surprised if the jackdaw bit of borrowing made a false claim. But it is genuine here; once you recognise that Ferdinand has an obvious though unavowable motive, because he secretly assumes that his family are like racehorses whereas the rest of mankind are like carthorses, you find this puzzled attempt to excuse himself almost likeable, and terribly pathetic even if not. (The story about money is improbable, but then, we cannot be expected to plumb how these characters get hold of money.)

The horoscope of the first child foretells a violent death, whereas it alone survives, becoming duke of Malfi. I wish I could believe that Webster had enough nerve to present a mistaken horoscope, but probably he just felt he was making the incident consistently sinister; the hurriedly scribbled calculation is cast aside in anger or despair when it is found to be disastrous, and is therefore picked up by the spy in the midnight courtyard. The idea that Antonio was untidy because he didn't have a search for it is surely comical; he could not admit that it existed, and could only hope that it had been destroyed. We may assume that the horoscope was not wrong; at the end of the play the poor child has still ample time to die a violent death, though it probably grew up and did justice in Malfi for a brief period beforehand.[21]

We do not hear much of the administrative work of the duchess, a thing rather out of the convention of the play; but at the beginning of Act III Antonio tells the trusted Delio how public opinion stands in Malfi. The duchess, he explains, has born him three children, and

> The common rabble do directly say
> She is a strumpet.   (III. i. 25–6)

One is relieved to hear this, because if the very existence of the children were kept secret, presumably by never letting them out of the castle dungeons, they would be leading very unhealthy lives. He adds that the people think the duchess indulges him by letting him make his fortune, on a calculation that this will make him treat the people generously in his turn; hence the contented people never suspect that he is married to the duchess. Maybe this detail does not smack of much real experience in public work, but Webster must have written it in for the specific purpose of showing that the duchess was not 'irresponsible' or 'at odds with life' and did no harm to Malfi when she married the man who was already best fitted to handle its affairs. In the next lines of this wonderfully compact play, the raging Ferdinand arrives on a visit, and at once tells the duchess that he has found a sufficiently aristocratic husband for her. She answers, on hearing the name of the man chosen, that he is a stick of sugar-candy:

> ... when I choose
> A husband, I will marry for your honour.   (III. i. 43–4)

She genuinely thinks she has done so, feeling the same kind of pride as her twin does, though in a less lunatic manner; so for the moment, making contact with her at an unconscious level, he is content. She takes advantage of it at once:

> But, sir, I am to have private conference with you
> About a scandalous report, is spread
> Touching mine honour.   (III. i. 46–8)

He refuses to believe it, and tells her she may be safe in her own innocency; she therefore leaves him, no longer asking for a conference, and Bosola tells him about her three children, which we gather that anybody in the market-square could have told him. But in the next scene, where he catches her before her mirror still prattling to her lover, who has slipped out for a practical joke, it seems as if she fiercely denies what she has already admitted. Professor Clifford Leech says (p. 67): 'Ferdinand does not recall what she told him earlier that same night, but takes occasion to embroider on the common theme of reputation's fragility.' This complaint does not allow for their diplomatic manners. When the duchess told her brother she was being slandered, she only confessed what (as the audience had just learned) his spies were certain to have told him already. In answer to his reproaches after the discovery, she does not condescend to any further mention of gossip but does say 'my reputation/Is safe' (iii. ii. 118–19), safe on some higher ground evidently; that is, the people will no longer be able to call her a strumpet when they learn her secret. Ferdinand embarks upon reciting one of the symbolical fables which are the chief fault of Webster as a dramatist (he is hampered by a symbolist theory, so that he has practically no point of difference from Savonarola Brown in 1890); but the boring irrelevance does for once make a point here, because the speaker is intended to be mad. It marks his refusal to ask her what she means by saying she is married; after about fifteen lines of Chaucer-like prattling he feels he has made enough imitation of holding a discussion with her, so he lets fall his thunderbolt: 'I will never see you more' (136). Various critics have called this sequence contradictory, but the psychology seems to me good once you realise that what constitutes a marriage is the point at issue.

Glancing at all history and all the world, it is plain that good writing happens much more often than a good theatre; there are rather few great schools of drama. Of those we have heard about, the Elizabethan school is uniquely keen on madness; the authors seem to feel without knowing why that there is some mystery about madness which they must drag to light, however clumsily. *The Duchess of Malfi*, with *The Changeling* and *King Lear*, is one of the distillations of this prolonged effort, into which whatever had been discovered during the process was meant to be concentrated – such is what Webster's notebook amounted to. The duchess indeed remains sane, but she says she wishes she was mad, and some kind of unreasonable importance is attached to surrounding her with madmen. It is clear that any account of the play needs to reckon with this major element in it. Professor Clifford Leech says that the madness in Webster gives 'an image of unrelieved and terrible chaos'; after distinguishing it from two simpler ways of using madness in drama, he says (p. 84):

A playwright who uses the theme in this third way can have no easy faith in divine goodness: there are certain humiliations which not even the promise of Heaven can atone for.

These are handsome and likeable phrases, but I doubt whether Webster was very different from other Elizabethans in his thought; he seems different because, having distilled the Shakespearean liquor, he can dole it out in concentrated nips. He has nothing like Shakespeare's flow of invention in his mad talk, indeed most of it is simply bad; he sometimes hits on a surrealist phrase which gives an answering ring from far down in the unconsciousness, and you feel that he knows how good it is, but also that it doesn't apply especially to the case it is used for; he has been hoarding it in the notebook. The collection of madmen brought in to mortify the duchess are a very disappointing lot; as they would be in real life no doubt, and I suppose in the production they would hardly be audible, but Webster seems to use them only for dull stock jokes. The only good remark from the entire herd is a flash of rationalism, better suited to Voltaire than to this peak of the romantic upsurge:

3RD MADMAN. He that drinks but to satisfy nature is damned.
(IV. ii. 96)

It is a fundamental Catholic position, perhaps I should explain, that you are damned if you perform the act of sex without the intention to produce children. A serious alcoholic, in the same way, regards with contempt a man who drinks merely to satisfy a bodily desire; he ought only to drink for some spiritual or unnatural purpose, such as to entertain his companions by his drunkenness. I have laboured to explain this little joke because the critics of Webster who describe him as always shuddering at the inherent horror of life are unlikely to give him credit for it. The tradition about lunatics was that they can be expected to blurt out the low truth, and to that extent Webster is following the formula in this bit of satire; but the epigram strikes me as polished in a very unlunatic manner. The Japanese Noh plays often introduce mad characters, but the purpose is extremely unlike the Elizabethan one; under intense mental suffering a character will become dumb, unresponsive in a sinister manner, and at last break out into apparently random acts of violence; but these are the result of possession by the spirit of some other person, usually but not always dead. The Elizabethans considered that when mad, so far from becoming someone else, you showed what you really had inside you all the time; the madness of Lear (someone said) is like a storm so vast that it lays bare the riches accumulated at the bottom of the sea. This was a very good reason why they should be interested in madness; it gave a peep into the workings of the unconsciousness, and a dramatist needs to know about that. I suspect that the doctrines of Paracelsus, the chain of spirits relating soul to body, which were bound to encourage a general belief in unconscious mental activity, were more important in making the drama of individual character possible than we have yet been able to trace. But Webster always feels to me rather outside this movement; as Mr Arthur Waley said long ago, *The Duchess of Malfi* would actually make a Noh play; and her passive majestic endurance is very much in the style of the Noh heroines. Webster would have liked to write mad scenes like Shakespeare's, but after his ridiculous bit of scissors-and-paste work in *The White Devil* he seems to have realised that he had better give it up. He is a master of the approaches to madness, but not of madness, I think we must say.

People often say that the whole fifth act is otiose because the duchess is killed at the end of the fourth. This presumes that the play is nothing but a horror-comic; if you are interested in the basic story, let alone the subjects which have been discussed, you are bound to want to hear what happened to the wicked brothers; indeed you might feel that the death of the duchess is too much spun out.

Professor Clifford Leech finds that the last act gives a parallel to the duchess' marriage to Antonio; when the cardinal's mistress Julia offers love to Bosola, then hides him, as a bribe to make him satisfy her, where he may hear the cardinal's secret, then coaxes him till he tells it and therefore murders her to let it go no further. He says (p. 75): 'in both cases, a woman's frank avowal; in both, a hidden witness; in both, a woman's triumph leading to her destruction'. The details are charmingly neat, and I suppose the author must have known about them, but we need not deduce: 'they are sisters, Webster hints, in their passions and in their consequent actions'. As usual with refined neo-Christian insights, this is merely nasty-minded. Webster would mean a contrast rather than a comparison, if either; but neither impose themselves. He realised, we need not doubt, that the fifth act needed cockering up, for fear that simple people called the fourth the natural end of the drama; and the parallel of situation to the first act would help to make the last one feel relevant. Even so, our opinion of the duchess can hardly be altered by the parallel, as it does not occur till after her death, when we feel that her affairs are already settled. The effect of the incident is that Bosola learns how the duchess was murdered, and this apparently decides him to kill the cardinal; his emergence from hiding does not affect Julia, who is already poisoned. In fact, the two cases are so different that it was clever to notice the parallel. The only purpose of introducing Julia, I had always assumed, was to make the illicit loves of the celibate Roman Catholic priesthood a contrast to the honest Protestant marriage of the duchess. His mistress is sure to betray him in one way or another, but the reason why the effects are fatal to both is that his wickedness to his sister has by this time poisoned his whole life.

[*While this peroration rehearses much of the preceding argument, it yet provides a forceful concluding statement of Empson's position.*]

The most prominent problem of the play has yet to be considered: 'Ought the duchess to have married her butler? Was the marriage successful? Did it work to the good of her people?' One can only give a conditional answer; it would have worked well, if her brothers had not conducted a lunatic vendetta. She chose to marry the man who was in fact carrying out the administration, and if she had done it in public he would have taken the power from her and become duke; but as their agreement was private the unacknowledged marriage made a good partnership for seven years. She tells her brother that her subjects call her a whore but are satisfied by her rule; it is important to hear that they are satisfied, and also we should be glad to hear that the children are no longer a secret, because otherwise they would be leading very unhealthy lives. It has often been said that her brothers could not have left her alone for seven years, being such lunatics as we see in the play; well, the story was accepted as true, and quite well known. Webster would have done better, I agree, to alter the facts into something credible, but that wasn't his climbing-plant approach; and really it isn't at all hard to believe.

The wicked brothers both lived such insanely active lives, and were so likely to be killed, that it was only touch and go whether they ever found time to pay off their grudge against their sister. She nearly got away with her bet, so need not be blamed for attempting the impossible.

The question whether she was wicked to marry beneath her class should be reconsidered but cannot appear majestic. The Borgias, I am informed, were not really very good class by origin. From the point of view of the audience, the only thing we need to understand is that there had been a change within one generation; earlier, the major-domo of a quasi-royal house would be a minor aristocrat or at least a recognised landowner, later he could get by if he could scrape up the big money for the clothes. Compared to later England, the Elizabethans were creditably short of indications about a person's class, because the lords were mostly frankly new and had to prove they were romantic and old-world, so that at any rate no dialect sounded low class. The theme of this play made the question deserve prominence, and it strikes me that Webster treats it with splendid breadth and firmness, as he can afford to do because he has now isolated Bosola, the character who is both villain and confessor (and if anything else only by accident). Bosola while trying to make the duchess confess her marriage to Antonio confesses democratic opinions, saying that virtue ought to be the only consideration in mating, for one who plans to breed true; but at last asserts that he is a coward because he is low class (III. v. 117–19). I am not at all inclined to deny that the play is puzzling, indeed I expect the first spectators were rather puzzled, but I expect we can estimate the author's intention by considering the audience he was trying to work upon. Surely, for a predominantly artisan audience, the effect of the two contradictory sets of insinuations by Bosola is to make the genetic claims of titled persons absurd; the audience would laugh. It might be argued that his earlier democratic remarks are outweighed by his later class insults, even though both are known to be dictated by crude plots; but as he himself is known to be a poor man on the make his later assertion of class dogma is not likely to be thought the more sincere of the two, especially as it begins the process of tormenting the duchess, by a variety of lies, into a repentant death. Bosola then becomes ridiculous in an almost homely way, because his employers refuse to pay him for his crimes, so he repents, with considerable relief naturally, and from now on he treats Antonio with an earnest respect, except that he kills him by mistake. The sequence could not be enjoyed for its imagery or its shuddering vision of hell or anything else except its sheer intelligence and gift of the gab as a plain old high-thinking Bernard Shaw discussion drama.

PART II:

Shakespeare and the spirits

CHAPTER 9

Elizabethan spirits

(FRANCES YATES, *THE OCCULT PHILOSOPHY IN THE
ELIZABETHAN AGE*, 1979)

Something badly needed has got left out from the great structure
that Dame Frances Yates has been building as an exposition of her
view of the occult tradition. I have felt it since her book on Bruno
(1964),[1] though I am ill-equipped to complain. Still, my ideas
derive from a critic who had something of her own range of knowledge, and she seems to ignore his views, so I may speak up.

C. S. Lewis, in the first chapter of his survey of English sixteenth-
century literature (1954), said that earlier writers had treated magic
as fanciful and remote, but in this period they felt it might be going
on in the next street; and one reason was a thing they surprisingly
called 'Platonism': 'the doctrine that the region between earth and
moon is crowded with airy creatures who are capable of fertile
unions with our own species'.[2] Another reason for feeling at home
with the spirits was the doctrine 'that the invisible population of the
universe includes a whole crowd of beings who might almost be
called theologically neutral'.[3] That is, they die like the beasts, and
never come before the Judgment Seat; they are 'far from Heaven,
and safe from Hell'.[4] They are not *morally* neutral, being a mixture of
good and bad like ourselves: but they are not angels or devils,
permanently engaged in a Manichaean battle, wearing the uniform
either of God or Satan.[5] Clearly, this makes them likely to be useful
to us, perhaps even to tell the secrets of nature, if we have something
to offer in return. It is an important change. But Dame Frances will
have none of it, and so she does not mention the names of Puck or
Ariel.

Lewis used his dubious phrase about neutrality to introduce the
idea, I think, because the full doctrine is seldom stated. It would be

considered heretical, and would anyhow be shocking: but the feeling of it, or an approach to it, is widespread in the period. One of the chief reasons for wanting some kind of belief in Middle Spirits was the reverence felt for the newly recovered classics, together with the belief, often expressed, that it would be impudent to deny experiences which had once been generally attested. Apollo could not have been nothing, and it was very disagreeable to believe him a devil. It was clear that he had lasted a long time, say two thousand years, and pretty certain that he was now dead; to believe he had been a Middle Spirit fitted very well. It would be unfitting if he were summoned to the Day of Judgment, so the educated tended to assume that this would not happen. Cornelius Agrippa does not face the question, but he was a very adroit writer who maintains a splendid ease, considering how likely he was to be burnt alive; and maybe, if he *had* faced it, his treatise [*De occulta philosophia libri tres*] would not have been available in ten of the Cambridge College libraries, including Marlowe's, when Marlowe was up.[6]

The only man in the period who supports it thoroughly, I think, is Paracelsus, a roving magic doctor who did not publish the *De Nymphis* during his lifetime. But it was printed at Basle [in 1567] while Marlowe and Shakespeare were boys, first in German as the author had demanded, and two years later in Latin; and, though he had defied the doctors' organisations, his writing had continued to be searched for secret cures. A huge complete edition of them was published in Amsterdam from 1590 onwards, which proves that there had been an interest in the earlier texts. A grand house in London always had a library, if only for show, to which readers of Latin were admitted if properly introduced. And the *De Nymphis* is the only at all readable thing ever written by Paracelsus: only about five thousand words, and packed full of anecdotes which became sources for later German romantic authors. Some friends would be likely to put Marlowe onto reading this, even granting that he did not read much in Latin after leaving college.

Paracelsus[7] begins by saying that Middle Spirits are not spirits at all, having bodies made of more subtle kinds of matter than ours, but adds that a creature who can pass through a stone wall is bound to be called a spirit, and it is no use quarrelling with common language. However, all creatures with material bodies will eventually die, so if we find them around they must be capable of breeding, though not often as they are long-lived: whereas the angels and fallen angels, being real spirits and totally immortal, must be totally incapable of breeding, or they would clutter the place up.

A number of consequences follow from this, providing useful tests. For example, Middle Spirits can move at great speeds, but angels and devils do not really live in space, so they can poke into it anywhere, as if at an infinite speed. Also there are practical consequences. Devils can easily be induced to help men, because they want to corrupt them: but Middle Spirits do not consider that we have much to offer. Here there is a loophole: Middle Spirits are indignant at being rejected from Heaven, and want to go there, and Paracelsus agrees that it is very queer of God to have allowed humans to enter Heaven, but not these greatly superior beings. Of course, the acts of God are often beyond our understanding. But if a nymph has a proper marriage with a human man, she at once acquires an immortal soul, just as a woman marrying an American gets an American passport. Paracelsus earnestly warns his younger readers that it is dangerous to jilt a nymph: there have been several well-known cases where the result has been murder. And one cannot blame the nymph, he reflects: a human woman has no business to do it – what has she got to lose? – but a nymph has an infinite amount to lose. Undine and Melusina were already familiar. If Marlowe read this, he would at once feel that a passionate friendship between males must at least allow of a sacrifice in the same field. At any rate, the *De Nymphis* is enough to justify the assertion of C. S. Lewis.[8]

Perhaps Dame Frances would say that Paracelsus was being facetious. And it is agreed, after an exhausting day in the surgery (leaving him, as an honest man, anxious whether he had done good or harm), he would drink after his dinner, since he rejected sex, and dictate theories, getting sillier as the evening wore on. He might have a good reason for dictating the *De Nymphis*, even if he thought it nonsense: his patients were terrified of having devils inside them, and so he pretended the devils were far away. He also believed that their bodies could not even tick over normally without good spirits working for them, but he may have found that it did no good to tell them so. It has been suggested that he was merely echoing the beliefs of the miners, to whom he gave a good deal of time, inventing industrial disease to describe their troubles [in *Von der Bergsucht und andern Bergkrankheiten drei Bücher*]; but he also liked to insist that the learned professors were all wrong, and that the common opinion was more sensible. His assertions might be derived from the miners and yet be sincere. But he also argues from these beliefs, arriving at his own conclusions. In more specialist works, he also announced belief in independent resident spirits, themselves sometimes needing medical treatment, and governed by an 'archeus' for each region, like the mayor of a city subject to a central government. The archeus of the belly is the chief of them, but with no supreme power. This is a splendid insight and, as I understand, justified by modern medicine, though it can have been of no use in his time for a cure. He is imagining the internal affairs of the body as a reasonable system, just sufficiently democratic. He is not peculiar here: we are echoing the same deep confusion when we speak of aeroplane 'spirit' or to poisonous 'spirits of salt'. If you had shown one of the authors of the *Hermetica* magnified photographs of the germs of plague, with a full account of their behaviour, he would answer: 'Yes, that's just what I said – a very low form of spirit.' Apollo, who was the god of plague, was a spirit too, of a higher grade. All spirits, including men, had regular reincarnations, as animals or angels, up or down the scale: so for a pagan there was no problem about it. For a Christian trying to be 'syncretist' about pagan belief, this might make it slightly easier, though still a problem, to think that Middle Spirits, like animals, did not have to attend the Last Judgment.

The rigid distinction between angels and Middle Spirits, one being spiritual, the other material, which Paracelsus treats so entertainingly, is firmly present in Aquinas, at least so far as he insists that angels, having no senses, can have no direct means of knowledge whatever. Aquinas therefore invents something very like the pre-established harmony of Leibnitz, who ascribed it to mankind: the only relation between the minds of angels and devils and the world around them, which in our case is secured by the senses, is in theirs dependent upon innumerable miracles perpetually done by God.[9] This is clearly a tiresome theory, because for all we can tell the senses may be a miracle for us too, and once the belief in Middle Spirits had been forbidden there was no need to make a great stir early in the century by insisting that there could be no knowledge for any creature without the senses (obviously, it has become very unusual to accept Aquinas on the point); and this inclined people to suppose that angels were made of a subtle kind of matter, as indeed Augustine had thought. When Milton in *Paradise Lost* said this about angels he was not considered shocking at all.[10] But the change reflected back on those people who still believed in Middle Spirits (a few philosophers, and most of the countryside): it had now become hard to tell the difference between them and devils. King James in his *Daemonologie* (1597) is indignant at the idea of devils who live in the storm-clouds: probably he felt that this practically lets you get back to believing in the pagan demigods.[11] The familiar of Faust in the original German has never been to hell at all, and complains at having to live in the storm-clouds: of course the censor insisted upon altering this for the English translation. 'Occult' or no, there was quite a lot of busy discussion going on about spirits in the sixteenth century.[12]

Thus I can only give rather weak evidence for the belief that the Middle Spirits died like beasts. To suppose that any responsible creature could escape God's judgment was felt as radically bad, and perhaps could only be printed in Basle or Amsterdam. Paracelsus was reckless, and seldom tried to get his works printed, whereas Agrippa was careful about it. They both died in their forties, when the brief time of intellectual freedom was over, because both sides in the Wars of Religion had closed their ranks. Probably C. S. Lewis could have produced other examples. However, I have a good reference from Reginald Scot: his *Discoverie of Witchcraft* (1584) is mainly a denunciation of the witch-burners, but he adds an appendix *A Discourse concerning Devils and Spirits*, having a broad interest in the subject. He remarks that the father [Fazio] of the famous [Girolamo] Cardan (himself born in 1600, so we are back in the springtime of the movement) had a spirit in his power for many years, and the spirit would still pay visits after it had been released, sometimes bringing its friends, but then it usually told lies. 'They said that their soules (and ours also) died with their bodies.' Scot treats this evidence as contemptible, but Cardan was famous for telling truth – probably old Cardan had some kind of planchette.[13]

More than a century later, the belief is firmly expressed in *The Secret Commonwealth* by Robert Kirk (1691), a Scots witness and believer, who says: 'They are not of such stuff that they can come before God; they are far from Heaven, and safe from Hell.'[14] So the belief had hung on in Scotland, more than England. It is implied in some of the Border Ballads, and even in the legends of *The Celtic Twilight*, collected by Yeats and his friends in Ireland. So it was fairly widespread: but what we need here is evidence from London in 1590–1600.

General readiness to believe in Middle Spirits does seem to have collapsed by then, but the belief in changelings was quite sturdy: usually doubted by men, maybe, but forced upon them as practical behaviour by wives, midwives, and nurses. The recent book by A. L. Rowse upon Simon Forman, a popular and successful medical practitioner, shows him treating the belief as a matter of course.[15] To discover that your baby is a moron is a slow, painful process, and then men cannot feel it decent to interfere with any palliation for the mother such as letting her be told that her real child is being much appreciated among the fairies. The trouble is that it has lost its chance of Heaven, but it will live unusually long. This comfort was often enough. It made baby-watching a very responsible business, and probably increased the unhealthy shutting of windows, because the fairies flew in there, but to speak against it would be callous. If the baby had been stolen by devils, that would be horrible, and there could be no connivance in the belief. This proves, I submit, that it was still usually accepted, if only in a half-way manner.

The whole movement, as Dame Frances has done so much to make clear, started with the translation of the *Hermetica* from Greek to Latin by Ficino, in 1463, so that Cosimo de' Medici might read it before he died. The manuscript had recently been fetched in from Greece, and was widely believed to be by an Egyptian tutor of Moses: it deserved reverence.[16] It is now dated at about AD 250 and ascribed to a group of pious people in Alexandria, perhaps helping at the hospital there as the attitude is so medical, much influenced by Plato but opposed to Christianity. It expresses quite opposite views on at least one topic, sometimes praising love and nature, sometimes asceticism: so the authors wrote independently. But they all carry the same tone of feeling. They are full of information about spirits, and on the whole give a strong warning against them; a reasoning man should try to rise above them, though they enter the most intimate parts of his body. It is readily admitted that they are 'both good and bad in their natures': the Manichaean separation had not yet started.

One long document had been translated early into Latin and survives only in that form; it was known in the Middle Ages, and considered very shocking. Hermes is addressing the father of medicine (this is 'Asclepius III'), and tells him how wonderful it was that man, though of modest station, has such great powers; he is the fashioner of the gods who dwell in temples. 'Thus man not only receives the light of divine life, but gives it also; he not only makes his way upward to God, but he even fashions gods.'[17] 'Do you mean statues, Trismegistus?' asks the doctor timidly, and is rebuked: these statues really do make prophecies and heal or inflict diseases. Then there is a long denunciation of Christians, who despise the creation; if they win, only bad spirits will remain around (pp. 24–6). After this he speaks again of the delightful experience of training up a spirit to be a god. Our ancestors had to learn gradually: 'being unable to make souls, they invoked the souls of daemons, and implanted them in the statues by means of certain holy and sacred rites'.[18] Of course the spirits of great men may also be valuable here [by way of euhemerisation]: both Hermes and Asclepius, it turns out, have grandfathers of the same name who preside over temples, but their consciousness is in Heaven; only their influence performs the miracles in the temples (p. 37).

I am using the translation of Walter Scott, whom Dame Frances describes sadly as too free;[19] he is excluded from her indexes. She translates the above sentences as 'not only does he receive life, but he gives it in his turn. Not only does he progress towards God, but he *makes gods*.' And: 'after having evoked the souls of demons or angels, they introduced these into their idols ... ' (This is in her *Bruno*.)[20] It is true that the Latin says 'daemons or angels' [*daemonum vel angelorum*], but this is nonsense: clearly an angel would not be enlightened by being used in this way.[21] Probably the translator hoped that the phrase would give an impression of a neutral spirit, 'both good and bad' like ourselves, which by this date (perhaps 360, Scott thinks)[22] had become hard to recapture. The Latin for the earlier sentence is: *non solum inluminantur, verum etiam inluminant, nec solum ad deum proficit, verum etiam conformat deos.* So there is no doubt that the priests 'enlighten' an at first dubious imp; till now, his highest mental flight has been some practical joke, but soon he will be responsible and benevolent, and will sound like it too. When Dame Frances summarises the passage for her new book, she says it describes 'how the Egyptians attracted celestial influences into the statues of their gods' (p. 45), and reports that Agrippa believed these statues were worked by number-magic, cabalistic presumably.[23] No doubt: but what Hermes himself said, when the doctor asked him, is that the imp would be coaxed to stay by jewels and scents: 'And would you know why frequent sacrifices are offered to do them pleasure, with hymns and praises and concord of sweet sounds that imitate heaven's harmony? These things are done to the end that, gladdened by the oft-repeated worship, the heavenly beings who have been enticed into the images may continue through long ages to acquiesce in the companionship of men.' And really they can do a great deal: they 'assist, like loving kinsmen, in the affairs of men',[24] whereas the gods that push the stars round pay no attention.

A comparison to the education of a prince is hard to avoid and was probably intended. He too cannot be beaten so he has to be coaxed: flattery and sweets if he behaves tolerably, and pained silence when he does not, and an appeal to his vanity all the time. There are painful failures, but it is remarkable how often the technique succeeds. It shows, feels Hermes, that the Cosmos is really good. The doctor is rather startled to hear this, and no doubt Hermes assumed that man must handle it properly to get good results. '[Y]ou may well hold man to be a marvel; he surpasses all other creatures.'[25] One wants to know how old this priest is, and what has really happened in his temple. It is like putting up a pigeon-loft, and finding that some pigeons come of their own accord (though that may lead to trouble with the neighbours). The passage might well give encouragement, around 1500, to the study of nature.

But any such sympathy depends upon *not* believing that all spirits are either angels or devils, all drilled and in uniform and for ever at war and under direct orders either from God or Satan. If you believe in the Principle of Plenitude, or Great Chain of Being – that is, believe that God has caused life wherever there is room – it seems plain that there is room for life between ourselves and Heaven; and it would be against the principle if these creatures were yet more enslaved than ourselves. That military concept is essentially Manichaean; and Aquinas, who is anti-Manichee, did actually resist it, though in moderate terms. The Platonists, he says,[26] maintained that all the gods were good, whereas some of the daemons were good and some bad; and by daemons they meant the intellectual substances which are beneath the lunar sphere, yet higher than men in the order of Nature. 'Nor is this opinion to be rejected as contrary to faith', because God rules everything through the angels. Consequently, he goes on with his odd detachment, 'there is nothing to prevent us from saying that the lower angels were divinely set aside for presiding over the lower bodies'. This is far short of saying that the Middle Spirits can interbreed with mankind, also never come to judgment, also are sometimes both good and bad: but surely it should relieve some of the anxiety which must lie behind the campaign of Dame Frances. It would be hard to lay down how low a lower angel might get; and no one supposes that the imp seduced by Hermes committed an actual sin.

Coming now to Cornelius Agrippa, one should realise that he was a cautious writer, and had reason to be: dying in bed was an achievement, and so was his wide acceptance in the Cambridge College Libraries. To print his spoof-book [*De incertitudine et vanitate scientiarum*, 1531], saying that *no* branch of learning was any good, while not actually implying that magic was any worse than physics or history, shortly *before* he finally printed his great treatise on magic [*De occulta philosophia*, 1533], was an inspiration:[27] but a more placid competence had already taught him that the dons would like a summary of what other people had thought, particularly the Byzantine authors of around AD 1000, not otherwise well known. He hardly ever expresses his own opinion, though he sometimes allows it to emerge. We do not reach the spirits till his third and final Book [of *De Occulta Philosophia*], and must begin it by reading many chapters of determined piety. At last he explains that among his authorities the magicians, as apart from the theologians, 'established Angels as Ministers for the disposing of these things which are below ... Hence the gods of the Woods ... Satyrs ... Nymphs of the Sea ... the Graces, the Genii, Hobgoblins and such like ... and they who have written the Chronicles of the Danes and Norwegians, do testifie that spirits of diverse kinds in those regions are subject to mens commands; moreover some of these to be corporeall and mortall, whose bodies are begotten and dy, yet to be long lived is the opinion of the Egyptians and Platonists, and especially approved by *Proclus*. *Plutarch* also ... affirm[s] the same ... ' This is the English version of 1651, by J. F. (chapter 16).[28] Augustine says that he does not believe angels have no matter, but allows them an airy matter. Psellus thought that the nature of spirits is not without a body, but that the angels and devils are without matter (p. 402). So it goes on till in chapter 32 Agrippa appears to feel he may speak in person, though with a let-out to some unnamed previous occasion: 'There is moreover as hath before been said, a certain kind of spirits not so noxious, but most neer to men, so that they are even affected with humane passions, and many of these delight in mans society ... He therefore that will call them, may easily doe it in the places where their abode is, by alluring them with sweet fumes, with pleasant sounds, and by such instruments as are made of the guts of certain animals' (p. 450). He has just named these creatures by saying: 'the Fairies, and hobgoblins inhabit champian fields; the *Naiades* fountains ... the *Nymphs* marshes, and ponds ... ' Surely it would surprise a pagan nymph, in her horse-pond, if she were summoned to a Christian judgment? It is hard to believe that Agrippa expected that. He is frankly conscious of the state of public opinion, of what it will let him say. Soon after this he is saying with relief: 'all now believe that *Merline*, a British prophet, was the son of a Spirit, and born of a virgin' (p. 453). Of course he could not be the son of a devil – that is agreed. It is at least a step towards accepting Middle Spirits.

Agrippa is much more hopeful than the *Hermetica* about these spirits, saying in a splendid passage that they may in their three grades bring inspiration to a technician or an artist or a philosopher, and Dame Frances gives this due prominence (*Occult Philosophy*, p. 53). But she spells them as 'demons' not as 'daemons'. The *OED* makes clear that English writers in the sixteenth and seventeenth centuries were conscious that a 'daemon' in Plato is quite different from a 'demon' in a sermon, and used the spellings for the distinction; it was given up in the eighteenth century, perhaps out of distaste for pedantry, and perhaps Dame Frances feels the same.[29] So she quotes Milton as confessing, in 'Il Penseroso' (lines 93–4), that he has some contact, during his reading at night, with 'those Demons that are found ... underground'.[30] Milton printed 'daemons', and had mentioned the spirit of Plato just before; he would be indignant at this misspelling, regarding it as typical of the ignorant slander by which he was persecuted. And I think the habit may be shown to mislead Dame Frances herself, in the book now under review. She is saying that the cabala is very important, in Agrippa's scheme, as 'a guarantee of safety' against evil powers. 'The three stages of inspired melancholy described by Agrippa would seem to be much in need of such protection since the inspiration is definitely said to be of a demonic nature' (pp. 55–6). But at least the daemons of the third stage, who tell you about God, are plainly meant to be of the highest goodness and purity. Of course, bad spirits often do break into a seance, and if the pitiful cabalist number-magic helps to keep them out, it had better be used: but this gives no excuse for suspecting the noble daemons themselves. In effect, Dame Frances adopts the position of Calvin, who thought them simply devils, though she can hardly intend to.

This book says several times that Agrippa and Bruno and such characters wanted to give Christianity greater power by magic, without discussing what kind of power. It does seem an improvement; in her book about Bruno she appears shocked at his corruption (whereas he was plainly an excessively innocent man) whenever he thinks of making his magic any use. Well, the Lord's Prayer says, 'Give us this day our daily bread', a definitely materialist attempt to secure gain, and there has probably never been a war in Christendom in which the priests on both sides did not pray God for (in effect) the death of the opposing troops in battle. The moral position of the Winter King in Bohemia [Frederick V], ancestor of our royal house, becomes at least decent if he had expected to win by magic. The pacifist doctrine is hard to carry out, but need not be handled as badly as he handled it. When he accepted the crown he put himself in a military situation, but after one defeat he left in his carriage, and his supporters were to suffer. If this was one of the decisive cases where magic failed to work, he looks just a bit better. No such considerations ever occur to Dame Frances, when she praises him in *The Rosicrucian Enlightenment* (London: Routledge and Kegan Paul, 1972).

The end of the chapter on Agrippa says: 'Though the genuine Hebrew cabalist might be shocked by Agrippa's interpretation of cabala solely as white magic, yet this interpretation served a purpose in fortifying man for intellectual and spiritual endeavour' (p. 47). It 'fortified' him by giving insurance against being caught by devils and sent to Hell; she has just explained that, and no doubt a real cabalist might be 'shocked' because his science was meant to teach deep truths about God. But Agrippa does not seem under strain when he says it is easy to raise a nymph in a water-meadow, and gives brief instructions for it; nor does he mention any high purpose there, intellectual or spiritual. He seems to assume that anyone would like to do it. Considering the fierceness of his opponents, it was only sensible to make the standard claims for his line of study, but he does not regard himself as perpetually struggling against devils.

Indeed, one might feel in more immediate danger from the horseplay of the Middle Spirits. Scot remarks that people used to be afraid of Robin Goodfellow (but now they are only afraid of witches, he goes on), and Robin had never been thought a killer. It is rather a hard matter to assess. 'They laugh and are glad and are terrible', says *The Immortal Hour*. 'And they dwell in the hills, the hollow hills.'[31] It is good poetry, but Robin [i.e. Puck in *MND*] at least was a more homely kind of spirit. Jan Kott, in *Shakespeare our Contemporary*, argued at length that he was a devil, and found direct proof of it when the players, running in terror from Bottom and his ass' head, tear their clothes on the brambles. Kott has set out to be grim and manly, forcing his readers to recognise the dire truth, but here he has to become quaintly maidenly: 'Oh, their poor jerkins! I can't bear to think of it.'[32] Shakespeare would consider this reaction unsoldierly: but one may suspect that he did not himself enjoy the horseplay which is so prominent in his earlier plays, and gave it up when he could afford to. The story, in any case, presumes that Puck is not malignant. Oberon is at first angry enough with his wife to intend a painful humiliation. He says: 'Wake when some vile thing is near' (II. ii. 33). Puck is presumed to stage-manage what happens next, and he presents to her the translated Bottom, so Oberon gets the Indian changeling and a small bit of revenge, all he really needed, without upsetting her. And at the end, as Puck says, 'The man shall hath his mare again, and all shall be well' (III. ii. 463). It was rather hard for the playwright to keep the story from appearing too soft. Anyhow, to say that Puck and Oberon are devils (or, for that matter, angels) is mere misreading.[33]

Teachers usually have a down on horseplay, having been swots when at school and being exposed to the rough young afterwards. I feel with my colleagues there entirely. I would greatly dislike having to engage in horseplay, let alone be horseplayed upon. But it is no use talking as if only low-class criminals behaved like this: within living memory, the chief danger at the universities was from young men who were heirs to titles. Nor is such behaviour always hated by people who feel they cannot afford it: towards the end of the career of Faust, Marlowe calls an indignation-meeting of people who think he has fooled them, and even these characters, when an indignant man tells how the horse he had bought melted into the village horse-pond, cry out all together: 'O brave doctor' (IV. v. 41). He is a very popular character in the German Faust-book too, especially in the additions made during the first year, when the book had succeeded. The reactions of such people, even if muddle-headed, are in their way generous-minded, and one does not really become more spiritual by calling them the work of the Devil.

The Tempest is more cautious than the *Dream*, having to be shown before James (indeed, it might be said, in partial defence of Jan Kott, that Shakespeare was teasing his audience in the *Dream*, allowing hints that Puck was a devil, before making clear that he wasn't). Ariel is so much a nature-spirit that he positively wants to dissolve into the more handsome parts of nature, and renounce all contact with mankind. But he likes playing practical jokes (both he and Puck are obeying their masters, and help on the plot by it, but they do it with evident pleasure); and he is lying sanctimoniously when he pretends to be obeying the supreme powers, and not a human magician. For their foul deeds, he tells the villains:

> The powers, delaying, not forgetting, have
> Incens'd the seas and shores, yea, all the creatures,
> Against your peace. (III. iii. 73–5)

Prospero praises him afterwards as a good actor who said all that he was told to. He is, in fact, clearly another Middle Spirit, and not an angel. And surely nobody says he is a devil.

I am not maintaining that Dame Frances says anything wrong here: she merely ignores the characters who do not fit her account. But these ones are usually considered important elements in the two plays. The fairies who really do fit her account are those of the *Merry Wives*. They are related to the Virgin Queen 'through their loyalty and through their fervent defence of chastity' (p. 148). Well, the story is that the queen wanted to see Falstaff in love, and the Bard turned out this play very rapidly; such, then, is the impression it made at the time. Giving the queen precisely what would please her need not be 'occult'. We are also told, what seems a support for the theory, that these fairies took to pinching because the Vestal herself was accustomed to pinch the sluts who waited upon her, as a punishment for their foulness, so that she would accept this detail as a simple compliment. Dame Frances calls these fairies 'imagery' (p. 148), as if they were merely allegorical: but there seems no reason why she should not agree with Aquinas and accept such beings as the very lowest grade of angel. Still, if Puck may count as a fairy, it is hard to say that all the fairies are devoted to chastity, considering that he gave Titania a craving for Bottom.[34]

A number of interesting pictures in the book are intended to illustrate the passage in Agrippa (largely quoted on her page 53) which says that discovery and inspiration are often produced by daemons, and that they do it by giving a trance-like melancholy, as in the great engraving by Dürer (who could have seen an earlier version of the book in manuscript). I think she proves that [George] Chapman [in *Shadow of Night*] had read this impressive passage, but if the artists other than Dürer were trying to represent such a melancholy they failed. At least, the attempt to capture the memorial bust of Shakespeare goes too far. She says that 'the fixed gaze, the trance-like expression, the half-open mouth' showed him as one who never blotted a line because he wrote when entranced (p. 162). Surely the air of surprised rueful uneasiness, as of one awaiting the next spasm deep within, should also be considered. I suggest he has just come from a city banquet, with a series of grand courses and a round of wines, and is wondering whether he will keep it down. He has started writing to his doctor but now it seems too late. And yet he keeps a certain assurance: 'I'll be all right if I'm not joggled', he may be saying to some anxious lady. There is a suggestion of the later Evelyn Waugh.

Still, though the method can produce boss shots, the sturdy indifference to received opinion, the basic earnestness and the eye open to the whole scene, allow her to come out with important judgments. Marlowe's *Dr Faustus*, as it now stands, is not only disgusting but a betrayal of all he might be expected to stand for: in effect, it is a vote to bring the witch-burnings and their attendant corruption to England. It ought not to be praised with an air of simpering connivance, and I hope very much that Dame Frances will affect opinion there.[35] But she is unjust when she tries to show that other plays by Marlowe are similar. Marlowe does not whitewash Edward II, but we are expected to feel sorry for him, and indignant with his murderers, by the time he is tortured to death at the end. Marlowe has evidently studied the sources about Tamburlaine: he was a ruthless conqueror, but a man of taste – at least, his architecture was admired. The chief emphasis is on the strangeness of such a man. If you recognise the fondness for horseplay of the Elizabethans, you regard the Jew of Malta as a kind of Punch, though of course you are pleased to have him stopped at the end. The B-text of *Dr Faustus*, the worst of which always gets printed now as part of Marlowe's play, builds up to a laborious but powerful piece of sadism intended to make the audience hate Faust and gloat over his agony as he approaches his eternal torture. No other play by Marlowe ends like this at all. One can imagine a travelled expert on the subject assuring his stay-at-home audience that, though of course nothing could touch the real thing, *Dr Faustus* came far nearer than any other play to catching the atmosphere of a witch-burning.

I think, and hope to prove, that the A-text is right, and all the nastiness was added to Marlowe's play after he had been murdered by government spies (not for that purpose, but it might turn out convenient).[36] [See *Faustus and the Censor: The English Faust-book and Marlowe's 'Doctor Faustus'*, ed. John Henry Jones, Oxford: Basil Blackwell, 1987.] A play needs a plot, and Marlowe made Faust try to escape Hell by becoming a Middle Spirit; he bought the help of Mephistophelis, who was a Middle Spirit, not a devil, by promising him his immortal soul. Neither of them dare say this because the Devil would overhear, but the Chorus to Act II, which is mysteriously missing, explained what they were hinting at; a Chorus was needed because the Devil could not overhear it. By the end of Act II Faust is already certain that he has been cheated, and is damned; he takes to horseplay to stave off his terrors; but after his terrible final speech denouncing Hell he cries 'Ah, Mephistophelis', and dies in his friend's arms with ecstasy, finding that his plan has worked after all. Of course the censors could not realise from the script how the play would be produced, and when they found in 1590 that the audience were delighted at the escape of Faust they clamped down on it, demanding total silence, until a thoroughly sadistic version had been prepared for 1594. The story of Marlowe's version did not seem pointlessly improbable, because it was a means of saying to the audience: 'You and I dare not say what we think, living as we do under a censorship, just like these characters.' It was what Marlowe would want to do next, after *The Jew of Malta*, and no wonder the government never forgave him.

However, the important thing is to recognise, as Dame Frances does, and as all our moral critics seem unable to do (although Bernard Shaw could),[37] that the B-text of *Dr Faustus* is disgusting, and had a harmful political intention. If one is allowed to feel this, it is fairly easy to recognise that the bad parts are not by Marlowe.

CHAPTER 10

The spirits of the 'Dream'

I

I am aiming towards a reconstruction of what the first audiences of Elizabethan plays thought of Marlowe's *Dr Faustus*, because there is clearly something wrong with the two surviving texts; so I have to estimate what the first audiences would think about magicians. The view of the forces of nature presented in the *Dream* is majestic and profound, and the theme had never before been treated with such grace and poetry; but probably, so far from baffling the first spectators, it seemed rather old-hat when it was new, a harking back to an earlier theatrical fashion. Also what I have to say about it can be said quite briefly. But I need to make it prominent in my scheme because the earlier surviving examples are not so impressive, though equally good as evidence about the audiences. First I must give some report of the recent studies on the magicians of the sixteenth century, which are bound to alter our reading of its literature; but I should avoid repeating at length what is already known from works carrying more authority. An attempt to pick out the decisive points at issue should be more within my range.

The crucial question, granting that there are spirits of more than one kind, and the Bible gave pretty unbreakable support for angels and devils, was whether there are neutral spirits, not wearing the uniform either of God or Satan. And if so, of course, whether we can get on comparatively workaday terms with them. It would be excessive to say, as some experts did, that these Middle Spirits are 'neither good nor bad'; they are merely like ourselves. Taking a more open-eyed view of the classics, as well as getting more texts to read, and making a wide variety of new contacts with societies outside Christendom, one found a surprisingly broad agreement with what unregenerate Christians had never been successfully prevented from saying. A man building a bridge over a river, almost anywhere at any time, would think it sensible to pay his respects to the river-god, and not feel surprised if he made difficulties; but only very bad behaviour from a river-god would make you suspect that he was even *possessed* by a devil, let alone that he *was* one. The Christian authorities while struggling to stamp out paganism naturally rejected all such middling belief; but it left them in a very Manichaean position, practically with two armies equipped and deployed by two equally powerful gods. Aquinas, who was against being Manichaean, clearly does not like this situation, but he sees no way to avoid it; except by saying, as if to nasty children: 'Why, but *of course* Satan can only do what God lets him'. There was never a strong Christian argument against the existence of Middle Spirits; the point was rather that they ought not to be worshipped, and always received worship when believed in. The churches never yielded on the matter all through the sixteenth century, and this time they were lucky; their resistance finally merged into a general common-sense rejection of spirits. And yet, revival of the belief in spirits coincided with the unique West-European breakthrough into genuine science, which must always remain a matter for curiosity. The feeling that you can *deal with* nature, as an explorer in the Maritime Expansion would feel sure he could deal with the natives wherever he beached, learning their language so fast that the process need not be recorded – surely this must have been an essential factor. The breakthrough in chemistry comes too late to be relevant, but in medicine the contact was always close. A broken bone heals of its own accord; this is an astonishing thing, and to thank a spirit for coming is only decent; but the spirit isn't sensible, and a reasoning man has to tie the splint right, or the bone will heal crooked. If God simply chose to make the bone heal crooked, so as to punish somebody, that is not open to negotiation. A good deal of magic, I must not deny, claimed not to deal with spirits at all, but offered a bogus scientific technique for dealing with nature. This attracted genuine believers, but it was often used merely as a protection against being burned alive for dealing with spirits; Aquinas indeed made a joke against them, saying: 'What are your *spells* then? Why write, if there is no one who reads?' This seems to me a hopelessly infertile side of magic; indeed, I began reading the magicians hoping to find more anecdotes about spirits such as those that bubble up in the mind of Shakespeare for the *Dream*. But they are very rare. It is not that they all failed to make contact with spirits; Dr Dee met them, or his medium did, and the results were astonishingly like a modern seance. The record was published by an enemy under Charles II, and may have been forged, as his supporters say, but even so they are a wonderful prevision of a modern seance.[1] Plainly this is no good for us; we need the spirits to be different from ourselves. But Dr William Gilbert, who wrote the book on the *Magnet* (1600), a very realistic and practical doctor, who for years had kept open house in London for maritime explorers – he was certain that the whole earth is a living creature, and not at all shy about saying so. The belief was not whimsical in the way it is expected to be now.[2]

This movement was not at all new. In 1463, Marsilio Ficino (1433–99) was settling down in Florence to translate Plato, but Cosimo de' Medici, who was dying, begged him for the ancient wisdom of Hermes Trismegistus, a manuscript recently arrived from Macedonia. It was done in time, so he died happy, in 1464, and the first edition [*Mercurii Trismegisti Pimander*] came out in 1471 [running through sixteen editions by the end of the sixteenth century]. This was the *Corpus Hermeticum*; a Latin text of the *Asclepius* had long been available, and considered wicked, though perhaps (it was conceded) the worst part had been foisted in, during translation to Latin, by the flippant author [Lucius Apuleius of Madaura] of the *Golden Ass*. The first edition giving both together was delayed till 1507; by that time, the Borgia Pope Alexander VI had given powerful support to the magical tenets of Pico della Mirandola, mainly from the cabala.[3] There were various other sources for learned magic, but Hermes had been accepted into the church, as a forerunner, by Lactantius (third century), though rejected by Augustine (fourth), and both of them said he was immensely ancient, influencing perhaps Moses no less than Pythagoras.[4] As a means of reconciling the ancient sources he had to be taken seriously, and his stuff was warm-hearted and high-minded; very refreshing to read, as the Wars of Religion boiled up. Of course the views of the Borgia pope were rejected by both Reformation and Counter-Reformation, but outside opinion, both in the universities and the centres of government (not to think only of royalty), seems hardly to have cared what the clergy thought about magic; it was not their business to reject the practical experience of all mankind. No court would have rejected a man who actually could tell the future or make gold, and most were ready to test applicants. Even Queen Elizabeth paid visits to Dr Dee, though he had to take his project to the emperor [Rudolf II].[5] The libraries of about seven Cambridge colleges, in Marlowe's time, had copies of Ficino's translation of Hermes, and thirteen, a majority which included his own, had copies of the *De Occulta Philosophia* of Cornelius Agrippa.[6] As for the poor, they had retained their folklore, usually rather grim, even under occasional persecution. It is therefore absurd for modern experts (e.g. R. H. West in *The Invisible World*, 1939) to quote from the theological treatises of the time as giving the only beliefs that theatrical audiences could possibly have heard of (even the publisher of Hooker had to be subsidised, because so few would buy).[7]

Part of the mystery and majesty of the Hermes material, one may expect, came from its being written by a number of different authors, though all Greeks around AD 100 and 200. Some of them are ascetic, urging you to renounce the body so that your spirit may enter Heaven, some worship the secondary God, the world-spirit, and recommend love through the body (evidently there is an adequate supply of girl philosophers, and we hear nothing of the loves of Plato); if you are accustomed to 'syncretism', such a completely contradictory teacher is bound to feel profound. But they still have a certain likeness, an obviously good quality in common, though not an easy one to define; perhaps it is freedom from fear. Man was intended to be a kind of god, but he fell in love with God's creation; so in a sense he has fallen, but the entanglement is not much to his discredit; one might feel, it was rather dashing of him. The practical question is how soon one should renounce the world, and most people had better settle for several more lives on earth. There is a hell, for purification before rebirth, if necessary; but the long-term prospects are assumed to be bright:

Souls of the nature of creeping things change into things which dwell in the waters; souls which dwell in the waters change into beasts which dwell on land; souls which dwell on land change into birds of the air; souls which fly in air change into men. And human souls, when they have attained to a beginning of immortal life, change into daemons, and thereafter pass on into the choral dances of the gods; that is the crowning glory of the soul. (*Herm.* x. 7, pp. 191–3)[8]

(Coleridge at the end of 'Religious Musings' looks forward to it.) Here the daemons are better than ourselves, as in *Herm.* xvi, 17: 'the daemons are dependent on these spheres; and men are dependent on the daemons' (p. 273); but *Herm.* ix, an ascetic work expressing contempt for the world, regards them as usually bad, causers of disease. Clearly it is not necessary that these authors disagreed about fundamentals, but their difference about daemons may be a matter of definition. Beings may be invisible to us and ubiquitous, but of a different nature; and the 'daemons' of *Herm.* ix seem to be beings like cholera germs, each causing a specific disease. There might be others like the white corpuscles of the blood, always needed to do beneficent work inside the body, and yet be of subhuman status entirely unlike the daemons of *Herm.* x. I am not sure of which sort it is said:

Organic bodies cannot receive their generic forms save by the fiat of the gods; nor can they be fashioned into their individual shapes without the ministration of daemons. (*Asc.* 1. 5, p. 293 note 8)

In any case, these daemons are intimately concerned with our bodily machinery, and most of their work is beneficent.

There is no reason why the frequent mention of Egypt need be a fiction, and it is tempting to think of these pious communities, some of whom had renounced meat, as growing their vegetables in the suburbs of Alexandria, where there was a prominent medical school. Anyway, there is a passage about the beauty of the human body which excites conjecture:

Who is it that has shaped the heart into a cone, and joined the sinews to it, that has made the liver broad, and the spleen long, and hollowed out the cavities of the lungs, and made the belly capacious? ... See how many crafts have been employed on one material, and how many works of art are enclosed within one compass! All are beautiful, all true to measure, yet all are diverse from one another. (*Corpus Hermeticum*, v. 6–7, pp. 161–3)

Surely this must record a visit to the dissecting room of a teaching hospital. Medical students themselves would not be likely to talk in this way, but the battlefield and the torture-chamber are places where hardly anyone would do it. Besides, Asclepius, who is a prominent character in the dialogues, turns out to be the grandson of the Egyptian priest [also Asclepius] who invented medicine, and became a god (just as the Hermes who teaches him is the grandson of the god Hermes, or rather the Egyptian god Thoth). So this Asclepius, though not a doctor, has a strong medical connection; probably, before the dialogues were composed, the holy men were accustomed to be useful around the hospital. It would be particularly welcome and astonishing in 1500 to hear about the beauty of the liver and lights; and Paracelsus made a good deal of use of the book's medical ideas.

I am now to report the passage from *Asclepius* III which was found particularly shocking in the Middle Ages, being already available in Latin; and it is a great pleasure to use the English translation by (the recent) Walter Scott. Other scholars usually mention his work in a snide manner, ostensibly because he altered the order a good deal; but his text gives full information about the original order, and I think they are jealous because he writes so well.[9] He treats the final section *Asc.* III as by one author, an Egyptian priest, devout but not ascetic, 'attached to the temple of one of the local deities of the Fayum' (p. 77), writing in AD 270 or thereabouts. He would thus have witnessed what he pretends to prophesy, the destruction by Christian mobs of all that he reverences; I cannot see the need for this late date, as it must have been easy to prophesy, but anyhow we may presume that he has done what he describes, or rather has been an enthusiastic subordinate while the work was in progress.[10] In the text, Hermes is admitting Asclepius to full discipleship, and must therefore tell him a very grave secret about the god enshrined in the temple, which would excite mockery among the impious if it became known. First he explains how fortunate is the position of man, at least if he has been endowed with goodness:

it is ordained by God's will that man is not only better than all mortal beings, but also better than the gods, who are made wholly of immortal substance. (p. 337)

These are the gods of heaven, who watch over him with loving mercy. God made those ones, but, in the same way,

so man is the fashioner of the gods who dwell in temples and are content to have men for their neighbours ... Do you wonder at this Asclepius? Or do you too doubt it, as many do? – *Asc.* I am amazed, Trismegistus; but I gladly give assent to what you say, and deem man most highly blest, in that he has attained to such felicity. – *Trism.* Yes, you may well hold man to be a marvel; he surpasses all other creatures. (p. 339)[11]

It is like the French diplomat in Oscar Wilde, who tells Lady Windermere that the English language ought to be more widely known. The translation is exquisitely tender here, going up to the edge of admitting the absurdity of the situation without ever ceasing to be ingenuously noble-minded; whereas if you read the passage in

G. S. R. Mead, [a theosophist] who believed in it all, it is mere pomposity.[12] The medievals decided it was intentional satire, fobbed into his Latin translation by the scoffer Apuleius;[13] so Scott cannot be told that he is dragging in an irrelevant modern sophistication. And indeed the person speaking, whether the author felt remote from him or not, is bound to know that he is telling a secret which would appear shameful to the world, and might even ruin the temple. He is a bit long-winded, but this is not flat if it marks his anxiety to secure the loyalty of the disciple before blurting out the secret:

> Mankind is ever mindful of its own parentage and the source whence it had sprung, and steadfastly persists in following God's example; and consequently, just as the Father and Master made the gods in heaven eternal, that they might resemble him who made them, even so do men also fashion their gods in the likeness of their own aspect. – *Ascl.* Do you mean statues, Trismegistus? – *Trism.* Yes, Asclepius. See how even you give way to doubt! I mean statues, but statues living and conscious ... statues which have foreknowledge ... statues which inflict diseases and heal them, dispensing sorrow and joy according to men's deserts. (pp. 236, 339–41)

But now, just as we are agog to learn the technique, he starts a long diatribe [*logoi* 24–6] against the Christians who are going to destroy all such temples, and the entire happiness of Egypt, once the favoured of God. The Christians are blasphemers because they refuse to worship nature, who is God's first-born, 'whereby the will of God operates in that which he has made, ungrudgingly favouring man's welfare' (p. 343), but prefer death to life, making religion a burden and thus bringing continual bloodshed. Even those who like myself think this indictment largely true are bound to pause before committing themselves to a fraudulent oracle; the conflict of opinion could not be expressed more sharply. And yet, to an outsider, there is a complete trip-up in this drama; the temple really does contain a spirit (so what has he got to laugh at?); the terrible confession is merely that it is a low-class one.

At last we are told something about the procedure for the marvellous work of making gods, and here I need a rather long quotation (*Asc.* iii. 37):[14]

> Our ancestors were at first far astray from the truth about the gods; they had no belief in them, and gave no heed to worship and religion. But afterwards, they invented the art of making gods out of some material substance suited to the purpose. And to this invention they added a

supernatural force whereby the images might have power to work good or hurt, and combined it with the material substance; that is to say, being unable to make souls, they invoked the souls of daemons, and implanted them in the statues by means of certain holy and sacred rites. We have an instance in your grandfather, Asclepius, who was the first inventor of the art of healing, and to whom a temple has been dedicated in the Libyan mountain, near the shore of crocodiles. There lies the material man, that is, the body; but the rest of him, – or rather, the whole of him, if it is conscious life that constitutes a man's whole being, – has returned to heaven. And to this day he renders to the sick by his divine power all the aid which he used to render to them by his medicinal art. Again, there is my grandfather Hermes, whose name I bear. Has he not taken up his abode in his native city, which is named after him, and does he not help and safeguard all mortal men who come to him from every quarter? And Isis too, the wife of Osiris, – do we not know how many boons she confers when she is gracious, and how many men she harms when she is angry? For terrestrial and material gods are easily provoked to anger, inasmuch as they are made and put together by men out of both kinds of substance. (pp. 359–61)

Asclepius asks how the daemons are induced to stay, and is told that they are given herbs and stones and scents 'which have in them something divine' (p. 361), and frequent sacrifices, with hymns and praises and special music.

These things are done to that end that, gladdened by the oft-repeated worship, the heavenly beings who have been enticed into the images may continue through long ages to acquiesce in the companionship of men. Thus it is that man makes gods.

And you must not suppose, Asclepius, that the operations of the terrestrial gods are to no purpose. (pp. 361–3)

Realising that the disciple has received the confession without enthusiasm, the master is goaded into a yet more damaging one. As a matter of fact, he goes on, the high gods are no use; they just follow their general rules: the daemons are the only ones who answer prayers at all:

but these our gods on earth below see to things one by one, predict events by means of sacred lots and divination, foresee what is coming and render aid accordingly; they assist, like loving kinsmen, in the affairs of men. (p. 363)

The ancestors come in at the start, I suppose, as part of the apology; when they discovered that this technique would work, they did not realise how blasphemous it would come to seem. The Latin for my quotation actually begins 'Quoniam ergo' (p. 358): '*Because* they were so ignorant and irreligious, they stumbled upon ...' But this might be merely a bemused idea of the Latin translator; who also puts 'daemons or angels' [*daemonum vel angelorum*], here and elsewhere, for the Greek 'daemons', to show that it does not simply mean devils; obviously, the capture of an angel for the statue is not in question here.[15] And Hermes certainly does not mean, as some renderings suggest, that the trick was only played long ago; it is alarmingly close to them, when the two grandfathers are involved. I used to think, or take for granted, that they congratulate themselves on having genuine culture-heroes for their own temples; after all, there are other places in the *Hermetica* where heroes become daemons. But here it is insisted that the consciousness of the elder Asclepius has been promoted entirely to heaven, so all the healing done in his name, though it may succeed because of his influence, has to be planned by others. Still, the cub daemon who is his perpetual locum has submitted to training decently enough; not like that frightfully embarrassing one who pretends to be the Queen of Heaven.

What we are to think of here is the education of a legitimate prince, trying to coax the little beast into a command of decent impulses, though you aren't allowed to beat him; we can't complain that it is hard to imagine, because nowadays all education has become like that. The pouting daemon cannot be given sweets, but it is given smells and noises that it likes, and maybe some of the sacrifices to it operate like a whipping-boy, appealing to its pity. It looks as if this author had been on a priestly committee, in his temple, which kept an eye on how the new god was developing; he does not underrate the difficulties, but feels you can bring the trick off sufficiently often. (Maybe the dean who made the crucial decisions would need to be rather more disillusioned.) We get a glimpse of a busy well-intentioned life which can perhaps never be presented in a novel. I see no way to tell whether it is literal or humorous; in either case the author understands the subject intimately. Ficino went too far [in *De Vita coelitùs comparanda*] when he regarded the passage as a foreshadowing of Christianity, but he was right to feel that the intention is not disruptive or sarcastic.[16] Nothing could be better calculated to make one believe in these petulant, greedy, muddled, but not really stupid or ill-natured, elementals. Perhaps the trust of the Hermetics in nature derived from the welfare state, the fairly recent Pax Romana of the Empire, which as an economic machine, though it got steadily worse, lasted for a long time; but the author of *Asclepius*, III was expecting total destruction from Christians, so he is not too cosy.

Cornelius Agrippa (1486–1535) had written most of the *De Occulta Philosophia* by 1510, and was showing it to his intimates, though it was not printed till 1533, soon before he died.[17] It is a survey of magical opinion, quoting many authorities, mostly old; he seldom claims to have done anything himself, though he is not above being mysterious (III. 41):

I will not here relate those things which I have seen with mine eyes, and felt with mine hands, lest by the admirable wonderfulness and strangeness of them I should by the incredulous be accounted a liar.[18]

(I quote from the translation by John French, 1651, which is in the British Museum; I don't know of any other complete English translation. It is eloquent and sympathetic, but rather prone to write 'angels' for daemons, no doubt to avoid misunderstanding.)[19] The final words of the book are a powerful enticement to turn back:

Let no man be angry with me, if we have folded up the Truth of this Science with many Enigmas . . . for we have not hidden it from the wise, but from the wicked and ungodly, and have delivered it in such words which necessarily blind the foolish, and easily may admit the wise to the understanding of them. (p. 556)

It was much the most widely read of the books on magic; the only one we can be sure that Marlowe had skimmed through, and Shakespeare had heard quoted. The publication of *De Vanitate Scientiarum* (1526) no doubt helped to make the book permissible, as it seemed to confess that his magic was false; but the title is correct – the book laughs at all forms of learning, though they obviously can't all be renounced, and the occasions where he relents, admitting one part of knowledge to be real, are as frequent inside magic as outside.[20] It is only monks who are invariably absurd. One might think he was lucky to die in his bed, but the censors were very permissive just before the Reformation got going.

The book is divided into three parts, natural, celestial, and ceremonial (or religious) magic; and the spirits come only in the third. All religions are on the same level (though Agrippa remained faithful to the pope); there is a particularly impressive moment (III. 34, pp. 453–60) when he advises us to pray to daemons who were once men, as they tend to be more sympathetic; the saints, for example ('as concerning our holy heroes we believe that they excel in divine power'), and Pan used to be a man, too. He is sometimes clear about the distinction between daemons, who have bodies of a subtle kind, and wholly spiritual beings such as angels and devils; thus daemons can move at great speed, but angels are not really in any place, and can manifest themselves elsewhere immediately. But as a rule he is only quoting opinions; the most one can say is that he wishes to recommend the ones he gives strong authority. Thus in III. 16, he says positively that there are three kinds of spirits: the supercelestial, the celestial, who govern the world through the stars, and thirdly (p. 391) 'Ministers for the disposing of those things which are below':

some of these to be corporeall and mortall, whose bodies are begotten and dy, yet to be long lived is the opinion of the Egyptians, and Platonists, and especially approved by *Proclus*. *Plutarch* also and *Demetrius* the Philosopher, and *Æmilianus* the Rhetorician ... (p. 393)

This is going very far. (I do not know where Hermes says that they are mortal. I take it that 'long lived' implies 'mortal'.) The chapter begins with a firm statement:

But I call Angels [Daemons] here, not those whom we call usually call Devils, but spirits so called from the propriety of the word, as it were, knowing, understanding and wise.[21]

The intelligences who rule the stars are immortal, he says, and he does not exclude them from being 'daemons', but we are closer to the ones who, though long-lived, eventually die. Dying and reproducing go together, or the state of things could not be permanent; and the kind who breed, a long tradition asserts, can breed with us. Augustine said it was impudent to deny that devils could breed with women, but then, he was determined to say that Jupiter (for example) was a devil.[22] More sober opinion agreed that Jupiter was a mortal demon, though long-lived. Agrippa does not spread himself on the subject, but mentions Plato and Merlin [see *infra*] as well-accredited cases, during historical times, of men whose fathers were daemons.[23]

The *De Nymphis* of Paracelsus (1493–1541), 'A Book on Nymphs, Sylphs, Pygmies, and Salamanders, and on the other Spirits' [*Liber de nymphis, sylphis, pygmaeis et salamandris et de caeteris spiritibus*] says the

Latin title, was printed in the original German in 1566 and in Latin translation, as part of a selection of his work, in 1569. He was a great centre of controversy and curiosity, and this book is much more readable than his others, as well as shorter (about 11,000 English words), but people interested in the others might pass it over as trivial. It was important later, for the German Romantic Movement. There is an English translation by Henry E. Sigerist (*Four Treatises of Theophrastus von Hohenheim called Paracelsus*, Baltimore: The Johns Hopkins Press, 1941). Around 1590 it was likely to be in one of the libraries of the big houses in London, but was not well known.

One biographer, to save the face of the great man, explained that he wanted to save his patients from feeling frightened of spirits inside them, causing their pains, so he pretended to believe in remote ones; but this is so wrong as to be quite interesting.[24] He did believe in spirits inside them, useful ones which were needed for their bodily functioning (and surely he would have said so); the most important one was the 'archeus' of the belly [*Archeitas Stomachi*], a sort of lord mayor, subject to the king but with considerable powers of local administration.[25] (He had probably read this into the *Hermetica*, even if it is not really there.) Also he was keen on distillation, and called any distillate (such as whisky or petrol) a 'spirit'; also he used the technique metaphorically, so that he will speak of the body as distilling an essential spirit from the blood. Obviously he did not think of all these chemicals as independent conscious beings; even an archeus, though capable of purposive action, did not need to think. It was bad luck that he had to use such confused language, and that real chemistry took so long to come; but his basic ideas were remarkably sound. On top of all this, he tells us in the treatise itself that these 'elementals', highly intelligent creatures of earth, air, fire, and water, are not spirits at all; because they have bodies, unlike angels and devils. This was too much paradox for the Latin translator, who called them spirits in his title; obviously a creature who does not notice passing through a brick wall must be a spirit. There was another apology with more force in it: that Paracelsus was merely reporting the opinions of his patients, especially of the miners among whom he had laboured so unselfishly. He admired them, but he might yet poke fun at their more absurd opinions, especially as it made such good talk (he is reported as being accustomed to dictate his books, with a drink beside him, after a hard day at the surgery). This has a ring of truth, but one must realise that he earnestly thought the miners much more likely to be right about such things than the professors at the church-ridden universities. The book rises to an impassioned paragraph at the end, saying that shortly before the Day of Judgment the people will be shown to be right and the false scholars to be wrong. At least, he does not quite say that all the people are on his side, but the English translation conveys a pressure from this idea at the back of his mind:

> Blessed will be the people, in those days, whose intelligence will be revealed, for what they produced will be revealed to all the people as if it were written on their foreheads. For that time I also recommend my writings for judgment ... (p. 253)

It was a pretty stubborn reader who took this for a scholarly joke against the peasantry.

The chief difference in his account is that he thinks the elementals are emotionally dependent on mankind. Agrippa (one suspects) had found them hard to get, but the overwork of Paracelsus had left him no time for a trial. Anyone who goes in for it, he expects, becomes positively pestered by the creatures:

> One who has a nymph for a wife, should not let her get close to any water, or at least should not offend her while they are on water. And one who has a mountain manikin [gnome] with him, should not offend him, particularly not at places where they get lost. But they are no much obliged to man and so closely bound to him, that they cannot get away from him, unless there is a reason for it, and this happens at the place from which they come. (p. 241)

Nymphs especially (it appears to be a term for female water-spirits; anyway we are told there is a shortage of male ones) are keen for men, so they very sensibly form a Venusberg ['a group ... of nymphs']:

> such people also convene and assemble in one place, where they may live together and seek intercourse with man, for they love him. (p. 243)

However, though they have this reliable impulse, there is also a practical reason for their interest in man. They have no souls, so they cannot go to Heaven, but with our help they can get a soul. If a man marries a nymph, she has a soul; so it is very important not to jilt a nymph; she will kill you – it has happened quite often, and quite right too. Here he thinks of a soul as an invitation card or ticket of entry; but at other times he finds it strange that these excellent creatures, so superior to ourselves in every way, can live as they do without souls. Almost at the end, when he is considering giants, who are abnormal but very kind, we get the strongest expression of the problem. They have no souls:

in spite of the fact that they have been found performing good deeds, works, etc., sincere to each other and with qualities usually associated with the soul. But just as the parrot can talk and the monkey imitate man and many such things occur, their innate nature is equally able to perform and accomplish such things ... I cannot feel that they were seeking salvation; this would be hard to believe, but rather that they acted like clever animals. Truly, if a fox or a wolf could speak, they would not be very different. One must concede a good deal to natural understanding that does not serve the purpose served by one who has a soul. (pp. 248–9)

His purpose is to avoid Hell and get to Heaven, and so he can never perform a disinterested good action, as these giants do. It is tempting to regard this as deliberate satire on Christian doctrine, but probably he is just bumbling about, trying to sound pious while recommending the beliefs of the people he admires. There is a rather similar bumbling about Venus, or rather the previous holder of the title, who reigned a long time (since classical times?) and was more vigorous than the present one. The elementals do not get old and have wrinkles; they just blow out suddenly.

There are many tales about her. Some people believe that she will live until the Day of Judgment, meaning: she and her seed, not she alone. And on the Day of Judgment, all these beings will appear before God, will dissolve and come to an end ... But this is not true, for all beings end in death and nothing remains, neither they nor other people, nothing is without an end. It is on account of the seed that all kinds survive to the Day of Judgment. (*Tractatus*, IV, p. 244)

Surely this leaves no eternity for us, any more than the elementals? But, again, he seems to mean nothing out of the way.

When he comes to the novelty in his doctrine he feels the need to cite an authority or otherwise show the source of his knowledge, but this can only be given as universal experience:

A water woman takes a man from Adam, and keeps house for him, and gives birth to children. Of the children, we know that they follow after the father. Because the father is a man from Adam, a soul is given to the child, and it becomes like a regular man, who has an eternal soul. Furthermore, this also is well known and must be considered, that they are saved before

God and by God like other women. It has been experienced in many ways that they are not eternal, but when they are bound to men, they become eternal, that is, endowed with a soul like man. (*Tractatus*, III, p. 238)[26]

He goes straight on to put this on a broader footing, so that even a male gnome employed as a technician, if working closely with his master, might achieve the status (p. 238):

God has created them so much like man and so resembling him, that nothing could be more alike, and a wonder happened in that they had no soul. But when they enter into a union with a man, then the union gives the soul. It is the same as with the union that man has with God and God with man, a union established by God, which makes it possible for us to enter the kingdom of God. If there were no such union, of what use would the soul be to us? Of none. But now there is that union with man, and therefore the soul is of use to man, who otherwise would have no purpose. This is demonstrated by them also; they have no soul, unless they enter into a union with men, and now they have the soul. They die, and nothing remains of them but the beast. And a man who is not in divine union is just like them.

It has been suspected that he dictated this kind of thing while half drunk.

One is not sure even if he realises, in the last sentence quoted, that he is rejecting the belief in Hell. A vigorous mind and a keen imagination are at work, but he is not interested in making a consistent theory, tidying up all possible objections; he is reporting beliefs firmly held by a community; but some of them excite his curiosity, and these ones he tries to make more philosophical or coherent.

He says two or three times that the elementals move extremely fast, while he is giving a list of their qualities, and lets drop that they know all future, present, and past 'affairs', but does not seem interested (p. 239). His spirits of the air do not go high up, or otherwise behave like Ariel; perhaps he feels that would make them too like angels. They are 'sylvestres', living in the woods, and 'cruder, coarser, longer and stronger' than the water people, rather like trees in fact; 'the nymphs can speak in the languages of the countries; the forest people, however, cannot, though they learn easily.'

[T]here is danger with the fire people [vulcans], because they are commonly possessed, and the devil thus rages in them, which causes great harm to men. (p. 240)

But any sort of elemental may be possessed, just as we may, and they get similar diseases, too. Where they do have an advantage over us is in not having to work:

Man is the most earthbound of creatures. What he must have and wants, he must make for himself, and he obtains nothing by wishing and desiring it. But those people have what they need and desire ... They have it without work. (p. 241)

But the gnomes like work, just as they like money; it is their whim. This short book, as I have tried to show, is astonishingly full of bits of folk-tale that have been used by later literature; they seem to rise from its pages like steam.

[E]verything lives in chaos, that is: everything has its abode in chaos, walks and stands therein. Now, the earth is not more than mere chaos to the mountain manikins. For they walk through solid walls, through rocks and stones, like a spirit; that is why these things are all mere chaos to them, that is, nothing. That amounts to: as little as we are hampered by the air, as little are they hampered by the mountain, by earth and rocks ... And the coarser the chaos, the more subtile is the creature; and the more subtile the chaos the coarser the creature. The mountain people have a coarse chaos; therefore, they must be the more subtile; and man has a subtile chaos; therefore, he is all the coarser. (p. 232)

One more worthy must be paraded, though he would snort at finding himself in such company, the philosopher Pietro Pomponatius, or Pomponazzi (1462–1524). There is an excellent account of his position by A. H. Douglas (1910), who gives long quotations, in English but with the Latin below.[27] His first book *De Immortalitate* (1516) denies the possibility of any ghost, soul, or spirit operating apart from a body; a soul's only means of gaining knowledge or making contact with other souls is through its sensory equipment – or, at least, we cannot conceive of any other procedure. It is useless to pretend that only a low-class kind of knowledge comes through the senses; if you see the face of God you have eyes, or else the word 'see' here has some completely unknown meaning. Thus a great deal of superstition may be swept away, and though the relation between soul and body remains a mystery it is made a consistent one. Pomponazzi retained his chair, and his books remained in print, though apparently some additions had to have orthodox rejoinders added at the end. A. H. Douglas considers philosophy only, but I do not know why he should assume that this rebuttal had no philosophy in it. There was an easy way out; only remember the resurrection of the body, which is so basic that it is in the Creed, and the main Christian tenets can be restored at once. This would entail the Mortalist heresy, which makes the soul revive with the body on the Last Day; it was considered a very bad heresy under Cromwell, but many people, including Milton, believed it secretly; they might consider that Pomponazzi had made it essential.

In his second book, *De Incantationibus* [*De Naturalium Effectuum Causis, sive de Incantationibus*] (1556), he is concerned to show that his position is not paradoxical; it does not deny common experience. Most people think it possible to see ghosts, and believe that 'incantations' can raise spirits; he takes a liberal view here, and does not call all such cases delusions. Anyway, the delusion need not be caused by a man; the senses of the victim may be 'directly affected by the secret agency of the heavenly powers' (p. 280). Pomponazzi was an astrologist, believing that everything is fixed by the Intelligences who act from the planets; he wrote here *a corporibus coelestibus*, which needed expanding into 'the secret agency of the heavenly powers'. They are much less human than God; there is never any attempt to find a reason for their decisions. Finally, says Douglas, Pompanazzi:

supposes that a secret power may act directly on the *air*, causing in it an unusual perturbation and producing an unusual appearance ... [R]eal apparitions of the sorts above described he holds to be possible; nor is there conclusive reason to doubt the possibility of their being produced by human ingenuity, by those who should gain sufficient knowledge of the conditions which regulate their occurrence. (p. 281)

This is expressed very dryly, as a grudging confession one would think; or perhaps it has the gleeful absurdity of the pure logician, as when Aristotle said that a man might be in love with his own wife. But it has opened the floodgates. Pomponazzi could not find 'reason to doubt' that such an apparition might last for two thousand years or so, like a Middle Spirit, which would make it a lot more substantial than we are. He believed that we are 'only the stars' tennis-balls', with no free-will, so that we too are hardly more than apparitions. Contrariwise, the idea that the Middle Spirits are merely apparitions gets at least one very firm expression in the *Hermes*; or rather in the extra part collected by Stobaeus, an anthologist of about AD 500, who may be recording late imitators of the original works. Hermes is again addressing his son Tat (*Stob.* excerpt VI):

And besides this, my son, you must know that there is yet another sort of work which the Decans do; they sow upon the earth the seed of certain forces, some salutary and others most pernicious, which the many call daemons. *Tat.* And what is the bodily form of these beings, father? *Hermes* They do not possess bodies made of some special kind of matter, nor are they moved by soul, as we are; for there is no such thing as a race of daemons distinct from other beings; but they are forces put in action by these six and thirty gods.[28]

(Or they 'lack distinction', like the ghosts of Yeats, in the sense that they move about in herds actuated by common impulses.) The Decans have no character either, as they are merely intervals of ten degrees on the circle round the zodiac, hardly more than conveniences for calculating horoscopes. If the daemons are dependent on them, and we are dependent on the daemons, we are in a parlous way. Maybe the sixteenth-century reader would regard this kind of disclaimer as merely a way to avoid persecution. Still, it seems clear that Pomponazzi had been told, after his first publication, that he had neglected the evidence about the daemons, and then looked it up; he could claim that his interpretation of the *Hermetica* was as well documented as that of Agrippa.

We may be sure that he did not himself use the resurrection of the body as a protection, because he argues at length, in this second book (and Mr Douglas reports him very finely), that the life of virtue does not depend upon belief in a heavenly reward, which indeed only tends to corrupt it. The bareness of his position has a Roman grandeur, though it may well have seemed as improbable as that of Agrippa. Anyway he was an accepted authority; of the Cambridge college libraries when Marlowe was at Corpus, Trinity had the *De Incantationibus* and John's had the *De Immortalitate*. The young Marlowe would probably have a brief period of reading him with sardonic fascination, but anyhow he was regularly working with people who had read him. Consider, this author does positively say that, if a man calls up a devil and the devil seems to come, what he has got is only some kind of flimsy neutral spirit.

It seems best to fit in here a few remarks about recent treatments of the sixteenth-century views on spirits. The best comes in the first chapter of C. S. Lewis's survey of the period (*English Literature in the Sixteenth Century excluding drama*, Oxford: Clarendon Press, 1954), and his testimony is the more impressive as he was in general prone to

deny any major change at the Renaissance. The same beliefs as
before crop up in the writings, but there is a change, he says, in the
tone; magic is no longer mysterious and remote, as in the *Morte
D'Arthur*, but a thing which, though the writer himself does not
claim to do it, men quite nearby can do, and any competent man
could take it up. (There had been the same tone in the early twelfth
century, he tells us in *The Discarded Image*, 1964.)[29] As to spirits, he
quotes Michael Drayton saying casually that, as the parentage of
Merlin does not concern him, 'I will not play the humorous Platonist' about it; and Lewis comments:

Platonism primarily means to him the doctrine that the region between
earth and moon is crowded with airy creatures who are capable of fertile
unions with our own species.[30]

This doctrine may not seem prominent in the admitted writings of
Plato, but he had learned a secret doctrine from ancient Egypt, from
Hermes in fact, which he transmitted to Plotinus and suchlike. The
magicians were not the only ones who claimed to be heirs; the
Family of Love, though not at all interested in spirits, also claimed to
derive their best doctrines from the tradition of Plato [see *Essays on
Renaissance Literature*, 1]. Coleridge still believed that Plato did trans-
mit a secret doctrine about Middle Spirits, even when he himself
had stopped believing in them. It is a telling quotation, because it
forces us to notice a strong, widely rooted, long-lasting set of assumptions which we have been brought up to ignore.

Lewis is very untroubled, with a touch of swagger perhaps, about
a question which has troubled a number of authors both in the
sixteenth and twentieth century; that is, whether Cornelius Agrippa
(say) really used devils, though he pretended not to. Lewis says:

What permits his own magic to be 'high' ... is the belief that there are
many potent spirits besides the angels and devils of Christianity.[31]

He therefore averts his eyes from any unworthy assumption of
Agrippa; rightly I think, though it is rather a surprising indifference
in so active a Christian. Agrippa does not make the division absolute; one could enter into diplomatic relations with devils without
vowing allegiance to them, and they might be a help in getting a
contact with Middle Spirits – who are inclined to take no interest in
us, so that Hotspur makes a central point when he says: 'Will they
come when you call for them?' I expect that, as a thoroughgoing

investigator, Agrippa had tried to raise devils (by the less fatal procedure) and had failed, rather to his relief; whereas, with the gentler spirits, it was less plain whether one had failed or not. The raising of zombies, ghosts who cannot speak, is the only thing that seems to worry him; he is sure it can be done (he still believes that, even in the *De Vanitate*) and yet they seem so pointless – he feels about them much as we feel about poltergeists.

About the higher reaches he remains uncertain; as C. S. Lewis remarks:

Agrippa in one place limits the power of our ceremonial to calling up the *mundana numina* or even their inferior daemons, in another he hints a more direct access to 'the perfection of heaven'.[32]

(So far as I know, these 'earthly spirits' are simply the daemons in general; probably Lewis wants to remind us of some other writer on the subject.) Agrippa might well be unsure, but to insist upon it was tactful; the hermetic doctrine that man is naturally a god was particularly offensive to a Christian, and a timid handling of it was the only way to make it seem decent. Modern critics are still eager to denounce the bumptiousness of Faust, a cad who did not know his place, when he uses language which was merely normal for a mage. There is one part of Agrippa's position which could be called a weakening of the usual standard; though it might as well be called idealistic. He does not deny that magicians should be holy men, if they are to succeed (celibacy, it should be explained, he considers positively unholy), but he thinks they will become so if they persevere with their magic; indeed, he thinks that much of the ritual or technique of magic is only needed to help them over this initial obstacle. There is a fine passage to that effect in the chapter on sacrifices, which the translator admired so much that he treated it rather too ambitiously.

And these are (as *Orpheus* calls them) keys which open the gates of the elements and the heavens, that by them a man may ascend to the supercelestials; and the intelligences of the heavens, and the demons of the elements, may descend to him. Now men that are perfect, and truly religious need them not, but only they, who (saith Trismegistus) being fallen into disorder, are made the servants of the heavens and creatures; who because they are subjected to the heavens, therefore think they may be corroborated by the favour of the celestiall vertue, untill they flying higher be acquitted from their presidency, and become more sublime than they. (Book III, chapter 59, pp. 536–7)[33]

There is also a side of Agrippa very like Benjamin Franklin; both of them liked giving advice to ambitious young men:

In what virtue thou thinkst thou canst most easily be proficient in, use diligence to attain to the heights thereof.

At the time the volume by C. S. Lewis [*English Literature in the Sixteenth Century*, 1954] excited resistance, and there was even talk of commissioning a more worthy volume to replace it, though now I suppose it is the only one of the series that is still remembered. Far apart from the Lewis influence, though no doubt subject to the same large causes, magical cults had a revival among angry young people, especially in America, and this produced a backwash; learned books appeared debunking the mages, of which a good example is *The Occult Sciences in the Renaissance* by Wayne Shumaker (1972). It is much sweetened by its frank anxiety to save the modern students from corruption, but very little at leisure to consider the mind of the sixteenth century in Europe. Shumaker is right to say that the *Hermetica* is plainly by different authors, some of whom being other-worldly mystics hate nature and therefore think all daemons bad; but absurd if he means to deny that in many parts of it some daemons are considered good. The point of historical interest is that the sixteenth century seized upon it eagerly as containing a religious praise of nature.[34] There perhaps our difference may rest; but an older book, specifically about spirits in Elizabethan plays, needs to be rebutted here, and besides, it gave me a lot of useful information. This is *The Invisible World* by R. H. West (Athens, Georgia: University of Georgia Press, 1939, second edn. 1969); evidently a popular work, and it has great efficiency as a means of delusion.

The subtitle says it is 'A study of pneumatology in Elizabethan drama', and a hope is expressed that this will contribute to an understanding of the plays. Mr West admits that various doctrines were then current, but explains that he will only give the official view of the church (that is what he *means* by using the term pneumatology), because the audiences in the public theatres would know of no other. These audiences after all were made up of simple people, so they had to agree with T. S. Eliot, because they didn't know any better. Surely it is only in America that this fantastic idea could be put forward; in Europe, the people were never so totally subservient as it implies. Mr West gives a learned documentation of the official belief, but his procedure is mere hypnotism, as nobody denies what he says, and the only question is why the plays ignore it. As to the *Midsummer Night's Dream*, he casually remarks in a footnote that he will omit all consideration of fairies, as they have been fully considered by others (p. 234); but there you have a grass-roots belief which the people had never abandoned, even under persecution from the clergy. The orthodox opinion, as he rightly shows, was that there could be no spirits other than angels or devils, wearing the uniform either of God or of Satan, so he finds the language of Agrippa deceitful. Agrippa, he says (p. 22):

uses the word *daemon* sometimes of good angels, sometimes of devils; consequently leaves it uncertain, in spite of an occasional pious explanation, whether he does not conceive the moral nature of some daemons according to pagan rather than Christian doctrine.

This is an interesting point. C. S. Lewis was a highly conscientious Christian, and had studied theology a good deal; he certainly had not found anything in Christian doctrine to forbid belief in these spirits of nature, some of them better than others, but none of them wearing uniform. He regarded it as a natural result of the Principle of Plenitude, that all possible forms of life exist in the Great Chain; indeed, if one refused to believe in creatures between men and angels, one might get saddled with embarrassingly low-class angels, as happened to poor Dr Dee. (Lewis of course enjoyed the belief, as well.) Both Rome and Geneva had forbidden it, but that was a point of discipline, on the same level as forbidding priests to marry; and the Church of England, as a body, never even forbad it. I think this mistake about doctrine explains why Mr West seems so blinkered.

Later on in his book, or rather in the long section of notes at the end, one finds a far more liberal attitude being taken; but this is a matter of allowing special indulgences to one favoured genius or another. He is aware that he will be ludicrous if he calls Ariel a devil (and he has already wriggled out of calling Puck a devil), so he says (p. 248):

The rationale of Prospero's art and world was an antique one which allowed for the elemental spirit Ariel, in a manner intolerable to Renaissance orthodoxy but quite acceptable to Agrippa, who found no difficulty in classing the nature spirits of Neo-Platonism as good angels deputed to earth, and letting it go at that.

'At that' is often a baffling locution, and what is 'let go', from what tie-up? It is very contorted, but if it means that Shakespeare had heard talk about Agrippa, and knew that there was learned support, in a general way, for his conception of Ariel, that is clearly true;[35] if it means that the play could not be acted at the Globe, because it was so antique that it would have affronted the people's theology, that is absurd. (Surely the phrase 'Renaissance orthodoxy' is rather absurd too.) But the book goes on considering difficult points in the plays, difficult, that is, for his theory, and the effect is quite illuminating. Rowley's *The Birth of Merlin*, for example (p. 93):

contradicts contemporary theory squarely in its principal pneumatological fact

– and he quotes Agrippa saying:

All now believe that *Merline*, a British Prophet, was the son of a Spirit, and born of a virgin . . .[36]

(This seems to deny virility to the spirit, but it can equally well mean, as supporting evidence, that she was known to have no human lover.) The daemon father [in *The Birth of Merlin*] is 'substantial enough to propagate truly and to be enclosed in a rock' (p. 239).[37] Surely nobody supposes that Rowley was writing this stuff for any audience more learned or refined than the public theatres, or that they would resist it because of their theology? Mr West tells us that 'the plays, with only one or two exceptions, seem orthodox in general pneumatological scheme' (p. 239), but does not give examples of what he means. Most Elizabethan plays do not have any spirits; a fair minority have ghosts, which were forbidden by Protestant orthodoxy anyhow; but very few have fairies. Perhaps by 'orthodox in general' Mr West meant that the incidental remarks about such matters are not controversial; but when a spirit is brought onto the stage, even if it is said to be a devil, it is always humanised a great deal. At least, I cannot think of a contrary example; the full bleakness of the Christian doctrine is not suited to the stage, and is felt as a great strain in *Dr Faustus*.

However, considering his examples, I realised a point which may be familiar; that most of them come from the time around 1590.[38] The habit of printing plays was only beginning then; some of the cases we have only survived accidentally, and many earlier ones may have got lost; but it does not seem a fashion which would last very long, and we know there was a fashion for battle-pieces around 1580. *Dr Faustus* in fact might have started a new vogue; but this is not likely, because Nashe in 1589, writing the Preface to Greene's *Menaphon*, speaks with some contempt of the plays about Oberon touring up and down the provinces [quoted below]. Even if Marlowe's play was already out, it could not have had this remote effect so soon; and anyway, I think it presumes an audience already accustomed to plays about spirits.[39] Evidently most of them were far more like the *Dream* than like *Dr Faustus*; indeed we may expect that Shakespeare was being bold, not in offering a fantasy which was too wild or learned for most of his audiences, but in recalling something so old-hat. The idea of very tiny fairies does seem to be his own;[40] Mercutio's 'Queen Mab' speech is the first time that fairies use insects as horses [*Romeo and Juliet*, I, iv. 53–94], and *Romeo* was almost certainly written during the long break for plague while he was a servant of Southampton; there he might well hear about Ficino, and have leisure to apply him in an unexpected manner.[41]

I had better give a list of spirit-plays about this time; most are dated 1590 or later, but we hear of earlier ones. *Friar Bacon and Friar Bungay*,[42] *A Looking-Glass for London*,[43] *James IV*,[44] *John a Kent and John a Cumber*. It is fortunate that I. A. Shapiro, in *Shakespeare Survey*, 8, put back the date of *John a Kent* from 1595 to 1590; the later date would be positively anomalous.[45] One should observe here that the magician's boy, called Shrimp, who is viewed jollily as the kind of boy who might turn cart-wheels, can get through the key-hole of a castle gate and thus open it from within. The technique is not discussed, but it is clear that he needs a clear hole; probably he can turn himself into a midge, and fly through. A devil would have no such limitation; Shrimp has not been given the powers of a devil, but of some kind of spirit, which was what Faust (in the play) demanded and obtained.[46] They are all comedies, with hardly any fear of Hell about them.

[*The following portion of the essay, to the end of this first section, is taken from a separate draft; though reiterative to a small degree, it otherwise expands Empson's observations with fresh material.*]

In *John a Kent and John a Cumber* (usefully restored by I. A. Shapiro to the date 1590) the winning magician has an apprentice called Shrimp. To defeat the wicked nobles it is necessary to enter a castle, and its front door is closed by magic, but he is casually told to use the keyhole of the back door, and they get in at once. Before puberty it was easier for a human to gain these powers, but I think they were always limited to turning oneself into some animal; Shrimp would not become a gas, but he could fly through the keyhole in the form of a midge. If the audience can accept this, with no explanation, they are not going to be surprised by Shakespeare's fairies. Being tiny was not a pathetic limitation but another of their many staggering skills. I do not deny that Shakespeare got tenderness into it too, but the tenderness is not stifling if you know the other half of the story.

There is a revealing paragraph in Nashe's Preface to Greene's *Menaphon* (1589), where the disdainful University Wit tells the actors that their wealth depends on the scholars who write for them:

Sundry other sweet gentlemen I know, that have vaunted their pens in private devices, and tricked up a company of taffety fools with their feathers, whose beauty if our Poets had not pieced with the supply of their periwigs, they might have anticked it until this time up and down the country with the King of Fairies, and dined every day at the pease porridge ordinary with Delphrigus.

Also in Greene's *Groatsworth of Wit* (1592) an out-of-date player says 'Why, I am as famous for Delphrigus, and the King of Fairies, as ever was any of my time.'[47] The lost play about Oberon must have been at least three years old when Nashe despised its antiquity, so even if you make *Dr Faustus* early, as I want to do, there is still an earlier play about supernatural characters, popular on tour; and a number survive from about that time. One of them was revived in 1594, when the theatres reopened, but not kept on; the fashion seems to have swung firmly against them, and even *Dr Faustus* gets some very low takings in *Henslowe's Diary*.[48] So we need not regard the first audiences of the *Dream* as astonished by the novelty of the conception; they were more likely (at first) to be affronted by being given something so old-hat. But it would not be hard to realise that the old form had been turned into something much larger and grander.[49] And yet Shakespeare does not seem to have cared about fairies; after throwing off the supreme treatment of them he drops the subject altogether, except for *The Tempest* at the end of his career, a study of a magician, probably wished on him, with the marriage of the princess coming up, by colleagues who remembered this old wedding celebration.[50]

The deep interest of the account of the fairies, though one usually does not recognise it, comes from regarding them as the spirits who actuate the normal workings of nature; and this philosophical view of them was not at all far out of reach, being inherent in the very prevalent 'Neoplatonism' of the time, to be found even in the *Zodiac* of Palingenius, a standard text-book for grammar schools. Not too obvious there; but the *De Occulta Philosophia* of Cornelius Agrippa (1533), where it is quite plain (in Latin, of course), was in thirteen of the Cambridge college libraries, about half of them, including the Corpus of Marlowe. Nothing like that could be printed later in the century, because the clergy controlled printing, but the dons were not seriously against it (whereas both were against Copernicus). But talk, if we can believe the reports of spies, was extremely free; everybody knew about the forbidden subjects, or rather, everybody who could read Latin. Thus there is an obvious reason for the sudden interest of Shakespeare in the Middle Spirits of Neoplatonism around 1592–4, when the theatres were closed for plague, and he became a servant in the household of Southampton, where he would hear these subjects discussed a great deal. As a friend of Marlowe, he might even find himself considered an expert on the subject, or at least informed about the doings of the rival faction; and to talk for effect would be almost a duty of politeness there. The brief speech about Queen Mab by Mercutio (*Romeo and Juliet*, I. iv. 53–94) is surely an echo of the way he was talking then; the huddled appearance of it as prose in the second quarto has been explained, but why was only this addition in prose? Because he felt a personal unwillingness to use it in the play, making one or other kind of obstacle, though the dramatic effect is so extremely good. Here is the first time the fairies use insects as horses, and the effect is careless fun, but the method is satire against human types. There is a pretence to be using ancient peasant wisdom, though really the joke was against philosophers of the current century:

> Her chariot is an empty hazel-nut,
> Made by the joiner squirrel or old grub,
> Time out o'mind the fairies' coachmakers.　　(I. iv. 59–61)

She brings dreams, and most of the passage is about what dreams people want, soldiers about cutting foreign throats, parsons about jobs with better salaries. But there are two bits about 'sluts', who are not said to be dreaming, and this is a concession to current fashion. One of the recent changes in fairies had been produced by the queen, who while visiting a country house, and walking in its park, would frequently encounter a fairy, suitably dressed and ready with a poem of welcome, who next handed her a fairly valuable piece of jewellery.[51] This gave her a good opinion of them, but she wanted them also to have a moral side, and she was herself much addicted to minor torments for her female servants, so the fairies took to pinching sluts: a term which combined being idle about washing or tidying and being too free with their sexual favours. There is only a breath of it in Mercutio, and none at all in the *Dream*. Already in Mercutio the fairy is not confined to being tiny, but finds it necessary for part of her work:

> This is the hag, when maids lie on their backs,
> That presses them and learns them first to bear,
> Making them women of good carriage. (I. iv. 92–4)

and here Romeo shuts him up. He has explained that Mab needs sometimes to be heavier than the average lover: for that matter, she could hardly plait the manes of horses if she stayed tiny.

In the twenties, when I was young, it was usual to say that the Renaissance revival of belief in neutral spirits marked a renewal of trust in nature, and this led to the discovery of the sciences. Since then a vehement reaction has denounced all such opinions, and I agree that trust in nature has often been sadly mistaken, but the steady part of the doctrine was permanently expressed by C. S. Lewis in his great survey of the sixteenth century. He of course was not in the least a propagandist for this change in tone towards magic and the fairies, but he regarded it as obvious for any scholarly reader of both periods:

The medieval author seems to write for a public to whom magic, like knight-errantry, is part of the furniture of romance; the Elizabethan, for a public who feel that it may be going on in the next street. (*English Literature in the Sixteenth Century*, p. 8.)

I do not know why he went on to call the *Dream* a fantasy, therefore unimportant beside *The Tempest*, which gave the current view of a magician (p. 8); he was very perceptive, and disliked science, and perhaps disliked the sexual implications of the *Dream*. Surely it is very understandable that Shakespeare, having caught up for its comedy value the belief that Shrimp could turn himself into a midge, might next reflect that a midge is an eerie object in itself. Or take those bright red specks moving with apparent decision across a tree-trunk, one cannot be sure whether with six legs or eight, what kind of machinery can be inside them? How do they work? No doubt it is some universal principle, enormous in its application. Such is the mood of the writing about fairies in the *Dream*, and it really does give a prevision of what the sciences are going to tell.

Also it makes a firm acceptance of something they had already been told. Shakespeare makes his fairies, when at leisure, fly round the world in a temperate latitude so as to remain always in the dusk of the dawn. This bold fancy has been remarkably ignored; I have not found any mention of it in the voluminous discussions of the play, though of course I have not read all. Previous accounts of the spirits of the air always make them travel fast, but never define their speed, let alone make it suit a purpose. Fairies had always tended to work at night, but Oberon appears in daylight without comment in *Huon of Bordeaux*,[52] and even in the *Dream* he protests that he is not confined to darkness as ghosts are [III. ii. 388–9].[53] Also, it is notable that the extravagant procedure is never regarded as an effort; even Titania, who does not seem an athlete, thinks of it as a time for a restful chat. This is the more notable because we are encouraged to view the flights of Puck as astonishing, quite unlike this placid routine; and yet both require speeds which were then unknown to mankind. I propose a simple explanation. C. S. Lewis, in a concentrated sentence, remarks that 'Platonism' meant to Michael Drayton:

the doctrine that the region between earth and moon is crowded with airy creatures who are capable of fertile unions with our own species. (*English Literature in the Sixteenth Century*, p. 10)

It means, among other things, that they could go a long way up, out of the wind, probably into a different kind of air. The daily rotation of the earth, I submit, had come to be accepted by a considerable part of Shakespeare's audience, though still with a lingering alarm. To suppose the earth in trustworthy hands could hardly be unwelcome. Oberon and Titania handle the fertility of the whole planet, and presumably they must survey it; after going high up, into an abode of peace, they have only to stay still and watch while the earth turns beneath them. The royal creatures hold a continual durbar. At one stroke, it takes us an immense distance from the trivial little beings who used to fidget around the village in the twilight.

A number of objections come to mind. 'How could this be meant, if it is not said? Shakespeare could have said it very well. How could he mean to imply half the Copernican theory, and not the other half? The spirits could hardly be at rest while they were dashing round the sun. And how could he support either half, with his patron in a faction opposed to the pro-Copernican men? It is agreed that *Love's Labour's Lost* pokes fun at Ralegh and Northumberland.' To begin with the last: Southampton may have supposed all along that both plays were poking the same fun; it would make him rather a bad literary critic, but that need not cause surprise. He could not complain of finding no mention of the theory which was to be attacked, because there was no mention of it in *Love's Labour's Lost* either. Maybe Shakespeare, in both plays, merely dared not explain what was being hinted at, because the government was so incalculable in its suspicions and so horrible when they were roused. But we have no reason to suppose that Southampton wanted him to attack the theory. Southampton would be keenly on the side of Essex, eager to jeer at his rivals, even before coming of age; but this need not make him anti-Copernican. You might as well say he disapproved of English colonists in America; as soon as Ralegh was safely in the Tower, he became head of the Virginia Company himself. For that matter it would be out of place, in a satire, to allow any serious opinion to the mathematicians – they could not even add up.

The two plays are remarkably different, though they are linked by a gimmick; both present an amateur performance, in which a lordly audience is to be admired for insulting the humble actors. As a rule, two such plays were written consecutively; Shakespeare felt there was more to be extracted from the gimmick, and wanted another go with it at once (the bed-trick in *All's Well* and *Measure for Measure*; the rope-ladder in *Two Gentlemen* and *Romeo*). But the large-mindedness of the *Dream* follows very oddly upon the extreme small-mindedness of *Love's Labour's Lost*. Many critics have thought that both were written to amuse the teenage earl, at private performances in his house, while Shakespeare was dependent upon him to avoid, if not starvation, at least an ignominious return to Stratford, since the theatres were closed. To jeer at Ralegh for losing all favour with the old queen by her discovery of his secret marriage, while he was supposed to be remaining chaste for her sake, is fair enough as the situation is so ridiculous; though the way he is presented as seducing one of the servants would be an insult to his wife. And then the sin of Ralegh was made the excuse for an official drive against atheism, in which Marlowe was murdered by government spies and Kyd tortured so that he died the next year; it does not look well for Shakespeare to write a comedy laboriously supporting the government, insinuating that such people were vain and silly and deserved no sympathy. To do him justice, Southampton was not a pro-government man of this type, but what seemed a good jeer to him happened to suit the government too. So it came about that the first quarto of *Love's Labour's Lost* (1598) says cosily: 'As it was presented before her Highnes this last Christmas. Newly corrected and augmented By W. Shakespere.' This was the first of the quartos to give Shakespeare's name, and after that it was seldom omitted. No wonder he apologised to the shade of Marlowe in *As You Like It*, the following year. No wonder, at least, if you find so much consistent attack upon the School of Night in the play as many recent commentators have done, but even that is doubtful; I find it hard to believe (as Dover Wilson does) that an *unpublished* poem by Thomas Harriot would be hinted at with any confidence of public ridicule.[54]

The marriage of Ralegh was discovered in May 1592, and the theatres were closed for plague that autumn; it was not till April 1593 that the drive against atheists began, and Marlowe was murdered on 30 May. Dover Wilson thinks that *Love's Labour's Lost* was written for a private performance around Christmas 1593. This makes things worse; I hope the play was written for Christmas 1592, when the news about Ralegh was fresh and the drive against his fellow atheists had not started. (The evidence for the later date seems quite flimsy.) The theatres remained closed for plague till spring 1594, so this leaves comfortable time for a first draft of the *Dream* to be written, again for a private performance, with another play-within-the-play as that had amused his patron before. Here Dover Wilson's dating is a great help. The first revision of the *Dream*, he considers, was for a grand marriage in January 1595, and almost all the fairy scenes as we now have them were added for it, as well as much of the humour of the artisan scenes. During 1594 Shakespeare became established on his own legs, no longer afraid of starving if he failed to gratify the patron, and free from any duty to attack the rival faction. Probably Southampton, when he came of age in October 1594, bought Shakespeare a share in the company; it was already acting his plays. I used to think that Dover Wilson's theory was impossible, as he was leaving nothing for the first draft of the play, but I see now that a short performance could include plenty of spiteful fun, pleasing to the teenage earl. Perhaps Shakespeare went rather to the other extreme in trying to rescue his play afterwards, but 'Lord, what fools these mortals be' remains part of its basic structure.

As Dover Wilson sees it, much the strongest bit of evidence for a rewriting in late 1594 is a joke against King James in Scotland. On 30 August 1594, while James and his queen sat at dinner celebrating the baptism of Prince Henry, a blackamoor drew in a triumphal car; this, says, the record,

should have been drawne in by a lyon, but because his presence might have brought some feare to the nearest, or that the sights of the lights and torches might have commoved his tameness, it was thought meete that the Moor should supply that room.[55]

Somebody thought this very funny, and it is echoed in the anxiety of Snug the Joiner. I agree that coincidence here is unlikely, and the artisan scenes keep on coming back to the joke; a lot of changes would be needed to fit it in. James however was an object of keen interest in London, and the joke (for those who thought it funny) would not be forgotten in one year. The marriage of Elizabeth Vere on 26 January 1595 seems too soon for all the rewriting and subsequent preparation (the joke itself would take at least a fortnight to arrive in London): and, what is more important, Shakespeare was a known *protégé* of Southampton, who had paid £5,000 rather than marry Elizabeth Vere.[56] She would hate having to accept this play at her wedding, and we have no evidence that it was forced upon her. Also the wedding of Southampton himself in 1598, which Dover Wilson regards as the occasion for the final revision of the play, was a legal duty satisfied during a brief secret visit to England, and when he next returned he was sent to the Tower. He could not have put on a show for it. The wedding of Elibabeth Carey, granddaughter of the lord chamberlain, at Blackfriars on 19 February 1596 is thus the only one, of those listed by E. K. Chambers, at all plausible for a performance; the lord chamberlain might well call on his own company for a fanciful entertainment, and the rather unconventional or daring play could hope for a sympathetic reception.[57] The second revision, in which *Puck* instead of *Robin* is used as a speech-heading, was for the longer productions at the Globe; the detailed analysis of Dover Wilson seems to fit this very well.

One might of course say, as many people do, that the play was written in 1595, and altered not long after for public performance, probably not very much (the mystery about the magic flower, which appears to be a personal compliment, was inserted then and *intended* to remain a mystery). The joke about King James comes to very little. No doubt people wanted an excuse to laugh at his cowardice, but any man, however heroic, must be free to decide that his captive lion is not tame enough to appear at a christening party; the joke has the unfairness of boys tittering at a schoolmaster. And the joke made by Shakespeare is entirely different; the scruples of the amateur actors, concerned not to frighten the ladies (hardly a matter the king would worry about) and therefore to make certain of the failure of their attempt at a stage illusion, excite reflections about the nature of tragic drama and indeed of all imaginative activity. It seems a typical example of the totally mistaken 'historical source'. And yet, the young Southampton would laugh more than anyone at this report from Edinburgh; he would certainly thrust it upon the attention of his acquaintance. The play is a rich mixture or a precarious balance, and can hardly have been written straight down. And we know that Shakespeare had gone through an earlier phase, when he spoke about the fairies in a conventional way, as teasing and unimportant creatures, from the speech of Mercutio. At all events, whether or not you believe in an earlier version of the *Dream*, the surviving version was not written while he was committed to the feuds of Southampton's party. It is not clear that Southampton was either; after 1592, Ralegh was not formidable again till the sea voyage of 1596, and we do not hear of Southampton quarrelling with him before that. Essex himself seems to have taken the accusation more seriously than anyone else; in his attempted rebellion he vociferated to the citizens of London that he was in danger of being murdered by Lord Cobham and Sir Walter Ralegh, atheists and caterpillars as they were, but no man regarded him.

We need here a broader view of the state of opinion, and the best book I know is an old one, F. R. Johnson's *Astronomical Thought in Renaissance England* (1937). Either the earth must revolve or the fixed stars, known to be enormously remote; and the old view had come to be found exasperating by a new class of skilled mechanics (Puck calls Bottom and his friends 'rude mechanicals' in III. ii. 9). Johnson (p. 171) actually produces such a mechanic, who prefaces his book on the magnetic dip [*The New Attractive*, 1581] with just the foreseen sentiments; and the rebuttal of them by a foolish archdeacon (p. 242) is no less neat:

But, although such [arguments] as these are, may goe current in a mechanicall Trades-man shop, yet they are very insufficient to bee allowed for good, by men of learning, and Christians by profession, who know right well, that it is great folly for to oppose that which we call difficult, vnto an omnipotent power.[58]

Belief in the astronomy of Aristotle, though always an effort, had been possible while everything above the moon had been made of the fifth element, a different kind of matter with an inherent tendency to move in circles. This reduced the stars to a kind of shadow play. The appearance of a very bright *nova* in 1572, which stayed firmly in its position among the fixed stars for the fifteen months that it lasted, refuted the rule that the heavens were incorruptible and thus made it inherently likely that matter on the outmost sphere was like matter on earth. This was a turning-point. Dr William Gilbert's *De Magnete* (1600) does not decide whether the earth goes round the sun but insists upon the daily rotation, driving it home with indignant rhetoric.[59] A preface is supplied by a moderate convert (Johnson, p. 218), who says that a quarter of a mile a second (.28) for the solid ground at the equator is nothing compared to the alternative, five thousand miles a second for the outmost sphere; and the Bible does seem to deny an orbit round the sun, but the earth may have an irremoveable centre and yet rotate. The date of publication is long after the *nova*, and far too late for the book to have influenced the *Dream*: but the great doctor had kept open house in London for years, exhibiting his collection of nautical equipment, so that navigators would come and tell him what their compasses had reported in remote parts. Then, when the queen was failing, he closed his house, and printed his book disordered and incomplete, and spent the rest of his life trying to save her. His opinions would certainly be influential in the London of 1590; one might say, the publication marked the date when he stopped being an influence. There is a quaint bit of evidence from the quarrelsome archdeacon (Johnson, p. 238–9), who claimed to have made Gilbert's experiments with magnets *twenty years* before he published them; well, he had to make it as long as that, or he could have no priority.

Johnson does not discuss censorship, but will praise an author for implying Copernican views by irony, or say that another 'took pains to give his reader a definite hint' at them (p. 270), as if no more could be expected. Christopher Hill has maintained that there was a censorship, but I think one needs to add that it was of an evasive English kind, trying not to be recognised. Harriot wrote to Kepler in 1608:

Things with us here are in such a condition that I still cannot philosophize freely. We are all stuck in the mud. I hope Almighty God will soon put an end to it.[60]

Still presumably means that he had hoped for more freedom of publication under the new reign. Harriot had been much slandered for supposed atheism, and was running errands for Ralegh and Northumberland, unjustly confined to the Tower; he might understandably have become rather neurotic; on the other hand, he knew the situation, and we don't. There was certainly no general prohibition of books supporting Copernicanism, under Elizabeth, because the *Perfit Description* of Thomas Digges went on being reprinted. It is a unique case which must be looked at in some detail.[61]

A Perfit Description of the Caelestiall Orbes (1576) is a supplement to a work by Digges' father, *Prognostication euerlastinge*, first printed under Edward VI. It is small and looks cheap, and even this first version went through many editions. It begins with astronomy, without any thought of Copernicus of course; there are circles showing the relative sizes of the planets. Perhaps the most impressive prognostication gives you the hour of high tide at London Bridge on any day for all future time; this requires an elaborate set of tables. The father was a respected mathematician, but the popular almanacs were often laughed at, and this book would be deemed a variant of them. He died in 1558. The son Thomas made detailed observations of the great *nova* of 1572, published [in *Alae seu Scalae Mathematicae*, 1573] and praised by Tycho Brahe [in his *Progymnasmata*, 1602]; and in 1576 he brought out another reprint of his father's book, adding at the end about 10,000 words of impassioned defence for Copernicanism, rising at times to high ecclesiastical prose. But the start is very moderate, saying that the reader should be informed about the new theory, so that he can judge for himself.

Presumably the added material would have to be licensed, though there seems to be no record of the procedure; but anyway it seems well calculated not to alert a licenser, but to slip through as merely filial action, keeping in being father's old book. This was before

Whitgift was appointed archbishop (1583), and he took the censorship more seriously; under him, it is reasonable to suppose, Thomas'
additions could not have appeared. But once licensed they could be
reprinted indefinitely, so long as they were not altered at all. Seven
editions are known, the last in 1605, and probably there were others,
as even of these only one or two copies survive; almanacs got worn
out fast. It was kept strictly unchanged, though there are signs of
hasty production and the author must have wanted to add more. He
went on writing books, about military techniques and their
mathematical applications, till near his death in 1595; and in 1591,
in a preface to one of them (Johnson, p. 170), he renounced further
publication in Latin, as he was concerned only to help his own
people. In 1588 Tycho Brahe had allowed him to see a copy of the
privately printed book which announced the new plan to make the
earth stand still; and the last edition of the *Prognostication euerlastinge*
during Digges' lifetime came out in 1592. He was prone in his last
years to lament that he had printed so little, owing to much press of
business. He thus had every inducement to make short decisive
additions to his most popular book; he must, I submit, have had a
legal obstacle in the way. It might be objected, indeed, that Whitgift
would not have endured a legal obstacle on *his* side, but here we find
the English formalism at work – the government did not want to be
seen to be suppressing a learned theory. Probably Scotch James,
when he realised what was going on, stopped the book at once (it
was republished in 1605 but never again).

Thus the mechanics in Shakespeare's audience would know the
main idea of the Copernican theory, and know that it was officially
frowned upon, as in the case of the fairies; but this need not make
them believe in it. The author is hard-hitting about the necessity for
the earth's daily rotation, and seems confident that his audience are
with him; he can rely on their intuitive sense of dynamics to reject a
rotation of the fixed stars. But on the orbit round the sun, though
just as convinced in himself, he feels at a loss. They cannot appreciate the beauty of the mathematics, he tells them, and (quoting
Copernicus) makes the theory sound like some queer religion. The
sun deserves to be the centre, 'for not vnfitly it is of some called the
lampe or lighte of the worlde',[62] and 'Trismegistus called hym the
visible God'.[63] This might impress philosophers but hardly
mechanics. The only plain-man argument Digges can offer is that
Mars looks brighter when Copernicus makes it nearer to us, and

then he lets drop that Ptolemy also made these distances vary (the argument had been used against the theory of Aristotle). Maybe it would be easy to put right, but it needs doing. He wanders off into grumbling about sailors, who can't be believed in their reports of what the compass does in remote parts (no doubt that came from Dr Gilbert, who had taken up a practice in London during 1573). And, though he is more confident about the daily rotation, one can hardly say that his arguments are stronger. The opponents said that, if the earth revolved, we would be thrown off; he says the effects would be worse if the outmost sphere revolved, but he cannot say why we are not.

As this was the only convenient book for Shakespeare to read about modern astronomy, we may expect him to rely on its figures. Digges is sound on the distance of the moon, as a multiple of the diameter of the earth. He gives that as 6,873 miles, too small by about one part in seven; Gilbert does the same in the *Magnet* (1600), so it had not been improved since 1576. The distance given for the sun is about a twenty-third of the right value, which would have a rather muddling effect. The speed of the earth in its orbit round the sun is about 18 miles a second, but this estimate makes it about three-quarters of a mile a second, close to the speed of the working fairy: it is definitely not 'of another order'. But no doubt the audience would not have wanted it anyway.

If the earth goes round the sun, it is on the same footing as the other planets, and this suggested that they might be inhabited by creatures like ourselves. The deduction was immediate; as soon as Copernicus published his book, Melanchthon said it must be wrong because Christ died only for men on this world.[64] Of course, if the earth revolved because the universe is infinite, and the fixed stars are all suns, there are pretty sure to be other inhabited planets anyway, but they are much further off, and the inhabitants may be angels. Digges and Gilbert, even allowing for their tact and caution, do not seem to feel that their public is pressing for an answer to such questions. More likely an instinctive or childish fright is what needs to be combatted; as in a man trying to raise the nerve to look over a cliff. The spinning earth was frightening, even if a spinning heaven would really be worse; and such a public might well be encouraged by the thought of guardian fairies, who could move at the right speeds to look after the world properly.

Still, the next thing you got saddled with was infinite space, and that is much more horrifying. It is a plausible view that Aristotle invented the impenetrable sphere of the fixed stars solely in order to shut out infinite space. He argued that the space outside this closed sphere would not really exist, because nothing could happen there; but Digges answers with tough humour that something would happen when the outmost sphere exploded into it:

without the Heauen there is no body, no place, no emptynes, no not any thinge at all whether heauen should or could farther extende. But this surelye is verye straunge that nothinge shoulde haue sutche efficiente power to restrayne some thinge . . .[65]

Fair enough, and yet the modern physicist is just as sure that his curved space-time is the only place where matter could be; one can rig up imaginary dimensions so as to treat the closed universe as Euclidean, and they are infinite, but they are not real. Copernicus had also remarked that the fixed stars, in his scheme, could be at varying distances, but he does not expatiate on infinity; Digges on the other hand exults in it, in his most splendid paragraph (p. 165 of Johnson). Blurring from the air made the fixed stars appear to have discs, so that they must be very big if at such great distances, and the rhetoric implies that they get bigger and bigger as you go further out. Only on one point does his nerve fail him, or caution stay his hand, or perhaps he has an intuitive foreknowledge of the inverse square law, which would make his infinite heaven infinitely bright. He decided that light is switched off after a finite, though large, distance, so that we cannot see the final splendours of the divine throne. (About eighty years later, Wilkins can be found still regarding this as an accepted scientific law of optics.) The absence of parallax in the fixed stars entails their being very distant if the earth goes round the sun, and this was commonly used as an argument against the theory, but Digges used it to convey overwhelming awe. One almost gets beyond being frightened; and incidentally the idea that all these bodies rotate round our twopenny-halfpenny earth every day has come to feel shameful nonsense. The subject was really not found dull, nor even 'materialistic', as modern critics are liable to suppose.

A Study of 'Love's Labour's Lost' by Frances A. Yates (1936) has been a very formative book, and it ends:

Hariot's calculations lead straight on through Newton to the whole modern world, which is so rich in the things of the mind and so poor in the things of the spirit, so ready to trample underfoot those social graces, based on respect and love for the immortal souls of men and women, which alone make life worth living. Perhaps something of this was already visible to one whose eye could pierce to 'the prophetic soul of the wide world, dreaming on things to come'.[66]

This frame of mind is still with us, and probably makes the strongest obstacle to my theory of the *Dream*. But, even supposing that Shakespeare looked three centuries ahead, we may be sure his audiences didn't. Southampton had a noble craving to be a hero, and would become ribald if told that social graces were all that made life worth living. The government drive against 'atheism', which the Bard is presumed here to support, had spelt misery and death for those two of his colleagues who had most influenced him; Frances Yates, all unknowing, was making him out a very bad character here. And what he was likely to think is quite different. I gravely doubt whether he believed in fairies, and he at least did not go on bothering about the rotation of the earth; but he recognised that they went together – they were parts of a large movement of advanced thought, widely discussed though always with a sense of danger.[67]

II

The middle three acts all take place in the magic wood. The first act, with majestic economy, arranges for the four lovers and the mechanicals to go there, assuming that the duke may go hunting without comment; and the last act, though it appears to be an irrelevant joke, may be viewed as a reflection on the stories which have already been brought to a happy ending. Thus the fairies dominate the play; modern critics and producers often try to snub them, but this is a distortion through prejudice. It is no use trying to snub them.

In II. i, when the audience first enter the wood, Puck meets a fairy, and says: 'Whither wander you?' She says she is going everywhere. She has to bring dew to all the cowslips; their smell, she explains, comes from the brown freckles on the yellow flowers, and somehow this is why she must 'hang a pearl in every cowslip's ear' (15). She has to look for the dew before applying it, and she must also apply it to all fairy rings. We do not hear how large an area she has to cover, but clearly this work, with the cowslips all coming out at nearly the same time, needs to be done at great speed; and also it is such finicking work that a tiny creature could do it best. She needs to be rather like a bee, which is solidly enough built to go at a good pace. When we meet her she is human (or child) size, but she has resumed that form for a short rest, panting slightly, with her back to a tree-trunk. 'Whither wander you?' was a stock phrase, and did not require travel at the moment. As to her speed, she remarks at once that she goes 'swifter than the moon's sphere' (7); this would not be definite when first heard, but we get an echo of it at the other end of our time in the wood, early next morning. The two royal fairies are about to set off; they must fly round the world, to avoid full daylight, and they must be quicker than usual, as they are to reappear and dance good fortune upon the wedding of Theseus at midnight:

> Trip we after night's shade:
> We the globe can compass soon,
> Swifter than the wandering moon.   (IV. i. 95–7)

Also Puck remarks, at the end of the play, that it is the custom of fairies in general (even Peaseblossom and Mustardseed?) to fly round the world all the time, 'Following darkness like a dream' (v. i. 372), so as to remain in the dawn. This is said at midnight, when they are all blessing the three marriages; it seems inconsistent, but no doubt only proves that they can break their rule for a special occasion. Anyway, it should leave the audience in no doubt that such is their rule. An Elizabethan had no idea that poetry ought to be vague, and would be prepared to speculate on the velocities involved.

Swifter than the moon's sphere is a confusing phrase; the traditional sphere is concentric with the earth and has no velocity at the poles, but at its equator has the same velocity as the moon, which rides on it. The fairy might just as well mean 'faster than the round moon'. As the distance of the moon is about 60 times the radius of the earth, and the moon goes round the earth in about 30 days, it goes about twice as fast as the earth's surface at the equator – a bit more. The speed at the equator is a little over 1,000 miles an hour, nearer a quarter than a third of a mile a second. 'More than twice' that may be put at two-thirds. At the latitude of Athens the cruising royalties, as they keep pace with the dawn, go at about 800 miles an hour, almost a quarter of a mile a second. The working fairy goes almost three times as fast as they do, but they can catch up with it if they try. And Puck, who can put a girdle about the earth in 40 minutes, goes at 10 miles a second if he means he can get to any point on the earth's surface *and come back* in the time, 5 if he only means he can get there. The lower speed makes him go about 7 times as fast as the working fairy, which is quite enough to make a boast. The two methods of indicating their speed, by the earth and the moon, fit together well, and the social arrangement is credible.

But if we assume the old astronomy the arrangement falls to the ground.[68] The sphere of the moon has now to go round the earth every day, with only a minor lag to produce the changes for the month; having got as far as the moon, we already encounter the monstrous consequences of Ptolemaic astronomy, far worse when it reaches the fixed stars. Now the working fairy goes 60 times faster than the surface of the earth at the equator, 20 miles a second. This is at least twice as fast as the racing fairy and more probably four times. And Puck heard the fairy say it but made no protest. And consider the claim of Oberon, when he is setting off at dawn for his usual trip round the world, but remembers that he must get back at midnight to dance a blessing on the marriage of Theseus. He does not need to go twice as fast as usual, only about half as much again; and he only says that he *could* go twice as fast if necessary:

> We the globe can compass soon,
> Swifter than the wandering moon.   (IV. i. 96–7)

But, if the astronomy is Ptolemaic, this would mean going 60 times as fast, arriving back after less than half an hour; in full daylight, which he cannot endure. Oberon does not use the word *sphere*, as the fairy did; it might involve some technical trip-up between the spheres of Aristotle and Ptolemy, so the words are clearer without it. But there is now another possible confusion; he may mean that they go *round the world* quicker than the moon does, in angular velocity (the world standing still). But this tells us nothing, because we already know that they can stay in the dawn, going round as quick as the sun, and the moon goes round slower than the sun, by about one part in thirty. And we can hardly suppose that the original fairy meant this too, in saying 'Swifter than the moon's sphere', because the fairy is doing a job and has no thought of going round the world; but the two remarks seem intended to be parallel. Thus the only coherent interpretation is the Copernican one, but it may be agreed that the phrases are arranged to leave even an alert spectator confused.

Or perhaps he should find them quite clear. They are arranged to sound like legal quibbles, adequate to protect the author in court if he is accused of heresy, but not intended to deceive any sensible person. There was not nearly enough danger to require this procedure, but a pretence of it would be dramatic and entertaining. Suppose the first main performance is for the marriage of the granddaughter of the Lord Chamberlain in 1596; his own company is putting on a fanciful comedy. There will be children and dependents about, on this domestic occasion, as well as a fair lot of grandees; even more of a mixed audience than the Globe ones. Surely it would include science-minded men who found a play about fairies pretty footling, and they would be just the ones who could recognise the hints at the banned astronomy, which would cheer them up very much. Some critics have taken the phrase 'moon's sphere' to be in itself an acceptance of the old astronomy, as the 'sphere of Mars' would be; but the moon still went round the earth under Copernicus and thus defined the 'sublunary region', the abode of Middle Spirits; so nothing can be deduced about the fairy's astronomy from her use of the term. Whether obscure or not, a speed considered remarkable has been mentioned in the first words of the superhuman creatures, and Puck mentions a yet more startling one in the same scene, ten minutes later.

Also they are made to seem very large, as soon as the fairy has been established as doing work suited to a tiny creature. The king and queen have just arrived from India for the royal marriage, so they live on a global scale;[69] and the long speech of the queen describing the bad weather brought by their quarrel, though much of it is in homely English terms, must imply a threat of famine over a large area of the world. 'Fairy' was just a homely term for the Middle Spirits believed in universally, and perhaps it is used here to disarm the resistance of the spectators; but they at once find themselves far away from village fairies and among the powerful spirits of continental Neoplatonism. If you called it Pythagoreanism you would presume that Copernicus would be lurking round the corner.

The tininess of the fairies is brought smartly back in the next scene; the back curtain opens upon Titania in her bower, and she instructs the fays about their toil before she goes to sleep. It seems likely that Shakespeare took advice about astronomy, but at this point he must be given credit (since the thought is so much embedded in the writing) for his grasp of what the operations of nature require. Not only must there be tidy accurate work in bodies too small for us to see (for example, in an insect so small that we cannot be sure of counting its legs) but also in times too short for us to grasp. These are particularly hard to believe in, and they can only be put on the stage clumsily, but the attempt is firmly made:

> Come, now a roundel and a fairy song;
> Then for the third part of a minute, hence:
> Some to kill cankers in the musk-rose buds ...   (II. ii. 1–3)

They sing her a lullaby, taking at least five minutes, and then leave her asleep; they do not return, so the incident does nothing to make sense of the instruction, but we are left with a respect for the mystery of their dealings with time. Oberon comes and poisons her eyes, hissing 'Wake when some vile thing is near' (II. ii. 33); by the way, Dover Wilson was wrong to make him 'hover' in flight over her[70] – he is never more like a creeping thing, and it would be awkward to 'hover above' her when she is on the inner stage. The fairies are now adequately defined, and the next revealing detail comes later, at III. ii. 24. Puck is boasting to Oberon about how he confronted Titania with the translated Bottom; his friends left him alone when they saw his head:

> ... at his sight, away his fellows fly;
> And at our stamp, here o'er and o'er one falls;
> He murder cries, and help from Athens calls.   (III. ii. 24–6)

Commentators [after Dr Johnson, 1765] have emended to 'at a stump', or explained that Puck is using the royal 'we' (which he would certainly not do when talking to his master).[71] The phrase sounds odd to us because we are little accustomed to magical stamping, but precedents have been found, and playgoers who had seen the recent fairy plays would no doubt feel at home with it. 'Our stamp' means 'the magical kind which we both know how to do' – probably Oberon has taught him. He should give one stamp in illustration here, and a deep-voiced gong should answer briefly from under the stage. After his second flight, when he is trying to hurry things up before dawn, he stamps about the stage enjoying the confusion but also preparing a spell:

> Up and down, up and down,
> I will lead them up and down;
> I am fear'd in field and town:
> Goblin, lead them up and down.   (III. ii. 396–9)

A gong at every step here; he is playing at being a devil, so that Jan Kott can hardly be blamed for mistaking him for one [see the following section for a detailed drubbing of *Shakespeare Our Contemporary*, by Jan Kott]. But his actions have now become wholly beneficent; the young men have reached the point of trying to stab each other in the dark, and he prevents them by imitating both voices (pretending to be in the dark was one of the elaborate skills of an Elizabethan actor). Within sixty lines he is using the magic juice for the last time, and pronouncing a real though not too solemn benediction (III. ii. 450).

These two uses of the drums are a preparation for the main drumming; but first (not to lose the order of development) I must consider the problem about the fairies' reaction to daylight. Oberon again orders Puck to put matters right for the lovers, and he answers with a warning: it must be done fast, because dawn is on its way (III. ii. 380). Ghosts have to vanish at dawn, or rather they choose to vanish, out of shame; and the ones who appear are all damned spirits, yet they return to their graves, not to hell. 'But we are spirits of another sort', says Oberon (388), and no one will doubt it; the only question is whether they are devils, but Puck does not mention devils at all.[72] Oberon boasts, rather pathetically:

> I with the Morning's love have oft made sport;
> And like a forester the groves may tread
> Even till the eastern gate, all fiery red ...   (III. ii. 389–91)

– 'makes the sea look golden', to paraphrase him. He evidently feels it is plucky of him to last out that long. The effect is not that he removes himself out of shame, like the wicked ghosts; full sunlight is regarded as physically painful, hard to endure. Puck addresses him as 'king of shadows' a few lines earlier (347). On the other hand, Titania in her first scene is asked how long she will stay in the wood, and says perhaps till after Theseus' wedding-day (II. i. 139). I suppose, if you notice the contradiction, it is enough to reflect that the wood gives plenty of cover, and she can take her sleep in the middle of the day. Anyway the fairies are much concerned with natural growth; the seed in the ground and the child in the womb require to grow in darkness, so it is fitting for Oberon as well. It seems evident that this idea has occurred to Shakespeare. But he is aiming at something different; he is teasing his audience, or a part of it, by making the creatures seem particularly likely to be devils, by the accepted criteria, just before they become plainly beneficent.

This happens just before they fly away. Titania was woken in her right mind, or at least agreeing with her husband's contempt for Bottom, and all five humans have been magicked so as to wake up normal. Oberon has obtained the changeling and loves his wife again; it is plain that all three stories are concentrating upon the happy ending; and yet no one could expect what happens next. Perhaps Titania does, as she has called for music to keep the humans asleep; but then Oberon, as usual feeling no need to explain his wishes to his attendants, calls for music again:

> Sound, music! Come my queen, take hands with me,
> And rock the ground whereon these sleepers be.   (IV. i. 84–5)

They are extremely heavy if they can rock the ground; no wonder the mortals need special magic, not to be frightened by waking. Big drums under the stage, echoing every step, are essential, but perhaps riveters' hammers might be employed; the theatre ought literally to shake. Titania has just seemed particularly flimsy in the bower, twining herself like ivy round the oak of Bottom, but now she is weighty, and yet immediately after the dance she is as light as air again, when the crane lifts them for their world flight. (Their two cars had better be immediately available, hidden behind the foliage of the bower.) Before he gets into his car, Oberon announces that he will hurry the trip slightly, so as to return and dance again at midnight in the palace after the royal wedding; so the audience is left wondering: 'Will they make all this noise in the palace?' They should not, of course, compete with the lateral movement of Puck; it is easy to assume that they wait for that till they have risen high. The only words while they are rising should be the four lines of Titania: 'Come my lord, and in our flight /Tell me ...' (IV. i. 98–9); she is settling down peacefully. The hunting horn of Theseus is already sounding before the cars are out of sight.[73]

I want now to examine the boast of Puck just before his first flight, which seems likely to have some point to it; at any rate, it would be a grand place to fit in a hint for the wise few, if such a thing were available. Modern editors have an odd tendency to keep secret the folio text of the passage. Oberon describes to Puck how a herb in the West became magical, and orders:

> OBE. Fetch me this herb, and be thou here again
>   Ere the leviathan can swim a league.
> PUCK I'll put a girdle about the earth, in forty minutes.
> OBE. Having once this juice,

I'll watch Titania when she is asleep . . .
[cf. Brooks, Arden Shakespeare, II. i. 173–7]

Puck is talking prose, and he does not say the word 'round'; neither Dover Wilson's *New Shakespeare* nor the 1972 *Riverside*, though both in their different ways concerned about the text, recognise the omission. Both quarto and folio print the sentence as prose [and indeed as one line], but the [first] quarto has 'round', making a line and a half of verse, fitted to the next words of Oberon. I agree that this fitting is intentional; Oberon talks as if his servant had addressed him in the blank verse which he commonly uses himself. But Puck has no blank verse throughout the scene; he talks to the fairy in rhymed couplets, is dumb while Titania is present, and then replies to Oberon in very curt, almost surly, prose. He is now the technical expert; a loyal servant, but on his subject bleak and unshakeable. At the end of the scene, confident that he can fulfil the demand, he speaks one line rhyming with the last line of his master. This plan is very crisp, and is quite spoilt if he is given some verse in the middle.

Ignoring the folio [1623; New Variorum edition] could be justified if it were 'only the reprint of a reprint', but Dover Wilson says (p. 78) that it

contains alterations which prove that the copy of the Jaggard Quarto [1619] from which it was set up had either itself served as a playhouse prompt-book or had been 'corrected', for the purpose of publication, by some scribe working with the prompt-book before him.

Riverside endorses this, and I cannot see why it entails rejection of the folio text.[74] The prompt-book author is supposed to make a series of bold inventions, creating very good lines where the quarto was nonsense. He is supposed not to know any acting tradition, nor yet have access to any tattered previous prompt-book, because the *Dream* was never acted except at two or three society weddings. Thus he invents when he puts 'I am amazed at your passionate words' (restoring the dropped word *passionate*, III. ii. 220), 'Now is the mural down between the two neighbours' (for *moon used*, V. i. 204);[75] a mis-spelling by his printer here), 'Thy stones with lime and hair knit up in thee' (for *knit now againe*, V. i. 189). And the removal of the word *round*, so that Puck may continue to speak prose, is of the same decisive kind. Dover Wilson expects all printers' errors to be of certain kinds which he has analysed, so he wants these to be wild inventions; but surely anybody who had read proofs has met random unexplainable errors by the printer. And the power to emend so well and so often is a rare gift; it is far more likely that this man knew the answer. Also we are told that a play was not released to the printers till it was no longer a draw, therefore the Globe was not acting the *Dream* in 1600. It is recognised now that quite a number of quartos, 'good' in the sense authorised by the management, were printed during 1598–1600, because the company needed to pay for building the Globe; even the Falstaff plays were printed then, and they were certainly still very popular. The *Dream* does not make its appearance among a job lot of old failures. I grant that, if you ignore all the topical and intellectual interest of the play, it might seem footling to the coarse audiences at the public theatres, much as it did to Pepys ['the most insipid ridiculous play that every I saw in my life'];[76] but this only proves that you had better not. Dover Wilson has further arguments to show that the altered copy of Q2, from which the Folio text was derived, was designed for a performance in a private house; the chief one is that Bottom in the Folio rises from the dead and offers to dance the bergomask – necessary, says Dover Wilson, because the hall would have no back curtain to hide the corpses (p. 149). But it would be funnier to have Bottom insist upon leading the dance; also, this is a particularly bad argument from staging. A curtained recess big enough for two corpses could be rigged up in any hall; and in any case Bottom's play would not be acted on the inner stage. As is familiar from *Hamlet*, the placing of a stage audience is rather tricky; here the duke and his guests had better sit in front of one of the side doors, with the other one curtained for the use of the actors, who perform in front of it. The middle curtain is open, but merely to show we are now in the palace not the wood; the throne may be discovered there, if Theseus needs one, but it would be enough to have a tapestry and a carved oak sideboard, having rolled away the shrubs in tubs. The reason why a new prompt-book was needed is that the old one had got worn out by frequent use (textual experts never seem to realise that this would often happen), not because the play was never acted unless hired for a society wedding.

A more general reflection can perhaps be made against this theory. We need not suppose that Shakespeare was very keen on the fairies, or believed in them earnestly. He writes a play about them when he was first becoming established, and then drops them altogether, though he still uses ghosts and witches; till at last on the eve of his retirement he writes another play about magic and spirits, again giving prominence to a spirit who flies; this is printed first in the collection of his plays, after his death, and edited with special care. Surely it looks as if he had been asked for another one, because the public especially enjoyed this kind of play. I will be told that the wedding of the Princess Elizabeth was coming up, and plays like this were considered particularly suitable for grand weddings, in fact that was all they were fit for. *The Tempest* was indeed acted among many others on the occasion, but it had been acted at court the year before (1 November 1611); and this is before the death of Prince Henry, so postponing the marriage because of that does not explain it. James was afraid of wizards and disbelieved in Middle Spirits [see *Daemonologie*, 1597], so it is not a matter of suiting his peculiar tastes; his children presumably coaxed him into allowing the play. Ariel like Puck boasts of his speed immediately before one of his flights:

> I drink the air before me, and return
> Or ere your pulse twice beat.　　(*The Tempest*, v. i. 102–3)

This proves that he sometimes did a rapid flight sideways, like Puck, though more often he hovers. But it is perfunctory; Shakespeare's imagination is no longer working on the subject. Puck is much more global; he would have flown over to Milan any day and fetched the books that Prospero wanted.

Originally, then, he said he could 'put a girdle about the earth in forty minutes', and the printer added *round*, which suggests completing a circuit. Puck is thinking about going to fetch something, not about going on round. A girdle does not have to be squeezing you all the time; when passed through loops in a gown it may be left with the two ends dangling on either side.[77] Thus he claims to be going at about five miles a second, not at ten; this is about seven times as fast as the working fairy, surely enough. Also it is the speed at which we would have no weight, so that if Puck went faster he would have to pull himself down. Major Gagarin went at this speed, not far from the earth, at the first entry of man into space; he had only just enough power to start and stop, so for most of the time he was in free flight.[78] That is, the distance he fell at each instant from the tangent to his orbit was just enough to keep him on the circle. This would not concern Puck, who has no trouble about power, but there is another way of looking at it. If the earth rotated 15 times as fast as it does, moveable objects such as ourselves, if at the equator, would just float up into the air. It is usually supposed that Puck, even if he means anything, only gives a round number, but this may be doubted. With modern values for the earth's radius and the acceleration the answer is between 42 and 43, but if you take the radius as 6873 miles, the value of Digges, with which Gilbert agrees, and presume Thomas Harriot content with 32 for the acceleration, it works out as just over $39\frac{1}{2}$, 40 to the nearest minute. If this could be said effectively on the stage it must have been known as a kind of trade-mark, at least within a certain group; and this explains why the figure for half-way is chosen. For a complete orbit, a conscientious scientist would have to say 79 minutes, and this could rouse no enthusiasm, but 40 for half-way was correct to the nearest minute. But could anybody in 1596 know the importance of acceleration, let alone the number 32, let alone how to solve this particular problem?

I used to think that Shakespeare could only have done it by magic, but that is too drastic; Galileo was already at work, and there was a considerable buzz of interest in such matters. Galileo would not have told the secret even if he had already found it out, but it was well within the range of interest of Harriot to time the rolling of balls down an inclined plane, and thus arrive at the number 32. What Harriot had achieved and refused to print is a considerable mystery. He had a group of admirers, who warned him that he was losing his fame by refusing to print, and Marlowe was accused of his acquaintance by a police spy, so he was not beyond the reach of Shakespeare. We may be sure that he tried to solve this problem, even if he failed. It was a standard objection to belief in the rotation of the earth that we would be thrown off it, and the only real answer would be to say 'not below a certain velocity'. The formula for this velocity is $v^2 = gr$, where 'r' is the radius of the earth and 'g' the acceleration of fall at its surface; a very straightforward answer, and a man with those interests would be tantalised to feel it was only just out of reach. It may be said that his lack of calculus would frustrate him, but elementary calculus feels very like doing what you were forbidden to do in your previous lessons. Newton having got his results by calculus refused to print them till he had found laborious means of doing without, because the method was suspect; and failing to achieve this might well be one of the reasons why Harriot refused to print. I shall give the proof that seems [*sic*] open to him, once he had found by laborious timing that the distance fallen is $\frac{1}{2}gt^2$. An approximation has next to be accepted.

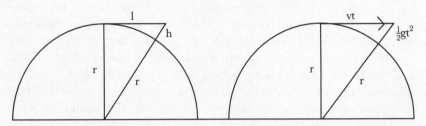

In the first picture, r is the radius of the earth, h the height of a cliff or mountain, l the length of the view one gets from it. By Pythagoras,

$$r^2 + l^2 = (h + r)^2 = h^2 + r^2 + 2hr$$
$$l^2 = 2hr \text{ nearly.}$$

There is only one term neglected, and it can easily be put back. If the mountain is a mile high, the full answer is $l^2 = 8000 + 1$; one can see for nearly 90 miles, and to add in the neglected term only gives another 10 yards. This is encouraging. In the other picture v is the velocity round the earth, so the distance l after a short time is vt, and the height h has been found by experiment to be $\frac{1}{2}gt^2$. Thus

$$v^2t^2 = 2r.\frac{1}{2}gt^2.$$
$$v^2 = gr.$$

This gives the result, but one might object that the formula $\frac{1}{2}gt^2$ is derived from a body which acquires a real velocity towards the centre of the earth, which the projectile never acquires. It seems a likely discovery for Harriot, because it entails no hypothesis – not even forces, let alone an inverse square law for them. But for the same reason it is not a fertile result, suggesting anything further; Harriot's papers were treated badly after his death, and it might easily get forgotten. The slogan 'forty minutes', I am presuming, was already familiar among Harriot's friends when Shakespeare used it in the play, and this too is not unlikely; to claim priority in a discovery by a riddle, such as an anagram, was a regular foible of the period. I grant that the whole series of events, ending in oblivion, is unlikely; but the alternative is a very improbable coincidence.

I am sure anyhow that Puck ought to say it as a slogan. Commentators explain to us that *forty* was then 'used frequently as an indefinite number',[79] and the *OED* has some examples which fit the description, but that is not the way Puck is talking here. It is his last word before taking off on a flight of well over 3,000 miles, and he has been distinctly tight-lipped while receiving his instructions. (Actually, the time he takes would be impossibly short even at 10 miles a second, but this could be theatrical convention, and I was surprised myself to find that Athens is so far away.) The number needs at least to excite conjecture, not to be met with the bored presumption that it is 'used as indefinite'. To start with, the purpose of making him fly is to prevent the fairies from seeming footling. His flight is not an illusion, even in the secondary sense that the audiences of Peter Pan want to be able to pretend to themselves that Peter is flying; when Puck did it, you were expected to admire the pluck and skill of the actor. But the shock of the spectacle altered the whole tone of your reaction to the fairies.

Shakespeare planned it first for the hall of a mansion, necessarily, because it could not be done in a public theatre till the building of the Globe.[80] The hall would have a high ceiling and be broad enough for Puck to swing on a long rope into the 'wings', the area invisible to the audience at the sides of the stage, where strong men would catch him. The eye is quick to grasp the truth if he merely swings, but if there is a sharp jerk on the rope from above just as he takes off he seems to zoom satisfactorily. The trouble was that the Elizabethan public stage had no 'wings', on principle as one might say; you could fly up on the crane, but rapid flight sideways was not possible. The Globe, however, extended the stage beyond one side of the octagon to the two adjacent sides, thus putting the two main doors at an angle; then the other halves of these two sides, above and below, became the 'lords' rooms', used by the twelvepenny men, who entered the theatre by the stage door. They were thus safe from contact with the groundlings but on patronising terms with the actors; they would not mind being asked to make room for an occasional trick, especially as they got an intimate view of it. (I accept the theatre design of J. C. Adams, and think that most of the recent attacks upon it have been footling, as I am trying to show elsewhere [see 'The Globe Theatre', *Essays on Shakespeare*, Cambridge University Press, 1986]; but I agree with some of the critics that the inner stage was 8 feet high, instead of 12, and correspondingly less deep.) The flight of Puck, which would nowadays take a great deal of insurance money, was from (say) the righthand end of the inner stage to the front end (towards the main audience) of the

upper lefthand 'lords' room'. The lefthand end of the long rec-
tangular opening in the 'heavens', which could be opened for the
uses of the crane, lies exactly above the halfway point of this
trajectory; the rope attached to Puck's shoulders comes from there,
and a separate string to his shoulders, held by a man hidden on the
balcony, must release the cord just before he gets so far. For the
second half he is in free flight. He actually leaves the stage, flying
over the staircase which comes up from hell, and he is coming out
towards the audience – only by 15 degrees, a quarter of a right
angle, but that is enough for the effect. He starts as if diving, from a
tree-trunk in the forest, but the cord should at once make him zoom,
and it is still pulling him up when it is unhooked, so that he is
levelling off, with a slight loss of velocity, when he vanishes from the
main audience and crashes in the recess. A bank of steel springs with
thick goose-feather cushions over them should be enough; he had
better turn his back to them just before he lands. It is a comfort to
observe that, after the second flight, he is assumed to need no time to
recover; he is back on the stage again after eight ceremonial lines.

The strongest piece of evidence for all this, I suggest, lies in the
exultant cry of Puck before he starts on his second flight:

> I go, I go, look how I go!
> Swifter than arrow from the Tartar's bow.   (III. ii. 100–1)

If he had made that boast and then merely scampered off, any
Elizabethan audience would have hooted him. Of course, the lines
can be cut from a performance with no flight, but the author must
have intended a flight when he wrote them. It is a reasonable view
that Puck never flew on the public stage, but did fly at the original
wedding, and perhaps at some later ones; if so, one has next to
consider how the lines survived in both quarto and folio. We are told
that the quarto was printed from Shakespeare's 'foul papers', with
some improvements written onto them, but with none of the changes
that would be needed for the public theatre, and the folio was
derived from that. Maybe it was a lie to put on the title-page of the
first quarto 'As it hath been sundry times publickely acted, by the
Right honourable, the Lord Chamberlaine his servants', but
publishers often did tell lies. I have already given what arguments I
have against this theory, and may now produce a rival theory,
which is often a stronger aid to conviction. The *Dream*, I submit, was
a show-piece for the new Globe, permitting an astonishing display of

its powers, and had been acted there fairly often for a year by the
time the quarto was published (it had been registered on the 8th
October 1600). Some extra bits had been written in, because the
wedding party would hardly have wanted a full-length play; so 'as it
was acted' on the title-page meant 'the full revised text'. The reason
why the *Dream* was held back till 1600, the last year of the series of
publications, was the rapid growth of its fame. And I suspect that
the couplet just considered, with the proud boyish cry 'Look at me!
Look!', was part of the additions for use at the Globe.

The second flight of Puck is very absurd. On the first flight he goes
more than 3000 miles in only 70 lines of the text, a majestic affair; in
the second he has only to look round the wood and fetch Helena.
Both exits are preceded by a grand boast. It is true that an excuse is
provided for the absurdity; Oberon scolds Puck for confusing the
two young men, and he becomes petulant, explaining that he likes to
have things in a muddle anyway. Then he uses his full powers, to
show that he thinks an unnecessary fuss is being made: and he finds
her quickly. The by-play is mildly amusing, but it has no function
except to introduce a second flight. At the great wedding, when
Puck was jerked on a rope into the wings, the audience would see
much the same from either side; but at the Globe, as he flew almost
towards the audience on one side or the other, many people would
want him to do it twice, once on each side. Besides, some people
would fear they had missed some detail, and would be hoping for
another look. The company too, after getting the machine ready
with so much fuss, would feel it only sensible to have two whacks,
and there was an overall need to make the play long enough for the
public stage. The easiest place to add to the length was in the
misunderstandings of the lovers, and the second flight could fit in
with that – its immediate effect is only to add to the confusion. E. K.
Chambers thought that III. ii. 177–344 could be later work, as it had
an increased proportion of feminine endings and mid-line pauses;[81]
probably he would use his judgment first, and arrive at this explanation afterwards. The addition had a serious drawback: it makes
the troubles of the lovers go on too long, and they are often despised
as shallow merely because they continue to suffer with unabated
vigour. The lengths of the acts, in round numbers, are 360, 420, 660,
270, 440, making about 2,150, still rather short but evidently
padded in the third act. The two flights are 550 lines apart, more
than half an hour, which gives time for moving the crane from one

end of the aperture to the other. We know that the Globe had three large huts above the stage, presumably to hold machinery; and unless some use of it was made for the flight, of a kind particularly attractive to the audience, there would be no need for this slight fault in the construction.

III

I wish now to report and comment on some other views of the play, briefly, because that seems to me a good way to recommend my own. Soon after the Communist victory in Peking [in 1949] the British Council representative was organising a short performance in English by students of the National University, giving the worker scenes from the *Dream*, and a deputation of them came to ask me whether this was not a plot to make them express contempt for workers. Of course I said that all the critics thought these scenes very tender, and that Shakespeare wrote for a mass audience, largely consisting of workers, and that these ones were skilled artisans who had been through an apprenticeship like Shakespeare's father, and that there was nothing absurd about the play except that its style was out of date, and so forth, but they remained convinced that these scenes were patronising, even if nothing worse, and quite unsuitable for them, even if not selected out of malice. The resulting coolness between the university and the council was never afterwards overcome. I feel now that I should have said more; that Shakespeare takes great care to preserve the manly dignity of the chief worker; but it would have been to no avail.

Though rather sad, this made an agreeable contrast with another reaction from a Communist country, that of Jan Kott in *Shakespeare our Contemporary* (1965). He thinks the play disgusting too, but he likes that. Witchcraft is always sordid and spiteful, so the fairy court is made up of prostitutes and leering old rips, delighted to see Titania degrade herself with a stinking hairy worker, barely human. The Night is a kind of Sabbat, an orgy of unavowable lust, and they all wake from it in an agony of shame:[82]

Titania wakes up and sees a boor with an ass's head by her side. She slept with him that night. But now it is daylight. She does not remember ever having desired him. She remembers nothing. She does not want to remember anything.

TITANIA   My Oberon! What visions have I seen!
          Methought I was enamour'd of an ass.
OBERON   There lies your love.
TITANIA   How came these things to pass?
          O, how mine eyes do loathe his visage now!   (IV. i)

All are ashamed in the morning: Demetrius and Hermia, Lysander and Helena. Even Bottom. Even he does not want to admit his dream:

Methought I was ... but man is but a patched fool, if he will offer to say what methought I had. (IV. i)

Even for a critic of Shakespeare, this is an astounding amount of misreading; lying one would have to call it, if the author were not eager to give the quotations which prove him wrong. To say that a vision was beyond words and then try to describe it is quite usual, and Bottom plans to boast about this one for the rest of his life. Titania asks her husband to *tell* her what happened while they are touring; the human lovers feel bemused, but in no discomfort – they agree to *tell* each other their dreams on the walk to Athens. Jan Kott quotes 'Never so weary, never so in woe ... I can no further crawl' (III. ii. 442–4) from the previous night as if it were said in the morning. Undeniably the night was a fierce experience, but they feel now, or they are ready to hope, that it has put things right again. As to the fairies, the essay does not literally assert that the first performances showed them as it recommends; it is more concerned to affect the productions of the future.

Remarks like this would not disturb the supporters of Jan Kott. There is already a vocabulary for defending this kind of production, and it does not imply any appeal to theatrical tradition or the intention of the author. The inner plot or the structural play may be what you aim at; and I can't deny that a husband who drugs his wife to make her copulate with 'some vile thing' might be regarded less cordially than the text of this play invites us to do. The limits of 'interpretation' are hard to set. Still, the reason for making this assumption about the couple is merely a stubborn refusal to believe that they are spirits, or rather that a proper manly audience can be asked to believe that they are. The Victorian tenderness must be avoided at all cost. An odd result of this is that flying through the air is more than once held up to contempt, as a downright sissy thing to do: 'The fairies' wings and Greek tunics are simply costumes; not even poetic but carnival costumes' (p. 178). This at least shows a willingness to consider the first performance; the interest of it was to lie in subtle hints at the bold sex lives of the smart audience. Maybe, but this would not prevent them from being interested in spirits as well. In the future, says Jan Kott, when we realise that both Puck and Ariel are devils, and that Prospero is 'an embodiment of Faust',

Ariel, who is all thought, intelligence, and the devil, will never more appear as a ballet dancer in tights, with little gauze wings, who floats over the stage with the help of stage machinery. (p. 172)[83]

I agree that wings are quite unsuited to creatures who command astronomical speeds; they would tear off at once; and no fairy in the *Dream* is said to have wings. A general contempt for flight, as somehow unmanly, is a very odd turn of Puritanism; the successful resistance among theatre managers to flying actors has been mainly due to the high cost of the insurance, and by this time they are pretty safe against a revival, because nearly all the Victorian theatres which were equipped to do it have been torn down. As in some other fields, the determined pursuit of the *avant garde* has ended in bleak incapacity. But the Elizabethans were not too proud to enjoy flights on the stage. Dr Dee when a student arranged one for a college performance ['the *Scarabeus* his flying up to Jupiter's pallace' in a production of Aristophanes' *Pax* at Trinity College, Oxford, in 1546], and was considered a warlock ever after, so that the mob burned his library when he went abroad [in 1583].[84] However, I have no wish to deny that a Kott performance could be very entertaining; for that matter, the Victorians were fond of burlesques of Shakespeare, too. They are praised in *The Way of All Flesh*, but Ernest does not say 'This is the real Shakespeare!'; he says 'What rot Shakespeare is after this.'[85] It is remarkable, I think, that the two criticisms just considered, Chinese and Polish, both come from Communist countries; surely Jan Kott might have realised that Shakespeare in handling Bottom is rather set on preserving the dignity of the worker.

The essay by Kott may be called left-wing or proletarian; it feels gleeful about the supposed orgy, and the misreading is important because it is so radical. But the political angle cannot be decisive, because authors with the opposite policies can make the same misreading. I instance the chapter on the *Dream* in Glynne Wickham's *Shakespeare's Dramatic Heritage* (1969), which is totally authoritarian and reactionary, eager to lick the boots of any tyrant available. The purpose of the play, he says, is to show 'the perils of sex for adolescents'; older people have self-command, but the youngsters' 'discovery of sex . . . makes them heedless of either parental advice or the law of the land'.[86] Surely any dramatist, if he wanted to recommend this moral, would present a tolerable law, a decent parent? Hermia's father gives no reason at all why she may not marry the man of her choice, merely asserting that she must marry the man he has chosen or he will kill her as the law allows (or imprison her perpetually). Theseus makes no attempt to defend this law. When he grants her petition, sordid old father tries to whip up the rejected suitor to help him have her killed. Wickham tacitly admits that the one change of mind by Demetrius (the only unreliable action before magic is employed) is not enough to make all love among young people ridiculous; for this purpose, Shakespeare very cleverly drags in a working man. Fancy a prole making love! Why, it's a scream. And now he can use the fairies, assuming that they are all nonsense, to keep the social incident free from feeling too real. What we actually see is:

a delicate and sophisticated lady with a mind of her own . . . and a good looking young workman whose tastes and conversation are as brutish and banal as his physique is striking . . . For her it is love at first sight. Bottom is honest enough to express surprise . . . (p. 187)

But he remains 'obstinately gross' – 'To the audience he is an emblem of all brainless bullies' (p. 187). All through the alarming affair he treats the lady with great tact and kindness, and I think Wickham, who cannot see that, is the one who is gross.

As Titania wakes from her thraldom so she is consumed with shame and disgust at the folly of her conduct . . . The destruction of sensuality is thus achieved in this instance by sensuality itself. (p. 188)

Please remember, if she did anything wrong, she was forced into it by a drug which her husband administered. The reason why she stops desiring Bottom is that her husband applies a counteracting drug, not that she has had an orgasm with Bottom, which the text makes impossible; she does not, of course, express shame at all; and the first audiences would be as impatient as I am with the moral thought of Wickham, that an orgasm with Bottom would throw her out of love with him. Of course the defence of the misreading would be that the plot is only a pretence; it is an allegory, 'shadowing' a more dull and frequent social event. But no audience, however coarse and unphilosophical, can hold this belief steadily in mind.

Kott and Wickham, I submit, have been driven into the same corner from opposite directions because they refuse to treat the fairies as real, to accept them as having a different mode of being. But there is not the slightest reason to believe that the first audiences would make this refusal; the play is written for people who are interested in theories about spirits, and so they actually were.

IV

An earlier part tried to show how powerful the spirits are in the *Dream*, and how thoroughly their activities are built into the course of nature. This fourth one is about their relations with mankind. The topic has been partly considered already, because the plot makes the two interact, but there is still a basic question: 'Why do the spirits take so much interest in us?' Gods are no use unless they answer prayers, but these creatures are not inherently connected with us, and we seem to have little to offer them. That indeed was why magicians were so readily suspected of traffic with devils, who are at least ready to pay attention (angels would only help a scheme of piety).

I must first come back to the theory of Kott: that the fairies *are* devils and get their pleasures from tormenting us. Oberon and Titania accuse one another of loving mortals, but their love may be of a sadistic kind (Kott does not say this, but he would have to say it if his theory were to hold water). Puck does call the lovers fools, and enjoys teasing them, but perhaps he would say the same about Titania. The human characters are also prone to practical jokes, and not in this play alone; many critics have been distressed by distaste at the tendency of the earlier plays to become heartless romps; it is hardly less marked in *The Comedy of Errors* than in *The Taming of the Shrew*. Even when agreeing that this is a fault, one is not committed to saying that all such characters are meant to be devils, or even rootedly malignant. Professor Kott, in his eagerness, gets himself into a comical position here. For example, Puck reports gleefully that the artisans, when they saw Bottom wearing the ass' head, fled through the wood tearing their clothes on the brambles, and this proves that his only pleasure is sadism. Kott is being tremendously tough, forcing upon us the full horror of life; and it makes him talk like a Victorian maiden lady. Their poor jerkins! He cannot bear to think of it. But Puck is quite willing to make the humans comfortable again, after he has teased them a bit ('The man shall have his mare again', III. ii. 463). One may suspect that he would not bother to do it if the grown-up Oberon did not tell him to, but even that is not diabolical. Rather in the same way, Kott expects us to be sickened by the monstrosity of nature when the fays in the bower of Titania sooth her with a comforting lullaby:

> Weaving spiders, come not here;
> Hence, you long-legg'd spinners, hence!
> Beetles black, approach not near;
> Worm, nor snail, do no offence.   (II. ii. 19–22)

Typical materials for witchcraft, thinks Kott. Not quite in the same way, because his reaction here is what the Victorians called 'townee'; it is based on fear of anything you might find if you stepped off the city pavement. Shakespeare would regard telling a snail to commit no offence as 'comic primness', not as a revelation of an inherent horror.

An unexpected truth, however, lurks behind this argument of Kott, and gives much interest to his collection of examples. Later in his career, Shakespeare takes care to explain that any magic he is introducing is not black magic, but here he teases his audience by insinuating that his fairies are devils, though only a fool or a witch-burner would believe it. Puck pretends to be a devil too; we have him stamping up and down, creating a fog, and saying he is a goblin (III. ii. 399), a dubious term, but usually taken to mean a devil; and when he first appears the fairy says she has heard that he often does mischievous tricks, but

> Those that Hobgoblin call you, and sweet Puck,
> You do their work, and they shall have good luck.   (II. i. 40–1)

The 'Hob', it seems, was short for Robert, and meant a countryman, a type who would wear hobnailed boots. He is flattered when addressed as this humble kind of devil; he will then become a domestic pet. Of course he is native English, whereas the others are international, but it seems that Middle Spirits often did pretend to be devils (as it made them seem important) and sometimes had real dealings with them. Anyway, it is as well to flatter Robin, as he can be quite rough.[87]

I fully share the distaste for horse-play which is so usual among

critics. Still less do I like being horse-played upon. Like my colleagues, I think that Shakespeare in his early comedies was only
struggling to gratify his coarse audience. But the horseplay of Puck is
treated rather differently; it is admitted to cause real suffering, and
we have to be assured that it will not go too far. The author seems to
know more about it, and it is not hard to see how he could have
learnt. At his trial, the Earl of Southampton was accused of bringing
a private army to the support of Essex, but pooh-poohed the tale; he
only came with ten or twelve men, he said, 'my usual train'.[88] To
enter the household of the earl must have required some adjustment,
and the early sonnets (especially 26) insist that Shakespeare has
become the servant of the dedicatee; then at 33 (*Full many a glorious
morning*) there has been a mysterious betrayal, and not till 40 (*Take
all my loves*) has it become an intelligible one. Shakespeare can make
the earl cry by scolding him for the first betrayal, so he has to be
forgiven (34), but we never hear of his putting the matter right. I
think the bodyguard ragged Shakespeare, when he first joined the
household, and the earl refused to punish them for it; they would
have felt he was being unfair, as the Bard was practically *asking* to be
ragged, and it was important to keep on the right side of one's
bodyguard. But quite soon Shakespeare has won them over, and can
afford to look down on the subject benignly, as Oberon does.

The suffering of Hermia when ragged by Puck is made important
for us by her poetry. The lover she has run away with abandons her
before she wakes, because he has been magicked by Puck; but she
wakes calling for his help, having foreseen his absence in a nightmare:

> Lysander, look how I do quake with fear.
> Methought a serpent ate my heart away,
> And you sat smiling at his cruel prey.   (II. ii. 147–9)

The premonition is not brought by the fairies; it seems a usual
experience for earnest natures such as hers. She feels that the
collapse of Lysander's love is a metaphysical exposure, making all
appearances unreal, as Troilus felt about Cressida:

> The sun was not so true unto the day
> As he to me. Would he have stol'n away
> From sleeping Hermia? I'll believe as soon
> This whole earth may be bor'd, and that the moon
> May through the centre creep, and so displease
> Her brother's noon-tide with th'Antipodes.
> It cannot be but thou hast murder'd him ...   (III. ii. 50–6)

She accuses Demetrius, and the two young men do start trying to kill each other, almost at once. (No other Shakespeare play drags in astronomy like this; it is in keeping here because the local astronomy of earth and moon has been made a centre of attention.) But in any case they expect life to be very bad – 'Brief as the lightning in the collied night' (I. i. 145) is the only course in prospect for true lovers such as Hermia and Lysander, and sure enough, after they had lost their way in the wood where the royal hunters are coming, they could have nothing to hope for unless the fairies had intervened. The behaviour of Helena, betraying them to Demetrius and then chasing after him 'to enrich her pain', is as prankish as anything that Puck could devise. For her, at any rate, the happy ending is entirely the gift of the fairies. These considerations ought to be enough to refute the Kott theory, but perhaps they are irrelevant; I suppose, at bottom, his chapter on the play was just a scheme for acting it so as to nullify the author's intention.

Thus the question 'Why are they interested in us?' has yet to be answered. One might think that the king and queen of the fairies answer it at once; they come on quarrelling about a human changeling, both wanting it, and they quarrel by accusing each other of infidelity with human lovers. Love for mankind could hardly be made plainer. And yet, something shadowy about these loves can be felt at once. Shakespeare is very bold here, and is not following Agrippa or Paracelsus, but presumably his ideas were derived, early in life, from the evil spirits in the New Testament. Such a being can 'enter into' a man and 'possess' him, and will then speak through his mouth. Having got so far, it is natural to suppose that he shares the bodily pleasures of the man; thus a spirit is like a human *voyeur*, except that he is much more efficient at it than we are, sharing a real and not an imaginary pleasure. It may seem unlikely that Shakespeare, who surely wanted to keep at bay the dogma that fairies were really devils, would recklessly confuse them at this crucial point. But the audiences would not be so technical; 'what the Gospel says about spirits is bound to be true, and it never says there are no middle ones – the reason why it reports only bad ones is that they come in stories about cures. So probably the middle ones have the same equipment as the bad ones.' Of course, the other main line of tradition about spirits was the classical culture, given such importance by the Renaissance that it became hard to maintain total disbelief in gods and demigods; but they had to be assimilated into the other information about spirits. The Shakespeare fairy became the established literary model at once, and the first audiences were much more likely than the modern ones to realise what is going on in their speeches.

There is only one crucial passage, the quarrel between Oberon and Titania, which I quote in full:

> OBE.   Ill met by moonlight, proud Titania.
> TITA.   What jealous Oberon? Fairy, skip hence;
> I have forsworn his bed and company.
> OBE.   Tarry, rash wanton; am I not thy lord?
> TITA.   Then I must be thy lady; but I know
> When thou hast stol'n away from fairy land,
> And in the shape of Corin, sat all day
> Playing on pipes of corn, and versing love
> To amorous Phillida. Why art thou here,
> Come from the farthest step of India,
> But that, forsooth, the bouncing Amazon,
> Your buskin'd mistress and your warrior love,
> To Theseus must be wedded, and you come
> To give their bed joy and prosperity?
> OBE.   How canst thou thus, for shame, Titania,
> Glance at my credit with Hippolyta,
> Knowing I know thy love to Theseus?
> Didst thou not lead him through the glimmering night
> From Perigenia, whom he ravished;
> And make him with fair Aegles break his faith,
> With Ariadne and Antiopa?
> TITA.   These are the forgeries of jealousy:
> And never, since the middle summer's spring ...
>
> (III. i. 60–82)

– never since then has she been able to get through a ritual dance with her attendants without his upsetting it; and the fertility of one part of the countryside or another depends on a dance being completed there, so the weather has been frightful, and there is a famine coming up. Oberon does not deny it, but says it is her own fault. The main interest is in the anecdotes; presumably we are not expected to believe in the official denials of them.

The early examples are not decisive; we are let into the subject gradually. Oberon might have appeared as a double of poor Corin, so as to cheat him, a trick sometimes played by classical gods; but then, from what we are told later, it is surprising that Oberon can appear by daylight. There is no problem if he is 'possessing' Corin, because then he is protected from sunlight by a human body. *In the shape of Corin* would usually be said of a separate figure made in imitation, but the words are better suited to Corin's own unique shape, which now has Oberon inside it.[89] And surely the busy Phillida would not listen to him all day? He practises all day, and on a day when Oberon comes he feels inspired; he looks forward to his evening performance with confidence. In the second case, we might decide that the fays are just being silly, and cannot imagine a real infidelity. Among mankind, to attend the wedding of an ex-mistress usually means accepting the new situation, and makes no one jealous. But this is feeble, whereas the alternative view has at least a mild human interest. Theseus is already middle-aged and somewhat battered by his heroic exploits, while his Amazon bride is in full vigour; if he is possessed by a demigod on his wedding-night, he will be pleased to have put on so good a show. His expressions of impatience beforehand may be acted as a polite routine. In the reply of Oberon, which evidently denounces Titania for the same fault, we come closer to overhearing what it actually is. If she wants Theseus for herself, why does she supply him with human women? And how can her husband call that infidelity? On any view, it is hard to see how she *makes* him break his faith, except by some action of her own. And the two lines about Perigenia, which are the same in all texts, are very specific. Titania, says the accusation, out of love for Theseus, led him *away from* Perigenia, in half-darkness, so he was presumably trying to hide or escape from someone; and at some time he ravished Perigenia; presumably we see him when he has just done it, and that is why he needs to escape from her father or her household. And Titania has been present, perhaps to help tie her down. There is no need to deny that a human woman might do this, but surely it would be eccentric behaviour, deserving a word of comment; Oberon takes it in his stride. There seems only one way to make sense of the story. Titania 'entered into' Perigenia, as a New Testament devil might do, and this enabled Theseus to ravage her; afterwards Titania appeared separately, though only in a ghost-like form, so as to show him the means of escape. As it was night-time, she could emerge 'glimmering' without discomfort from her human cover.

This theory, I may be told, does not survive looking up the case in North's *Plutarch*, which was certainly used by Shakespeare for other details and names in the play. The father of Perigouna (another form of the same name) was one of the wild criminals rightly killed by Theseus on his journey to Athens; those who entered his land were torn apart by pine-trees. His daughter, when he was killed, hid in a grove of thorn-bushes, and swore never to cut or burn them if they would help her. But Theseus called to her and promised not to hurt her, so 'she came out of the bushe, and laye with him, by whom she was conceyued of a goodly boye' who is named, and later had a son by another man to whom Theseus gave her.[90] One of the sons colonised Caria, where they still carry out her promise to the thorn-bushes. So she retained her status, and Theseus did not rape her, and probably she was the one who led the way out of the thorn-bushes. Plutarch is sure about the story here, but in the case of Ariadne he says 'there is no trothe nor certeintie' (p. 10). Theseus is usually thought to have behaved shamefully in marooning her on Naxos, after she had saved his life and escaped under his protection, but there are other versions; perhaps she died in childbirth on Cyprus, having demanded to be put off there because she was sea-sick. Shakespeare might well reflect that stories about Theseus were fair game, and that a jealous husband could have a quite different story about Perigouna – whose name for that matter might well be improved, giving it a more piercing vowel and the shake of an extra syllable (we need not reject this form as a mistake made by the printer).[91] Clearly, he makes free with the details of the legend; the name of the hero's father, Egeus, is given without comment to the villain of the play. So it feels refreshing, like a voice from an older world, to have all the commentators assume that Shakespeare wanted to copy out North's details about Perigouna exactly, but happened to say the opposite out of mere incompetence, which should be tactfully smoothed over. He invented very telling details, which necessarily imply possession.

The poetry is magical, all the more so as it pretends to emerge from a scolding. I have no idea of debunking it. No one denies that Theseus treated his ladies unscrupulously; certainly Oberon does not. But Shakespeare does not feel it his duty to join in the work of blame, and the reaction expected from his audience is: 'How wonderful it would be to have a Middle Spirit arranging everything like that.' The answer of Titania to Oberon is merely, 'These are the forgeries of jealousy', but we need not take her to mean that all the stories concerning herself are false; she is both more plausible and more humane if she means: 'I never arranged any cruelty for the girls, as you suppose I did for Perigouna; nor for Ariadne either.' I thus claim to explain *why* the lines are magically beautiful; they call up a world of delight which is only just beyond our grasp. Not far from rough fun either, come to that.

It may be said: 'Perhaps Shakespeare has these louche fancies; but they can have nothing to do with the play, because they are too hard for the audience to deduce.' I answer that the first audiences were ready to pick up such hints, being interested in how one might actually use fairies. But, in any case, the theory is needed to explain what happens next in the play. Having gained nothing by the quarrel scene, Oberon decides to punish his wife, or make her give up the changeling, by a special magic which Puck hurries off to fetch; it will make her love the first creature she sees when she wakes, probably an animal. Most of the animals he mentions would not be expected to respond to her sexually, but the 'meddling monkey, or ... busy ape' (II. i. 181) would be; and by the time he anoints her eyes he is malignant enough to say 'Wake when some vile thing is near' (II. ii. 33). We may suppose that Puck arranges for her to love Bottom with an ass's head, though he pretends gleefully to his master that it was an accident (III. ii. 33); here he is a very good servant, making his master's act of spite work out much less unpleasantly than was probable (also more funnily, but only for those who prefer comparatively mild forms of fun). Oberon intercepts her while she is leading Bottom to her bower, and she sends a messenger to hand over the changeling at once, but he does not at once relieve her from her delusion; he leaves her to continue with her pleasure. Complacent husbands [wittols] were familiar to the first audiences and were jeered at extremely fiercely, especially if, as here, the husband permitted his wife's adultery to gain some advantage for himself. Surely even a modern audience would raise an eyebrow at this point, if it had not been bludgeoned into expecting nothing but a mawkish unreality throughout. Kott deserves sympathy for feeling that a bit of fresh air is needed here, though he need not have smashed the windows at random. The initial quarrel, I submit, by exciting a general curiosity about the sexual nature of the fairies, makes this part easier to put over.

Both quarto and folio stage directions tell us that, when Titania and Bottom arrive at her bower, where they are expected to make love, they are spied on by her husband from the start. This would do Oberon no good with the audience so far; the peeping husband was thought particularly absurd and disgusting. But the production may allow him to play a decisive part, which he should do. When Bottom says he is sleepy, however the actor interprets the absurd words ('I have an exposition of sleep come upon me', iv. i. 38), some of the audience will assume that he is making a tactful approach to a show-down. Here is the one point, no more than the space between two lines, where a Kott production may insert a heroic miming of an act of sex. I do not deny that Bottom has become willing to inquire how far she is prepared to go; he would be an ass if he did not mean that. But Oberon should stretch out his wand (he will be wearing his cloak of invisibility) and administer a deep instantaneous anaesthetic; the polite lie becomes a decisive truth, and some of the audience may at first think he has killed them. We know that he can impose sleep, as he does the same thing just afterwards to the four lovers, though by music only as they are asleep already:

> Titania, music call; and strike more dead
> Than common sleep, of all these five the sense.   (iv. i. 80–1)

They must have a deep sleep not to hear the magic shaking of the ground. But before this he addresses Puck, immediately following upon the impassioned tenderness of Titania to Bottom: 'O how I love thee! How I dote on thee!' 'Welcome, good Robin' are the first words of Oberon (iv. i. 45), and they are much easier to say if he has just performed some decisive action.[92]

I had better quote the main part of what Oberon says to Puck, over the two immobilised bodies, because it has often been taken to present Titania as a repentant adulteress who has won back her husband by her tears. Very hypocritical; but perhaps it is to the credit of Oberon that he wants to put a good appearance on the affair:

> Her dotage now I do begin to pity;
> For, meeting her of late behind the wood
> Seeking sweet favours for this hateful fool,
> I did upbraid her and fall out with her:
> For she his hairy temples then had rounded
> With coronet of fresh and fragrant flowers;
> And that same dew, which sometime on the buds
> Was wont to swell like round and orient pearls,
> Stood now within the pretty flowerets' eyes
> Like tears, that did their own disgrace bewail.
> When I had at my pleasure taunted her,

And she in mild terms begg'd my patience,
I then did ask of her her changeling child;
Which straight she gave me, and her fairy sent
To bear him to my bower in fairy land.
And now I have the boy, I will undo
This hateful imperfection of her eyes.   (iv. i. 46–62)

It is easy to get an impression that she wept; but no, the flowers she had stuck into the donkey's fur of Bottom were the only creatures that wept. Titania asks her husband to be patient with her infatuation, but evidently with no idea of renouncing it. Nor did he want her to, because her concentration upon Bottom was what made her willing to give away the changeling. Oberon expresses genuine disgust for Bottom, but this is probably on grounds of class; Puck does not find him disgusting, though foolish, of course (the fairies do not realise how artful he is). The public mind now has been much stuffed with cooked-up sex-thrills, and the thrill here is to think: 'a lady is being tricked into bed with a stinking hairy worker, practically an animal'. I would not be sure that anything is quite absent from this rich work, but the first audiences would have much more acquaintance with donkeys. Even in recent times, many a girl child has fallen in love with her donkey on the sands at Margate; 'And kiss thy fair large ears, my gentle joy' (iv. i. 4) sums up her feeling exactly. The whole affair is very lyrical; I am not sure why the flowers are weeping, but it is not because an ass' ears are not of good enough class for them. That is, I do not know the profound reason, but a practical reason, in terms of handling the audience, is very clear. Bottom and Titania have just begun 'sleeping together', and sleep they must, while her husband makes this speech looking at them. An Elizabethan audience might continue to regard the scene as farce (after all, they were being encouraged to laugh a moment before), and then their reaction to the fairies would get badly out of hand. The general masterfulness of Oberon, who is now tidying everything up, is a great help, but also, beside it, the mysterious weeping of the flowers is needed to keep mockery at bay. Besides, if someone in the audience needs to believe, like the modern critics, that Titania repented, they had better be given a loophole. The apparent vaguenesses in the play are engineering techniques to handle the floodwaters of audience reaction.

What Bottom was thinking about is another question; but, of course, a theory about the spirits in the play is no good if it does not make the play satisfactory as a whole, so I must deal with the other characters, however briefly.

The two pairs of lovers are already in a knot when the play begins, and not only because of wicked old father. Demetrius has switched over to a passion for Hermia, distressing both her and his previous love Helena, and the support of father is merely an aggravation. Hermia and her true love Lysander decide to escape from Athens through the wood; she has a rich dowager aunt only twenty miles away, outside the law of Athens. Demetrius follows, meaning to kill Lysander, and Helena follows him 'to enrich her pain'. Oberon, while fixing up an ungentlemanly punishment for his own wife, overhears Demetrius rejecting Helena brutally; he disapproves and decides to reverse the situation for a punishment. This bit of magic is never undone; so far from melting away like a dream, it is one of the foundations of the happy ending. The fairies are not only well-disposed towards men (apart from some rough fun) but intimately percipient about us, or (in the case of Bottom) rather too confident in their snap judgments. In this play, of course, there is no magician, no man trying to make contact with the fairies; they are doing that towards us, and it is natural to suppose that they have some deep habitual purpose. A reader may object that this view of the fairies cannot be presented on the stage; I have seen it done, at Stratford, Ontario, in 1968, but I grant that it seemed a lavish thing to do. Twenty or thirty fairies, almost naked, never saying a word, lay about (for perhaps a third of the performance) in attitudes of strained attention, yearning, sometimes moving an elbow to get closer. Someone said it was obscene, but I thought it just explained the fairies.[93] However, they were disappointed; no act of sex takes place during the Midsummer Night. In the case of the couple who run away together, one might be tempted to call Shakespeare his own Bowdler for keeping them chaste. He was prone to keep up appearances before the mass audience; the most absurd case is in bawdy *Pericles*, where he pretends (unlike his source) that the young prince went to the brothel where he finds Marina merely to inspect and correct it; but the preference is innocent enough, being merely intended to avoid trouble. Here, I think, his account of the character's motives for chastity rings very true. Hermia is not seriously frightened, but she is tired and uncomfortable, and her man has lost his status by losing the way. This is no occasion for yielding her virginity; she tells him to leave her alone but stay in ear-shot. It is almost archetypal. And it is necessary for the plot, since finding them asleep like that made Puck sure that he had found the ungracious Athenian who deserved the punishment of a 'love forbid'. Lysander wakes to see Helena, and is forced to love her; she is certain that all the other three are mocking her, and Hermia waking alone goes off seeking death. We cannot call the situation trivial, though the author makes us laugh at it.

v

Finally the reactions of the humans to the fairies are to be considered, and the first question is: 'Why does Bottom not respond to the advances of Titania?' Maybe this makes no great problem to the actor; the character may be shy, or artful, or unattracted, in various degrees, and he need not show which: but there has been disagreement among critics. The Kott view, that he responds vehemently in miming though there is no sign of it in the words, must I think be rejected because it makes the dramatist so incompetent. We had better follow the sequence, from his first entry wearing the ass's head.

Quince says at once 'We are haunted!' (III. i. 99) and all the actors run away. Bottom appears unconscious of the head throughout, except as a general source of irritation; it makes him want to scratch, so he thinks his hair wants cutting. This of course is accepted as a kind of allegory; a fool does not know he is a fool; but it would have to be imposed upon Bottom by a separate act of magic, so it does not prove he is a fool in other ways. Not knowing why the others are frightened, he supposes that 'This is a knavery of them to make me afeard' (III. i. 107–8); he suspects he is being ragged – as Helena does, also rather gratuitously. Perhaps all these characters, in the youth of the world, are prone to teenage fun.

But I will not stir from this place, do what they can; I walk up and down here, and I will sing, that they shall hear I am not afraid. (III. i. 117–19)

He sings a song about birds, and pauses after the lines about the plain-song cuckoo, 'Whose note full many a man doth mark, And dares not answer nay –':

for, indeed, who would set his wit to so foolish a bird? Who would give a bird the lie, though he cry 'cuckoo' never so? (III. i. 129–31)

Such is the moment when he becomes aware of the doting Titania. Dover Wilson notes at this point: 'Bottom's comment shows that he entirely misses the point.'[94] Can he never have seen George Robey? His blindness here is astonishing, far beyond what he attributes to Bottom. It is the method of this type of comedian to 'reprehend the true meaning of what he is saying'; Bottom (or the husband he is impersonating) regards it as totally beneath his dignity even to admit that he knows what the bird means. I grant that, when such a character is put into a play, it is hard to be sure that he understands the joke, because he is struggling to pretend that he doesn't; but surely the actor of Bottom does not have to be unconscious – he ought to be putting the joke over, and it is hard for him to avoid suggesting that the character understands it too. Anyhow, the testing moment finds Bottom already in a facetious and competitive frame of mind. She says she loves him, and he answers:

Methinks, mistress, you should have little reason for that. And yet, to say the truth, reason and love keep little company together nowadays. The more the pity that some honest neighbours will not make them friends. Nay, I can gleek upon occasion. (III. i. 137–41)

The easiest way to prove yourself at home in the great world is to express contempt for it; love, indeed! he is a long way above that. It is an entirely successful speech, in which he makes himself out almost as nasty as Hamlet. At the end of it, he feels so sure of its effect that he asks the audience for applause (a usual practice for clowns). To *gleek* meant to make snooty cracks; not really in his line, but the proper thing to offer a lady. The force of *Nay* is: '*You* thought I wouldn't be able to handle this very embarrassing situation, but I can.' One's heart bleeds for Bottom, who has got off entirely on the wrong foot; but it turns out not to matter as a goddess cannot realise that she is being snubbed. After a lengthy harangue, telling him that she will purge him and so on, she calls up his attendants; these turn out to be almost babies, tots who can just speak, and he has actually to invent details about fairies so as to amuse them. This makes him feel entirely at home, and by the end of the second session, in the bower, I think he really has become willing to have a shot at going to bed with her (that is, I expect a performance treating it so would be all right). But he may naturally want to know more about the set-up before he commits himself; that was a very sinister-looking fairy who came up while they were on the way to the bower, and just what is involved in being purged? She is obviously very unpredictable too. One had better keep open an escape route.

As the tots are the making of this party, which would otherwise be a sad failure, it is natural to ask where they come from. We need not doubt that they are the children of fairies. But how can there be so many, immediately available? The authorities do not tell us just how long the Middle Spirits (or 'Longaevi') may expect to live, but it must be well over 2,000 years, as classical spirits were known to have been raised in the sixteenth century. To keep their numbers steady, they must breed very much less frequently than we do, say 30 times. In fact, they might be changelings, human children who had been 'purged', but I have not heard of anyone who says so: and Shake-speare wants his fairies to be spirits of natural fertility. Titania might have ordered these tots beforehand, expecting Bottom to like them, but she has had no time to plan. However, it is not surprising to find rarities around a court; no doubt Titania collects them, and they have a few elegant lessons there, all coming briefly in rotation perhaps. One might be disappointed that they tell us so little about their lives; it is Bottom who invents the quaint details about what they are to do for him. But he is not supposed to be ignorant; he knew a good deal about fairies before, like most of his audience. And he is told their names, which are enough to prove that his folklore is not a delusion. Still, it seems plain that these fairies are not really going to do what he invents; they are to enjoy imagining they will, just as human children would do. Titania indeed, just before she calls them in, says of the fairies who will attend on him, 'they shall fetch thee jewels from the deep' (III. i. 151), but she need not regard these few tots as the only ones.

> The spirits tell me they can dry the sea,
> And fetch the treasure of all foreign wrecks

– so Faust had been told by an encouraging magician (*Dr Faustus*, I. i. 144–5), and these spirits are distinctly grown-up. The effect of having a man inventing suitable activities for baby spirits is to make the whole scene credible, as hardly anything else would have done. And it solves his problem of how to handle Titania; he does not have to address her again at all in their first scene together, and in the other one she appears to have started 'playing up', or accepting her role:

TITA.   Or say, sweet love, what thou desir'st to eat.
BOT.   Truly, a peck of provender; I could munch your good
        dry oats. Methinks I have a great desire to a bottle
        of hay: good hay, sweet hay, hath no fellow.

TITA. I have a venturous fairy that shall seek
The squirrel's hoard, and fetch thee new nuts.   (IV. i. 30–5)

It sounds very much as if, in saying this, she knows that his stomach cannot accept hay, though the donkey's mouth wants it, but she hopes that nuts may satisfy both of them. She has been reduced to being tactful to him. Of course, if Bottom realises his situation, he may be seriously anxious about what he can manage to eat, but to us, as to her, he remains impenetrable. The effect is that he treats her like a girl of six who has taken a fancy to him on the sands at Margate; he jollies her along, feeling 'no need to bother – the parents will turn up soon enough'. The method would not have worked with the Venus of Shakespeare's recent *Venus and Adonis*, because she was in a state of bodily desire, whereas Titania, though ecstatic, seems as yet to have no specific craving, except for the reassurance that he provides. Her last words before she sleeps –

... the female ivy so
Enrings the barky fingers of the elm.
O how I love thee! How I dote on thee!   (IV. i. 42–4)

– do not sound as if she needs immediate activity from Bottom, or even as if she feels capable of sustaining it. No doubt the audience and her husband would not be inclined to rely upon that, but even so they can hardly jeer at Bottom as 'this lack-love, this kill-courtesy' (II. ii. 76). Bottom has better luck than Adonis, but also he is allowed to cut a better figure. By the way, when Bottom chooses the music of the tongs and the bones, the folio stage direction mutters 'Musicke Tongs, Rurall Musicke', but the quarto says nothing. Commentators have often assumed that Titania must 'pass over', in embarrassed silence, a request for music suited to the lower classes; but magic knows a better honour than that. If the bones were a nuisance to provide, the line asking for them would be cut; both editions give evidence that they were sometimes provided. Stage directions often get dropped. The scene is very short, and a fairy dance to the bones could help it a good deal; perhaps we could have a steel band.[95]

The conversation of Bottom and his attendants (III. i. 172–89) is almost entirely about food, or rather about the strangeness of the whole procedure of eating. The one he addresses first gives the name Cobweb, and Bottom says he will use him if he cuts his finger; this is not about human food, but the spider gets good by spinning from its entrails, and the power of the web to stop blood has an eerie suitability. In their other scene Cobweb is sent to catch a humble-bee, and Bottom will eat the honey-bag. The next attendant is Peaseblossom, almost too plain a case, and no great fun can be extracted from his parents Squash and Peascod. Perhaps the children have a lurking fear that the monster is going to eat them; if so the third name, Mustardseed, is a great help, because the mustard bites back. Bottom pretends that it is the wicked beef who eats the mustard, but no one believes him; it makes his eyes water. Probably this case had another interest for the children, rather hard to make explicit while keeping the smooth tone. I have not noticed mustard still biting while being evacuated, but I sometimes have the curry; and this of course makes it plainly a spirit; it has emerged from the great tube (as long as a cricket-pitch) without loss of identity. Finally the case of Moth has to be considered; he has been reduced in the folio to one mention of his name in a stage direction, and even in the quarto, though he speaks, he is not endowed with any flow of fancy by Bottom. No doubt it was hard to keep four such young children available for a public theatre, and three are quite enough. *Moth* was then specifically a word for the kind of moths who eat clothes, so queerness about eating was provided again. It has been argued that Shakespeare used this form for 'mote', so that Moth was an intestinal bacterium, and one would like to hear Bottom's instructions to it, but more probably he addressed a clothes-eating moth.

Marcel Proust has a fine passage, easy to find because it is exactly in the middle of 'Combrai', the first long section of his great novel [*Du Côté de chez Swann*]; he is describing his life at about the age of nine, when he first realises that he is being given good cooking. Apparently the asparagus is what he admires in the kitchen and can then smell in his own farts late in the night:

I felt that these celestial hues indicated the presence of exquisite creatures who had been pleased to assume vegetable form who, through the disguise which covered their firm and edible flesh, allowed me to discern in this radiance of earliest dawn, these hinted rainbows, these blue evening shades, that precious quality which I should recognise again when, all night long after a dinner at which I had partaken of them, they played (lyrical and coarse in their jesting as the fairies in Shakespeare's *Dream* [*dans leurs farces poétiques et grossières comme une féerie de Shakespeare*]) at transforming my humble chamber into a bower of aromatic perfume. [trans. by C. K. Scott Moncrieff]

As I read this I felt certain that it was very penetrating, but I could not remember any coarse jests that the fairies had made (apart from Puck, in whom they are no paradox). The idea that the mustard gives you a last bite in the tail, though only implicit, must I think have occurred to Proust, because it is the only definite example of what he describes. And this impression of getting on easy terms with the spirits, intimate and domestic, really was a major novelty in the play, and has been used in very various ways ever since, for example in *The Ancient Mariner* and *Through the Looking-Glass*.

But though accepted as a way of feeling, then and later, it actually followed from a theoretical doctrine of the new medicine. Paracelsus had maintained that we have 'spirits' inside us which make our bodies tick over normally; every section of the body has a governor or mayor who handles the immediate situation and also passes information higher up – the most important one is the 'archeus' of the belly. These are quite different from the Middle Spirits, who live independently and take little interest in us, also from the bad spirits who may sometimes enter us and cause our diseases. The first complete edition of Paracelsus (in Latin) was coming out in Amsterdam during 1588–92, so his views were being discussed, probably in the hearing of Shakespeare; but Shakespeare does not follow them, as he assumes that his Middle Spirits can take possession of us directly, like the bad spirits in the gospels. He is a bit reckless, it would seem at the time, in making practically no attempt to distinguish them from devils, except by maintaining firmly that they are beneficent.[96]

There is also a long-term reason for making the fairies work inside us, though it had better be kept in the background. The last act discusses imagination, meaning all that Wordsworth did by the term so far as I can see, without a glance at the fairies except in the first words; apparently it is all about plays, and poetry maybe, possibly also religious fanatics. It is found hard to be sure where imagination begins; how much the eye and ear 'half-create, And what perceive'.[97] It is not denied that imagination, though often ludicrous and delusory, may sometimes tell us truths which we could not otherwise have known. Inspiration by a muse cannot be far out of sight, and how is that less than possession by a spirit? Most critics have been content with the negative side of this, thankful that the Bard ends by laughing off the belief in fairies. He does sound sensible, but no such negative has been asserted.

Such being the main point about the adventure of Bottom, I must next try to answer a few of the many accusations against him. His friends once or twice call him *bully*, which to them meant 'good all round'; the use of it to mean 'brutal and overbearing' came in with the Restoration. In the rehearsal scenes, though he is full of ideas, he always accepts the ruling of the producer (he roars like any sucking dove). He does not scratch because he has fleas but because the donkey's hair irritates the human skin (as he nearly explains: IV. i. 25). Perhaps his finest moment is a retort to the duke while acting Pyramus. 'Curs'd be thy stones for thus deceiving me!' he has said to the wall (V. i. 179), and the duke interrupts with: 'The wall, methinks, being sensible, should curse again':

No, in truth, sir, he should not. 'Deceiving me' is Thisbe's cue: she is to enter now, and I am to spy her through the wall. You shall see it will fall pat as I told you: yonder she comes. (V. i. 182–5)

Perhaps he is feeling the inevitability of the tragedy, but he would enjoy knowing better anyhow. And, childish though the retort may appear, the audience on the stage are behaving like much nastier children; he actually silences them for nearly twenty lines, so that some of the necessary business can go forward. I do not know why critics keep saying he is typically working-class; he is a trained artisan, the same class as Shakespeare's father, whether Shakespeare had become unclassed or not; and surely he is the life and soul of many a city boardroom. He is brave, resourceful, and generous; his vanity is a tyrant over him, and might often lead him wrong, but it lets him sail through the situations that confront him in the play. In short, he is a fundamental kind of man.

There is also a learned problem about the meaning of 'Bottom'. The word was not used for a part of the body till the later eighteenth century; also, as a name it was suited to a weaver, as it could mean 'a nucleus on which to wind thread, or the thread so wound' (a pern, Yeats would say). This is all right, if we may allow other meanings of the word to comment upon bottom; 'the base on which a thing stands, an abyss, a valley, an alluvial hollow, the most remote or inmost part, the foundation, the soil in which a plant grows, the essence or reality of something, financial stability' (*OED*): all these are at least seventeenth century. Clearly, Bottom is a fundamental character, well fitted to confer with nature upon the bases of life. It has often been found that a joke in Shakespeare was not so aggressive as it now appears; thus, leaving his wife his second-best bed was not offensive (the best bed would be in the guest-room), but Shakespeare of all men would know it was funny. If anyone doubts that the name Bottom was meant to be funny, it seems enough to quote the passage where Venus recommends her body, as a landscape, to Adonis:

> 'Within this limit is relief enough,
> Sweet bottom grass and high delightful plain,
> Round rising hillocks, brakes obscure and rough ...'
>
> (*Venus and Adonis*, 235-7)[98]

The human fundament could be a prominent example of a bottom, before it was called one. And there is a supporting pun, familiar at least to actors who feel at home with Shakespeare, in ASS and ARSE, which I think is plainly meant though it looks improbable in the *OED*. Each word is given only one pronunciation, with the vowels different, and the 'r' comes into all the spellings of words cognate to *arse* in Northern Europe.[99] However, Helge Kökeritz (*Shakespeare's Pronunciation*, 1953) says that London and the Midlands had a standard difference here, and London around Shakespeare's time was coming to be accepted as having the classier version.[100] When Shakespeare was a lad in Stratford he would say BARSTARD, but when acting a lord in a London theatre (though perhaps not when swearing) he would say BASSTARD.[101] This greatly improves a line by the Dauphin describing the English aristocracy before the battle of Agincourt; they are

> Normans, but basstard Normans; Norman Barstards.[102]

In the same way, ASS could be regarded as a genteel way of saying 'arse'; indeed, that has remained normal in America. I am not sure of the reverse operation, but the play twice rhymes *ass* with *pass*:

> ... it came to pass
> Titania wak'd, and straightway lov'd an ass. (III. ii. 33-4)

Of course it is quite possible to pronounce *pass* rhyming with 'mass'; I used to have relations who did, but they regarded it as regional. A vowel-shift is likely to run through a whole group of words. An actor might pause for attention and then pronounce the word that didn't rhyme, but that would be making rather too much fuss about it. The only basic idea about Bottom is that he is sturdy and unrefined, vigorous and necessary. No grave faults need result from that.

We may take it then that the name of Bottom pilloried or defined the clown of the play, almost as much then as it does now. Oddly enough, all through the fourth act, but there only, his speeches are headed 'Clown' or 'Clo.', as if Shakespeare felt the need to remind himself that the character must not rise above his nature. It is in this act that the danger arises, because Bottom brings off the chief surprise of the play. The four lovers have lain asleep on the stage while Puck cures Lysander, and then Titania arrives at her bower; she and Bottom are stricken unconscious, so we have six sleepers. Oberon restores Titania, they perform their dance and fly away; then Theseus and his train arrive hunting, and awake the lovers, who are forgiven; then the lovers discuss the situation, and return to Athens. Then Bottom awakes, and the delay has excited the curiosity of the audience. Will he rejoice, in some absurd manner, at the release he has been demanding? But no, he has swung round completely. He is overwhelmed by the privilege that has been granted to him; he has had a vision of the divine, and he will boast of it for all the rest of his life.

A surprise about a character had better allow of being accepted after a brief reflection, and the audience are not under much strain here. It is easy to reflect that Bottom has been brought up to worship Greek goddesses, and Titania is as near to one as makes no difference. He attempts rhetoric in a ludicrously muddled way ('The eye of man hath not heard, the ear of man hath not seen', IV. i. 209 ff.), and does not deny that he hopes to gain by turning pious. Besides, the others have all said they feel somehow better for being ragged by the fairies; so his change fits in well enough. But there is another factor here. The *Riverside Shakespeare*, tirelessly concerned to make the text as dull as possible, has a note to this speech: 'A parody of 1 Corinthians 2: 9' [Bishops's Bible];[103] and the *OED* is unusually confident that a *parody* is an imitation intended to mock. But the theatre of Shakespeare did not ridicule the New Testament; that was one of the things the censor was employed to prevent. And the passage was very well known; even if missed at the start, it would soon be spotted. Shakespeare may have had to plead for it, saying that it was just an apposite quotation, but why was it apposite? The words as used by Bottom merely say that the revelation given to him cannot be expressed; to make him happen upon the words of St Paul says to the audience: 'Don't think you're the only ones; people with other religions have revelations too.' This would not come under the blasphemy laws, but it would be a good deal more than the *Riverside* edition means to allow.[104] And I must urge that it is not cancelled by the details which allow Bottom to remain in character. The fool says:

man is but a patched fool if he will offer to say what methought I had. The eye of man hath not heard, the ear of man hath not seen, man's hand is not able to taste, his tongue to conceive, nor his heart to report, what my dream was. I will get Peter Quince to write a ballad of this dream: it shall be called 'Bottom's Dream', because it hath no bottom; and I will sing it at the latter end of a play, before the Duke. Peradventure, to make it the more gracious, I shall sing it after death [*at her death*: quartos and folio]. (IV. i. 208–17)

These are the final words before we leave the magic wood. After his absurd but laboured piece of rhetoric, saying that the experience cannot be expressed, Bottom is at once sure that a poet can express it. (And why not? It is no more than his due, after an experience of such profundity.) There is no slyness about his shift from one to the next; they all seem radiantly true. The audience may be tempted into further thoughts, such as 'If you can't believe in nature you are in no fit state to believe in God' and 'Bottom is just the kind of man who does see the fairies'. Anyhow, it is important for the shape of the play that his speech should come out strong. I have accepted Theobald's emendation to 'after', at the end, because *at her death* sets the audience an untimely puzzle. There is no chance of getting the ballad ready for tonight's audience, and Bottom's mind does not run on Thisbe anyhow. But to sing it after his own death, on or off the stage, is a plan adequate to his vanity, and gives the resonant exit line that must have been intended.[105]

I need finally to say something about Theseus on imagination in the last act, as he in effect tells us how to take the play, and students usually write down that he is a hard-headed rationalist, totally against belief in fairies. They find this a relief, as they have resisted fiercely the earlier attempts in the play to make them accept fairies. Here is an important case where the initial joke sets the tone for the subsequent scene; supposing you know just enough about Theseus to recognise the joke. We do not easily realise how insistently classical even the elementary education was. One of the things the coarse audience was sure to know about Theseus was that, before his time in this play, he had been shipped to Crete with other youths and maidens of Athens to be fed to the Minotaur; but on the way he jumped overboard and sank without trace. 'I suppose we ought to

chain them', said a depressed Cretan guard; 'of course, they all
know what's in front of them'. But after half an hour the hero
surfaced again, carrying a typical product of the sea, a very large
pearl necklace, which he would need for seducing the princess
Ariadne. The boat had passed over one of the palaces of his sea-
nymph mother Amphitrite. Now, such being his note, the audience
are keen to hear what he will say about the appearance last night of
fairies in his hunting-park. His bride, though she had given a rather
worldly impression so far, remarks that what the lovers report is
strange.

> THE. More strange than true. I never may believe
> These antique fables, nor these fairy toys.
> Lovers and madmen have such seething brains . . .
> The lunatic, the lover, and the poet
> Are of imagination all compact:
> One sees more devils than vast hell can hold;
> That is the madman: the lover, all as frantic . . .
>
> (v. i. 2–10)

This madman sounds very like Martin Luther. Theseus has jumped
right away from laughing at a village superstition, and is affronting
a belief particularly attractive to the clergy. Sir Thomas Browne
said it was a kind of atheism not to believe in spirits, and it certainly
was hard to combine with a literal acceptance of the Bible.[106]
Whether you can believe in anything, beyond the next meal,
Theseus might appear to be questioning; and yet his following words
do not deny that the lover and the poet may hit on something true
by using their imagination – he only says they are absurdly liable to
be wrong.

> Such tricks hath strong imagination,
> That if it would but apprehend some joy,
> It comprehends some bringer of that joy:
> Or, in the night, imagining some Fear,
> How easy is a bush suppos'd a bear!   (v. i. 18–22)

A series of critics, claiming to know the style, have explained that
the last two lines cannot possibly be meant there; at least, a lot of
lines must have been added [see for example Furness, *New Variorum*,
p. 202]. Probably they were, but the final jolt is left in because it is
still intended. Theseus is host, and fears he is becoming a bore, and
breaks off his speech with a deliberately absurd example, well suited

to the beginning of it, but not to the sympathy with lover and poet expressed in-between. I needed to glance at the whole speech, but the greatest impact would come from the first two lines. The maker of legends, halfway through making them, says: 'I never can believe in all those stuffy legends, can you? They seem to mean nothing to me.' It is terrifically smooth and sporting; and of course cannot really prevent you from believing in the legends about him.[107]

He says very little that is damaging. Of course, he would have no business to, being a demigod himself, and due to become a Middle Spirit after his death; and surely he has seen Titania at least once, when her glimmering shade led him through the night from Perigenia? If he visits his mother, he has seen a great deal of the spirits. And the only thing he sticks to in his nay-saying is that imagination may always be wrong; of course, I agree that his remarks are intended to relieve members of the audience who feel too glutted with fantasy. 'The best of this kind are but shadows; and the worst are no worse if imagination amend them' (v. i. 208–9); it is so mild that it pricks us on to say more. You cannot appreciate any play at all without using your imagination; nor yet understand what is going on around you. Whether you can sometimes learn things by using your imagination which you could not have learned otherwise – to deny that would be important, but Theseus comes nowhere near it. He does perhaps suggest that the fairies give an inadequate picture of the mysterious and beneficent powers of nature.[108]

Walter Pagel in his profound book on Paracelsus says that 'imagination' to Paracelsus meant the power to enter into the working of nature, as a doctor must do in grasping the needs of a patient; it would be imagination if one said, correctly: 'that branch of the tree will tear off, in this wind, unless I tie it back'. Probably he is right, but I was rather shocked to find that the German word he translates as *imagination* was also the ordinary one for religious faith.[109] It would be unfair to expect sixteenth-century authors to bowl us over with their scientific wisdom. But it is wonderful that Shakespeare had so much grasp of the challenging subject, and could put it into a cool and amused survey; to end with Theseus as a sceptic does not mean much, but allows of universal good humour.

Notes

INTRODUCTION

1 WE, letter to Terence Moore, 'Guy Fawkes Night 1981' (Cambridge University Press).
2 WE, letters to Christopher Ricks, 22 November 1981 and 10 September 1982.
3 WE, letter to Ian Parsons, 21 October 1975 (Chatto and Windus).
4 WE, letter to Boris Ford, 28 April 1959 (copy in Empson Papers).
5 WE, letter to Terence Moore, 15 August 1981 (Cambridge University Press).
6 WE, letter to Ian Parsons, 4 November 1972 (Chatto and Windus).
7 Typescript introductory passage from Clark Lectures (Empson Papers).
8 Arthur Freeman, *Thomas Kyd: Facts and Problems*, Oxford: Clarendon Press, 1967, p. 95.
9 J. R. Mulryne (ed.), Thomas Kyd: *The Spanish Tragedy* (New Mermaids), 2nd edn., London: A. and C. Black; New York: W. W. Norton, 1989, p. xx.
10 Undated loose-leaf letter, recipient unknown, in Empson Papers.
11 TS draft of an essay entitled 'Censorship in *The Spanish Tragedy* and *Dr Faustus*' (Empson Papers).
12 Ibid. Empson's argument may be supported by the following passage in Wilfred T. Jewkes, *Act Division in Elizabethan and Jacobean Plays 1583–1616*, Hamden, Conn.: The Shoe String Press, 1958, pp. 124–5: 'The play is clearly divided into acts, although the division is uneven. Act I has 606 lines, Act II, 427, Act III, 1367, and Act IV, 566. No Act V is indicated. The natural inclination is to suggest that Act III, since it is more than twice the average length of the others, was originally divided into two, and that what is marked Act IV is really Act V. *However, Revenge and the Ghost, acting as an opening chorus to each of the acts, only appear four times (exclusive of an epilogue at the end).* It seems clear that the author intended the play to be divided, and it is unlikely that he would divide it into four acts. Since one act heading is gone, *it must have been deliberately*

removed, perhaps for some reason connected with performance.' (Editorial italics.)

13 See Philip Edwards (ed.), Thomas Kyd: *The Spanish Tragedy* (The Revels Plays), London: Methuen and Co., 1959, rpt. Manchester and New York: Manchester University Press, 1977, pp. xxvii–xl.

14 John Henry Jones, *The English Faust Book: a Critical Edition, based on the Text of 1592* (Cambridge University Press, forthcoming). I am greatly indebted to Dr Jones for showing me the typescript of his edition.

15 See, for example, Janet Clare, *'Art made Tongue-Tied by Authority': Elizabethan and Jacobean Dramatic Censorship*, Manchester and New York: Manchester University Press, 1990; and Richard Dutton, *Mastering the Revels: The Regulation and Censorship of English Renaissance Drama*, London: Macmillan Academic and Professional, 1991.

16 'Still the Strange Necessity' (1955), rpt. in *Argufying: Essays on Literature and Culture*, ed. John Haffenden, London: Chatto and Windus, 1987, p. 121.

17 'The Hammer's Ring' (1973), in *Argufying*, p. 221.

18 'Obscurity and Annotation' (*c.* 1930), in *Argufying*, p. 83.

19 John Creaser, *'Volpone*: The Mortifying of The Fox', *Essays in Criticism*, 25, July 1975, 355.

20 Martin Butler, 'Introduction', in *The Selected Plays of Ben Jonson*, I, ed. Johanna Procter, Cambridge: Cambridge University Press, 1989, p. xvii; and Butler (ed.), *The Selected Plays of Ben Jonson*, II, Cambridge: Cambridge University Press, 1989, p. xvii.

21 WE, undated letter (1973) to Roger Sale (copy in Empson Papers).

22 S. Schoenbaum, 'The Humorous Jonson', in *Shakespeare and Others*, Washington: The Folger Shakespeare Library; London: Scolar Press, 1985, p. 202 note 6.

23 Lee Bliss, *The World's Perspective: John Webster and the Jacobean Drama*, Brighton: The Harvester Press, 1983, p. 232 note 12.

24 Frank Whigham, 'Sexual and Social Mobility in *The Duchess of Malfi*', *PMLA*, 100:2, March 1985, 183–4 note 20.

25 Frank Kermode (ed.), Shakespeare: *The Tempest* (New Arden), London: Methuen and Co., 1954, rpt. 1961, p. 108 (note to IV. i. 212), and Appendix B, pp. 142–5.

26 WE, letter to Terence Moore, 'Guy Fawkes Night 1981' (Cambridge University Press).

27 David Bevington and Eric Rasmussen (eds.), Marlowe: *Doctor Faustus: A- and B-texts (1604, 1616)* (The Revels Plays), Manchester and New York: Manchester University Press, 1993, pp. 27–9, 1.

28 Cf. D. Allen Carroll and Gary Jay Williams: 'As regards the date, nothing has altered our assumption that the play was written between 1594, not early, and 1596, not late, either narrowing this range or placing an emphasis within it, unless Harold F. Brooks' recent preference for the winter of 1595–96 should gather support' (*'A Midsummer*

Night's Dream': An Annotated Bibliography, New York and London: Garland Publishing, 1986, p. xxi).

29 John S. Mebane, *Renaissance Magic and the Return of the Golden Age: The Occult Tradition and Marlowe, Jonson, and Shakespeare*, Lincoln and London: University of Nebraska Press, 1989, p. 4.

30 David B. Pirie (ed.), Empson: *Essays on Shakespeare*, Cambridge: Cambridge University Press, 1986, pp. vii–viii.

31 WE, letter to Terence Moore, 15 August 1981.

32 Ibid.

I: 'THE SPANISH TRAGEDY' (1)

1 Cf, for example, J. R. Mulryne (ed.), *The Spanish Tragedy* (New Mermaids), 2nd edn., London: A. and C. Black; New York: W. W. Norton, 1989, p. xx; and note 4 below. See also Michael Hattaway, *Elizabethan Popular Theatre: Plays in Performance*, London, Boston, Melbourne and Henley: Routledge and Kegan Paul, 1982, p. 127.

2 Quotations from *The Spanish Tragedy* refer to the Revels Plays edition by Philip Edwards (London: Methuen, 1959; rpt. Manchester and New York: Manchester University Press, 1977); cited hereinafter as Edwards, *ST*.

3 It has since been pointed out to me [by Derek Roper: see the letter by Empson printed after the present essay] that 'thrust Horatio forth my father's way' could then mean 'out of his way', and evidently did because that makes a display of arrogance; the murder is described as removing an unsightly object from the duke's path. I thus lose the one bit of the text which appeared to tell the secret. But Lodovico would have been unlikely to tell it anyhow, so this does not refute the theory. The arguments against it which have kindly been sent me have left me all the more convinced. (WE) Edwards, *ST*, glosses 'forth' as 'out of'.

4 Hence Empson's essay (first published in 1956) is precisely seeking to address, by anticipation, Edwards' indifferent observation that 'it is very hard to justify the sub-plot. The Portuguese court could have been introduced more economically and the relevance of theme is very slight ... [N]o theory of revision can explain away what seems to be the pointless savagery of the murder of unoffending Castile. It may be that Kyd was trying to give a Senecan touch of the curse upon the house, but there are other considerations which make *condemnation* of Hieronimo rather irrelevant. In the first place, Castile was Andrea's enemy (see II. i. 46–7 and III. xiv. 111–13) and Hieronimo is the agent of destiny employed to avenge Andrea; Castile's death appears to make Andrea's peace perfect. Revenge is satisfied, and we had best try not to worry about the bloodthirstiness of it all' (Edwards, *ST*, pp. liii, lx). Cf. Fredson Bowers, *Elizabethan Revenge Tragedy 1587–1642*, Princeton University Press, 1940, pp. 70–1, 80. J. R. Mulryne noted too, 'Justice in

the familiar sense can scarcely be said to be done in the killing of Castile
at the play's end (even though he was Andrea's enemy)' (*The Spanish
Tragedy* (New Mermaids), London: Ernest Benn, 1970, p.
xxii); and
Eleanor Prossor: 'The killing has been justified on the grounds that
Castile opposed the love of Don Andrea and Bel-Imperia, but the
argument is not convincing. In the play itself, Castile is a sweet old man
who does not deserve blame, much less sudden death' (*Hamlet and
Revenge*, Stanford, California: Stanford University Press; London:
Oxford University Press, 1967, p. 51 note). Arthur Freeman yet insists,
'we may assume that if Kyd knew what he was doing, the death of
Castile finally is not, as some have suggested, either an accident or a
gross dramatic error in the interest of pure sensationalism' (*Thomas
Kyd: Facts and problems*, Oxford: Clarendon Press, 1967, p. 95) – though
without offering any satisfactory solution. Alternative interpretations
include those by Andrew S. Cairncross, 'Introduction' to Thomas Kyd,
'The First Part of Hieronimo' and 'The Spanish Tragedy', London: Edward
Arnold, 1967, p. xxviii; G. K. Hunter, 'Ironies of justice in *The Spanish
Tragedy*' (*Dramatic Identities and Cultural Tradition: Studies in Shakespeare
and his Contemporaries*, Liverpool University Press, 1978, pp. 228–9);
Sharon Dahlgren Voros, 'Thomas Kyd and Pedro Calderón: Toward a
Semiotics of Revenge Drama', in Louise and Peter Fothergill-Payne
(eds.), *Parallel Lives: Spanish and English National Drama 1580–1680*,
London and Toronto: Associated University Presses, 1991, pp. 116–17.
5 Algernon Charles Swinburne, *A Study of Shakespeare*, London: Chatto
and Windus, 1880, p. 162.
6 See, for example, Edwards, *ST*, pp. xxxiv-xl; Freeman, *Thomas Kyd*,
pp. 98–100. Cf. Mulryne (ed.), *The Spanish Tragedy*, 2nd edn., p. 119
note to lines 165–7 and 179–82.
7 Edwards, reviewing the evidence for identifying Jonson as author of the
additions, concurs with Empson to this extent (*ST*, p. lxv): 'the search
for traces of Jonson's known style is hopeless. Yet it is important not to
return a flat "impossible" to Jonson. The principle of decorum has to be
remembered ... we need to try to imagine what Jonson would have
written for *The Spanish Tragedy*. Must he not have indulged a more
romantic vein, with its own type of language ... when he tried to fit
scenes to an old "romantic" play? Would anything that is truly Jonsonian have done?' Freeman (*Thomas Kyd*, pp. 122–30) contends that
Jonson could not have provided the extant additions. But cf. Anne
Barton's affecting hypothetical reconstruction of the circumstances
under which the 1602 additions were composed, in *Ben Jonson, Dramatist*, Cambridge: Cambridge University Press, 1984, pp. 12–28; and
David Riggs, *Ben Jonson: A Life*, Cambridge, Mass.: Harvard University Press, 1989, pp. 87–91. Roslyn L. Knutson stresses, 'although Kyd
scholars have not wanted to assign the additions of Q1602 to Jonson
(they object, primarily, on stylistic grounds), none has been able to

prove that the additions are *not* his, due to the 25 September 1601 and 22 June 1602 payments in *Henslowe's Diary* ... On the presumption that *The Spanish Tragedy* as printed in Q1602 represents substantially the performance text of the 1597 revival, we have a gauge for the combined pressures of commercial duplication and generic growth. When the Admiral's Men brought the play out of retirement [in 1597], it must indeed have looked old-fashioned – not in rhetorical style – but in relation to what revenge drama had become since *The Spanish Tragedy* was last on the stage in 1592–1593' ('Influence of the Repertory System on the Revival and Revision of *The Spanish Tragedy* and *Doctor Faustus*', *English Literary Renaissance*, 18, 1988, [257–74], pp. 258 note 5 – which also provides a convenient list of references to the various opinions of Kyd scholars on the subject of the 'additions' – and p. 270). Knutson's article further supports Empson with the observation, 'It is possible that the additions Jonson was hired to provide in 1601–2 were meant to accommodate *The Spanish Tragedy* to the most recent revenge plays (namely, *Antonio's Revenge* and Shakespeare's *Hamlet*) as the additions in Q1602 apparently imitate *The Jew of Malta* and *Titus Andronicus*' (p. 271).

8 Cf. Bowers, *Elizabethan Revenge Tragedy*, pp. 78–9.

9 See Philip Edwards (ed.), *Hamlet, Prince of Denmark* (New Cambridge Shakespeare), Cambridge: Cambridge University Press, 1985, pp. 3–7, for a good account of the relation between *The Spanish Tragedy, Hamlet* and *Antonio's Revenge*.

3: 'THE SPANISH TRAGEDY' (II)

1 'This demand and situation [the ghost's reason for revenge] closely parallels the reported ghost of Achilles in Seneca's *Troades*; but it is a piece of Senecan ethics undigestible to English audiences' (Fredson Bowers, *Elizabethan Revenge Tragedy 1587–1642*, Princeton University Press, 1940, p. 66 note; see also pp. 68, 74).

2 Quotations from *The Spanish Tragedy* refer to the Revels Plays edition by Philip Edwards (London: Methuen, 1959; rpt. Manchester and New York: Manchester University Press, 1977); cited hereinafter as Edwards, *ST*.

3 Cf. J. R. Mulryne (ed.), *The Spanish Tragedy* (New Mermaids), 2nd edn., London: A. and C. Black; New York: W. W. Norton, 1989, p. xx.

4 Empson felt egged on to write this further essay on Kyd's play in part by reading both '*The First Part of Hieronimo*' and '*The Spanish Tragedy*', ed. Andrew S. Cairncross (Regents Renaissance Drama Series), London: Edward Arnold, 1967, and Arthur Freeman, *Thomas Kyd: Facts and Problems*, Oxford: Clarendon Press, 1967. 'Silly of me not to have found out it was there', he noted of the so-called *1 Hieronimo*. 'It is not decisive help, and I think one has to conclude that the censorship mangled the

plot, so as not to allow disrespect for royal marriages (and the first audiences would still know what it was all about) ... What needs correction most is the refusal to see Andrea when appearing in SP *does not think he needs revenge.* He only finds that out when he has seen what appears in the first *two* acts. He does not learn that Lorenzo tried to murder him, in the first play (and why do Hier. and his son say it's a good thing he didn't get their letter?) but he can see Lorenzo needs killing. The idea of not having a fair fight is too medieval and remote [...]; it does not occur to Andrea. I think the idea that he had to be murdered for a dynastic marriage is the only way out'. Freeman's book Empson considered 'sensible ... good at exposing the imbecile pedantry of the tittering critics'. (Empson Papers). Apropos the 'mangling' of *Dr Faustus*, see Empson, *Faustus and the Censor: The English Faust-book and Marlowe's 'Doctor Faustus'*, ed. John Henry Jones, Oxford: Basil Blackwell, 1987.

5 See J. E. Neale, *Queen Elizabeth I* (1934), Harmondsworth: Penguin, 1960, pp. 240–50, 252, 257–9.

6 See for example Richard Dutton, *Mastering the Revels: The Regulation and Censorship of English Renaissance Drama*, London: Macmillan Academic and Professional, 1991, pp. 58–9.

7 See Janet Clare, *'Art made Tongue-Tied by Authority': Elizabethan and Jacobean Dramatic Censorship*, Manchester and New York: Manchester University Press, 1990, pp. 26–7.

8 Cf. Philip Edwards (ed.), *The Spanish Tragedy* (The Revels Plays, 1959); rpt. Manchester: Manchester University Press, 1977, pp. xxiv–xxv ('Kyd is innocent of contemporary allusions'); hereinafter cited as Edwards, *ST*. But, as Empson noted, Freeman 'makes nonsense of Edwards' struggle to exclude reality' from the play. Kyd assuredly worked with the recent history of Spain and Portugal; among other details, Freeman remarks, 'Philip II's institution of the office of Viceroy in Portugal did, in fact, follow Spanish practices in Naples, Sicily, Sardinia, and the New World, and while the Viceroy was, as Edwards points out, a nephew of Philip himself, he was also native Portuguese' (*Thomas Kyd*, p. 53).

9 Philip Edwards, like Bowers before him, concurs with Empson's line of thought here: 'The Elizabethan revenge-play, and *Hamlet* in particular, is concerned with exploration, not preachment. It devotes itself to the whole issue of the legitimacy of violence and the responsibility of the individual in pursuing justice, finding in the revenge convention an extraordinarily rich source of conflicts to exhibit and illuminate the many faces of violence and redress. To prejudge the plays by saying that for the Elizabethans revenge was of course evil or was of course acceptable is to defeat them completely ...' (*Hamlet, Prince of Denmark* (New Cambridge Shakespeare), Cambridge University Press, 1985, p. 39).

10 Wilfred T. Jewkes, *Act Division in Elizabethan and Jacobean Plays 1583–1616*, Hamden, Conn.: The Shoe String Press, 1958, pp. 28–9. (For an account of line numbers in the four given acts, and deductions by Jewkes which may very well support Empson's argument, see pp. 124–5 – quoted in Introduction note 12 above.) Further page references to Jewkes are given in the text.

11 Empson's citation of Tilney's directive is taken from *The Book of Sir Thomas More* (Malone Society Reprints no. 26, Oxford: Oxford University Press, 1911, pp. xiii–xiv), a corrected transcription is given in Anthony Munday and others, *Sir Thomas More* (Revels Plays), ed. Vittorio Gabrieli and Giorgio Melchiori, Manchester and New York: Manchester University Press, 1990, p. 17. In a detailed discussion of the text and additions, and of Tilney's hand (pp. 17–33), Gabrieli and Melchiori effectively quash the notion that Tilney was really rather indulgent in his intervention: 'In spite of the Additions meant to disarm censorship, the surviving parts of the original contained enough objectionable matter (the sympathy with the reasons of the May Day rioters in I. i and I. iii, the treatment of More's resignation and Fisher's arrest in IV. i. and odd allusions here and there) to induce Tilney to write, in 1593–94, his signed injunction on the first page, amounting to a veto to the performance of the play' (p. 27). See also G. Blakemore Evans, who remarks that Tilney's order 'would imply the deletion of something like a quarter of the play!' ('*Sir Thomas More*: The Additions ascribed to Shakespeare', *The Riverside Shakespeare*, Boston: Houghton Mifflin Company, 1974, p. 1683); and Clare: 'Clearly, Tilney was not remotely interested in the effects of his censorship on the play ...' ('*Art made Tongue-Tied by Authority*', p. 32). Cf. Dutton: 'The effect of the censorship he proposed would have been both to suppress potentially inflammatory scenes of rioting and to keep the depiction of More's rise and fall at a more restrained, less contentious pitch. If this is what he had in mind, it was both shrewd and circumspect of him, though it may have left the actors with a play hardly worth performing as it stood ... [T]he issue at stake is the Act of Supremacy ... Yet, with specific changes, Tilney was apparently willing to see it appear on stage (though we do not know if it ever did so)' (*Mastering the Revels*, p. 86).

12 Edwards concurs with Empson's approval of Bel-imperia (*ST*, p. liv).

13 See also S. Viswanathan, 'The Seating of Andrea's Ghost and Revenge in *The Spanish Tragedy*', *Theatre Survey*, 15, 1974, 171–7; Michael Hattaway, *Elizabethan Popular Theatre: Plays in Performance*, London, Boston, Melbourne, and Henley: Routledge and Kegan Paul, 1982, pp. 115–16.

14 'At the end of II. v, there is some inconsistency in the directions for removing Horatio's body from the stage, and it might be argued that Hieronymo's Latin dirge was struck out by the theatre and a direction inserted to close the scene before the dirge' (Edwards, *ST*, p. xxxii; see

also pp. 44–5 and notes). Cf. Hattaway, *Elizabethan Popular Theatre*, p. 109.

15 This is not the only occasion on which Empson made up the words to supply a story that had been suppressed: see Christopher Ricks, ' "*Doctor Faustus*" and *Hell on Earth*', *Essays in Criticism*, 35:2, April 1985, 102.

16 See previous essay, note 7.

17 Algernon Charles Swinburne, *A Study of Shakespeare*, London: Chatto and Windus, 1880, p. 162.

18 Helen Gardner, 'Milton's "Satan" and the Theme of Damnation in Elizabethan Tragedy', *English Studies 1948* (Essays and Studies, new series 1), 63; rpt. in *A Reading of 'Paradise Lost'*, Oxford: Clarendon Press, 1965, pp. 117–18.

4: 'VOLPONE'

1 Edward B. Partridge, *The Broken Compass: a Study of the Major Comedies of Ben Jonson*, New York: Columbia University Press, 1958, p. 80.

2 Quotations from *Volpone* refer to the edition by John W. Creaser, *Volpone, or The Fox* (London Medieval and Renaissance Series), London: Hodder and Stoughton, 1978. See also the following, later essay by Empson, written in response to a preparatory article by John W. Creaser.

3 Partridge, *The Broken Compass*, p. 99.

5: 'VOLPONE' AGAIN

1 John Creaser, '*Volpone*: The Mortifying of The Fox', *Essays in Criticism*, 25 July 1975, 329–56; Creaser reproves Empson's earlier article as 'an extraordinarily uneven argument' (p. 355).

Quotations from *Volpone, or The Fox* refer to Creaser's excellent later edition of the play (London Medieval and Renaissance Series), London: Hodder and Stoughton, 1978, which amplifies material from the preparatory article that Empson takes to task in this essay. However, since this Empson piece was drafted (1975–6) before the appearance of Creaser's volume, quotations from Creaser in the text and footnotes here refer only to his first offending article in *Essays in Criticism*.

For an outline of the conflicting schools of criticism on *Volpone*, see R. B. Parker's Revels Plays edition (Manchester University Press, 1983), esp. pp. 37–8, 44. Equally informative is the prefatory matter to the play in *The Selected Plays of Ben Jonson*, 1, ed. Johanna Procter (Cambridge University Press, 1989); Martin Butler, in an Introduction, salutes Creaser's 1975 essay – 'Much the most eloquent and sympathetic account of Volpone' – while rebuking Empson's earlier article as 'provocative and untrustworthy' (p. xvii). See too Joan Lord Hall, '"Wee cannot ... returne to our selves": *Volpone*', in *The Dynamics of Role-Playing in Jacobean Tragedy*, London: Macmillan, 1991, pp. 95–114, which takes good stock of the critical heritage.

2 According to Creaser, 'the Volpone of Acts I–IV needs too much to feel superior and invulnerable to relish taking risks. He only bets on near-certainties, and has nothing of the delight in arbitrary risk so characteristic of, say, the medieval Reynard' (p. 346). Creaser allows that Volpone is 'courageous in one crucial episode' (p. 338).

3 John W. Creaser, 'Marvell's Effortless Superiority', *Essays in Criticism*, 20:4, October 1970, 403–23; see also 'Raw Material' (a review of *The Art of Marvell's Poetry* by J. B. Leishman), *Essays in Criticism*, 17:1, January 1967, 103–7.

4 'So far as possible, everything is calculated: he goes out of doors in disguise and checks that it has not been perpetrated ...' (Creaser, '*Volpone*: The Mortifying of the Fox', p. 346).

5 Creaser does not actually quote this line in his essay, though he does discuss the speech in question on pp. 348–9.

6 'A character like Volpone, who draws the audience's attention to his zest and skill in acting, sharpens our conscious pleasure at the nature of theatrical experience, and makes us collaborate in the performance' (Creaser, ibid., p. 345); 'Almost all Jonson's vital and engaging characters, from Bobadill onwards, are narcissists ... those Jonsonian characters who are virtuosi of self-devotion invent the selves which they act out in front of others. They are exhibitionists to a man' (pp. 339–40).

7 'Tormented himself [in Act V], he must himself torment others ... Volpone is out less to perform than derisively to inflict pain' (Creaser, ibid., p. 349).

8 Creaser remarks on the possibilities of the pun: 'Volpone thus implies that the sentence is both hideous and inappropriate' (p. 352).

6: 'THE ALCHEMIST'

1 For an up-to-date, generously informative discussion of the critical heritage, see Martin Butler (ed.), *The Selected Plays of Ben Johnson*, II, Cambridge: Cambridge University Press, 1989; and R. V. Holdsworth's fine introduction to his volume *Jonson: 'Every Man in his Humour' and 'The Alchemist'* in the Casebook series (London: Macmillan Press, 1978).

2 A student objected that Face must needs be presented morally, because he repents:

> They'll tell all.
> (How shall I beat them off? What shall I do?)
> Nothing's more wretched, than a guilty conscience.

> (v. ii. 45–7)

Face is afraid of losing his confidential relation with his master, and snatches every occasion to beg the sympathy of the audience, with comic despair, from here to the end of the next scene, rather over a hundred lines, when he invents the plan of marrying his master to the fortune. No one denies that the characters use moral language; I only say that this is not an impressive repentance. It may have served the purpose of coaxing the audience to forgive Face. (WE)

3 Quotations from *The Alchemist* refer to the Revels Plays edition by F. H. Mares (London: Methuen, 1967; Manchester University Press, 1974).

4 I used to think there is a bitter irony when he says:

> This lip, that chin! Methinks you do resemble
> One o' the Austriac princes   (IV. i. 55–6)

– because the Hapsburg jaw came to be the standard example of the degeneration caused by dynastic interbreeding. But Jonson wrote before the sinister change had occurred; the prominence of the jaw might still be taken to mark decisiveness and firm will, with which we know Doll to be endowed. (WE)

5 W. B. Yeats, 'Preliminaries', *On The Boiler*, Dublin: The Cuala Press, 1938, p. 12.

6 C. G. Thayer, *Ben Jonson: Studies in the Plays*, Norman, Oklahoma: University of Oklahoma Press, 1963, p. 93.

7: 'MINE EYES DAZZLE'

1 Clifford Leech, *Webster: The Duchess of Malfi*, London: Edward Arnold, 1963 (Studies in English Literature no. 8). Leech initiated the fashion for disparaging the duchess in *John Webster: A Critical Study*, London: Hogarth Press, 1951 – 'a warning to the rash and the wanton' (p. 108). Critics who largely concur with his stance include James L. Calderwood, '*The Duchess of Malfi*: Styles of Ceremony', *Essays in Criticism*, 12:2, April 1962, 133–47; Robert F. Whitman, 'The Moral Paradox of Webster's Tragedy', *PMLA*, 90, 1975, 894–903; Joyce E. Peterson, *Curs'd Example: 'The Duchess of Malfi' and Commonweal Tragedy*, Columbia and London: University of Missouri Press, 1978. More kindly assessments include 'The Tragic Indeterminacy of *The Duchess of Malfi*', in Charles R. Forker, *Skull Beneath The Skin: The Achievement of John Webster*, Carbondale and Edwardsville: Southern Illinois University Press, 1986: 'The correlative factors of the Duchess's secrecy and Antonio's humble birth of course complicate – and are intended to complicate – our response to her fatal decision to remarry. But ... critics have been too ready to assume a condemnatory attitude on the part of Webster and his audience. Clandestine marriages, usually contracted for emotional reasons, were understandable in an age when parents or higher authorities tended to think principally in political

and financial terms. Such unions were often stringently punished, but it is unreasonable to believe that popular sympathy would be universally withheld' (p. 299). Gunnar Boklund (*'The Duchess of Malfi': Sources, Themes, Characters*, Cambridge, Mass.: Harvard University Press, 1962) proposes that the character of the duchess' defiance is 'Utopian': 'She points towards the establishment of an order of love and nature which she wants to uphold against the old system of law and social custom' (p. 90). John L. Selzer, who reviews the critical contretemps in 'Merit and Degree in Webster's *The Duchess of Malfi*' (*English Literary Renaissance*, 11:1, Winter 1981, 70–80), builds on Boklund's suggestion in arguing that the play exhibits 'an unblinking assertion of the primacy of personal worth over inherited position' (p. 70). Joan Lord Hall declares in a note: 'My own view is that the Duchess's *hamartia* . . . is not emphasised as morally culpable within the play' ('Creative Role-Playing: *The Duchess of Malfi*', in *The Dynamics of Role-Playing in Jacobean Tragedy*, London: Macmillan, 1991, p. 230). See also G. K. and S. K. Hunter, *John Webster: A Critical Anthology*, Harmondsworth: Penguin, 1969.

2 Empson is slightly misremembering a flourish by J. A. Symonds, with regard to 'the tainted crew' on whom Vendice 'treads and tramples' in *The Revenger's Tragedy*: 'They are curling and engendering, a brood of flat-headed asps, in the slime of their filthy appetites and gross ambitions' (*Webster and Tourneur*, intro. and notes by John Addington Symonds (Mermaid Series), London: T. Fisher Unwin, no date, p. xiv).

3 Dawn L. Smith likewise stresses the fact that Webster's England felt 'an intense xenophobia toward Catholic countries, particularly Spain'; in the Jacobean theatre, 'Spaniards and Italians were stereotyped as cunning, jealous, bloodthirsty, and untrustworthy. Webster's play with its Italian setting and villainous Spanish brothers is thus in tune with contemporary chauvinism and xenophobia' ('Text, Stage and Public in Webster's *The Duchess of Malfi* and Lope's *El Mayordomo de la Duquesa de Amalfi*', in *Parallel Lives: Spanish and English National Drama 1580–1680*, eds. Louise and Peter Fothergill-Payne, London and Toronto: Associated University Presses, 1991, p. 84).

4 F. L. Lucas (ed.), *The Complete Works of John Webster*, II, London: Chatto and Windus, 1927, p. 12. Yet Lucas also says (p. 22), 'The fatal error of the Duchess – fault we cannot call it – is that she ever fell in love with Antonio. Weakness is the least dramatic of human qualities; and the play, as well as his mistress, suffers from its presence in him . . . Such as he is, for all his sensitiveness, a juster and happier fate would have wedded him, not to the Duchess, but to Cariola.' Cf. Boklund, '*The Duchess of Malfi*', p. 179 (ch. 4, note 6), on Belleforest's moral attitude. William Painter's version of the tale, from *The Palace of Pleasure*, is now available in *The Duchess of Malfi* (Revels Plays), ed. John Russell Brown, London: Methuen and Co., 1964; rpt. Manchester University

Press, 1976, Appendix 1, pp. 175–209 (hereinafter cited as Brown, *DM*).

5 See also Bob Hodge, 'Mine Eyes Dazzle: False Consciousness In Webster's Plays', in *Literature, Language and Society in England 1580–1680*, ed. David Aers, Bob Hodge and Gunther Kress, Dublin: Gill and Macmillan, 1981, pp. 117–18.

6 *The 'Summa Theologica' of St Thomas Aquinas*, literally translated by Fathers of the English Dominican Province, Third Part (Supplement), QQ. XXXIV–LXVIII (19), London: Burns Oates and Washbourne, 1920, p. 121. See also F. L. Lucas (ed.), *The Complete Works of John Webster*, II, p. 140: 'By the canon law *sponsalia de presenti*, in which the pair recognized each other as wife and husband at the time of speaking, were valid ... The Council of Trent (1563) insisted on all marriages taking place henceforward *in facie ecclesiae*; but in Protestant countries the canon law remained in force (it had been abolished in England by Henry VIII, but was restored under Edward VI) though such a union had to be consecrated subsequently by a religious service, under pain of certain penalties'; Brown, *DM*, pp. 35–6 (footnote to I. i. 479); Lawrence Stone, *The Family, Sex and Marriage in England 1500–1800*, London: Weidenfeld and Nicolson, 1977, pp. 31–2.

7 Quotations from *The Duchess of Malfi* are taken from the Revels Plays edition by John Russell Brown (Brown, *DM*: note 4 above), even though Empson once commented on Brown: 'He is rather sweet, I suppose, but madly permissive. Lucas is still much the best, and it is a shame that they forbid him to clear up the text.' (Empson Papers) All the same, it seems best to make reference here to an accessible, modernised edition.

8 Cf. Peterson, *Curs'd Example*, pp. 66–7. M. C. Bradbrook suggests that these lines refer to the sacrament of penance (*Themes and Conventions of Elizabethan Tragedy* (Cambridge: Cambridge University Press, 1935, p. 206); Brennan concurs with Empson that the point is marriage (New Mermaids, pp. xxiv, 111). Cf. Boklund, '*The Duchess of Malfi*', p. 118: 'The Duchess's reliance on the sacrament of marriage at this point is in marked contrast to her self-sufficiency in the wedding scene, with its challenging references to the church.' Empson (in his notes) snapped at Boklund's remark, 'So he doesn't get the point at all'; and yet he thought Boklund finally: 'Blind on the points I want, but well done otherwise, and with no positive bad feeling; except perhaps when he says she proposes just after her brothers have threatened her because she is "unable to restrain her passion" [pp. 85–6]'. Cf. Forker: 'Fundamentally Christian values inform both the attitudes and actions of the Duchess. She regards her secret union, despite its irregularity, as "a sacrament o' th' church" (IV. i. 39) and clearly intends to have it publicly solemnized as soon as this should become feasible ...' (*Skull Beneath The skin*, p. 323). But Forker also remarks, 'Webster implants a

few hints that in spite of her admirable resistance to tyranny, the Duchess is less than totally honest with herself ... In making Cariola witness to her legal contract *"Per verba de presenti"*, she stresses that concealment is everything ...' (p. 322).

9 Cf. Cecil W. Davies, 'The Structure of *The Duchess of Malfi*: An Approach', *English*, 12, 1958, 92–3; and Forker: 'But, of course, the religion of the Duchess is not free of conflict or inconsistency. Feigning a pilgrimage ... gives her conscience no pause ...' (*Skull Beneath the Skin*, p. 324).

10 See also Elizabeth M. Brennan (ed.), *The Duchess of Malfi* (New Mermaids), London: Ernest Benn, 1964, p. xii. Cf. Bliss: 'In this context, the audience's own feelings about second marriages are irrelevant: unconcerned with her duchy's political health, the Duchess seeks private happiness at the expense of public stability. As a ruler, she can no more be lauded for the example she sets than her brothers ... She should not be – and does not strive to be – a ruler at all. The Duchess does not so much misuse or evade public responsibility as seem unaware of its claims' (*The World's Perspective*, p. 145).

11 Cf. Bob Hodge: 'What is especially interesting about this is not the relationship itself ... but its invisibility. No character ... seems aware of this motive, and the audience is encouraged to share the characters' bewilderment and misconceptions. The infra-plot, as it can be called, not only concerns unconscious motivation, it remains at that level for the audience' ('Mine Eyes Dazzle', p. 115). Boklund finds it 'improbable' that Ferdinand is to be regarded as incited by incestuous love – 'since the tenor of the decisive passages is almost the same in Painter as in Webster – only tangentially relevant and possibly detrimental to the effect of the pertinent scenes and the play as a whole' ('*The Duchess of Malfi*', p. 99). Cf. McD. Emslie, 'Motives in Malfi', *Essays in Criticism*, 9, 1959, pp. 391–405; Brown, *DM*, pp. lii–liv; Bliss, *The World's Perspective*, p. 233 note 17; and James L. Calderwood, '*The Duchess of Malfi*', p. 134: 'most critics have acknowledged as least plausible the case made by F. L. Lucas and supported by Clifford Leech that Ferdinand acts from incestuous jealousy'. See also Brennan, *The Duchess of Malfi*, p. xiv. Frank Whigham, in a forceful psychosocial essay, concurs with Empson's view in describing Ferdinand 'as a threatened aristocrat, frightened by the contamination of his ascriptive social rank ... Ferdinand's incestuous impulse is determined by class paranoia ... His lycanthropia, unitary wolf at last, brings him to his logical end in total isolation. Walled in alone, not in a secret garden but an inward hair shirt, he is finally *sui generis*, unique, a peerless class of one – a final entropic apotheosis of the superb Renaissance hero' ('Incest and Ideology', in *Staging the Renaissance: Reinterpretations of Elizabethan and Jacobean Drama*, ed. David Scott Kastan and Peter Stallybrass, New York and London: Routledge, 1991, pp. 266, 268, 270). Whigham specifically

endorses this passage from Empson's essay on p. 271 note 9. Empson could not later identify a source for his remark *vis-à-vis* the Elizabethan view of the Borgias, which he probably came across in the 1920s, but he had no misgivings on the matter. 'What I fear is that the attribution to family pride may be classed as my invention, and it is the only part that adds a critical sidelight on the *Duchess*', he wrote to Whigham on 12 August 1982. 'But I will still believe it myself even if no authority is found. The pride of the Borgias was notorious, and the incest of the Pharaohs as a religious duty had long been well known' (Frank Whigham).

12 Giovanna d'Aragona, the original of the duchess, was married in 1490, at the age of twelve, to Alfonso Piccolomini, who became duke of Amalfi in 1493.

13 See also Empson's remarks on the play in 'Literary Criticism and the Christian Revival' (1966), reprinted in *Argufying*, pp. 634–5.

8: 'THE DUCHESS OF MALFI'

1 Clifford Leech, *John Webster: A Critical Study*, London: Hogarth Press, 1951, p. 82.

2 As in the previous essay, the text for all quotations from *The Duchess of Malfi* is that of the Revels Plays edition by John Russell Brown (1964), rpt. Manchester: Manchester University Press, 1976 (Brown, *DM*).

3 R. W. Dent, *John Webster's Borrowing*, Berkeley and Los Angeles: University of California Press, 1960; hereinafter cited as Dent, *JWB*. 'Good sensible book,' wrote Empson in his notes. 'But are we to take the borrowings to mean that he was "conventional-minded"? I think he was very conventional about literature but not about moral judgments – hardly noticed when he was disagreeing in fact. But to go as far as that is almost agreeing with Dent. [...] I expect that all writers echo fashionable phrases more than we realise. The control experiment would be hard to do, and Dent does not try. [...] I probably agree with him more than I think.' (Empson Papers).

4 Dent, *JWB*, pp. 36–7.

5 'As [F. L.] Lucas observes, even in his favorite source, Sidney's *Arcadia*, he made little use, if any, of the verse ... Thus, insofar as Webster's imitation is evidence of his reading, we have little indication that he read the most famous poetry of his age ...' (Dent, *JWB*, p. 45).

6 Dent, *JWB*, p. 71.

7 'There are a good many parallels and dubious echoes, especially to Shakespeare, but relatively few clear signs of direct verbal borrowing' (Dent, *JWB*, p. 46).

8 'According to Lucas, "The episode that follows is full of echoes of Shakespeare; some will feel, too full." But except for the parallel to Ophelia's distribution of flowers, the supposed "echoes" are probably

coincidental' (Dent, *JWB*, p. 157). Dent had, in fact, anticipated Empson with this footnote: 'Parallels to Shakespeare, verbal and otherwise, are more numerous and more obvious in *The White Devil* than in *The Duchess of Malfi*. One possible cause is that Webster wrote the second play, but not the first, for Shakespeare's company and audience' (p. 46). Cf. Leech, *A Critical Study*: '[T]he scene of Cornelia's madness echoes passages from *Hamlet, Macbeth* and *Lear* ...' (Ibid., pp. 116–17).

9 Cf. Gunnar Boklund, '*The Duchess of Malfi': Sources, Themes, Characters*, Cambridge, Mass.: Harvard University Press, 1962, pp. 130–1; Charles R. Forker, *Skull Beneath The Skin: The Achievement of John Webster*, Carbondale and Edwardsville: Southern Illinois University Press, 1986, p. 365.

10 See John Russell Brown, 'On the dating of Webster's *The White Devil* and *The Duchess of Malfi*', *Philological Quarterly*, 31:4, October 1952, 358–62; Brown, *DM*, pp. xxv–xxvi.

11 See John Bossy, 'The Counter-Reformation and the People of Catholic Europe', *Past and Present*, 47, 1970, 57; Lawrence Stone, *The Family, Sex and Marriage in England 1500–1800*, London: Weidenfeld and Nicolson, 1977, pp. 31–2.

12 M. C. Bradbrook, *Themes and Conventions of Elizabethan Tragedy*, Cambridge: CUP, 1935, p. 206; hereinafter cited as Bradbrook, *TCET*.

13 Cf. Joyce E. Peterson, *Curs'd Example: 'The Duchess of Malfi' and Commonweal Tragedy*, Columbia and London: University of Missouri Press, 1978, pp. 66–7.

14 F. L. Lucas (ed.), *The Complete Works of John Webster*, II, London: Chatto and Windus, 1927, p. 12; hereinafter cited as Lucas, *CWJW*.

15 Frank W. Wadsworth, 'Webster's "Duchess of Malfi" in the light of some contemporary ideas on marriage and remarriage', *Philological Quarterly*, 35: 4, October 1956, 394–407.

16 Bradbrook, *TCET*, p. 203 (Empson's italics).

17 *Ibid.*, p. 201.

18 *Ibid.*, p. 202.

19 Brown (*DM*, pp. lxv, 110–11) argues that the stage-direction was probably authorial, 'and we may suppose that Webster aimed at a maximum horror and cruelty'. Empson observed in notes on Brown's edition: 'argument that he can't have meant *child* because the stage directions were added specially after setting up the page. Still an easy mistake. Brown's idea [p. 111] that she would easily *forget* the children were dead is very unlike her. That is what she is thinking about all along.' (Empson Papers) Cf. Elizabeth M. Brennan (ed.), *The Duchess of Malfi* (New Mermaids), London: Ernst Benn, 1964, p. 111.

20 'Antonio's son lives to inherit his mother's duchy, not only violating primogeniture but apparently proving the dismal horoscope false' (Forker, *Skull Beneath The Skin*, p. 367).

21 Lucas, *CWJW*, II, pp. 147, 153; Brown, *DM*, note to II. iii. 56–64.

Johnstone Parr ('The Horoscope in Webster's *The Duchess of Malfi*', *PMLA*, 60, 1945, 760–5) notes that Webster had a fair understanding of the technicalities of horoscopy, since the horoscope is hypothetical but accurate; he concurs with Empson that 'we are left with the thought that attempts will be made to restore "this yong hopefull Gentleman" [the base-blooded son of Antonio] to his proper titles. But there will be difficulties. The Duchess had an elder son – her heir apparent – by her first husband ...' (p. 764).

9: ELIZABETHAN SPIRITS

1 Frances Yates, *Giordano Bruno and the Hermetic Tradition*, London: Routledge and Kegan Paul, 1964; hereinafter cited as Yates, *Bruno*. 'Rather a horrid book', Empson remarked in his notes; 'she has had her temper spoiled by teaching I think'. (Empson Papers)
2 C. S. Lewis, *English Literature in the Sixteenth Century excluding Drama*, Oxford: Clarendon Press, 1954, p. 10.
3 Lewis, *English Literature in the Sixteenth Century*, p. 9.
4 'W. P. Ker thought the philosophers and theologians believed in daemons but the elves of folklore were "far from heaven, and safe from hell" – the other way round in fact', Empson quipped in his notes. 'Probably he was wrong.' (Empson Papers) His source is Minor White Latham, *The Elizabethan Fairies: The Fairies of Folklore and the Fairies of Shakespeare*, New York: Columbia University Press, 1930, p. 43; 'A fussy book,' thought Empson, 'and he [*sic*] never sees the point, but plenty of information' (Empson Papers). Latham quotes too (p. 41), as Empson noted, from *A Discourse concerning Devils and Spirits*: 'Many have insisted upon the Natures of these Astral Spirits: some alledging, That they are part of the faln Angels [...] others, as Del rio, Nagar the Indian Magician, and the Platonists affirm, That their nature is middle between Heaven and Hell; and that they reign in a third Kingdom from both, having no other judgment or doom to expect for ever' (Reginald Scot, *The Discoverie of Witchcraft*, (1584), London: Elliot Stock, 1886, p. 495). Empson wrote further, in his notes: 'I don't find any case of someone doing what Faust did, joining the M[iddle] S[pirits] to escape Hell, in Miss [*sic*] Latham's book. It would have been considered an unlikely bit.'
5 Manes of Persia (*c.* 215–75) taught a radical dualism, a contest between the two ultimate forces of good and evil.
6 Empson's source here is H. M. Adams, in a letter of 12 November 1975 (Empson Papers).
7 Empson's source for *Liber de nymphis, sylphis, pygmaeis et salamandris et de caeteris spiritibus* is the translation by Henry E. Sigerist, *A Book on Nymphs, Sylphs, Pygmies and Salamanders, and on the Other Spirits*, in *Four Treatises of Theophrastus von Hohenheim*, eds. C. Lilian Temkin, George

Rosen, Gregory Zilboorg and Henry E. Sigerist, Baltimore: The Johns Hopkins Press, 1941, pp. 213–53. Cf. Robert H. West, *Shakespeare & the Outer Mystery*, Lexington: University of Kentucky Press, 1968, pp. 88, and 191–2 note 9: 'Paracelsus is the principal writer of the Renaissance to assert true cohabitation and issue between elementals and human beings ... Antiquity provides endless tales of union between mortals and gods or demons, and Renaissance writers, both pneumatologists and others, picked up these tales in profusion ... For the orthodox view that angels, whether elect or damned, never begot true issue upon women, see Thomas Aquinas, *Summa Theologica*, Q. 51. Art 3. Most orthodox writers on sexual relations between spirits and women parrot Aquinas.'

8 Lewis calls *De Nymphis* a 'pleasing little tract [which] mainly gives a pseudo-scientific form to local and contemporary folklore, mostly of a very innocent sort' (*English Literature in the Sixteenth Century*, p. 12).

9 Aquinas, *Summa*, Q. 57, Art. 2. See *Faustus and the Censor*, ed. John Henry Jones, Oxford: Basil Blackwell, 1987, p. 106.

10 *Paradise Lost*, I, 423–31; VI, 328–34, 344–53. In addition, Milton most notably denotes 'middle spirits ... Betwixt the angelical and human kind' (III. 461–2).

11 As Jones points out (*Faustus and the Censor*, p. 90n), King James does not specifically mention storm clouds; Empson is perhaps offering a (not misleading) shorthand version of James' diatribe in *Daemonologie* (1597): 'all Devils must be lyars; but so they abuse the simplicitie of these [witches] ... that they make them beleeve, that at the fall of *Lucifer*, some Spirites fell in the aire, some in the fire, some in the water, some in the lande ... But the principall part of their fall ... the falling from the grace of God ... they continued still thereafter, and shal do while the latter daie, in wandring through the worlde, as Gods hang-men, to execute such turnes as he employes them in. And when anie of them are not occupied in that, returne they must to their prison in hel' (*Minor Prose Works of King James VI and I*, ed. James Craigie, Edinburgh: Scottish Text Society, 1982, p. 14). Empson may also have been thinking of a passage from *A Discourse of Devils and Spirits* to the effect that 'an organicall bodie must have bones, sinewes, veines, flesh, &c.: which cannot be made of aier. Neither (as Peter Martyr affirmeth) can airie bodie receive or have either shape or figure. But some ascend up into the clouds, where they find (as they saie) diverse shapes and formes even in the aier. Unto which objection P. Martyr answereth, saieng, and that trulie, that clouds are not altogether aier but have a mixture of other elements mingled with them' (quoted in Robert Hunter West, *The Invisible World: a Study of Pneumatology in Elizabethan Drama*, Athens, Georgia: University of Georgia Press, 1939, p. 26).

12 For a sceptical survey of the actually impressive diffusion of Hermetic influence both on the Continent and in England, see Wayne Shumaker,

The Occult Sciences in the Renaissance: A Study in Intellectual Patterns, Berkeley, Los Angeles and London: University of California Press, 1972, pp. 232–48; hereinafter cited as Shumaker, *Occult Sciences*.

13 Reginald Scot, *The Discoverie of Witchcraft*, p. 418; Scot adds that 'these histories are ... grosse and palpable ... ' G. Cardano (1501–76) was a mathematician, astrologer, physician, polymath; see Henry Morley, *The Life of Girolamo Cardan*, London: Chapman and Hall, 1854. J. B. Bamborough notes that Cardano's 'two encyclopaedic works, *De Subtilitate* (first published 1550) and *De Rerum Varietate* (first published 1557), were ... valuable sources [for Robert Burton in *The Anatomy of Melancholy*], and Burton draws on them for a variety of subjects (in particular demonology: although he was sceptical about witchcraft, Cardan had much to say about demons, and Burton quotes, for example, his account of the conversation which his father Fazio Cardano had with seven devils "in Greek apparel" in August 1491)' ('Burton and Cardan', in *English Renaissance Studies Presented to Dame Helen Gardner in honour of her Seventieth Birthday*, Oxford: Clarendon Press, 1980, p. 183). Like Empson, K. M. Briggs points to the theory 'that the fairies, nymphs and spirits of the Gentiles were not devils but an intermediate creation between humanity and pure spirits, of an ethereal body, a life longer than human life but still mortal, and an eternal destiny still unfixed, so that they were capable of salvation. Such spirits were those that Cardan claimed to have seen raised by his father ... ' (*The Anatomy of Puck: An Examination of Fairy Beliefs among Shakespeare's Contemporaries and Successors*, London: Routledge and Kegan Paul, 1959, p. 169).

14 Latham, *The Elizabethan Fairies*, p. 43 (citing Robert Kirk, *The Secret Commonwealth of Elves, Fauns, & Fairies: A Study in Folk-Lore and Psychical Research*, London: David Nutt, 1893). C. S. Lewis, writing about the kinds of Fairies or *Longaevi* ('Longlived'), notes that the first theory of their nature is that 'they are a third species distinct from angels and men': 'In the fourteenth century the family of Lusignan boasted a water-spirit among their ancestresses.' [Lewis' source is S. Runciman, *History of the Crusades*, II, 1954, p. 424. Cf. A. S. Byatt, *Possession: A Romance*, London: Chatto and Windus, 1990] Later still we get the theory of a third rational species with no attempt to identify it. The *Discourse concerning Devils and Spirits*, added in 1665 to Scot's *Discoverie*, says "their nature is middle between Heaven and Hell ... they reign in a third kingdom, having no other judgement or doom to expect forever" [see also above]. Finally, Kirk in his *Secret Commonwealth* identifies them with those aerial people whom I have had to mention so often already: "of a middle nature between Man and Angel, as were Daemons thought to be of old" ' (*The Discarded Image: an introduction to Medieval and Renaissance Literature*, Cambridge: Cambridge University Press, 1964, p. 135). 'Surely it wasn't *hard* to "identify" them,' crabbed

Empson; his opinion of *The Discarded Image* as a whole is pertinent to the present essay: '[Lewis] is too bland, seeing no harm in anything, and he is keen not to allow the Renaissance to have occurred. However, that Ficino was *recovering* Trismegistus need not be denied' (Empson Papers).

15 A. L. Rowse, *Simon Forman: Sex and Society in Shakespeare's Age*, London: Weidenfeld and Nicolson, 1974, p. 210.

16 Yates, *Bruno*, pp. 12–14; Shumaker, *Occult Sciences*, pp. 201–51; and Peter J. French, *John Dee: The World of an Elizabethan Magus*, London: Routledge and Kegan Paul, 1972, pp. 66–88 (hereinafter cited as French, *John Dee*). John S. Mebane gives a lucid overview in *Renaissance Magic and the Return of the Golden Age*, Lincoln and London: University of Nebraska Press, 1989, pp. 17–35; on Ficino's attitude to these daemons (Middle Spirits, as Empson would say) – 'stellar and planetary souls ... mediators ... the demigods of pagan religions' – see especially pp. 31–2 (hereinafter cited as Mebane, *Renaissance Magic*.) The most recent, and authoritative, translator includes a succinct review of the reception of the text in the Renaissance and after: Brian P. Copenhaver, *Hermetica: The Greek 'Corpus Hermeticum' and the Latin 'Asclepius' in a new English Translation, with Notes and Introduction*, Cambridge: Cambridge University Press, 1992, pp. xli–l (hereinafter cited as Copenhaver, *Hermetica*).

17 Walter Scott (ed. and trans.), *Hermetica: The Ancient Greek and Latin Writings which contain Religious or Philosophic Teachings ascribed to Hermes Trismegistus*, I, Oxford: Clarendon Press, 1924, p. 339 (hereinafter cited as Scott, *Hermetica*).

18 Scott, *Hermetica*, I, p. 359; III (1926), pp. 151–6. Copenhaver takes this view: 'Instead of a theory of magic, the theoretical *Hermetica* [now under discussion, as opposed to the 'technical' texts] present a theory of salvation through knowledge or *gnosis*, yet this theory was the product of a culture that made no clear, rigid distinction between *religion* as the province of such lofty concerns as the fate of the soul and *magic* as a merely instrumental device of humbler intent ... Magic comes closest to philosophy, perhaps, in the famous "god-making" passages of the *Asclepius* (23–4, 37–8) which show that material objects can be manipulated to draw a god down into a statue and thus ensoul it' (Copenhaver, *Hermetica*, pp. xxxvii–xxxviii). On the significance of the god-making passage from the *Asclepius* both to Ficino and to Pico della Mirandola, see Mebane, *Renaissance Magic*, pp. 24–5, 43–5; Shumaker, who is insistent upon the philosophical aspect of Hermetism, palliates it as 'exceptional' in the theoretical *Hermetica* (*Occult Sciences*, pp. 206–7).

19 Yates, *Bruno*, p. 22 note 2. Shumaker, too, warns that 'Scott, although an excellent Greek scholar, emends the text boldly and rearranges both sentences and whole sections, especially in the *Asclepius*, in ways that he thinks will produce greater coherence' (*Occult Sciences*, p. 211); and Copenhaver, the latest translator, calls Scott's text 'a jungle of exci-

sions, interpolations and transpositions so distantly related to the
manuscripts that Scott's translation can only be regarded as a translation of Scott, not of the Hermetic authors. Apart from the text and
translation, however, Scott's volumes remain indispensable, and some
of his textual insights are brilliantly right, others brilliantly wrong. His
commentary is copious and learned ... ' (*Hermetica*, p. liii). Scott's
commentary is indeed a stupendous, highly stimulating achievement,
just as Empson found it; however, serious scholars place a higher value
on *Corpus Hermeticum, texte établi par A. D. Nock et traduit par A.-J.
Festugière*, Paris: Société d'Édition 'Les Belles Lettres', 4 vols., 1945–54.
20 Yates, *Bruno*, p. 37; also pp. 9, 169. Copenhaver cannily renders the
latter passage thus: 'But then they discovered the art of making gods.
To their discovery they added a comfortable power arising from the
nature of matter. Because they could not make souls, they mixed this
power in and called up the souls of demons or angels and implanted
them in likenesses through holy and divine mysteries' (*Hermetica*, p. 90).
French (*John Dee*, pp. 85–6) gives his own translation, along with this
commentary: ' ... Hermetic texts not only exalted man as magus but
approved both natural and demonic magic ... [T]he idols commended
by Hermes, the most pious of priests who foretold the coming of
Christianity, were very different from those condemned in the Bible –
the creation of the Egyptian terrestrial gods involved only good demons
... Such reasoning led ... to Dee's attempts at demonic magic, about
which he always protested that his practices were pious and religious
because he never dealt with evil demons. One of his chief sources for this
argument would have been the approval of demonic magic in the
Asclepius' (p. 86). Empson commented on *John Dee*, 'Thin and rather
evasive, I think'; and he remarked too, unfairly: 'Peculiar in sticking to
it that Dee (and Paracelsus and all) were invoking "angels" not spirits'
(Empson Papers); he was irked by the fact that French does not allow
for any distinction in spelling between 'daemon' and 'demon': see
further below, and note 28.
21 Scott, *Hermetica*, I, p. 358. 'The words *vel angelorum* have probably been
added by the translator' (Scott, *Hermetica*, III, pp. 175, 223). Copenhaver helpfully refers us to a work by Franz Cumont, *Lux Perpetua*
(Paris: Librairie Orientaliste Paul Geuthner, 1949), which 'discusses
texts in which angels and demons were not distinguished as good and
evil'; furthermore, apropos sections 25 and 37 of *Asclepius*, 'Cumont,
Lux, notes the synonymy of "angel" and "demon" and their equivalent
moral status' (*Hermetica*, III, pp. 242, 255).
22 Empson is misremembering here; following a review of the extensive
evidence for dating, Scott judges that 'the Greek original of *Ascl.* III as a
whole was written in AD 268–73'; as for the Latin translation, 'any date
between about 280 and 426 is possible' (*Hermetica*, I, pp. 76, 79).
According to Copenhaver, the Latin *Asclepius* 'seems to have been

written in the latter part of the period in which scholars generally locate the theoretical *Hermetica*, 100 to 300 CE' (*Hermetica*, p. xliv).

23 Yates, *Bruno*, pp. 137–43, 146–7.
24 Scott, *Hermetica*, I, pp. 361, 363.
25 Scott, *Hermetica*, I, p. 339. Cf. Shumaker, *Occult Sciences*, pp. 227–9.
26 Aquinas, *Summa Theologiæ*, London: Blackfriars/Eyre and Spottiswoode; New York: McGraw-Hill, 1963, 2a2æ. Q. 94. 1, pp. 20–3; also *Summa*, Q. 63, 7. Cf. *Faustus and the Censor*, p. 100n.
27 D. P. Walker, *Spiritual and Demonic Magic from Ficino to Campanella*, London: The Warburg Institute, 1958 (Studies of the Warburg Institute, vol. 22), pp. 90–1; French, *John Dee*, pp. 52–3.
28 *Three Books of Occult Philosophy, written by Henry Cornelius Agrippa, of Nettesheim*, trans. J. F., London: printed by R. W. for Gregory Moule, 1651, pp. 391–3. Briggs names 'J. F.' as J. Freake (*The Anatomy of Puck*, p. 173); French, who identifies him as James French (*John Dee*, p. 28 note 2), discusses Dee's indebtedness to Agrippa in his chapter 5.
29 Lewis distinguishes 'daemons' from 'demons' (*English Literature in the Sixteenth Century*, p. 9); as does Mebane: 'I have adopted the spelling *daemon* or *daemonic* in order to distinguish the spirits regarded by the Neoplatonists as benevolent from those evil spirits which the spelling *demon* normally brings to mind' (*Renaissance Magic*, p. 214). See also West, *The Invisible World*, esp. pp. 15–34, and 230–1 note 51.
30 Yates, *Occult Philosophy*, p. 180; but compare Yates, *Bruno*, p. 280.
31 Empson is recalling, after a gap of many years, *The Immortal Hour* by Fiona MacLeod (the pseudonym of William Sharp), a drama in two acts (a musical version was performed at Cambridge in the late 1920s):

> How beautiful they are,
> The lovely ones
> Who dwell in the hills,
> In the hollow hills
> ...
> They laugh and are glad
> And are terrible:
> When their lances shake
> Every green reed quivers
>
> How beautiful they are,
> How beautiful
> The lordly ones
> In the hollow hills.
>
> (*The Immortal Hour*, Edinburgh and London: T. N. Foulis, 1908, pp. 30–1.)

For the ancient Gaels, MacLeod explains (p. ix), 'the Hidden People (the *Sidh* or *Shee*; or *Shee'an* or *Sheechun* of the Isles) were great and potent, not small and insignificant people'. The play is founded on the 'Celtic legend of Midir and Etain (or Edane)' – Etain being 'a Gaelic

Eurydice, Midir a Gaelic Orpheus who penetrated the dismal realm of Eochaidh ... a humanised Gaelic Dis'. Cf. Latham, *The Elizabethan Fairies*, p. 46.

32 Empson is not quoting but spoofing Kott's argument in 'Titania and the Ass's Head', *Shakespeare Our Contemporary*, London: Methuen, 1964.

33 Cf. Latham, *The Elizabethan Fairies*, pp. 180, 219, 224, 231, 256–8. One of the very few other critics to identify Shakespeare's fairies as 'intermediate spirits between heaven and earth' is L. A. Beaurline, who also explicitly compares these 'aerial spirits' to 'Ficino's good daemons' (*Jonson and Elizabethan Comedy: Essays on Dramatic Rhetoric*. San Marino, California: The Huntington Library, 1978, p. 87).

34 James L. Calderwood observes that Titania continually manifests 'a desire for mortality' ('*A Midsummer Night's Dream*: Anamorphism and Theseus' Dream', *Shakespeare Quarterly*, 42:4, Winter 1991, 424; now incorporated in Calderwood's New Critical Introduction to *A Midsummer Night's Dream*, Hemel Hempstead, Herts.: Harvester Wheatsheaf, 1992) – though not for the reasons that Empson argues at greater length in *Faustus and the Censor*.

35 Yates does not explicitly lament the apparent moral of *Dr Faustus*, as Empson seems to suggest; she merely reports what she sees as Marlowe's anti-Agrippan, witch-hunting message: Marlowe 'certainly knows something about Christian Cabala as propagated by Henry Cornelius Agrippa and by "Franciscan Friars" and he is violently against it as diabolical ... *Faustus* looks something like an attempt to overwhelm Elizabethan Christian Cabala in a witch craze' (*Occult Philosophy*, p. 120).

36 See Janet Clare, '*Art made Tongue-Tied by Authority*': *Elizabethan and Jacobean Dramatic Censorship* (Manchester and New York: Manchester University Press, 1990, p. 56 note 12), for a critical notice of Empson's work on *Dr Faustus*; and Richard Dutton: 'to the best of our knowledge, Christopher Marlowe never had problems with the Revels Office' (*Mastering the Revels: The Regulation and Censorship of English Renaissance Drama*, London: Macmillan Academic and Professional, 1991, p. 87). Dutton takes Empson to task on p. 88, and then again in 'Shakespeare and Marlowe: Censorship and Construction', *The Yearbook of English Studies*, 23, 1993, 1–29. Mebane, though unwilling yet to jettison the B-text, still believes like Empson that 'the entire Christian conception of reality' is 'insidiously questioned in *Dr. Faustus* by the protagonist's skepticism with regard to traditional doctrine and by systematic allusion to the heretical philosophies of scientists and occult philosophers such as Bruno and Harriot' (*Renaissance Magic*, pp. 122–3). Leah S. Marcus proposes an excellent resolution of the critical–historical impasse: 'Textual Indeterminacy and Ideological Difference: The Case of *Doctor Faustus*', in *Renaissance Drama*, ed. Mary Beth Rose, new series, 20, Evanston, Ill.: Northwestern University

Press and The Newberry Library Center for Renaissance Studies, 1989, pp. 1–29.

37 In a review of a production of *Dr Faustus* by the Shakespeare Reading Society at St George's Hall, 2 July 1896; G. B. Shaw, *Our Theatres in the Nineties*, London: Constable, 1932, II, p. 182. 'Bernard Shaw said that Marlowe was a nasty young boy trying to make our flesh creep with a Hell in which he no longer believed; and he had in mind chiefly the passages now in question' (Empson, *Faustus and the Censor*, p. 166).

10: THE SPIRITS OF THE *DREAM*

1 Meric Casaubon (ed.), *A True & Faithful Relation of What passed for many Yeers Between Dr: John Dee ... and Some spirits*, London, 1659. See also Frances A. Yates, *Giordano Bruno and the Hermetic Tradition*, London: Routledge and Kegan Paul, 1964, pp. 148–9 (hereinafter cited as Yates, *Bruno*); Peter J. French, *John Dee: The World of an Elizabethan Magus*, London: Routledge and Kegan Paul, 1972, pp. 11–13, 113–22.

2 'As for us, we deem the whole world animate' (William Gilbert, *De Magnete*, trans. P. F. Mottelay, 1882; rpt. New York: Dover, 1958, v, 7, p. 309). T. Walter Herbert celebrates 'the animist frame of mind' in his tiresome *Oberon's Mazéd World*, Baton Rouge and London: Louisiana State University Press, 1977; while Wayne Shumaker deprecates it: 'The Hermetic universe was ... vitalistic, permeated with life. So is the universe of the low savage, the *Naturmensch* ...' (*The Occult Sciences in the Renaissance: A Study in Intellectual Patterns*, Berkeley, Los Angeles and London; University of California Press, 1972, p. 225; hereinafter cited as Shumaker, *Occult Sciences*).

3 Yates, *Bruno*, pp. 3, 9, 12–17, 113–16, 172–4; Shumaker, *Occult Sciences*, pp. 201–51.

4 Yates, *Bruno*, pp. 6–12. See Lactantius, *Div. Inst.*, II, iii (Migne, *Pat. Lat.*, VI, col. 266); Augustine, *De civitate Dei*, VIII, xxiii–iv; also Aquinas, *Summa contra gentiles*, III, civ.

5 Frances A. Yates, *The Rosicrucian Enlightenment*, London: Routledge and Kegan Paul, 1972, pp. 37ff; R. J. W. Evans, *Rudolf II and his World*, Oxford, 1973, pp. 218–28; Yates, *The Occult Philosophy in the Elizabethan Age*, London, Boston and Henley: Routledge and Kegan Paul, 1979, pp. 87–9 (hereinafter cited as Yates, *Occult Philosophy*).

6 Empson's source is H. M. Adams, in letters dated 12 November 1975 and 14 January 1976 (Empson Papers).

7 For a notable discussion of Ficino and Agrippa, as well as Paracelsus and Pomponazzi (whom Empson cites below), see D. P. Walker, *Spiritual and Demonic Magic from Ficino to Campanella*, London: The Warburg Institute, 1958 (hereinafter cited as Walker, *Spiritual and Demonic Magic*). See also Charles G. Nauert, Jr., *Agrippa and the Crisis of Renaissance Thought* (which Empson studied), Urbana: University of Illinois

Press, 1965; Frances A. Yates, 'Renaissance Philosophers in Elizabethan England: John Dee and Giordano Bruno', in *Lull and Bruno*
(*Collected Essays*, 1), London, Boston and Henley: Routledge and Kegan
Paul, 1982, pp. 210–21; and Nicholas H. Clulee, *John Dee's Natural
Philosophy: Between Science and Religion*, London and New York: Routledge, 1988, p. 128ff. 'Recent studies', writes Clulee, 'indicate a considerably richer picture of magic in the Renaissance ... [D]emonic
magic can be an aspect of Ficino's spiritual magic, but there are also
examples ... where demonic magic is not based on a theory of the spirit,
the demons and angels being appealed to directly as separate intelligences or souls that act directly in the world and in man without the
medium of the spirit' (p. 129). See too John S. Mebane's study of the
occult philosophy of the period – it is after Empson's heart – *Renaissance
Magic and the Return of the Golden Age*, Lincoln and London: University of
Nebraska Press, 1989, esp. pp. 17–35 (Ficino), 53–71 (Agrippa): hereinafter cited as Mebane, *Renaissance Magic*. (Donne was deeply versed in
neo-Pythagoreanism and in the Hermetic and cabalistic writings: see
M. van Wyk Smith, 'John Donne's *Metempsychosis*', *Review of English
Studies*, new series, 24:93, 1973, 20–1.)

8 All quotations are taken from Walter Scott (ed. and trans.), *Hermetica:
The Ancient Greek and Latin Writings which contain Religious or Philosophical
Teachings ascribed to Hermes Trismegistus*, Oxford: Clarendon Press, 3
vols., 1924–6 (hereinafter cited as Scott, *Hermetica*: page references will
normally be given in the text).

9 See 'Elizabethan Spirits' above, note 18.

10 Scott, *Hermetica*, I, pp. 61–76; cf. Shumaker, *Occult Sciences*, p. 210.

11 Cf. Yates, *Bruno*, pp. 28, 35, 111.

12 G. R. S. Mead, *Thrice-Greatest Hermes: Studies in Hellenistic Theosophy and
Gnosis*, II: *Sermons*, London and Benares: The Theosophical Publishing
Society, 1906, pp. 348–51.

13 Symphorien Champier, a French Platonist, first suspected such a foist,
in his *De Quadruplici Vita*, 1507; see Scott, *Hermetica*, I, pp. 78–9; Walker,
Spiritual and Demonic Magic, p. 169; Yates, *Bruno*, pp. 3, 9, 172–4.

14 Cf. Yates, *Bruno*, pp. 9, 37, 169; Shumaker, *Occult Sciences*, pp. 206, 229.
Yates maintains that Shakespeare was familiar with this passage from
the *Asclepius* and made 'profoundly important' use of it in *The Winter's
Tale* (*Shakespeare's Last Plays: A New Approach*, London: Routledge and
Kegan Paul, 1975, pp. 90–1). Mebane begs the same question when he
too suggests that the restoration of Hermione in the form of a statue is
'obviously modelled on the account of the magical animation of statues
in the Hermetic *Asclepius*. Although Paulina's art is not literal magic, as
is Prospero's, the scene suggests the extent to which Hermetic sources
have stimulated Shakespeare's imagination ...' (*Renaissance Magic*,
p. 193).

15 '*Quoniam* is a mistranslation of *epei*; "after our ancestors had for some time been godless, they invented an art of making gods". Augustine misunderstood this passage, being misled by the word *quoniam*; see Aug. *De civ. Dei* 8. 23 *ad fin.* -24 (*Testim.*) ... The temple-gods then, according to the writer of *Ascl.* iii, are deified men; or more exactly, the souls of the temple-gods are deified souls of men ... The *deus terrenus* is a deified human soul embodied in a statue, and operating on earth; and it is by the action of men that this combination of body and soul is brought into existence' (Scott, *Hermetica*, iii, pp. 220–1). D. P. Walker substitutes '*quando*' for '*quoniam*' (*Spiritual and Demonic Magic*, pp. 40–1). On the speciousness of the phrase *vel angelorum*, see the previous essay, 'Elizabethan Spirits', note 21.

16 Walker, *Spiritual and Demonic Magic*, pp. 46–53; Yates, *Bruno*, pp. 20–43.

17 Yates, *Bruno*, pp. 130–43; *Occult Philosophy*, pp. 37–47.

18 *Three Books of Occult Philosophy written by Henry Cornelius Agrippa, of Nettesheim*, trans. J. F., London: printed by R. W. for Gregory Moule, 1651, p. 485. Further page references are given in the text.

19 Mebane notes likewise, 'I have found that the 1651 translation by J. F. is generally accurate, but occasionally (though certainly not always) the translator has toned down the heretical aspects of Agrippa's thought' (*Renaissance Magic*, p. 222).

20 Cf. Mebane, *Renaissance Magic*, pp. 61–71.

21 '*Dico autem daemones hic non illos quos diabolos uocamus, sed spiritus sic uouactos ex uocabuli proprietate, quasi scientes, intelligentes & sapientes*' (*De occulta philosophia*, iii, 16, p. 390). Mebane notes: 'J. F. translates "Daemones" as "angels," which, although a more cautious word, is precisely what Agrippa means' (*Renaissance Magic*, p. 223). Cf. West: 'The subsequent discussion leaves it plain that Agrippa's conception was a mixture of Christian, Judaic, and Neo-Platonic ideas of heavenly intelligences, and that the Neo-Platonic predominated. In spite of his assertion that he does not mean devil by the term *daemon*, he frequently uses *daemon*, as do his contemporaries, for evil daemon, meaning fallen angel' (*The Invisible World*, p. 219 note 21).

22 Augustine, *De civ. Dei*, IV, ix–xi, xvi; VII, ix–x.

23 *De occulta philosophia*, iii, 34. '[Agrippa] exposes what Ficino, rather feebly, had tried to conceal: that his magic was really demonic. He also mixes it up with magic that aims at transitive, thaumaturgic effects, whereas Ficino's effects were subjective and psychological' (Walker, *Spiritual and Demonic Magic*, p. 96); see also Shumaker, *Occult Sciences*, p. 152.

24 Henry M. Pachter, *Paracelsus: Magic into Science*, New York: Henry Schuman, 1951, pp. 71–4.

25 Walter Pagel, *Paracelsus: An Introduction to Philosophical Medicine in the Era of the Renaissance*, Basle, Switzerland: S. Karger, 1958, p. 107.

26 'Paracelsus is the principal writer of the Renaissance to assert true
    cohabitation and issue between elementals and human beings ...
    Antiquity provides endless tales of union between mortals and gods or
    demons, Renaissance writers, both pneumatologists and others, picked
    up these tales in profusion ... For the orthodox view that angels,
    whether elect or damned, never begot true issue upon women, see
    Thomas Aquinas, *Summa Theologica*, Q. 51. Art 3. Most orthodox writers
    on sexual relations between spirits and women parrot Aquinas' (Robert
    H. West, *Shakespeare & the Outer Mystery*, Lexington: University of
    Kentucky Press, 1968, pp. 191–2 note 9). Yet West finds evidence of
    cabalistic pneumatology only in *The Tempest*, not in *A Midsummer
    Night's Dream* which he considers belongs solely to folklore and not to an
    intellectual tradition (pp. 80–1).
27 Andrew Halliday Douglas, *The Philosophy and Psychology of Pietro Pompo-
    nazzi*, Cambridge: Cambridge University Press, 1910. See also Nauert,
    Agrippa and the Crisis of Renaissance Thought, p. 252.
28 Scott, *Hermetica*, I, p. 415.
29 Empson commented, in his notes, on C. S. Lewis, *The Discarded Image:
    an introduction to Medieval and Renaissance Literature* (Cambridge: Cam-
    bridge University Press, 1964): 'leaves little room for *any* novelty in the
    Renaissance'.
30 C. S. Lewis, *English Literature in the Sixteenth Century excluding Drama*,
    Oxford: Clarendon Press, 1954, p. 10. Empson added in another draft,
    after this quotation from Lewis:

Plato was considered to have nursed a secret doctrine, which had been transmitted to his disciples ... But anyhow the visible beliefs of Plato would be a
help. Socrates had a modest daemon who only said No, thus saving him from
active errors, and it was found hard to believe that such a man had a devil.
There is a fine passage about the spirits in the *Symposium*, which became
available in Latin and French translations well before the year in which
Shakespeare and Marlowe were born; Diotima is being reported, an Egyptian
priestess, and of course she may be wrong; but her speech is admired.

Love is a very powerful spirit ... and spirits, you know, are halfway
between god and man ... They are the envoys and interpreters that
play between heaven and earth, flying upwards with our worship and
our prayers, and descending with the heavenly answers and command-
ments; and since they are between the two estates they weld them
together and merge them into one great whole. They are the medium of
the prophetic arts, of the priestly rites of sacrifice, initiation, and
incantation, of divination and of sorcery; for the divine will not mingle
directly with the human, and it is only through the mediation of the
human with the spirit-world that man can have any intercourse,
whether sleeping or waking, with the gods.

They might as well be called angels, at this rate, but it is poetical talk in praise
of love, and we know that real interpreters are liable to act independently.

Cf. Walter Hamilton: 'Love, in fact, as Diotima goes on to show, is one of the links between the sensible and the eternal world. This is expressed mythologically by making him a being of intermediate nature between gods and men, one of the class known to the Greeks as spirits or daemons ...' (Plato, *The Symposium*, Harmondsworth: Penguin, 1951, p. 21).

31 Lewis, *English Literature in the Sixteenth Century*, p. 9.

32 *Ibid.*, p. 13.

33 Cf. West, *The Invisible World*, pp. 111–12, and 246 note 5.

34 Mebane concurs: 'Shumaker attempts [in *Occult Sciences*] ... to free the philosophical treatises which we now regard as the *Corpus Hermeticum* proper from any association with magic. As Yates points out, however, in *Giordano Bruno*, 44–49 et passim (drawing upon A. J. Festugière's authoritative *La Révélation d'Hermès Trismégiste*), the early philosophical works traditionally were understood as closely related to the magical treatises which were also attributed to Hermes. The *Corpus Hermeticum* contains much of the astrology and daemonology on which magic depends, and the idol-vivification passage in *Asclepius* [discussed above] occupies an important position in the philosophical works. The regeneration of the soul described in the *Corpus Hermeticum* often involves the defeat of evil daemons and an escape from astrological influences. Furthermore, operative magic is the logical extension of the optimistic conception of humanity as creator which we find in the Hermetic books ...' (*Renaissance Magic*, pp. 216–17). Yet Empson still remarked of Shumaker's work as a whole: 'A decent book, wants to make the young more respectable.' (Notebook in Empson Papers.)

35 Yates (*Shakespeare's Last Plays*, pp. 93–4) warmly endorses Frank Kermode's 'pioneering' conviction (Arden Shakespeare, 1954) that Cornelius Agrippa was 'a power behind Prospero's art' in *The Tempest*. According to A. Koszul, Shakespeare may have found the name 'Ariel' in *De Occulta Philosophia*, II, vii ('Ariel', *English Studies*, 19, 1937, 202–3); cf. W. Stacy Johnson, 'The Genesis of Ariel', *Shakespeare Quarterly*, 2, 1951, 205–10. Useful studies of Shakespeare's putative indebtedness to Agrippa include Barbara A. Mowat, 'Prospero, Agrippa, and Hocus Pocus', *English Literary Renaissance*, 11:3, Autumn 1981, 281–303; Mebane, *Renaissance Magic*, p. 180.

36 What completely contradicts contemporary pneumatological theory, says West, is 'the veritable generation of Merlin [in *The Birth of Merlin*] by an incubus'. He goes on: 'Most orthodox authorities preferred to say that the devil could use stolen human seed to generate, but they did not grant the child so begotten any extraordinary powers ... Merlin must be accounted for by the daemonology of legend rather than by the daemonology that professed to be a science. This means that he is fundamentally unaccountable, even in sixteenth century terms' (*The Invisible World*, pp. 93–4; see also pp. 26–7).

37 'These capacities,' West goes on to say, 'seem to indicate an elementary body according to the conception of Psellos, who attributed to daemons the power to reproduce. It was by a similar daemon that Sycorax conceived Caliban ... ' (*The Invisible World*, p. 239). Recently, Mark Dominik has devoted a detailed volume to the dubious old proposition that *The Birth of Merlin* (?1613–15) was co-authored by Shakespeare and Rowley – just as the first, posthumous, edition (1662) had claimed: *William Shakespeare and 'The Birth of Merlin'*, New York: Philosophical Society, 1985. A. R. Braunmuller and Michael Hattaway guess at a date of 1608 (*The Cambridge Companion to English Renaissance Drama*, Cambridge: Cambridge University Press, 1990, p. 432).

38 Douglas Brooks-Davies highlights the evidence of 'demonic (or angel) magic', as informed by the Hermetic writings, in the first three books of *The Fairie Queene* published at this same interesting date of 1590 (*The Mercurian Monarch: Magical Politics from Spenser to Pope*, Manchester University Press, 1983).

39 Nashe in his preface to Greene's *Menaphon* (1589), a very irritating piece full of half-information given in a state of confused ill-temper, says that the playwrights he dislikes, if they had not been able to crib from B. A. poets like himself, 'might have anticked it until this time up and down the country with the King of Fairies'. There is so much we don't know here; can Oberon have done the Northern Circuit, as in the 1890s, with Bradford, Huddersfield, and all that? (WE)

40 Latham, *The Elizabethan Fairies*, pp. 187–97. Cf. R. A. Foakes (ed.), *A Midsummer Night's Dream* (New Cambridge Shakespeare), Cambridge: Cambridge University Press, 1984, p. 8; hereinafter cited as Foakes, *NCS*. Harold F. Brooks demonstrates that there was in fact a goodly tradition of child-sized and diminutive fairies (*A Midsummer Night's Dream* (Arden Shakespeare), London: Methuen, 1979, pp. lxx–lxxv); hereinafter cited as Brooks, *AS*.

41 Biographers of Southampton often suggest that he may have taken Shakespeare 'into his household' during the crucial period of 1592–4 while the theatres were closed for plague – it comes in the sober and well-documented life of him by G. P. V. Akrigg (*Shakespeare and the Earl of Southampton*, London: Hamish Hamilton, 1968) – and what can have gone on in this household became a subject for fascinated though baffled conjecture. The teenage earl must have been furious with Burghley and the queen for robbing him almost to the point of ruin merely because his father was dead; and the plays shown only to his intimates in Southampton House would be chiefly satires on those two. The first three books of Spenser's *Fairie Queene* had been published in 1590, and the frustrated love-affairs of Elizabeth were an obvious target. Surely, if we date back the *Dream* so far, the original scenes between Bottom and Titania must have been very unlike what we now admire? It may be said that such behaviour would be impossibly

reckless, because certain to be betrayed, but maybe the queen did hear a belated echo of it in 1595, making her turn against him for ever. If Shakespeare felt himself trusted with secrets, that would justify the presumption of intimacy in his dedication of *Lucrece* (1594). But a damping question has to be faced: would Southampton have a 'household' at all, before his majority? Would he even be in London during the plague years?

There are only scraps of information. In October 1590 his mother writes thanking Burghley for entrusting her son to her for such a long visit; by then he has left Cambridge with an MA (choosing to be tested by an oral defence) and has become a member of Gray's Inn, but does not seem busy there. Next summer he visits Cambridge to see Rutland, a younger earl, who is studying there. In June 1592 he writes to Burghley's secretary, asking him to use his influence to avoid the 'great danger and decay' which threatened much of his inheritance through lack of maintenance, and the letter is from 'my lodging in the Strand' (A. L. Rowse, *Shakespeare's Southampton: Patron of Virginia*, London: Macmillan, 1965, p. 67). The refusal to marry Burghley's granddaughter has begun having dire effects, and he has still more than two years of his minority before him, but at least he is not imprisoned in Cecil House. One might think that the guardian ought at least to supply a bodyguard, but there would not be much room for them. His mother would live at Southampton House for most of the time (she was receiving her widow's-third from the encumbered estate). By June 1594, when she had remarried and left the house, the theatres were opening, and Shakespeare and other actors would be busy. The earl leased it out in November 1594, soon after he came of age (his guardian would not do anything helpful like that). His mother would quite like to have a play, but would forbid anything politically dangerous (she complained that he was difficult and unkind). It seems that in September 1592 he invested in a privateer [Rowse, p. 68], and one would expect occasional splashing of money about, as he would have to borrow money anyhow; but he would not have a regular establishment in London, and it is no longer maintained that Shakespeare went to Titchfield (where old retainers continued to live). He could provide what Shakespeare most wanted, an empty room where he could get on with his work, and I expect that Shakespeare was allowed to hand round drinks when he gave a party, but most of the time things were rather pinched. Early versions of *Love's Labour's Lost* and the *Dream*, of a more satirical character than the final ones, were however probably shown. (WE)

Amy J. Riess and George Walton Williams seek to confirm that *Romeo and Juliet* predates the *Dream* ('"Tragical Mirth": From *Romeo* to *Dream*', *Shakespeare Quarterly*, 43:2, Summer 1992, 214–18).

42 Completed about 1589–90: see Robert Greene, *Friar Bacon and Friar*

Bungay, ed. J. A. Lavin (The New Mermaids), London: Ernest Benn, 1969, pp. xii–xiii; Robert R. Reed, Jr., *The Occult on the Tudor and Stuart Stage*, Boston: The Christopher Publishing House, 1965, pp. 101–6. Empson's early remarks on the play (*Some Versions of Pastoral*, 1935, pp. 31–4) include the pertinent observation (p. 33) that Bungay:

> actually defends the claims of the earth-spirits ... Here at least M. [Denis] Saurat's theory [*Milton: Man and Thinker*, 1925] of the influence of the cabba-lists is not fanciful, for they are quoted, and Bungay is making just that claim for the value of matter –
> I tell thee, German, magic haunts the ground
> which M. Saurat takes as the essential novelty of the Renaissance. (Matter is not evil and made from nothing but part of God from which God willingly removed his will; one can therefore put more trust in the flesh, the sciences, the natural man and so on.)

43 *A Looking-Glass for London and England* by Robert Greene and Thomas Lodge, written *c.* 1590, printed 1594; normally regarded as a Tudor morality play.

44 Entered in the Stationer's Register on 14 May 1594, but probably written by 1591; see *The Scottish History of James the Fourth*, ed. J. A. Lavin (New Mermaids), London: Ernest Benn, 1967, pp. x–xii (Lavin characterises the play as 'a transitional Morality ... a homiletic comedy'). 'For the sustained high conception of Oberon, Shakespeare was probably indebted to Robert Greene's *The Scottish History of James the Fourth*', writes Reed; Greene 'elaborates at length upon [the] altruistic character' of Oberon, who assumes a major role (*The Occult on the Tudor and Stuart Stage*, p. 199). Cf. Arthur E. Pennell's curious comment: 'Unlike Shakespeare in *Midsummer Night's Dream*, Greene fails to dispose of the element of reality and as a result the fairy quality of his Oberon scenes contrasts sharply with the serious, "real" business of the main plot' (*An Edition of Anthony Munday's 'John A Kent and John A Cumber'*, New York and London: Garland Publishing, 1980, pp. 204–5).

45 I. A. Shapiro ('The Significance of a Date', *Shakespeare Survey*, 8, 1955, 100–5) observes that from 1589 there was evidently 'a demand for plays introducing magicians and "magical" effects, a demand created perhaps by the success of such a play [as *John a Kent and John a Cumber* or *Friar Bacon and Friar Bungay*]' (p. 102). See also Shapiro, 'Shakespeare and Mundy', in Allardyce Nicoll (ed.), *Shakespeare Survey*, 14, 1961, pp. 25–33. Nevill Coghill contends that *John a Kent and John a Cumber*, by Anthony Munday, was an obvious influence upon *A Midsummer Night's Dream* (*Shakespeare's Professional Skills*, Cambridge: Cambridge University Press, 1964, pp. 41–60): 'It is, in my opinion, impossible to suppose the parallels to be fortuitous ... Shrimp is used by Mundy [*sic*] in ways that are echoed not only in Puck but also in Ariel ... ' (pp. 42,

48). (Robin Goodfellow is mentioned by Munday in his comedy *Two Italian Gentlemen* (printed 1584), which also uses his other familiar name of 'Hobgoblin'.) According to Reed, 'Shakespeare was assuredly familiar with the minute details of Munday's sprightly story'; among the many attributes of the winsome, elf-like Shrimp, the magician's apprentice, is the ability to travel at superhuman speed: 'I fly, Sir, and am there alreadie.' However, Reed argues, while Shrimp appears in some ways similar to Puck, he more plainly foreshadows Ariel (*The Occult on the Tudor and Stuart Stage*, pp. 106–10). Mowat ('Prospero, Agrippa, and Hocus Pocus', p. 297 note 29) judges that 'Shrimp probably prefigures both Puck and Ariel'. Brooks provides an informative discussion of the likelihood of influence (*AS*, pp. lxiv–vi); but Foakes is not convinced by the 'tenuous' connexion between the two plays (*NCS*, p. 145). 'It is evidence (anyhow)', wrote Empson in his notes, 'that the magic in MND was very familiar, or it would not get copied so casually'.

Roslyn L. Knutson helpfully observes, '*Dr. Faustus* is the only tragedy in a set of friar-magician plays from 1589–1594. If Greg's date for Marlowe's text is correct, a plausible order of composition among the plays is as follows: *Friar Bacon and Friar Bungay*, 1589; *John a Kent and John a Cumber*, 1590; *John of Bordeaux, or 2 Friar Bacon*, 1591; *Dr. Faustus*, 1592. Another appeared in 1594: *The Wise Man of West Chester* [of which *John a Kent* was formerly believed to be a revision]. Although the text is lost, the title suggests a comedy about a magician' ('Influence of the Repertory System on the Revival and Revision of *The Spanish Tragedy* and *Dr. Faustus*', *English Literary Renaissance*, 18:2, Spring 1988, pp. 271–2).

46 Chapter I:4 of Reginald Scot's *The Discoverie of Witchcraft* (1584) – a text which is the source for several passages in *MND*, principally to do with Robin Goodfellow (*Narrative and Dramatic Sources of Shakespeare*, ed. Geoffrey Bullough, 1, London: Routledge and Kegan Paul; New York: Columbia University Press, 1966) – observes in addition that 'hurtful witches ... can go in and out at awger holes' (c5^v); see Standish Henning, 'The Fairies of *A Midsummer Night's Dream*', *Shakespeare Quarterly*, 20, 1969, 484–6.

47 Robert Greene, *Groats-worth of Witte*, ed. G. B. Harrison, Edinburgh University Press, 1952, p. 34. Cf. John Dover Wilson, 'The Copy for *A Midsummer Night's Dream*, 1600', in Sir Arthur Quiller-Couch and J. D. Wilson (eds.), *A Midsummer Night's Dream* (The New Shakespeare), Cambridge: Cambridge University Press, 1924, p. 94; hereinafter cited as *MND* (NS).

48 Empson is mistaken here; as Knutson notes, the Admiral's Men at the Rose gave *Dr Faustus* 'an extraordinarily long run of twenty-four performances' over a three-year period from September 1594 to the autumn of 1597 – by which time 'it was commercially exhausted'

('Influence of the Repertory System', p. 263). See R. A. Foakes and R. T. Rickert (eds.), *Henslowe's Diary*, Cambridge: Cambridge University Press, 1961. Reed observes too, 'the vogue of fairies as a dramatic device had virtually ... expended itself' by 1603 (*The Occult on the Tudor and Stuart Stage*, p. 205) – later than Empson proposes. H. W. Herrington ('Witchcraft and Magic in the Elizabethan Drama', *The Journal of American Folk-Lore*, 32:126, October–December 1919, 447–85) established that the fashion for fairy plays lasted through the 1590s; 'a decided shift in dramatic values' took place only just before 1600, when fairies flitted out of the general drama and into the court masque (p. 452).

49 'In *A Midsummer Night's Dream*, Oberon and the other fairies are nontypical in that they are functional to the plot. By and large, the fairies of the late Elizabethan stage are introduced into the drama merely for the sake of displaying them' (Reed, *The Occult on the Tudor and Stuart Stage*, p. 203).

50 The fate of Dr John Dee, as recounted by Yates, *Occult Philosophy*, may have a good deal to do with this hiatus or suspension of interest.

51 O. J. Campbell, *'Love's Labour's Lost Re-studied'*, in *Studies in Shakespeare, Milton and Donne* (University of Chicago Publications in Language and Literature vol. 1), New York: Macmillan, 1925, pp. 1–45; Richard David (ed.), *Love's Labour's Lost* (Arden Shakespeare), 5th edn., London: Methuen, 1956, p. xxxii; David P. Young, *Something of Great Constancy: The Art of 'A Midsummer Night's Dream'*, New Haven and London: Yale University Press, 1966, p. 26.

52 '[H]ewen of burdokes' was performed by Henslowe's company in 1593; it is a likely source for *MND*.

54 Quotations from *A Midsummer Night's Dream* refer to the Arden Shakespeare edition by Harold F. Brooks (London: Methuen, 1979), cited as Brooks, *NA*.

54 John Dover Wilson (ed.), *Love's Labour's Lost* (The New Shakespeare, 1923), 2nd edn., Cambridge: Cambridge University Press, 1969, pp. xvi–xviii, l–liii.

55 Quoted in Dover Wilson, *MND* (NS), p. 95.

56 Akrigg, *Shakespeare and the Earl of Southampton*, p. 39.

57 E. K. Chambers, *William Shakespeare: A Study of Facts and Problems*, Oxford: Clarendon Press, 1930, 1, p. 358. See also Paul N. Siegel, *'A Midsummer Night's Dream* and the Wedding Guests', *Shakespeare Quarterly*, 4, 1953, 139–44; Paul A. Olson, *'A Midsummer Night's Dream* and the Meaning of Court Marriage', *Journal of English Literary History*, 24, 1957, 95–119; John Dover Wilson, 'Variations on the theme of *A Midsummer Night's Dream'*, in *Shakespeare's Happy Comedies*, London: Faber and Faber, 1962, esp. pp. 191–207; Brooks, *AS*, p. lvi; Foakes, *NCS*, pp. 3, 68; Marion Colthorpe, 'Queen Elizabeth I and *A Midsummer Night's Dream'*, *Notes and Queries*, new series, 34:2, June 1987,

pp. 205–7. William B. Hunter, who perceives that 'the artificial verse of the play seems to me to come from an earlier period in Shakespeare's development', believes it may have been written for the Southampton–Heneage wedding on 2 May 1594 and revised for the Berkeley–Carey wedding in February 1596 ('The First Performance of *A Midsummer Night's Dream*', *Notes and Queries*, new series, 32:1, March 1985, 45–7); Steven W. May finds the play full of topical allusions to the Careys (*'A Midsummer Night's Dream* and the Carey Berkeley Wedding', in *Renaissance Papers 1983*, ed. A. Leigh Daneef and M. Thomas Hester, Raleigh, North Carolina, 1984, pp. 43–52); J. J. M. Tobin argues for the Berkeley–Carey wedding because *A Midsummer Night's Dream* exploits numerous borrowings from *The Terrors of the Night* (1584), by Thomas Nashe ('Nashe and Shakespeare: Some Further Borrowings', *Notes and Queries*, new series, 39:3, September 1992, 309–12). E. A. J. Honigmann promotes the occasion of the Vere–Derby wedding, 26 January 1595 (*Shakespeare: the 'lost years'*, Manchester University Press, 1985, pp. 150–3). But Stanley Wells remains sceptical about the wedding-play theory (*'A Midsummer Night's Dream* Revisited', *Critical Survey*, 3:1, 1991, 14–18).

58 William Barlowe (1618); quoted in Francis R. Johnson, *Astronomical Thought in Renaissance England: A Study of the English Scientific Writings from 1500 to 1645*, Baltimore: The Johns Hopkins Press, 1937, p. 242.

59 Cf. Haffenden, 'Introduction', *Essays on Renaissance Literature*, i, p. 43.

60 Jean Jacquot, 'Thomas Hariot's Reputation for Impiety', *Notes and Records of the Royal Society*, ix, 167; quoted in Christopher Hill, *Intellectual Origins of the English Revolution*, Oxford: Clarendon Press, 1965, p. 32–33 (Empson's immediate source).

61 Apropos Thomas Digges see also Empson's 'Copernicanism and the Censor' and 'Thomas Digges his Infinitive Universe' in *Essays on Renaissance Literature*, i, pp. 207–19. Leslie Hotson persuasively suggests that Shakespeare might have met Thomas Digges through his close friend, the actor John Heminges, who was Digges' neighbour in the 1590s; after Digges' death, another of Shakespeare's closest friends, Thomas Russell, wooed and won the widow Anne Digges (*I, William Shakespeare*, London: Jonathan Cape, 1937, p. 112–40).

E. A. J. Honigmann, who convincingly argues that *King John* dates from the notable year 1590, identifies Shakespeare's use of the phrase 'the bias of the world' (II. i. 574) as an early allusion to the heliocentric system (*King John*, Arden Shakespeare, London: Methuen, 1954, p. 52).

62 F. R. Johnson and S. V. Larkey, 'Thomas Digges, the Copernican System, and the Idea of the Infinity of the Universe in 1576', *Huntington Library Bulletin*, v, April 1934, p. 87.

63 'Trimegistus [*sic*] visibilem deum' (N. Copernicus, *De Revolutionibus Orbium Caelestium*, Thorn, 1873, p. 30). See also Yates, *Bruno*, p. 238.

64 See Grant McColley, 'The Seventeenth-century Doctrine of a Plurality of Worlds', *Annals of Science*, 1: 3, 1936, pp. 412–13.

65 Johnson and Larkey, 'Thomas Digges, the Copernican System, and the Idea of the Infinity of the Universe in 1576', p. 91.

66 Frances A. Yates, *A Study of 'Love's Labour's Lost'*, Cambridge: Cambridge University Press, 1936, p. 202.

67 Cf. French, *John Dee*, pp. 97–103. 'For a Hermeticist like Dee, the sun-centred universe of Copernicus would have been a mysterious, mystical and pregnant religious revelation. This is exactly the type of thing Dee would *not* discuss in print (as he consistently refused to do) since it was a matter for the *illuminati*, not the common man ... [A]lthough the Renaissance magus worked his magic within a geocentric system, he had a spiritual affinity with heliocentricity ... Renaissance Hermeticism prepared the way emotionally for the acceptance of Copernicus's revolutionized universal structure' (p. 103).

68 Cf. H. H. Furness (*A Midsommer Nights Dreame*, New Variorum edn., Philadelphia: J. B. Lippincott Company, 1895, p. 47), citing Furnivall: 'At the date of this play the Ptolemaic system was believed in, and the moon and all the planets and stars were supposed to be fixed in hollow crystalline spheres or globes'; hereinafter referred to as Furness, *New Variorum*.

69 Herbert (*Oberon's Mazéd World*, p. 169) remarks: 'Sixteenth-century *India* ... often (as the Oxford English Dictionary suggests) signified the territory beyond the Indus, but at times it meant something even less definite: lands to the east of the vague boundary of the Holy Land and east of "the East" that Antony speaks of as the home of Cleopatra. See the Introduction by S. L. Lee in *The Boke of Duke Huon of Bordeaux*, trans. Sir John Bourchier, Lord Berners (*ca.* 1534; London: N. Trubner, 1882–7), p. li.'

70 *MND* (NS), p. 24.

71 Cf. Dover Wilson, *MND* (NS), pp. 126–7. Both Brooks (*AS*, p. 64) and Foakes (*NCS*, p. 87) regard 'stamp' as quite warrantable.

72 Cf. Roger Warren, *'A Midsummer Night's Dream': Text and Performance*, London: Macmillan Press, 1983, p. 17. As Keith Thomas notes, the name 'Oberon' was that of 'a demon who had been frequently conjured by fifteenth- and sixteenth-century wizards, long before the title become associated with the King of the Fairies' (*Religion and the Decline of Magic: Studies in Popular Belief in Sixteenth and Seventeenth Century England*, London: Weidenfeld and Nicolson, 1971, p. 607. Furness cites testimony to show that 'Puck' was itself 'the generic name for a minor order of evil spirits', or 'an old word for devil' (*New Variorum*, p. 3). Anthony Harris observes, 'In many respects both Puck and Ariel are in the English tradition of the "knavish sprite", each being apparently more mischievous than evil. But ... just as Puck's alternative name, Robin Goodfellow, links him with the devil, so Ariel has clear demonic

associations' (*Night's Black Agents: Witchcraft and Magic in Seventeenth-Century English Drama*, Manchester University Press, 1980, p. 142).

73 Their dogs are chosen only for sounding beautiful in combination, not for being good at hunting ['Slow in pursuit, but matched in mouth like bells', IV. i. 122], and this also seems a plan for a magical contact with nature. One needs first to realise that hounds actually can sound very beautiful, but the brief speeches are themselves sufficiently knock-down: the figures of myth are on a par with the fairies. (WE]
See also Warren, '*A Midsummer Night's Dream*', pp. 26–8.

74 See Foakes (*NCS*, pp. 135–43) for a good account of the relationship of quartos and folio; the first quarto, he believes, is authoritative, perhaps deriving from an authorial manuscript – even though mislineations are a notable feature of that text.

75 This crux is discussed in detail in Brooks, *AS*, appendix II, pp. 159–62.

76 Samuel Pepys, 29 September 1662, *Diary*, ed. R. C. Latham and W. Matthews, III, p. 208; also quoted in Brooks, *AS*, pp. ix–x.

77 Brooks' note on the line (*AS*, p. 39) may be taken to work to Empson's advantage here: 'Among Whitney's *Emblems*, 1586, one on Drake's circumnavigation depicts that globe encircled by a girdle, of which one end is fastened to the prow of the *Golden Hind*, the other held in the hand of God (H. Green, *Shakespeare and the Emblem Writers* [1870] p. 413; quoted Furness).'

78 Cf. Jan Kott, *Shakespeare our Contemporary*, London: Methuen, 1965; 2nd edn. revised, 1967, p. 173: 'Shakespeare was not far wrong. The First Russian sputnik encircled the earth in forty-seven minutes.'

79 *The Riverside Shakespeare*, Boston: Houghton Mifflin Company, 1974, p. 228; Furness, *New Variorum*, p. 92.

80 Cf. Bernard Beckerman's tentative note: 'Actually the history of flying apparatuses in the Elizabethan theater needs further study. For the Globe, at least so far as the plays demonstrate, no machinery for flying existed' (*Shakespeare at the Globe 1599–1609*, New York: Macmillan, 1962, p. 94). See also Michael Hattaway, *Elizabethan Popular Theatre: Plays in Performance*, London, Boston, Melbourne, and Henley: Routledge and Kegan Paul, 1982, p. 32; Andrew Gurr, *The Shakespearean Stage 1574–1642*, 3rd edn., Cambridge: Cambridge University Press, 1992, p. 192.

81 E. K. Chambers, quoted in *MND* (NS), p. 86.

82 Kott, *Shakespeare our Contemporary*, pp. 188–9. Stanley Wells, who chose to ignore (and implicitly dismiss) Kott's book in the introduction to his New Penguin Shakespeare edition of the play (Harmondsworth; Penguin, 1967), still finds it – for all its large, and largely regrettable, influence – 'a piece of essentially belle-lettrist criticism' ('*A Midsummer Night's Dream* revisited', p. 25).

83 Kott, *Shakespeare our Contemporary*, p. 172. Like Empson, Brooks disputes the notion that there is 'anything potentially sinister about this fairy-land' (*AS*, pp. cvii–cviii).

84 French, *John Dee*, pp. 24, 44; Peter J. Zetterburg, 'The Mistaking of "the Mathematicks" for Magic in Tudor and Stuart England', *Sixteenth-Century Journal*, 2, 1980, 83–97. 'Dee attributed this invention to his predecessor in the worlds of magic and scholarship, Roger Bacon' (Harris, *Night's Black Agents*, p. 159).

85 Samuel Butler, *The Way of All Flesh* (1903), Harmondsworth; Penguin, 1947, p. 282 (*pace* Empson, who may be recalling the passage after a gap of decades, the context does not actually suggest that burlesques of Shakespeare are being praised).

86 Glynne Wickham, *Shakespeare's Dramatic Heritage: Collected Studies in Mediaeval, Tudor and Shakespearean Drama*, New York: Barnes and Noble, 1969, pp. 183–4.

87 'Hob', as all etymologists agree, is short for 'Robin' or 'Robert'; 'hob', meaning a rounded peg or pin, as in *hobnail*, is first recorded in 1589 (*The Barnhart Dictionary of Etymology*, H. W. Wilson Company, 1988). Furness discusses the provenance of the name 'Robin Goodfellow' in *New Variorum*, pp. 289ff. Unlike Robert Burton, who categorises the terrestrial demons ('Digression of the Nature of Spirits', *The Anatomy of Melancholy*, 1621), Shakespeare 'made no distinction between a puck and a Robin Goodfellow' (Reed, *The Occult on the Tudor and Stuart Stage*, p. 195). The best accounts of Robin Goodfellow are Minor White Latham, *The Elizabethan Fairies: The Fairies of Folklore and the Fairies of Shakespeare*, New York: Columbia University Press, 1930, esp. pp. 219–62; and K. M. Briggs, *The Anatomy of Puck: An Examination of Fairy Beliefs among Shakespeare's Contemporaries and Successors*, London: Routledge and Kegan Paul, 1959.

88 See Akrigg, *Shakespeare and the Earl of Southampton*, p. 125.

89 Furness (*New Variorum*, p. 59) appears to agree with Empson here; it is, he ventures, one of Shakespeare's 'strokes of humour'. Foakes (*NCS*, p. 29) poses what he calls these 'unanswerable questions': 'As spirits, can they only meddle vicariously in human love affairs, or are they also, like Greek gods, capable of intercourse with humans, as Theseus takes the shape of Corin to woo Phillida?'

90 *The Lives of the Noble Grecians and Romanes, compared together by that graue learned Philosopher and Historiographer, Plutarke of Chæronia*, trans. Thomas North, Imprinted at London by Thomas Vautrouillier and John Wight, 1579, p. 5.

91 Brooks suggests that 'Perigenia' (the Q1 version of the name favoured by Empson) 'is perhaps more probably the compositor's error ... than Shakespeare's ...' (*AS*, p. 31).

92 Brooks smartly seconds Empson's view here: 'even a controlled suggestion of carnal bestiality is surely impossible: jealous Oberon will not have cast his spell to cuckold himself' (*AS*, p. cxv). See also James L. Calderwood's sceptical discussion of the 'ravishing interpretation', in '*A Midsummer Night's Dream*: Anamorphism and Theseus' Dream', *Shake-*

speare Quarterly, 42:4, Winter 1991, 409–30, esp. 419–24; now incorporated in Calderwood's New Critical Introduction to *A Midsummer Night's Dream* (Hemel Hempstead, Herts.: Harvester Wheatsheaf, 1992). The 1992 Royal National Theatre production, directed by Robert Lepage, suffered Bottom to indulge in a braying bonking (happily, it enabled Puck to 'fly' in a spectacular way while hanging by one arm from a rope whipped by an assistant below – as in a circus).

93 For a detailed account of this production, directed by Jean Gascon and designed by Leslie Hurry, see Arnold Edinborough, 'Stratford, Ontario – 1968', *Shakespeare Quarterly*, 19, 1968, 383–3.

94 *MND* (NS), p. 123.

95 Cf. *MND* (NS), pp. 157–8.

96 David Woodman notes likewise: 'Oberon's interference in human affairs is almost consistently benevolent ...' (*White Magic and English Renaissance Drama*, Rutherford, Madison, Teaneck: Fairleigh Dickinson UP, 1973, p. 68). Brooks confirms that 'comparison of the *Dream* with its sources puts it beyond doubt that in respect of fairy benevolence [Shakespeare] is not innovating' (*AS*, p. lxxvi; see also p. lxxxiv). On Paracelsianism in Shakespeare, see Richard K. Stensgaard, '*All's Well that Ends Well* and the Galenico-Paracelsian Controversy', *Renaissance Quarterly* 25, 1972, 173–87; J. Scott Bentley, 'Helena's Paracelsian Cure of the King: *Magia Naturalis* in *All's Well That Ends Well*', *Cauda Pavonis: The Hermetic Text Society Newsletter*, new series 5:1, spring 1986, pp. 1–4. Robert Grudin further sifts the evidence of Paracelsian thought (*Mighty Opposites: Shakespeare and Renaissance Contrariety*, Berkeley, Los Angeles, London: University of California Press, 1979).

97 W. Wordsworth, 'Lines Composed a Few Miles about Tintern Abbey', lines 106–7.

98 See also Eric Partridge, *Shakespeare's Bawdy*, London: Routledge and Kegan Paul, 1947: *s. v.* 'bottom-grass'. John Roe rather humourlessly disputes this point: 'The modern imagination ... finds it hard to resist a pun on "bottom", but *OED* provides no contemporary evidence. In fact, "bottom" is a later, polite substitute for "breech" or "buttock". Despite Partridge's further offering of "brakes" (237) as "pubic hair", the analogy between landscape and anatomy works less in precise detail and more generally in terms of the pleasures and convenience each affords' (*The Poems*, New Cambridge Shakespeare, Cambridge: Cambridge University Press, 1992, p. 92).

99 See also Annabel Patterson, *Shakespeare and the Popular Voice*, Oxford: Basil Blackwell, 1989, p. 66: 'Bottom is not only the bottom of the social hierarchy as the play represents it, but also the "bottom" of the body when seated, literally the social ass or arse. It is typical of the Oxford English Dictionary's conservatism that it does not sanction this meaning of the word in Shakespeare's day, with the result that generations of editors have been satisfied with "bottom" as a technical term

for the bobbin in weaving. Yet as Frankie Rubinstein observes in her dictionary of Shakespeare's sexual puns, Shakespeare and his contemporaries took for granted that *ass*, as the vulgar, dialectical spelling of *arse* was the meeting point of a powerful set of linked concepts [*A Dictionary of Shakespeare's Sexual Puns and their Significance*, London: Macmillan Press, 1984, p. 17]: "Shakespeare ... used 'ass' to pun on the ass that gets beaten with a stick and the arse that gets thumped sexually, the ass that bears a burden and the arse that bears or carries in intercourse".'

100 Helge Kökeritz, *Shakespeare's Pronunciation*, New Haven: Yale University Press, 1953, p. 409.

101 Empson nursed this notion for many years: in a review entitled 'Next Time, A Wheel of Fire' (*Essays in Criticism*, 17:3, January 1967, 96) he argued that Shakespeare must have exploited the difference in pronunciation between the [a] of rural Warwickshire and the refined [æ] of London. He reiterated the point in a follow-up debate in the 'Critical Forum' pages of the periodical: 17:3, July 1967, 407–10; 18:2, April 1968, pp. 236–7. His sparring-partner was J. C. Maxwell (17:2, April 1967, pp. 257–8; 18:1 January 1968, p. 112).

102 *King Henry V*, II. v. 10; Empson's spelling. (The line is usually given to the Duke of Bretagne, as in the Arden Shakespeare ed. by J. H. Walter, London: Methuen, 1954).

103 *The Riverside Shakespeare*, p. 241; also p. 217. But Halliwell (1856) remarked: 'This kind of humour was so very common, it is by no means necessary to consider, with some, that Shakespeare intended Bottom to parody Scripture' (cited in Furness, *New Variorum*, p. 195). See also Patterson, *Shakespeare and the Popular Voice*, pp. 68–9

104 Cf. L. A. Beaurline, *Jonson and Elizabethan Comedy: Essays in Dramatic Rhetoric*, San Marino, California: The Huntington Library, 1978, pp. 90–3, 321; Ronald F. Miller, '*A Midsummer Night's Dream*: The Fairies, Bottom, and the Mystery of Things', *Shakespeare Quarterly*, 26:3, Summer 1975, 265–8.

105 Furness, *New Variorum*, p. 195–6, salutes Theobald's explanation as 'an *emendatio certissima*'. Cf. Brooks, *AS*, p. cxvii; Foakes, *NCS*, pp. 35, 113.

106 'I have ever believed, and do now know, that there are witches. They that doubt of these do not only deny them, but spirits; and are obliquely, and upon consequence, a sort, not of infidels, but atheists' (Browne, *Religio Medici*, Sect. xxx, quoted in West, *The Invisible World*, p. 1). Cf. Shumaker, *Occult Sciences*, pp. 241–4.

107 Brooks agrees that the Duke's 'assessment is further put in perspective by his equivocal status as its spokesman. Are we meant to reflect that this disbeliever in antique fables is something of an antique fable himself, despite his credentials from historical biography (Plutarch's *Lives*)?' (*AS*, p. civ.) Cf. Coghill, *Shakespeare's Professional Skills*, p. 60 and note 1.

108 He does not say which of the myths about him are not true, but the end of the story about the Amazons is even now being enacted. Blake has an even more splendid use of the same device:

> The Prophets Isaiah and Ezekiel dined with me, and I asked them how they dared so roundly to assert that God spake to them ...
> Isaiah answered, 'I saw no God ... but ... as I was then persuaded, and remain confirmed, that the voice of honest indignation is the voice of God, I cared not for consequences, but wrote.' ['The Marriage of Heaven and Hell', *The Poems of William Blake*, ed. W. H. Stevenson and David V. Erdman, London: Longman, 1971, p. 112.]

Many readers have taken this, with relief, as a confession by Blake that he did not really see visions, and meanwhile they are taking for granted that he really did dine with Ezekiel. We should remember, I think, that Theseus became a demigod with a cult of his own; his status is not really very different from that of Oberon, or at any rate it won't be in a few years' time. (WE)

109 See for example Pagel, *Paracelsus*, pp. 110, 122, 300.

Index

288

Woodman, David, 285
Wordsworth, William, 242

Yates, Frances A., 2; *Giordano Bruno and
the Hermetic Tradition*, 9, 155, 161,
165, 264, 275; *The Occult Philosophy*

in the Elizabethan Age, 12, 155–69,
264–71, 280; *The Rosicrucian
Enlightenment*, 165; *Shakespeare's Last
Plays*, 272, 275; *A Study of Love's
Labour's Lost*, 206–7
Yeats, W. B., 91, 96, 103–4, 159, 187, 243